WITHDRAWN
UST
Libraries

Andrew Bradford

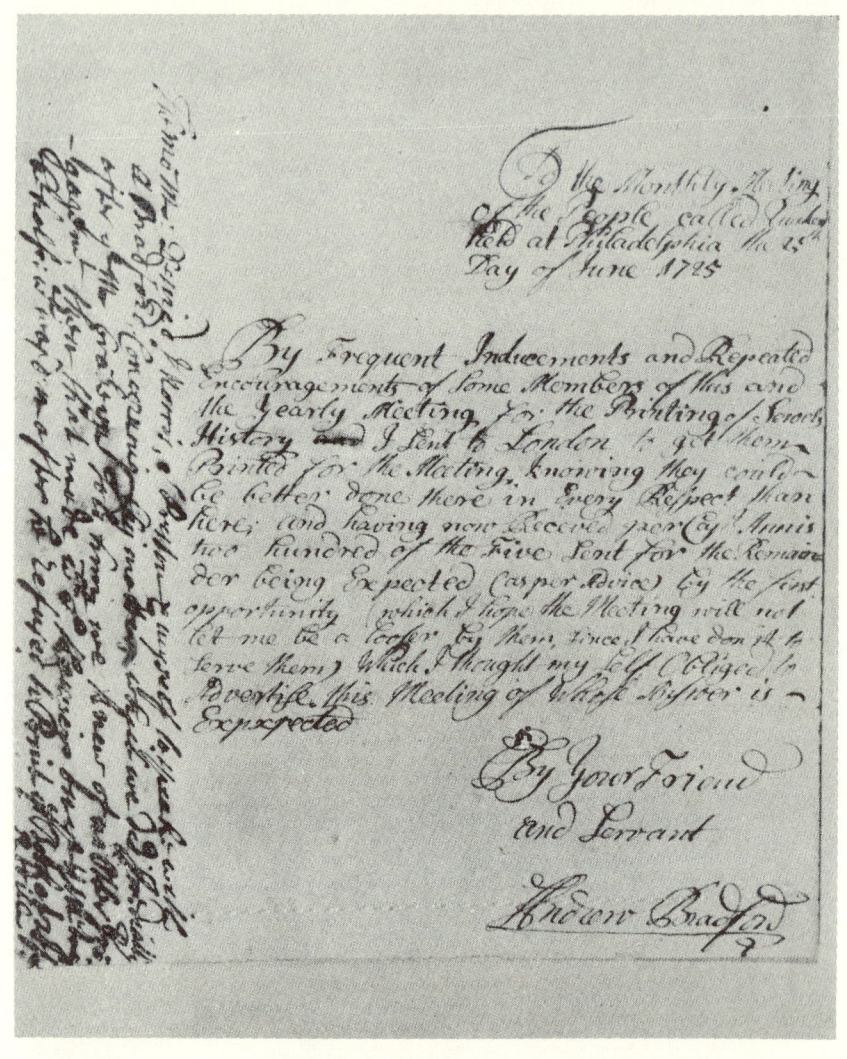

Letter of Andrew Bradford to the Society of Friends (see pages 25-26)
Courtesy of the Historical Society of Pennsylvania

ANDREW BRADFORD

Colonial Journalist

by
ANNA JANNEY DeARMOND

GREENWOOD PRESS, PUBLISHERS
NEW YORK

Reprinted by permission
of Professor J. DeArmond

First Greenwood Reprinting 1969

Library of Congress Catalogue Card Number 79-91758

SBN 8371-2429-8

PRINTED IN UNITED STATES OF AMERICA

Foreword

The first version of the following study in the history of colonial journalism was completed in the spring of 1934 when I was a graduate student at Columbia University. At that time the essay consisted of a summary of the development of printing in Philadelphia from 1685 to the arrival of Andrew Bradford, a biographical sketch of Bradford (later published in the *Pennsylvania Magazine of History and Biography*), and an analysis of the *American Weekly Mercury* during its first seven years. When I resumed work on the subject in 1944, various changes in the original plan seemed advisable. Accordingly, the introduction has been reduced to a few pages, with the intention of presenting only that background necessary to an understanding of Andrew Bradford's place among early Philadelphia printers. The chapter on Bradford's life has been enlarged and almost entirely rewritten, not only to include the results of further research, but also to correct certain errors of fact or emphasis. The section devoted to the *American Weekly Mercury* has been completely reorganized and expanded to cover the entire history of the newspaper. Finally, in order to complete the picture of Bradford's career as a journalist, a chapter on the *American Magazine* has been added to the earlier plan.

It is too much to hope, I believe, that we shall ever see Andrew Bradford in three dimensions. He left no direct descendants; moreover, despite a few dramatic episodes, his life appears to have been for the most part unobtrusive and conventional. We have no record of those details of his character without which a biography cannot come to life. But if the study of Bradford himself is restricted by lack of material, discussion of his newspaper suffers from no such limitation. The section on the *Mercury* is, I think, the first attempt to analyze a colonial journal both systematically and with reasonable completeness. Here the major problem was the selection and organization of material. Without sacrificing an impression of the unity and total effect of the paper, I have tried to bring into focus in successive chapters each of the divers elements of which the *Mercury* consists and, insofar as Bradford's journal is typical of its age, to suggest the essential characteristics of the early American newspaper in general.

I should explain in brief my handling of the problem of typography. I have not attempted to reproduce all the peculiarities in printing of the *Mercury,* the *American Magazine,* and the colonial records which I have used. Furthermore, I have generally avoided the use of *sic.* My practice has been to disregard such variations in type as the inconsistent and often pointless use of italics, large capitals, and black-letter, except in those places where special type would be employed today, and I have omitted hyphens in the titles of magazines and newspapers. I have reproduced — I hope with accuracy — the initial capitals, the punctuation, and the spelling of my sources, though I have silently corrected what seem to be mistakes of typesetting, especially in the *Mercury* and the *American Magazine.* Since the sources of all quotations are indicated, errors of accuracy or judgment may be readily discovered.

Space does not permit me to mention all the institutions and individuals who have contributed to the making of this book. I am particularly indebted to the New York Public Library, the New-York Historical Society, the New York Genealogical and Biographical Society, the Columbia University Library, the University of Pennsylvania Library, the Yale University Library, the Boston Public Library, the Massachusetts Historical Society, the American Antiquarian Society, the Henry E. Huntington Library, the Library of Congress, the Genealogical Society of Pennsylvania, the Bucks County Historical Society, and the Bibliographical Society of America. To the Library Company of Philadelphia, the Historical Society of Pennsylvania, and the Free Library of Philadelphia I can express only inadequately my gratitude for innumerable kindnesses over a period of several years. I am likewise grateful to the Overseers of the William Penn Charter School of Philadelphia, to the Philadelphia Yearly Meeting of Friends, and to Christ Church, Philadelphia, for the privilege of examining their original records. Several members of the Bradford family have shown friendly and helpful interest in the progress of my research; I should like here to express my appreciation to Miss Katharine N. Bradford, Mr. James Sydney Bradford, Miss Frances M. Bradford, Mrs. Eugene P. Pendergrass, and Mrs. Vincent L. Bradford. I am indebted also to Dr. Victor Hugo Paltsits, to Dr. Lawrence C. Wroth, to Dr. Clarence S. Brigham, and to Dr. Julian P. Boyd, as well as to Mr. Eustace M. Shilstone of the Barbados Museum and Historical Society. I owe a special debt to Dr. Ralph L. Rusk and the late Dr. Arthur E. Christy, who suggested this study; and to Dr. Arthur Hobson Quinn, Dr. Matthias A. Shaaber, Dr. Robert E. Spiller, and Dr. Allan G. Chester of the University of Pennsylvania, who have given me advice and assistance. To Dr. Quinn especially I am grateful for constant help and encouragement over a number of years and at various difficult points in my work. I should also like to thank Dr. John H. Powell of the Free Library of Philadelphia and Dr. Ned B. Allen of the University of Delaware for many practical suggestions and for unfailing interest during the course of my research. Lastly, I am indebted to Dr. Honor C. McCusker, of the United States Information Service Library in the Hague, who read the book in manuscript; and to Miss Sarah Dowlin Jones, of the Library of the University of Pennsylvania, who checked many references and who assisted me in reading the proof and making the index.

A. J. DeA.

Newark, Delaware
December 30, 1948

Errata

Page 6, note 23, line 1: *delete* in
Page 8, note 8, line 15: *delete* in
Page 14, line 3: *read* of Pennsylvania; 'Whereupon,
Page 47, line 4: *read* that *Mercury*, hopes,
Page 67, line 3: *read* on the trends of the
Page 81, note 131: *for* in addition to *read* besides
Page 112, line 37: *for* His *read* his
Page 136, line 10: *for* threatened *read* threatned
Page 149, line 11: *for* times *read* Times
Page 154, line 1: *read* of Ringing in England."²⁴⁶
Page 177, line 9: *for* Reflection *read* Reflections
Page 178, line 32: *for* light *read* Light
Page 180, line 9: *read* in what manner, shall I
Page 180, line 12: *read* you cannot, to your
Page 184, line 16: *read* thou propitious Power,
Page 200, line 26: *for* Fair *read* fair
Page 206, line 9: *for* Arm *read* arm
Page 215, line 1: *for* suggest *read* suggests
Page 216, note 35, line 3: *read* Jan. 5, 1726/27
Page 227, line 2: *read* a Correspondence is settled
Page 228, line 22: *read* Webbe was speaking the truth:
Page 233, line 33: *for* was *read* were
Page 246, line 28: *for* Elsewhere *read* Elswhere
Page 258, number 964: *delete* comma *and* 1738
Page 261, *American Magazine*, line 7: *for* 240 *read* 231
Page 261, *American Weekly Mercury*,
      line 4: *for* 48 *read* 55
      line 6: *for* 48, 112, 144, 192 *read* 55, 119, 151, 199
      line 8: *for* 192 *read* 199
      line 9: *for* 48, 112, 144, 192 *read* 55, 119, 151, 199
      line 11: *for* 192 *read* 199
      line 12: *for* 144 *read* 151
      line 13: *for* 192 *read* 199
      line 14: *for* 192 *read* 199
      line 16: *for* 144, 192 *read* 151, 199
Page 262, Bradford, Andrew, line 19: *for* 192 *read* 199
Page 263: *read* Bristol *Journal*,
Page 266: *read* Hyatt, Tacy Bradford,
Page 269, Philadelphia, line 6: *for* 112, 240 *read* 119, 231
Page 270: *read* Raylton, Tacy Sowle (Mrs. Thomas),

CONTENTS

Foreword v

Introduction: The Philadelphia Press from 1685 to 1713 1

Part I: Andrew Bradford............................... 7

Part II: *The American Weekly Mercury*

   Chapter 1. History of the *Mercury*..................... 39

   Chapter 2. Sources of the *Mercury*..................... 51

   Chapter 3. Foreign and Colonial Affairs in the *Mercury*... 66

   Chapter 4. Politics in Philadelphia and the Bradford-Hamilton Controversy 84

   Chapter 5. The *Mercury* as a Mirror of the Times....... 119

   Chapter 6. Editorials and Features in the *Mercury*........ 160

   Chapter 7. Literature in the *Mercury*................... 182

   Chapter 8. Popularity and Influence of the *Mercury*....... 211

Part III: *The American Magazine*......................... 223

Conclusion 240

Bradford Genealogy 242

Andrew Bradford's Will................................. 243

Cornelia Bradford's Will................................ 245

Bibliography 247

Index to the Issues of the *Mercury*........................ 252

General Index 261

ILLUSTRATIONS

Letter of Andrew Bradford to the Society of Friends   *Frontispiece*

Early Nameplates of the *Mercury*............... *Facing page* 55

Nameplate of the *Mercury*, Showing an Early View of Philadelphia .... *Facing page* 119

Advertising Page of the *Mercury*, October 9, 1735.. *Facing page* 151

Advertising Page of the *Mercury*, December 9, 1742 *Facing page* 199

Title Page of the *American Magazine*............. *Facing page* 231

Introduction
The Philadelphia Press from 1685 to 1713

Pennsylvania was the last of the British colonies to be established in North America in the seventeenth century. It grew more rapidly in population, however, than any other, and Philadelphia quickly transformed itself from the village of a few houses which Penn found on his arrival late in 1682 to the thriving town, perhaps of 4500 people,[1] which he incorporated as a city in 1701. But the development of Philadelphia was a phenomenon more complex than merely a steady influx of settlers and a healthy birth rate. At the beginning, British Quakers made up the greater part of the population, and for more than half a century they were the dominant element in the political, social, economic, and cultural life of the province. Indeed, even after they had been far outnumbered by other religious and racial groups, they maintained a disproportionate influence upon nearly all the activities of the colony. In spite of occasional derelictions, they were on the whole intellectually vigorous and liberal. The Great Law of 1682 allowed very nearly complete religious freedom;[2] the Charter of Privileges of 1701 gave the people of Pennsylvania political and civil rights which most other colonials won only after a struggle and many years later. The Friends also, like the Puritans, believed in the value of education; hence, in 1689, seven years after Penn's arrival, Philadelphia's first school was founded.[3] In short, the colony, especially its capital, showed a strong and early inclination towards both the ideal and the practice of intellectual freedom.

Favored by the comparatively tolerant atmosphere of early Pennsylvania, the printing press achieved immediate and lasting importance. In printing and the book trade, indeed, colonial Philadelphia gained a special eminence. Its first press, the second in the middle colonies,[4] was set up less than four years after the city had been laid out; the Rittenhouse paper mill, built when the settlement was but eight years old, was the first in British America. Philadelphia's first newspaper and the

---

1. Estimates of population for this early period are untrustworthy, but see Joseph Jackson, *Encyclopedia of Philadelphia,* IV, 1014, and *The New International Encyclopaedia,* second edition, XVIII, 475.
2. The only significant restriction was that, in effect, non-Christians and Unitarians were excluded from the franchise and from holding office.
3. This school, the well-known William Penn Charter School of Philadelphia, is still in existence.
4. Lawrence C. Wroth (*The Colonial Printer,* second edition, 39) has recently shown that Maryland takes precedence over Pennsylvania as the first of the middle colonies to have a permanent press.

first colonial paper outside Massachusetts, the *American Weekly Mercury*, was founded while many of the original settlers were still living; the earliest magazine was Bradford's *American Magazine* of 1741; in 1783 appeared both the first trade journal in the country, John Macpherson's *Price Current*, and the first daily paper, the *Pennsylvania Evening Post, and Daily Advertiser*. Moreover, in Philadelphia appeared the first American reprints of the Bible, both in English and in German,[5] and of the works of Shakespeare, Milton, Richardson, Smollett, as well as of other major English writers. Mr. Wroth sums up a most important aspect of Philadelphia's eminence as a colonial metropolis when he speaks of it as[6]

> a community where, during the eighteenth century, the press was to attain an unusual significance, steadily overtaking in interest and in bulk of production the publishing activities of Massachusetts, and surpassing in these particulars the output of any other colony. Here, in the Quaker colony, was the crucible of colonial America, here the conflict of races and creeds and of political difference was at its sharpest, here were wealth, education, and an enlightened people. Here, too, were the political leadership of New Jersey and Delaware and an economic connection so close as to make the three at times take on the semblance of a single colony. The Bradfords, Franklin, Bell, the Sowers, the German Baptists at Ephrata, the Dunlaps, Goddard, the Halls, and other printers in and near Philadelphia expressed in type the active intelligence of the community.

To this city in 1685 came William Bradford, bringing with him from London two recent acquisitions, his press and his young wife. The former, though affording him a livelihood, more than once got him into trouble. His wife, a more satisfactory partner, bore him about 1686 his first son, Andrew. The boy inherited from both sides of his family the tradition of the press. His paternal grandfather, William Bradford of Burwell (or Barnwell), Leicestershire, England, was a printer. His mother's father, for whom he was named, was Andrew Sowle, a well-known printer and publisher in London during the periods of the Commonwealth and the Restoration, whose press was the leading instrument in that city of the Society of Friends.[7] Sowle was, in fact, a man of dis-

---

5. The prospectus of Sower's famous German Bible may be found in *Mercury* 1161.
6. Wroth, 29-30.
7. Victor H. Paltsits, "William Bradford," *D. A. B.* Henry R. Plomer (*A Dictionary of the Booksellers and Printers*, 168) says: "... there is no doubt that he [Andrew Sowle] was the printer of most, if not all, of the early Quaker literature."

tinction in Quaker circles, a friend of both George Fox and William Penn, and one of the witnesses to the original charter of Pennsylvania.[8] In addition, though he never came to America, he was a "first purchaser" of land in the province, the holder of a thousand acres in Upper Dublin Township, County of Philadelphia.[9] It is not surprising that young William Bradford, an apprentice in Sowle's establishment, should have joined the Society of Friends and become interested in Pennsylvania. Accordingly, after his marriage to Elizabeth Sowle, a daughter of his master, he emigrated to the Quaker colony.[10] He arrived there well provided against the future, with a printing press and materials, with the personal sanction of Penn,[11] and with a letter from George Fox, introducing him to American Friends as " a sober young man."[12]

The first book to come from Bradford's press bore the incongruously pretentious title *Kalendarium Pennsilvaniense, or America's Messenger. Being an Almanack For the Year of Grace, 1686.* In the years immediately following this first venture Bradford's trade steadily increased, though less rapidly than he had hoped. In 1689, when he was thinking seriously of returning to England,[13] the Meeting "agreed to grant him, besides all the business which they could throw in his way," a yearly salary of £40, and two years later it further encouraged him by guaranteeing to subscribe for two hundred copies of every book printed by him at the advice of the Friends.[14] Of work not sponsored by the Meeting, his most numerous publications were almanacs, though his most famous secular production, probably, was Thomas Budd's *Good Order Estab-*

---

8. See facsimile in *William Penn's First Charter To the People of Pennsylvania, April 25, 1682*, edited by A. C. Myers.
9. See *Deed Books in the Office for the Recording of Deeds in Philadelphia*, F-5, 529-530, and also *Minutes of the Board of Property of the Province of Pennsylvania, Pennsylvania Archives*, Second Series, XIX, 435. The grant was made by deeds of lease and release dated August 22 and 23, 1682. The location of the land was near the head of what is now called Wissahickon Creek, a tributary of the Schuylkill.
10. Under date of February 4, 1685/86, in the *Minutes of the Monthly Meeting of Philadelphia, 1682-1714* (p. 22), the certificate of William and Elizabeth Bradford from Devonshire-House Monthly Meeting in London was ordered to be recorded. The certificate was dated August 12, 1685.
11. John William Wallace, *An Address Delivered at the Celebration . . . of the two Hundredth Birth Day of Mr. William Bradford . . .*, 23.
12. Quoted by Wallace, 24.
13. Henry Lewis Bullen, "The Bradford Family of Printers," *Americana Collector*, I, 153. Bullen quotes from Bradford's proposal for printing the Bible in 1688, wherein the printer speaks of having found "little encouragement" in the colony. Paltsits states that Bradford did leave the city and returned to England in July 1689, but that he came to Philadelphia once again at the earnest solicitation of the Yearly Meeting.
14. Wallace, 53. Wallace says this was told him by Nathan Kite, the author of "Antiquarian Researches Among the Early Printers and Publishers of Friends' Books."

lished in Pennsylvania and New Jersey. In 1690 he hazarded another business, of which he wrote in a letter to a friend in London thus: "Samuel Carpenter and I are Building a Paper-Mill about a Mile from thy Mills at Skulkill, and hope we shall have Paper within less than four months."[15] William Rittenhouse, as active manager of this very successful concern, became the founder of a Philadelphia business family as distinguished as Bradford's, and almost as intimately connected with the development of printing in the colony.

The course of William's affairs did not, however, run smoothly; four times during his residence in Philadelphia he found himself confronted with restrictions on his press. The first three skirmishes were unpleasant and disheartening, though not serious,[16] but in 1692 came a violent clash. In that year, although he continued to print for the Meeting, Bradford published some pamphlets for the Quaker apostate George Keith. Three years earlier Keith, a man of considerable scholastic attainment, had been brought from his position as surveyor-general of New

---

15. Wroth (pp. 126-127), from a colonization tract of 1691: *Some Letters and an Abstract of Letters from Pennsylvania.*

16. A difficulty arose with the publishing of Bradford's first book, the almanac for 1686. The minutes of the Provincial Council for January 9, 1685/86 (I, 165) contain the following entry:

> The Secretary Reporting to ye Councill that in ye Chronologie of ye almanack sett forth by Samll Atkins of Philadelphia, & Printed by Wm. Bradford, of ye same place, there was these words, (the begining of Governmt here by ye Lord Penn,) the Councill Sent for Samll Atkins, & ordered him to blott out ye words Lord Penn; & likewise for Wm. Bradford, ye Printer, and gave him Charge not to print any thing but what shall have Lycence from ye Councill.

It was customary at that time to set down in almanacs after each day of the year an important occurrence of which that day was the anniversary; the Council, however, objected to "ye Lord Penn" as a violation of the Quaker sentiment against titles.

The second restriction on Bradford's press is revealed by the following record in the notes of the Monthly Meeting of 1687:

> Ordered by this meeting that William Bradford the printer do shew what may concern friends or Truth before printing to the Quarterly Meeting of Philadelphia, and if it require speed then to the monthly meeting where it may belong . . . (*Minutes of the Monthly Meeting of Philadelphia, 1682-1714*, 41).

The third conflict occurred in 1689. On April 2, 1683, at a meeting of the Council the Charter of Pennsylvania had been read, signed, sealed and delivered (*Minutes of the Provincial Council*, I, 72). A few weeks afterwards, on May 23, at another meeting of the Council at which Penn himself presided, "It was Proposed to have an attested Coppy of ye Laws Printed. After some debate ye Govr put ye Question, & it was carried in ye Negative, they should not be printed" (*ibid.*, I, 74). To a considerable number of people the lack of a published statement of their legal obligations and privileges seemed altogether unjust. Finally, therefore, Joseph Growdon, a member of the Council, had the Charter published (*ibid.*, I, 277 ff.) on his own responsibility by William Bradford, whose name, however, did not appear in the imprint. There is, unfortunately, no sub-

Jersey to head the Friends' school in Philadelphia.[17] At once he proved a most unruly member of the Society, and his outspoken criticism seemed to threaten a division of the Friends. Since the government of the province was largely in their hands, it was to be expected that neither Keith nor those who presumably had supported him in spreading his subversive theories should escape the punishment of the secular power. A broadside entitled *An Appeal from the twenty-eight Judges to the Spirit of Truth* was considered by the Quakers sufficient excuse for legal action against Keith. Bradford too was taken into custody, not only for having printed seditious matter but also, by the revival of a dead-letter law, for the violation of the Parliamentary Press Act of 1662 against the publishing of pamphlets without the printer's name.[18] Keith was found guilty, but Bradford, after a court appearance in December, was released.[19] In spite of his acquittal, his difficulties were not over, for an entry in the minutes of the Provincial Council for April 27, 1693, states that a petition had been received from Bradford requesting the return of his "tooles and Letters," seized the previous September, without which he had been unable to pursue his trade and support his family.[20] The printing materials were restored to him at once, but the concession came too late to deter him from carrying through a plan, which he had prob-

sequent report on the matter in the Council minutes, but an account written by Bradford himself of his interview with Governor Blackwell on April 9, 1689, explains his stand (Wallace, 49-52; the passage quoted is from page 51):

> ... it is my imploy, my trade and calling, and that by wch I get my living, to print; and if I may not print such things as come to my hand, which are innocent, I cannot live .... If I print one thing to-day, and the contrary party bring me another to-morrow, to contradict it, I cannot say that I shall not print it. Printing is a manufacture of the nation, and therefore ought rather to be encouraged than suppressed.

It is probable that so spirited a reply won Bradford his freedom; and it was after this episode that the Society of Friends offered him the annual subsidy of £40 already mentioned.

17. Robert Proud, *The History of Pennsylvania*, I, 345.
18. Wroth, 31.
19. Isaiah Thomas, *The History of Printing in America*, I, 222. The story, famous in the annals of printing, runs that the frame from which the pamphlet was printed was reduced, perhaps intentionally, to pi, thus destroying the evidence of Bradford's having done the work. Bradford's view of his position is made clear by his own statement in a list of books printed and sold by him in 1692:

> And whereas it is reported, That the Printer, being a favourer of G. K. he will not print for any other, which is the reason that the other Party appear not in Print as well as G. K. These are to signifie, that the Printer hath not yet refused to print any thing for either Party; and also signifies that he doth not refuse, but is willing and ready to print any thing for the future that G. K.'s Opposers shall bring to him. (Quoted by Charles R. Hildeburn, *A Century of Printing: The Issues of the Press in Pennsylvania, 1685-1784*, I, 26.)

20. *Minutes of the Provincial Council*, I, 366-367.

ably been weighing for some time, to leave the city. On April 10 he had been appointed printer to the colony of New York, and in May or June, accordingly, Bradford set up his press in the neighboring province.[21]

The story of printing in Philadelphia for twenty years after William Bradford's departure can be reconstructed in only the most sketchy fashion. There was apparently a smaller amount of printing between 1693 and 1713 than in the comparatively few years when Bradford maintained his press in the city;[22] and for two periods, between 1693 and 1699, and again between 1706 and 1709, there seems to have been no press at all. A certain Reinier Jansen,[23] whose name appears in a good many imprints from 1699 to 1705, was the only important printer, and his press evidently belonged exclusively to the Society of Friends. His son, known as Joseph Reyners, carried on the business for a year,[24] and Tiberius Johnson[25] and Jacob Taylor[26] also figure briefly in the annals of this uncertain time. None of these men, however, is comparable in importance either to William Bradford, who preceded them, or to Andrew, who came after. With their work the first chapter in the history of Philadelphia journalism closes.

21. Wroth, 32.
22. According to Hildeburn, William Bradford printed 67 items in Philadelphia and Jansen about 33. Twenty other works were put out by minor printers in the interlude between the Bradfords.
23. John William Wallace (in *An Old Philadelphian, Colonel William Bradford, The Patriot Printer of 1776*, 8) expresses his belief that after William Bradford, Senior, had left Philadelphia he "had an agency in matters of printing there." Thomas (I, 223) thinks it probable that Jansen had been an apprentice of Bradford. Wroth (p. 30) believes that Jansen came "simply as the agent of Bradford." Kite ("Antiquarian Researches Among the Early Printers and Publishers of Friends' Books," *Friend*, XVII, 28) specifically denies his connection with Bradford.
24. Wroth, 30.
25. Tiberius Johnson was, like Joseph Reyners, a son of Reinier Jansen (Douglas C. McMurtrie, *A History of Printing in the United States*, II, 12).
26. Taylor was an interesting person, a jack-of-all-trades. In addition to being a printer, the surveyor-general of the province, and the compiler of one of the most popular American almanacs before *Poor Richard*, he was a poetaster and, possibly, for a time head of the Friends' school. (For the last point see the *Minutes of the Monthly Meeting*, 251-252.)

PART I

Andrew Bradford

Under date of May 9, 1712, in the votes and proceedings of the Assembly of Pennsylvania appears the following entry:[1] "The House taking into Consideration the great Use and Benefit it would be to the Country to have the Laws printed, and thereupon sent for Jacob Taylor to treat with him about the same: He informed the House, that according to the best of his Judgment, the Charges thereof would amount to about One Hundred Pounds, besides Paper. . . ." Evidently not satisfied with Taylor's answer, on the twenty-seventh of the same month the Assembly appointed a committee of four to inquire again of Taylor and of "the other Printers in Town" concerning the cost of printing the laws.[2] On the afternoon of the same day, when the report of the committee had confirmed Taylor's original estimate, a resolution was passed empowering a new committee to make the arrangements necessary for the publication of five hundred copies of the laws; this committee was granted fifty pounds outright, and the Assembly agreed "that what it amounts to more by a true Account of the whole Expence . . . . shall be a Debt chargeable on this Province . . . ."[3]

Apparently because of insufficient funds[4] the project languished through the summer, autumn, and early part of the winter. Then on January 13, 1712/13, the Assembly once again took action:[5] "It being agreed that the Printing the Laws of this Province is necessary, William Davis, Samuel Preston, and Thomas Stevenson, are appointed a Committee to treat with any Printer, or other Person or Persons of this City, about the Charge and Method of Printing the said Laws, and bring their Proposals in Writing to this House." Two days later the committee "brought in a Proposal in Writing from Jacob Taylor, which was read, and ordered to lie on the Table";[6] and very shortly afterwards, on February 3, 1712/13, "A Proposal from Andrew Bradford, Printer, was read, and ordered to lie on the Table."[7]

As we have already seen, Andrew Bradford was born in or near Phila-

1. *Votes and Proceedings*, II, 111.
2. *Ibid.*, II, 115. Thomas (I, 225) thinks that the "other Printers" were William and Andrew Bradford, who had come to Philadelphia expressly to bargain for the job of publishing the laws.
3. *Votes and Proceedings*, II, 115.
4. *Ibid.*, II, 121.
5. *Ibid.*, II, 125.
6. *Ibid.*, II, 126.
7. *Ibid.*, II, 127.

delphia, about 1686.⁸ In 1693 he moved with his parents to New York, where he spent the remainder of his childhood and his youth. Of his early life and education nothing is known; indeed the earliest record of him dates from 1706, when he signed his name as one of the witnesses to a legal transaction.⁹ He was trained to the press, no doubt in his father's shop, and on February 22, 1708/09, he was made a freeman of the city of New York and listed as "Andrew Bradford, printer."¹⁰ He appears, moreover, to have been in partnership with his father in 1710-1711, not long before he came to Philadelphia.¹¹ Some years before Andrew proffered his services to the Pennsylvania Assembly, and shortly after he had been admitted a freeman of New York, he had sought and then apparently declined a similar position, for in the colonial records of Rhode Island was penned the following entry in the proceedings of March 22, 1708/09:¹²

Voted, and be it further enacted, that whereas there is one Bradford, son of Bradford, the printer, of New York, who hath

---

8. Though 1686 is given as the date of Andrew Bradford's birth in all the secondary sources, there seems to be no reliable evidence in support of it. There is no extant record of his birth; the record of his burial does not mention his age, nor does the obituary in the *Gazette;* and the Bradford tombstone has long been either obliterated or completely destroyed. (It is not mentioned, for instance, in E. L. Clark's *Record of the Inscriptions . . . in the Burial-Grounds of Christ Church,* 1864.) Isaiah Thomas (I, 229) speaks of Bradford's having died in 1742 "aged about fifty-six years"; from such a statement writers on Bradford may have deduced his birth date as 1686. Possibly Henry Darrach, compiler of the Bradford genealogy, or Horatio Gates Jones, the earliest serious biographer of Bradford, both of whom give 1686 as the birthdate, had access to family records which are no longer available. None of three branches of the present Bradford family of Philadelphia, lineal descendants of William Bradford I, apparently possesses any record of Andrew's birth. The "Census of the City of New-York. [about the year 1703.]" (in *The Documentary History of the State of New York,* I, 404) lists William Bradford as the head of a family which included, among other members, two "males" between the ages of sixteen and sixty. Since there is no reason to doubt that Andrew was the first-born son, one of these "males" must have been he, and if he was sixteen or over in or about 1703, he could not have been born later than approximately 1687.

9. This document is a bond, dated February 2, 1705/06, from Peter Bayard to Martin Schenck and John Amerman. The earliest of the autographs of Andrew Bradford, it is in the possession of the Henry E. Huntington Library.

10. See "The Burghers of New Amsterdam and the Freemen of New York, 1675-1866," *Collections of the New-York Historical Society for 1885,* Publication Fund Series, XVIII, 89.

11. At least three books were printed jointly by the Bradfords: Daniel Leeds' *American Almanack for . . . 1711,* published in 1710; *A Plat-form of Church-Discipline, Gathered out of the Word of God, and Agreed upon by the Elders and Messengers Of the Churches assembled in the Synod At Cambridge in N.E.,* reprinted in New York in 1711; and *The Young Man's Companion,* 2nd edition, 1710.

12. *Records of the Colony of Rhode Island and Providence Plantations, in New England,* IV, 65.

offered himself to set up a printing press in this place, and to find paper and print all things that may relate to the colony and government, for £50 per annum, if it be but for one year or two:

The Assembly considering the premises, are, upon the conditions aforesaid, willing to allow him, the said Bradford, £50 for one year; and so yearly, if the colony see good to improve him.

Wallace believes that William Bradford was keeping paternal watch over the young man's career and, being for some reason dissatisfied with these conditions, prevented the completion of the transaction.[13] It is equally possible that the Bradfords were already looking towards Philadelphia as a particularly promising place in which to set up a new printing office, for in addition to the likelihood of an opportunity to print for the government, Philadelphia offered another inducement.

After William Bradford's departure for New York, the Friends, feeling the need of a printing establishment in the colony of Pennsylvania, tried diligently to obtain one. In 1697, since it seemed improbable — and, from their point of view, it was perhaps undesirable—that a private press would be set up, the Yearly Meeting decided that printing equipment should be imported at its expense from either Boston or England.[14] The following year, after the press and appurtenances had been ordered, it was further agreed that a printer should be sent for and offered £30 a year for doing the work of the Meeting.[15] But when the press was established and a printer, Reinier Jansen, employed, the Friends were not satisfied with his qualifications. In 1700, accordingly, the Monthly Meeting was urged "to get a Person that well Understands printing, that it may be better managed than heretofore";[16] and in 1704, the same year that the press was installed in the upper floor of the schoolhouse,[17] a committee was appointed to procure a printer from England, if necessary at as large a salary as £50.[18] Two years later, after Jansen's death, the Meeting once more tried to secure an English printer, but without success.[19] At the time that Bradford brought himself to the attention of the Assembly, the Quakers were still without any regularly trained printer. It is not unlikely, therefore, as Nathan Kite suggests, that he had "received encouragement from members of the Society of Friends."[20]

13. Wallace, *William Bradford*, 85.
14. *Minutes of the Yearly Meeting of Philadelphia, 1681-1746*, 63.
15. *Ibid.*, 68.
16. *Ibid.*, 76.
17. *Minutes of the Monthly Meeting*, 186.
18. *Minutes of the Yearly Meeting*, 97-98.
19. *Ibid.*, 105-106.
20. Kite, 44.

As it turned out, Bradford was fortunate enough to win the good will of both the government and the Quakers. Although there is no record in the votes and proceedings of the House or in the minutes of the Provincial Council of his employment by the colony, in 1713 was issued, from the press of Andrew Bradford in Philadelphia, the *Acts and Laws of the Province of Pennsylvania, October 14th, 1712 to March 27, 1713*,[21] the publication of which established him, though unofficially, as provincial printer. For the Friends within the next few years Bradford published several pieces, the earliest among them being Thomas Chalkley's *Forcing A Maintenance Not Warrantable from the Holy Scripture, for a Minister of the Gospel* in 1714; and in 1716 he took over the upper room of their school, with the press and its materials, as his printing office, for which he paid the Meeting an annual rent of £10.[22] He maintained his establishment there until 1724, when he moved to a house, also on Second Street, owned by Richard Hill,[23] a prominent Quaker with whom he had frequently had business dealings, both personal and in connection with his work for the Meeting.[24]

For ten years after his arrival in Philadelphia Bradford was the only printer in the colony. His publications, it must be admitted, were few in number and limited in scope. To the end of 1723, the year in which Keimer set up as his competitor, Bradford had published approximately seventy-five items, including at least three works put out jointly with his father.[25] Almanacs, the mainstay of the early eighteenth-century printer, predominated: Jacob Taylor's appeared annually; Titan Leeds' began in

21. It is possible that William and Andrew established their press in Philadelphia in 1712. Hildeburn lists Joseph Morgan's *Gospel Ordinances*, which bears their imprint, as having been published in Philadelphia in that year. Charles Evans' *American Bibliography*, I, 1573, gives New York as the place of publication.

22. *Minutes of the Yearly Meeting*, 175, 182. Accounts in the *Logan Papers* (XVII, 88, 95, 96, 100, 107, 112, 113) between Bradford and the Society of Friends show that he paid this amount regularly each year from 1716 to September 25, 1724, except that for 1723 (XVII, 109) he paid only £5. The deviation is probably explained by a letter of September 17, 1723, from Bradford to the Yearly Meeting, in which he says that he hopes the Friends will "abate" his rent for the ensuing year because, "Friends Letters being worn out," he now uses his own (*Logan Papers*, XVII, 106). The *Logan Papers* (XVII, 113) contain a summary of Bradford's account with the Meeting from 1716 to September 1723. Kite (p. 44) believes that Bradford took over the Friends' school room upon his arrival in Philadelphia, even though no regular agreement between him and the Meeting was made until 1716.

23. *Logan Papers*, XVII, 113.

24. *Logan Papers*, XVII, 89, 93, 106, 112; XVIII, 14, 23. Several transactions concern the printing of more than 1400 copies of *A Legacy for Children, Being Some of the Last Expressions, and Dying Sayings, of Hannah Hill*. Hannah Hill, Richard's daughter, died at the age of eleven.

25. The information in this paragraph is derived from Hildeburn. A new and complete bibliography of Bradford imprints would be desirable, but for our purpose Hildeburn gives a sufficiently accurate picture of the extent and variety of Bradford's publications.

1715 (published in 1715) and continued thereafter; John Jerman's appeared first in 1721 (published in 1720). More important were Bradford's publications for the government; in 1714 he issued *The Laws of the Province of Pennsilvania*, the first printed collection of the laws of the colony, intended to give in full all those which were then in force, with the titles of those which were obsolete.[26] In addition to this major production Bradford regularly printed the acts of the Assembly, as well as such other works as James Logan's charge to the grand jury in 1723, various Indian treaties, a petition of the Swedes in 1722, and several letters and proclamations of Governor Keith.[27] The government finally recognized and approved his services by making him "Printer to the Province," a title which appears first in his imprint in 1720.[28] Besides his work for Pennsylvania, Bradford printed at least two items for other colonies: Governor Burnet's speech to the Assembly of New Jersey in 1723, and *The Laws of the Province of Maryland* in 1718. The remainder of his work, about one-third of the total output, consisted of books and pamphlets on social, political, or religious matters. For the Friends, for example, he printed *The Christianity of the Quakers Asserted* and William Penn's *Key*;[29] in 1715 appeared an anti-slavery tract; his first edition of the popular handbook of local government entitled *Conductor Generalis* came out in 1722;[30] *The Young Man's Companion*, a business manual issued first by William Bradford in New York in 1705 and reprinted frequently thereafter by various printers, appeared in 1723;[31] and from the same year dates *The Husband-Man's Guide, being a Colection of very useful Directions and Receipts for Country People*.

On December 22, 1719, Bradford published the first number of the *American Weekly Mercury*. From the perspective of two centuries this newspaper appears the most important single project of Bradford's career. One of the longest-lived of early papers, it continued without

26. Hildeburn (no. 128) notes that there were a few omissions.
27. One of these, *A Letter to His Majesty's Justices of the Peace for the County of Chester*, 1718, is typographically interesting because the title-page is printed in red and black; this is believed to be the earliest example of American printing in more than one color.
28. The work was a proclamation of Governor Keith, dated November 5, 1720.
29. The complete title explains the nature of the work: *A Key opening a way to every common Understanding, How to discern the Difference betwixt the Religion Professed by the People called Quakers, and the Perversions, Misrepresentations and Calumnies of their several Adversaries*, 1717.
30. There were three Philadelphia editions of this book between 1722 and 1750 (Wroth, 241). Its imposing title is *Conductor Generalis; or the Office, Duty and Authority of Justices of the Peace, High-Sheriffs, Under-Sheriffs, Gaolers, Coroners, Constables, Jury-men, Overseers of the Poor, And also the Office of Clerks of Assize and of the Peace, &c. Collected out of all the Books hitherto written on those Subjects, whether of Common or Statute Law.*
31. Wroth, 243-244.

a break for more than twenty-six years; it had a wide circulation and carried a large amount of advertising; its handling of news, both local and "foreign," was generally dependable; and it brought to its readers not only information but entertainment as well. It was typical of its age; yet it had considerable individuality. When Bradford laid his plans for the *Mercury* the only paper in the British colonies was the Boston *News Letter*. The *News Letter* had been started in 1704, fourteen years after the appearance of the earliest American paper, *Publick Occurrences* of Boston, which had been suppressed after one number. Before the *Mercury* had actually come from the press, however, it had acquired a second rival in the Boston *Gazette,* the first issue of which appeared on December 21, 1719.[32]

The early numbers of the *Mercury* were sold by Bradford at "the Bible in the Second Street" and by "John Copson in Market Street." Copson, a Philadelphia merchant, did not remain long in the firm, for on May 25, 1721, his name was dropped from the imprint, and in the same paper an announcement of his opening a marine-insurance office probably explains why the arrangement had been dissolved. The loss of Copson was more than balanced, however, by the acquisition almost a year earlier of another partner: Number 25 expanded the ordinary imprint with the statement that the paper might also be had of "William Bradford in New York, where Advertisements are taken in." Once again we see evidence of the solidarity of the Bradfords in business matters, and until December 21, 1725, immediately after William had started his *Gazette,* this business arrangement between father and son continued.

During his first years in Philadelphia Bradford was fortunate or circumspect enough to avoid conflict with the government, but his trade made it unlikely that he would permanently escape difficulty. As Mr. Wroth has pointed out, "direct interference with the colonial press by the English authorities was most unusual, but the local governments — governor, officials, and both houses of assembly — were extremely sensitive to printed criticism, then a relatively new form of protest."[33] Between 1721 and 1723 political discussion in Pennsylvania centered upon the falling off of public credit and upon possible means of correcting the disordered condition of trade and finance. In 1721 was printed an anonymous pamphlet entitled *Some Remedies Proposed, for the Restoring the sunk Credit of the Province of Pennsylvania; with Some Remarks of its Trade. Humbly Offer'd to the Consideration of the Worthy Rep-*

32. The significance of the *Mercury* is more apparent if we remember that, though Pennsylvania was one of the younger colonies, it was the second to support a permanent newspaper. Massachusetts waited sixty-four years for the *News Letter,* New York a hundred years for the *Gazette,* and Philadelphia but thirty-eight years for the *Mercury.*
33. Wroth, 173.

resentatives in the General Assembly of this Province, By a Lover of this Country.[34] Neither "Philadelphia" nor the printer's name appeared in the imprint, but since Bradford's was the only press in the colony, the pamphlet could hardly have had any other source. His audacity in printing such a tract was emphasized by his assuming in his own name a position on the problem and bringing it into the columns of his paper. In the *Mercury* of January 2, 1721/22, the news items were concluded with the following pertinent, though scarcely impassioned, comment: "Our General Assembly are now sitting, and we have great Expectations from them at this Juncture, that they will find some effectual Remedy, to revive the dying Credit of this Province, and restore us to our former happy Circumstances."

The implications of such a sentence were not to be overlooked by a body that had troubled itself over the "Lord Penn" affair of William Bradford's time.[35] Under date of January 19 in the Council minutes we find the following entry:[36]

> Upon a motion made, that Andrew Bradford, Printer, be Examined before this Board concerning the publishing of a late Pamphlet, entituled 'Some Remedies proposed for the restoring of the Sunk Credit of the Province of Pennsylvania,' as also of the Weekly Mercury of the 2d of January instant, the last paragraph whereof seems to have been intended as a Reflection upon the Credit of this province; it is ordered that He, the said Printer, have Notice to attend this Board at the next meeting of Council.

The result of this order appears in the minutes of February 1:[37]

> The Board being informed that Andrew Bradford, the Printer, attended according to order, He was called in and

34. The author was Francis Rawle.
35. It is important to realize that the point at issue was not the truth or fallacy of Rawle's and Bradford's contention about the state of the province. Indeed, everyone knew and acknowledged how serious the economic situation was. On the very day on which the offending *Mercury* appeared, Governor Keith in a public address admitted the miserable condition of the colony. (See *Mercury* 108.) A week later, evidently without arousing any official objection, Bradford printed a letter from some merchants in Jamaica protesting against the deterioration in the quality of Pennsylvania flour and stating unequivocally: "Thus the Reputation of a Place once famed for the Best Flour in America, is perfectly lost." James Logan in a letter to his friend Henry Goldney said: "This Province is now exceedingly sunk in its Circumstances. We have very little Trade, and less money . . ." (*Papers Relating to Provincial Affairs in Pennsylvania, 1682-1750*, 77, under date of April 9, 1723). William R. Shepherd points out that about 1722 "hard money was so scarce that many were obliged to cut gold coin into six-pences for marketing" (*History of Proprietary Government in Pennsylvania*, 405 n.).
36. *Minutes of the Provincial Council*, III, 143.
37. *Ibid.*, III, 145.

examined concerning a late Pamphlet, entituled 'Some Remedies proposed for restoring the Sunk Credit of the Province of Pennsylvania'; Whereupon, He declared that He knew nothing of the printing or publishing the said Pamphlet; And being reprimanded by the Governour for publishing a certain paragraph in his News-Paper, called the American Weekly Mercury of the 2d of January last, He said it was inserted by his Journey-Man, who composed the said Paper, without his Knowledge, and that He was very sorry for it, and for which he humbly submitted himself and ask'd Pardon of the Govr. and the Board; whereupon the Governour told him, That He must not for the future presume to publish any thing relating to or concerning the Affairs of this Government, or the Government of any other of his Majestys Colonies, without the permission of the Governour or Secretary of this province, for the time being, And then He was dismissed and the Council adjourned.[38]

Bradford does not appear to have changed his business policy noticeably following his tiff with the government. Moreover, his own experience with the provincial authorities of Pennsylvania probably made him the readier to sympathize with James Franklin when in 1723 the latter found himself at odds with the government of Massachusetts Bay. Whatever the reason, in the *Mercury* of February 26 appeared a full report of "the Proceedings of the General Assembly at Boston against Mr. Franklin" taken from the *New England Courant* of January 21.[39] In addition, at the point where the account in the *Courant* ended, the *Mercury* continued with an outspoken commentary as follows:

> My Lord Coke observes, That to punish first and then enquire, the Law abhors; but here Mr. Franklin has a severe Sentence pass'd upon him, even to the taking away Part of his Livelihood, without being call'd to make Answer. An indifferent Person would judge by this Vote against Couranto, That the Assembly of the Province of the Massachusets Bay are made up of Oppressors and Bigots, who make Religion the only En-

---

38. Bradford's winning his freedom on such very flimsy evidence as his denial of knowledge of both the pamphlet and the disputed paragraph in the *Mercury* may possibly have been due to the presence at the Council meeting of February 1 of Andrew Hamilton and Governor Keith. Hamilton may have already possessed convictions about the freedom of the press; Keith was not only a personal friend of Rawle, but publicly supported his proposal that the colony should issue paper money.

39. *Courant* 77. Franklin introduced the account in his own paper with the remark: "We hear that the following Act is to be inserted in the *News Letter* and *Gazette* Three Weeks successively."

gine of Destruction to the People; and the rather, because the first Letter in the *Courant* of the 14th of January (which the Assembly censures) so naturally represents and exposes the Hypocritical Pretenders to Religion. Indeed, the most famous Politicians in that Government (as the infamous Gov. D———y and his Family) have ever been remarkable for Hypocrisy: And it is the general Opinion, that some of their Rulers are rais'd up and continued as a Scourge in the Hands of the Almighty for the Sins of the People.

Thus much we could not forbear saying, out of Compassion to the distressed People of the Province, who must now resign all Pretences to Sense and Reason, and submit to the Tyranny of Priestcraft and Hypocrisy.

Isaiah Thomas believed that the observations upon the news item — what he called "the following severe remarks" — were "unquestionably furnished by the Courant Club in Boston."[40] Whether or not this speculation is sound, Bradford's friendly attitude towards Franklin is shown by his willingness to publish so uncompromising an opinion. Moreover, these words, severe though they may have been, were hardly likely to get him into trouble. Despite the Pennsylvania Council's injunction against publishing anything relating to "the Government of any other of his Majestys Colonies," intercolonial solidarity was notably lacking in eighteenth-century America, and it was improbable that the government of Pennsylvania would concern itself about a possibly libelous attack upon the government of Massachusetts. On the other hand, the story itself was news, it was good reading, and its printing might gain Bradford credit in Boston — three sound reasons for his including it in the *Mercury* aside from any wish to go on record as opposing censorship of the press.

Subsequently, in 1727 and 1728, Bradford published a number of political pamphlets bearing such titles as *Some Necessary Precautions worthy to be considered by all English Subjects, in their Election of Members, to Represent them in General Assembly; wherein, neither Fear, Flattery, nor Gain, ought to byass* and *Advice and Information To the Freeholders and Freemen of the Province of Pensilvania* and *A Few Words in Favour of Free-Thinking.*[41] The titles sound daring, but it is probable that none of the pamphlets concerned itself with the

---

40. Thomas, II, 36.
41. Neither Hildeburn nor Evans locates a copy of the first; the third is known apparently only through an advertisement in the *Mercury* of April 4, 1726. The second provoked a reply, *Remarks upon the Advice to the Freeholders &c. Paragraph by Paragraph*, printed by Keimer. Both of these pamphlets are in the Historical Society of Pennsylvania.

work of the Assembly or the government as such, and the printer, therefore, escaped the displeasure of the Council. Still it must have been obvious which way the wind was blowing at the Sign of the Bible, and in 1729 Bradford was again brought before the authorities. This time he was dealt with severely and his defense was correspondingly vigorous.

On September 18, 1729, Number 31 of the *Busy-Body* series, then appearing in the *Mercury*,[42] was introduced by its editor, probably Joseph Breintnall, with a paragraph to this effect:

> In my No. 26. I mentioned the Receipt of an elaborate Epistle subscribed Brutus or Cassius, or both. I have since received three Packets of Papers, from Caska, inclosed under one Cover to the Printer. My Readers may think them too good to have been conceal'd; I shall therefore publish 'em without Alteration, not desiring to take the Praise of any Man's Performances to my Self. I have repeatedly invited the Learned and Ingenious to my Assistance, and have given proper Cautions to my Correspondents. I shall say no more to introduce the said Papers. The first mentioned is as hereunder: The rest (being on the same Subjects) will follow, as they are numbred, weekly; if in the mean Time I am not under a Necessity to postpone any of them.

Then followed an essay of which this sentence appears to be the thesis: "There is scarce any one of the Passions but what is truly Laudable, when it centers in the Publick, and makes that it's Object."[43] The article,

---

42. In the *Mercury* for January 28, 1729, Number 473, the famous attack on Keimer began. Three letters were cited — samples, so the Busy-Body said, of several epistles he had received from women denouncing Keimer, especially for *Instructor* 8, which, it was asserted, did the female sex particular injustice. Then followed the series of papers, thirty-two in all, Numbers 1, 2, 3, 4, 5, and 8 by Franklin, the later ones chiefly from the pen of Joseph Breintnall. (See Albert H. Smyth, editor, *The Writings of Benjamin Franklin*, II, 100 n.) They continued until September 25, one week before Franklin took over the *Instructor*, when, having accomplished his object by forcing the unfortunate Keimer to sell out, Franklin allowed the essays to come to an end.

43. The sentence is an exact quotation from the Cato letter of July 29, 1721, Number 39. "Cato" was the *nom de plume* of two English writers, Thomas Gordon and John Trenchard, who first became famous with the publication between January 20, 1720, and January 4, 1721, of *The Independent Whig*, subtitled "A Defence of Primitive Christianity," a series of fifty-three essays on religion, published weekly and written from a distinctly rationalistic point of view. When the South Sea Bubble burst in 1720, these men, calling themselves "Cato," began a series of letters which demanded vigorous action by the government against the perpetrators of the swindle. Between November 12, 1720, and December 7, 1723, a total of 144 letters appeared, first in the London *Journal* and later in the *British Journal*. (In September 1722 the London *Journal* became a thoroughgoing ministerial paper. Cato's last letter appeared in it on September 8. On September 22 appeared the first issue of the *British Journal* with a new Cato letter in it. See

however, quickly works around to the negative side of this proposition and stresses the dangers of those passions which are not subservient to the public good, emphasizing particularly the tendency of power to perpetuate itself. It then suggests a definite measure to prevent the undue extension of political influence — that is, rotation of office; and it ends with a vigorous challenge:

> Let us exert our Selves for Liberty, and don't Tamely sit by and allow any Part of it to be wrested from us by any Man, or Combination of Men whatsoever; but rather take care to transmit it to Posterity, rather Improved, than in the least Diminished, one Day, one Hour of Vertuous Liberty is worth a whole Eternity in Bondage. To be the Friends of Liberty, Firmness of Mind and Publick Spirit is absolutely requisite, and this Quality so Essential and Necessary to a noble Mind, proceeds from a Just Way of thinking that we are not born for our Selves alone, Nor our own private Advantage alone, but Likewise and Principally for the good of others, and Service of Civil Society. This raised the Genius of the Romans, improved their Vertue, and made them Protectors of Mankind, this Principle, according to the Motto of these Papers, Animated the Romans, Cato, and his followers, and it was impossible to be thought Great or Good without being a Patriot; and none could pretend to Courage, Gallantry, and Greatness of Mind, without being first of all possessed with a publick Spirit, and Love of their Country, I am, take which you will.
>
> Brutus, or Cassius, or both.

As the Busy-Body himself had already pointed out in Number 26, in his letter to "Brutus or Cassius, or both,"[44] the writer of the essay "had purloin'd [a Treasure] from *Cato*."[45] In the entire article very little but the concluding sentiment, quoted just above, was not plagiarized and certainly none of the ideas was novel. Had the essay not appeared just before an election, it might, therefore, have been allowed to pass un-

---

C. B. Realey, "*The London Journal* and Its Authors, 1720-1723," *University of Kansas Humanistic Studies*, V, no. 3, 25-26.) Gordon and Trenchard soon carried their discussions far beyond the ramifications of the South Sea scandal, so that when *Cato's Letters* was published as a book in 1724, in the first of many editions, it was actually, as the subtitle says, a group of "Essays on Liberty, Civil and Religious, And other important Subjects."

44. See *Mercury* 501, August 14.

45. The specific indebtedness of this paper to *Cato* may be summarized thus: paragraph 1 (in part) verbatim from *Cato* 39; paragraph 2 (almost entirely) verbatim from *Cato* 40; paragraph 3 (topic sentence and elsewhere) verbatim from *Cato* 40; paragraph 4, the same ideas on Whigs and Tories, expressed in different words, as in *Cato* 96. The crucial suggestion about rotation of offices, though phrased differently, may well have come from *Cato* 61.

noticed; but so carefully timed and so forcible a thrust necessarily perturbed the Council. From the minutes of that body it seems that Governor Gordon considered the problem of sufficient importance to warrant a special meeting on September 20:[46]

> The Governour acquainted the Board that he now called them together to lay before them a News paper published in this Province, printed & sold by Andrew Bradford, numbered 506,[47] in which a Letter signed Brutus or Cassius, or both, appears to reflect on the King & Government of Great Britain, & to incite the Inhabitants of this Province to throw off all Subjection to the regular & Establish'd Powers of Government. And the same being read & considered by the Board, It is their Opinion that it is a wicked & seditious Libell, tending to introduce Confusion under the Notion of Liberty, and to lessen the just Regard due to Persons in Authority. 'Tis therefore Ordered, that the said Bradford be immediately taken into Custody, & examined by the Mayor & Recorder of this City, or any other two Justices of the Peace, & that his Dwelling House & Printing Office be searcht for the written Copy of the said Libel, that the Author may be discovered, & that the Attorney General commence a Prosecution against the said Bradford for Printing & Publishing the same.
>
> This order being executed and the Original Copy found, it appeared to be wrote by one Campbell, a Parson of a dissolute Character, who had lived for some time in Newcastle County, but his scandalous Behaviour proving intolerable to his Hearers, there he removed to Long Island, from whence he sent that Paper with others of the same strain, by the Post, to Andrew Bradford, who without considering or knowing its Tendency, printed it as he did other Papers in his Mercury. His ignorance therefore, gave some Abatement to the Prosecution; he was however committed, & then Bound over to the Court.

This is the last we learn of the affair from the minutes, a record apparently of complete victory for the government. But the *Mercury* tells a different and more heartening story, for when Number 507 came out with its usual promptness on September 25, the *Busy-Body* essay had its accustomed position on the first page. Moreover, the author once more furnished an introduction, at the end of which he hazarded this independent statement:

46. *Minutes of the Provincial Council*, III, 369-370.
47. The issue of September 18.

I Thought I had said enough to introduce to the Publick the last Week's Paper, without Blame; But I've been mistaken, it has given Offence undesign'd, the Printer has been arrested, and the Sheriff ordered to confine him. I cannot think the Gentlemen, by whose Authority Mr. Bradford was call'd to Account, did of themselves conceive this rigorous Usage necessary; till the Matter had been misrepresented to them and aggravated.

I desire my Readers to believe me, and I do hereby truly assure them, that the Present Paper, hereunder, was writ before the above-mention'd came from the Press, and was design'd for this Day, and that I have not enlarg'd, lessened or altered it, for what has happened upon Publishing the other. These are my own Sentiments.

The essay, also, shows an increase in daring over the previous one: it particularly mentions the approaching election; it advises careful scrutiny of each candidate's actual record;[48] and finally it speaks in favor of the re-election of the city sheriff then in office.[49]

On the two occasions when he clashed violently with the provincial government Andrew Bradford offered no spectacular defense; the first time he listened politely and apologized as he was expected to do; the second time, so far as we know, he went quietly to jail and, when released, went quietly back to work again.[50] Ostensibly Bradford bowed to authority. Actually he seems to have gone steadily on his way, without making any real concession to the threats of the government; and in the 'thirties, certainly, the *Mercury* was bolder than ever. More than one historian, in fact, has considered Bradford's undramatic resistance to control of his press important in the story of colonial journalism,[51] and J. M. Lee paid Bradford this emphatic tribute:[52] "In supporting his case he set forth those principles that later enabled Andrew Hamil-

---

48. This section of the essay closely resembles *Cato* 69 and 70, one sentence in 70 being especially pertinent: "It is the Right and Duty of the Freeholders and Burghers of Great Britain, to examine into the Conduct, and to know the Opinions and Intentions, of such as offer themselves to their Choice."

49. The sheriff was Owen Owen, who had been commissioned on October 4, 1726. Charles Read, commissioned on October 4, 1729, succeeded him. (See John Hill Martin, *Bench and Bar of Philadelphia*, 100.)

50. James Melvin Lee (*History of American Journalism*, 32-33) says: "In colonial days editors did not seem to mind being locked up in jail: editing a paper from prison was always sure to increase the circulation." John Peter Zenger is a famous illustration; the New York *Weekly Journal* flourished during the eight and a half months that he managed it while he was imprisoned.

51. For example, see David Paul Brown, *The Forum, or Forty Years Full Practice at the Philadelphia Bar*, I, 287, and Livingston Rowe Schuyler, *The Liberty of the Press in the American Colonies Before the Revolutionary War*, 31.

52. James Melvin Lee, "Andrew Bradford," *D. A. B.*

19

ton, in New York City, to free John Peter Zenger in the most famous case for press freedom in colonial days."

II

During the years when Bradford was establishing himself as a printer and building the reputation of his newspaper, he engaged also in a good many other activities.[53] He had been made a freeman of Philadelphia on May 20, 1717,[54] and on October 3, 1727, he was elected a member of the city council, a position to which he was re-elected annually until the end of his life.[55] In 1726 he was appointed to the vestry of Christ Church, and he remained a vestryman for many years.[56] In 1728 he assumed the postmastership of the colony, a position of much responsibility and civic importance.[57] Two years before this appointment he had ventured into an unfamiliar field of business; he and eleven other men, nearly all of them distinguished citizens of Philadelphia,[58] had formed the Durham Iron Company "with an Intent to erect a Furnace and other Works for casting and making of Iron"[59] in Bucks County near the Delaware River. Accordingly the group took up a tract of land, totalling 5948 acres and embracing all of Durham Township, at a cost of £781 in Pennsylvania currency,[60] and on March 4, 1727/28, signed a partnership agreement

53. According to Wroth (p. 188) the colonial printer was frequently active in local affairs.
54. *Minutes of the Common Council of the City of Philadelphia (1704 to 1776)*, 126.
55. *Ibid.*, 276-408. The last meeting which Bradford attended was held on January 18, 1741/42.
56. The *Minutes of the Vestry of Christ Church* first mention his name under date of April 11, 1726; he was re-elected to the vestry from 1727 to 1732 inclusive. The minutes between October 6, 1732, and April 1735 are lost; but Bradford's name appears again in the minutes for 1735, '36, and '37. There are no minutes from July 28, 1737, to April 29, 1740, and from July 31, 1740, to April 19, 1742. Bradford's name appears for the last time in 1737.
57. See *Mercury* 431.
58. Jeremiah Langhorne (the only one of the twelve men who was not from Philadelphia), Charles Read, Anthony Morris, Clement Plumstead, William Allen, and James Logan were the most prominent members of the company. Robert Ellis, another member of the group, was Bradford's wife's brother-in-law. On both the deed (of March 4, 1727/28) and the partnership agreement Bradford signed for Ellis as his attorney.
59. Quotation from the original deed. Four of the original legal documents relating to the founding of the Durham Iron Company are written on one large parchment which is in the possession of the Bucks County Historical Society. Bucks County Deed Book 16 (also called F-1), 136 ff. and 119 ff., contains the deed and partnership agreement of March 4, 1727/28. The Bucks County Historical Society likewise owns several unpublished volumes prepared by B. F. Fackenthal, Jr., in which important documents are reproduced and in which the history of the company is fully discussed.
60. Three tracts of land were first separately conveyed to Samuel Powell of Philadelphia; then on February 10, 1727/28, Powell in turn conveyed the entire

to run for fifty-one years.[61] Even before the legal arrangements were completed, however, the company had put up a blast-furnace[62] and several other buildings. Bradford's interest in the company was, it is probable, rather financial than active; he continued, however, to hold his share in the business throughout his life and mentioned it specifically in his will.

A more conventional enterprise than the Durham Iron Company was Bradford's store. It was the custom, almost the necessity, of the printing shop to sell all sorts of commodities; for, as J. M. Lee says, "the colonial printer was willing to take almost anything in exchange for subscriptions" and often "sold over the counter the goods accepted in payment."[63] For this reason, perhaps, Bradford's advertisements for his own shop in the earlier numbers of the *Mercury* are a medley of the commonplace and the exotic. He sold molasses by the barrel, whalebone, live goose feathers, and "Barbadoes Rum"; corks; chocolate, the "pure nut"; "English pease"; and Spanish snuff, in half- or quarter-pound canisters; Jesuit's bark,[64] Bohea tea, "very good Pickled Sturgeon," and beaver hats, as well as a variety of patent medicines with such names as "Squires Grand Elixir."[65] Of articles answering an intellectual rather than a physical need there were few, but it is worth noting that Bradford's heterogeneous stock at one time included "A Curious Prospect of the City of New York" and "A Pair of Globes Nine Inches Diameter, with their Appurtenances."[66] Bradford's shop seems also to have been an unofficial bureau of inquiry, where lost or found articles might be reclaimed or deposited, where information about runaway servants might be sought, where queries regarding the buying and selling of Negro slaves or the purchase of houses and ground-rents might be made,[67] where tickets for lotteries might be obtained,[68] and where all sorts of miscellaneous questions might be asked and answered, as is illustrated in Number 129, in which Bradford tells of a letter received by him from

tract to the company. There were sixteen shares, of which four men held two each, and the other eight men one each. Bradford had one-sixteenth.

61. The partnership agreement was terminated in 1773 (Bucks County Deed Book F-1, 192 ff.), when Bradford's share was in the possession of his widow's niece-by-marriage, Cornelia Smith.

62. The date-stone of the furnace with "1727" clearly cut in it is in the museum of the Bucks County Historical Society.

63. Lee, *History of American Journalism*, 68, 72.

64. "Jesuit's bark" is better known as "Peruvian bark" (cinchona).

65. See the following numbers of the *Mercury* in the order given: 91 ff., 82 ff., 75 ff., 116 ff., 136 ff., 151 ff., 151 ff., 159, 206 ff. and 219, 11 ff., 331, 331, 209.

66. *Mercury* 114, 130.

67. See the following numbers of the *Mercury* in the order given: 32 and 143, 60 and 336, 148, 347 and 294.

68. See *Mercury* 358 and the New York *Gazette* of April 10, 1727.

"Hemstead Harbour in Long Island" requesting information about a medicinal spring supposed to exist near Philadelphia.

In later years the store assumed a more dignified air and increased the range of its stock and services. Though Bradford continued to sell feathers and "pease," beaver hats and "Pickl'd Sturgeon,"[69] the advertisements now announced the importation from Europe of such articles as "Super-fine Spectacles with Steel Bows and Joints, either with Fish-skin Cases or without, with several other sorts of Horn or Leather; also Reading and Burning Glasses, Pocket Compasses with Dials, very convenient to Travel with."[70] At various times a harpsichord and a virginal were for sale.[71] The shop imported "good English Red Leather," "English Cherry Brandy, and the Right Irish Usquebaugh in Quart Bottles," quadrants and sea-charts.[72] Bradford could give information about "A Shad Net almost New, Ninety Fathoms long, Twenty Foot deep, well hung," and about a copper still for brewing "which will Boyle off two Barrels compleatly."[73] When Colonel Spotswood lost a servant he advertised in the *Mercury* that information about the runaway should be sent to Andrew Bradford.[74] When Richard Dereham — son of Sir Richard Dereham, Baronet, sometime of the West Indies, and latterly of Maryland and Pennsylvania — inherited £500, the *Mercury* advertised to find him.[75] If a prospective traveller wished to book passage on the *Christiana* for Bristol, he might make arrangements at Bradford's shop.[76] When two casks of rice and a trunk from South Carolina, plus a letter with a key in it, had remained long unclaimed at the shop (which was also, we remember, the post office), Bradford had to threaten to sell the rice to pay the freight and the storage unless the owner put in a prompt appearance.[77] A lost gold girdle-buckle, the public was informed, should be returned to Bradford's store for a ten-shilling reward — and no questions would be asked.[78] A person who wanted a wet nurse or a housekeeper might hear of one by inquiring of the printer,[79] and a person qualified to keep school and desirous of living in the country might also be reached by asking at the shop.[80]

69. See, for example, *Mercury* 396, 533, 501-506, 641.
70. *Mercury* 882.
71. *Mercury* 367, 479-480.
72. *Mercury* 592, 480, 671, 756.
73. *Mercury* 576, 506. In Number 943 a "fishing sein" is advertised to be sold at auction.
74. *Mercury* 641.
75. *Mercury* 644. The advertisement seeking to locate a missing person was very common; see, for example, Numbers 554, 658, 675, 717.
76. *Mercury* 690, 699.
77. *Mercury* 713.
78. *Mercury* 793.
79. *Mercury* 824, 841.
80. *Mercury* 860.

Bradford imported looking glasses, either with plain walnut frames or japanned, and "sundry sorts of Picture Cards, as Love Cards, Nuptial Cards, Proverb Cards, Musical Cards, Stock-Jobbing (or the Humours of Change-Ally) Cards, Bubble Cards, Popish Miracle Cards. And a parcel of others, Fine and Coarse."[81] Any person who had occasion to purchase Maryland money might inquire of the printer, and those who wished to exchange their paper money for gold should also see him.[82] He had information about a second-hand two-wheel chaise; he sold "hand-engines, made of Tin, which will cast Water near Thirty Foot perpendicular, and are very convenient in watring Gardens, washing Windows, cooling Houses, or upon occasion to extinguish Fire."[83] Once he advertised: "Any Persons having any live Deer to Sell, are desired to repair to the Printer hereof, where they may hear of a Market."[84] And at least once he appealed primarily to the ladies with a consignment of "Superfine Womens black Velvet fit for Scharves and Hoods, fine and course Chints, black and other colour'd Taffeties and Persians, fine and course Callicoes, silver and plain Ribbons, Men and Womens Stockings, sewing and stitching Silk, Threads, Tapes, Spices of all sorts, choice Tea and Coffee, Starch, Powder-blew and Indigo, . . . with sundry other Goods too tedious here to mention . . . ."[85] So, on and on, run the advertisements, until we are quite sure that Bradford's shop, if it could be reconstructed, would pass very well as the American eighteenth-century collection in a well-stocked museum.

In addition to the oddly assorted objects of sale or inquiry which his store accumulated, Bradford gradually built up a more appropriate business as a stationer and bookseller. At a very early date the usual printer's advertisement of lampblack appeared in the paper,[86] and continued intermittently throughout. In January 1731, a sentence was added to the imprint of the *Mercury* informing those who were interested that there were at the Bible "all Sorts of Printing Work done cheap, and Old Books neatly bound; likewise Ready Money for Linnen Rags."[87] Some of these rags, perhaps, came back over the counter as writing paper, for there were many advertisements to this effect: "most sorts of Stationary

---

81. *Mercury* 919, 824.
82. *Mercury* 932, 576-577. See also Number 1109.
83. *Mercury* 973, 907.
84. *Mercury* 635.
85. *Mercury* 1113.

86. *Mercury* 133; sometimes, as in Number 1018, the lampblack advertisement is coupled with one of "Linced [linseed] Oil by the Gallon." *Mercury* 676 makes clear that Bradford owned a "House" for the manufacture of lampblack.

87. *Mercury* 575. The appeal for linen rags to be used by the local paper mill was a recurrent feature of the colonial newspaper. (See Wroth, 143-150.) Similar advertisements appear regularly in the *Mercury*.

Ware, Sold very Cheap."[88] But a considerable part of the paper was brought from Europe. In an advertisement of articles "Lately Imported from London," for instance, are listed the following items:[89]

> A Choice parcel of Blank Books, of Royal, Medium, Demy and Pot Paper. Also a parcel of good Slates. Choice Ink-Powder and Japan Ink, Sealing Wax and Wafers, Folio Letter-Cases fit for Merchants Desks or Counting Houses. Likewise a parcel of very good Paper, as Royal, Demy, Superfine large Post, Fools Cap and Pot; Ink Stands of several sorts, and most sorts of Stationary Ware. N. B. All sorts of Old and New Books neatly Bound and Cheap.

A similar list six years later mentions also "Slate Pencils, Spunges, Blank Books of several sizes (and may be made of any sort that's wanted either in Parchment, Vellum, or Calf-skin) Pocket-Books, Letter-Cases, fine Writing Paper of several sorts and sizes, Ink, Ink Powder, Pounce, Sealing Wax, Wafers of various sizes, black Lead Pencils silver'd with Caps and Cases."[90] Bradford advertised that he sold "glaz'd Press Papers" and that fullers might be supplied very reasonably,[91] and that he carried good writing parchment, wholesale or retail, and "English Glue."[92] He also imported "Books with Ivory Leaves," hornbooks, "Dutch Quills," "Crown and Half-Crown Wafers for Offices," gilt paper for letters, Aleppo ink, "Gum-Arabec," "fine Glass Ink Founts," and "Glass Viols."[93] Beginning in 1730, legal stationery also appeared in Bradford's stock, as we can see from an advertisement of "Penal Bills, Penal Bonds, Bail Bonds, Counter Bonds, Bonds of Arbitration, Letters of Attorney, Indentures, Bills of Lading, Bills of Sale for Ships or Sloops, General Releases; and several other Sorts of Blanks."[94] Commercial stationery, indeed, remained a staple of Bradford's trade throughout the existence of the shop.[95]

---

88. *Mercury* 626, and throughout. See also the advertisements in Felix Leeds' almanac for 1728, Hughes's for 1726, Titan Leeds' for 1724.
89. *Mercury* 574.
90. *Mercury* 882.
91. *Mercury* 1106, 1116.
92. *Mercury* 1166, 1167.
93. *Mercury* 756, 759. Horatio Gates Jones (*Andrew Bradford,* 19) says: "The importation of *gilt paper* indicates that the Province was growing in wealth and increasing in attention to points of elegance and etiquette. The use of this sort of paper for elegant or special correspondence was formerly considered quite a matter of propriety . . . ."
94. *Mercury* 525 ff.
95. Cornelia Bradford continued to do business as a commercial stationer after her husband's death. See, for instance, the advertisement in *Mercury* 1205. Wroth (p. 224) points out that the profit from the sale of legal forms was often regarded by the colonial printer as the "velvet" of his business.

Andrew Bradford

Though Bradford was not primarily a book dealer, his store frequently — in later years, nearly always — had books for sale. Hildeburn says that Samuel Keimer was the first printer in Pennsylvania to be more than a mere printer.[96] He was thinking, no doubt, of Keimer's reprints of *The Crisis* and *The Independent Whig,* of his publishing *Epictetus His Morals,* the first translation of a Greek or Latin classic to appear in America, and of his bringing out the largest single volume in the colonies before 1748, the first American edition of Sewel's *History of the Quakers.* Hildeburn adds that Franklin followed the lead of Bradford rather than Keimer, in that he printed chiefly the political documents which were commissioned from him and pamphlets and papers of ephemeral character. Yet Franklin, everyone admits, deserves credit for the books he imported as well as censure for whatever books he may be accused of having failed to print,[97] and the same may be said of Bradford. Fortunately Bradford had an excellent connection in London, his aunt Tacy Sowle Raylton, daughter of Andrew Sowle. John Dunton in his *Life and Errors* mentions her as "a Printer as well as a Bookseller, . . . [who] understands her Trade very well, being a good Compositor herself."[98] The Philadelphia Friends had business dealings with her,[99] and we know of at least one specific transaction between her and her nephew Andrew, probably the model of many others. It occurred when Bradford imported from London her second edition of Sewel's *History* in preference to printing it, thereby showing greater practicality than Keimer who, in attempting the gigantic task proposed by the Quakers, finished it only in 1728 after five years of labor, long after Bradford's importation had arrived in Philadelphia. Bradford's initiative, however, went unrewarded, for the Friends, having subscribed to Keimer's enterprise, preferred to wait until he had completed his edition and Bradford's books were left on his hands.[100]

96. Hildeburn, I, vii.
97. Wroth (pp. 222-223) notes that as late as 1765 a typical list of the annual publications of Franklin and Hall "shows such a paucity of works of a literary character as might lead one to believe that the Americans of this period were entirely without interest in polite letters." He goes on to say that this assumption is proved erroneous "by the known facts of the trade in imported books . . . . It was more economical at this time to procure works of European *belles lettres* in foreign editions than to attempt their republication in this country."
98. John Dunton, *The Life and Errors of John Dunton,* I, 222-223.
99. *Minutes of the Yearly Meeting,* 106, under date of 1706: "The Books sent for to England of George Bishop's Tacy Sowle hath sent in Part. . . ."
100. Bradford wrote "To the Monthly Meeting of the People called Quakers held at Philadelphia the 25th Day of June 1725" as follows (see frontispiece):

> By Frequent Inducements and Repeated Encouragements of some Members of this and the Yearly Meeting for the Printing of Sewels History I sent to London to get them Printed for the Meeting knowing they could be better done there in Every Respect than here. and having

The earliest book advertisement appeared in the *Mercury* of May 19, 1720, when three sober and improving volumes were listed to be "Sold by Andrew Bradford and John Copson Book sellers in Philadelphia":

> The Life and Works, of the most Illustrious and Pious Armand De Bourbon Prince of Conti. To which is added a Discourse of Christian Perfection, by the Author of Telemachus.[101]

> Sober mindedness Pressed upon Young People, by the late Mathew Henry a Book very Necessary for Youth of all Perswasions.

> An Account of the Torments, the Protestants Endure on board the French Galleys, by an Eye-witness.

For several years thereafter few books were advertised in the paper, and those few were almost entirely put out by Bradford's own press:

> now Receved per Capt. Annis two hundred of the Five sent for the Remainder being Expected (as per Advice) by the first opportunity (which I hope the Meeting will not let me be a Looser by them, since I have don it to serve them) Which I thought my self Obliged to Advertise this Meeting of Whose Answer is Expected.

The answer was hardly the one Bradford had hoped to receive, however, for to the manuscript of Bradford's letter is added this note:

> The Mo. M. Desired I Norris, S Preston & myself to speak with A Bradford, Concerning this matter, which we did Imediatly after the M brake up Told him we knew of no Other Ingagement, then that made wth S Keimer on ye Y Mtings behalf wch was done after he refused to Print ye Book at 20/s
> R. Hill

(This MS is in the *Logan Papers*, XVII, 114.)

The *Minutes of the Yearly Meeting* (pp. 303-304) explain the attitude of the Friends: "A Paper from Andrew Bradford was read, Setting forth that he had provided, a Quantity or Number of William Sewell's Historys, in Expectation that Friends would take them off his Hands, and containing Some Allegations, which occasion'd a Call upon, or Enquiry of the Friends, who were formerly appointed, or desired by this Meeting, to get that Book printed. And they declare, that after their earnest Desire, to give him the said Andrew the Preference, & pressing that he would undertake to print the sd Book; offering him a larger Price than they Could have it done for by another, the Treaty broke off, by his direct and absolute refusal, And that then, they fairly ended with him, and agreed with another, as he was then given to understand they would, - - - - Wherefore the said Friends do further Say, that Several of his allegations, Especially those which would Seem, to lay Friends under any obligation to buy the Books, are great Mistakes (to use no other Expression) Whereupon The Said Friends are desired to draw up a full answer in writing to ye Said Paper, to be used as there may be occasion, if he should persist in misrepresenting Friends in the Case, and also to speak with him, in order to Sett him right in this matter."

See also the advertisement of Sewel in *Mercury* 351.

101. *Les Aventures de Télémaque* (1699) was the best-known work of Fénelon, Archbishop of Cambrai, and tremendously popular in the early eighteenth century.

almanacs,[102] political papers,[103] an Indian treaty,[104] the *Conductor Generalis,* "An Essay on Scripture-Prophecy,"[105] as well as the imported edition of Sewel. Bradford's advertising space, however, was not limited to the columns of his paper; for it was apparently his custom to use the last pages of the almanacs he printed to cry his wares. The Titan Leeds for 1724, for example, contained the following list: the *Conductor Generalis; The Young Man's Companion; The Ancient Testimony of the People called Quakers, Revived; The Husband-Man's Guide; War with the Devil* (a dialogue concerning a young man's struggle with the powers of darkness) ; *The History of the Kingdom of Basaruah;*[106] Ellwood's *Sacred History; Essays on the Preservation and Recovery of Health;* two books on the art of navigation; a history of the later times of the Jews and the destruction of Jerusalem; and *The new Help to Discourse; or Wit and Mirth intermixed with more serious Matters.* Another almanac, that of Felix Leeds for 1728, called attention to several of the same collection and to these additional items: *Fruits of a Father['s] Love, being the advice of William Penn (late Proprietor and Governour of the Province of Pensilvania, to his Children, relating to their Civil and Religious Conduct. Written Occasionally many Years ago, and now made Publick for the General Good; By a Lover of his Memory*; Sewel; *The History of the Five Indian Nations depending on the Province of New York, in America;*[107] *The Life Works and Posthumous of Richard Claridge; The Whole Duty of Man; Comes Commercii, or the Traders Companion;* Culpeper's *English Physician;* and an assortment of spellers, arithmetics, and other such usual books. A third almanac, the 1726 version of John Hughes, presented among a list of familiar titles two additions: *The Testament of the Twelve Patriarchs, the Sons of Jacob* and *A New Version of Psalms of David, fitted to the Tunes used in Churches. By N. Brady, and N. Tate.*

Mercury 309, of November 18, 1725, was the first paper to advertise a large stock of books. Under the familiar heading "Lately Imported from London" was listed a supply of Bibles, concordances, psalters, grammars, spelling books, and an English dictionary. It was not until the 'thirties, however, that Bradford's shop appears to have offered any encouragement to book lovers. At the beginning of 1730, for instance, it was still advertising the *Conductor Generalis,* Sewel, Cadwallader

102. *Mercury* 58, 305, 399, 462, 506, etc.
103. *Mercury* 91, 109, 284, 453, etc.
104. *Mercury* 84.
105. *Mercury* 251. This was a joint publication of William and Andrew Bradford.
106. All of those so far mentioned were printed by Bradford himself, whereas the remainder were simply "Sold at the aforesaid Shop."
107. The famous work of Cadwallader Colden, originally printed by William Bradford.

Colden, *Fruits of a Father's Love*, books on navigation, the usual array of prayer books, Bibles, spellers, and "Primmers" — and very little else.[108] But at the end of 1731 came a change; *Mercury* 626 devoted an entire page, four columns, to the books on sale in Bradford's shop. Religious books predominated:[109] *Dialogues betwixt a Christian and a Quaker;* "Peter Martyre's Commonplace Book";[110] Calvin's "Institutions"; *The Popish Labyrinth; Examples of Virtue & Vice;* "Quakers Tracts"; Luther's *Catechism;* "Truths Triumph over Trent"; *Morning Exercises, or Sermons against Popery; The Secrets of the Jesuits;* and "Peter Burgundy on the Contempt of the World."[111] Science, pseudo-science, and philosophy were represented by such titles as Ward's *Mathematical Works*,[112] Whiston's *Astronomical Lectures*,[113] a *History of Magick*, Martin's *Physical Dictionary*, Read's "Anatomy of the Humane Body,"[114] Maydman's *Naval Speculations*,[115] Euclid's *Elements*, Newton's *Idea of Geography and Navigation*,[116] Moore's *Modern Fortification*,[117] and Clauberg's *Logick*.[118] A large collection of what might be called handbooks included such titles as Sydenham's "Cure for all Diseases,"[119]

108. *Mercury* 525.
109. The classification of the books listed here is mine, not Bradford's. Quotation marks, instead of italics, are used to point out peculiarities and possible inaccuracies in Bradford's titles.
110. The author was the Augustinian monk, Pietro Vermigli, who accepted the reformed faith, became Regius Professor of Divinity at Oxford in 1548, and helped Cranmer prepare the second Prayer Book. His *Loci Communes sacrarum literarum* was translated into English in 1583 as *The Common Places of . . . P. Martyr.*
111. In 1585 Petrus Burgundius translated into Latin from Italian from the original Spanish of Diego de Estella *De Contemnendis Mundi Vanitatibus Libri Tres.* A year earlier "G.C." had translated the Italian version of Estella's work into English; this translation reached a third edition in 1622. Thomas Rogers, chaplain to Archbishop Bancroft, also translated the work into English in 1608. I am unable to say whose version Bradford had for sale.
112. The work is probably that of Seth Ward, Bishop of Exeter and Salisbury, and a mathematician and astronomer.
113. Whiston's *Praelectiones Astronomicae* (1707) was translated into English in 1715 and 1728.
114. It seems probable that this work is *The Manuall of the Anatomy or Dissection of the Body of Man* (1634) by the distinguished physician Alexander Read (Reade, Reid, Rhead). This book went through several editions in the seventeenth century.
115. Henry Maydman's *Naval Speculations and Maritime Politicks* appeared in 1691.
116. This work by Samuel Newton was printed in London in 1695.
117. Sir Jonas Moore, the mathematician, published *Modern Fortification* in 1673.
118. This was evidently a translation of *Logica vetus et nova* by Johann Clauberg, the seventeenth-century German philosopher.
119. Dr. Thomas Sydenham's *Compleat Method of curing almost all Diseases* was a very popular medical book in England in the early part of the eighteenth century.

The Mystery of Husbandry, "Bradley on Cattle,"[120] a secretary's guide, *The Whole Art of Fishing,* and Hannah Wooley's "Lady's Delight."[121] The group of books relating to history began with the then-incomplete Burnet[122] and embraced titles like Temple's *History of the Irish Rebellion* and his *Observations on the United Provinces,* Petty's [*Political*] *Anatomy of Ireland,* a history of street robbers, a history of the Reformation, a "History of Ethiopia, with Cuts," "Hulsius's Right of K William to the Throne of Great Britain,"[123] Prideaux's *Life of Mahomet,* and Eusebius' *Church History.* Finally, the list contained books of a linguistic, belletristic, or antiquarian nature, of which the most interesting were "Erasmus of the Copiousness of Words,"[124] *History of Reynard the Fox,* Roger Boyle's *Parthenissa, The Phrases of the Poets,* "Virgil's Works" and "Lucan," a Greek concordance and a Greek dictionary, an anonymous *Essay upon Literature,* "Artemidorus of Dreams,"[125] Udall's *Key of the Holy Tongue,*[126] a Hebrew grammar, "Stobay's Sentences,"[127] a French and Latin dictionary, Selden's *Syrian Gods,*[128] and "Broun's" *Religio Medici.*

In November 1736, among a long list of books, were these: "P. Virgilii Maronis Opera Interpretatione et Noties [*sic*]," Cato's *Distichs,* "Lylly's Grammars," "Spectators," "Tattlers," "Guardians," "Craftsman," *Cato's Letters,* and "Pilgrim's Progress single, and the three Parts bound together."[129] Four years later Bradford imported a stock of altogether different titles, including several law books, a school edition of Æsop's fables, a translation of Horace's satires, epistles, and the *Poetics,* and translations of Persius' and Juvenal's satires.[130] Here and there in the *Mercury* appear other curious or significant titles: a pocket volume for accountants called *Interest at one View,*[131] *The General History of the*

---

120. This was probably *The Gentleman and Farmers Guide for the Increase and Improvement of Cattle* by Richard Bradley, professor of botany at Cambridge and a voluminous writer on various phases of agriculture.
121. The correct title was *The Ladies' Delight.*
122. *The History of His Own Times,* by Gilbert Burnet, Bishop of Salisbury, was published posthumously, 1724-34.
123. This was evidently a translation of Henricus Hulsius' *Jura Guilielmi III . . . in Regna Angliae, Scotiae, Hiberniae, &c. ex fonte naturali, et divino asserta,* 1697.
124. *De Copia Verborum et Rerum* (1512) was the Latin rhetoric prepared by Erasmus for the use of students.
125. Perhaps this was Robert Wood's translation of Artemidorus' famous work; Wood's version reached its twentieth edition in 1722.
126. John Udall's book was published at Leyden in 1593.
127. This was evidently a translation of the *Sententiae ex thesauris Graecorum delectae* of Joannes Stobaeus.
128. This appears to have been an English version of *De Diis Syriis.*
129. *Mercury* 882; this same advertisement, with occasional additions, ran for many weeks.
130. *Mercury* 1081.
131. *Mercury* 888.

Pyrates,[132] "Drilingcourt on Death,"[133] Fénelon's *Dissertation on Pure Love*,[134] *Several Discourses upon Practical Subjects* by George Whitefield and the first part of his autobiography,[135] *The Tryal of Capt. Samuel Goodere* concerning a sensational murder-case of the day,[136] and a collection "from the German" of material on Count von Zinzendorf.[137] Indeed, the list of books sold at various times in Bradford's shop might be almost indefinitely lengthened, but this selection, I think, gives an adequate idea of what intellectual nourishment Bradford offered his customers. Though the output of his own press was limited, his importations showed considerable variety and worth. The preponderance of religious and moral literature, invariably with a strong anti-Catholic bias, was inevitable. Manuals and other practical books were also much in evidence. But what impresses us is that such names as Selden, Erasmus, Virgil, Horace, Sir Thomas Browne, Addison and Steele, the "English Cato," and others of like merit appear so often. It seems unlikely that Bradford chose his books with special care; conceivably his English aunt did the greater part of the selecting,[138] and certainly his stock shared the heterogeneity of the articles on sale in the rest of the store, with here and there something of real value among a clutter of trash. Yet even admitting his limitations, we can see that Bradford did good service, for he must surely have helped to make Philadelphia aware of books, and by so doing he opened the way to a more frequent and systematic book trade with Europe.

Bradford's store must have been a lively place. For almost a decade it was the city post office; for twenty-six years it was the headquarters of an important newspaper; for more than twenty it housed an active printing establishment. From the number and regularity of its advertisements over many years the store itself seems to have been a profitable undertaking; and why not, when under one roof one could buy, as in a modern department store, a hat or a book, a barrel of molasses or a bottle

---

132. *Mercury* 263. This is advertised as sold by William Bradford, but it seems likely that Andrew also carried it.
133. Charles Drelincourt's *Consolations de l'Âme Fidèle contre les Frayeurs de la Mort* (1651) became very popular in eighteenth-century England, partly because of the publicity given it in Defoe's "The Apparition of Mrs. Veal."
134. *Mercury* 983; in Number 893 Bradford had advertised his intention of printing it and asked for subscribers.
135. *Mercury* 1034, 1082. Bradford printed many of Whitefield's sermons and letters (see Numbers 1039, 1048, 1065, etc.) as well as both defenses of, and attacks upon, him; see, for example, Number 1078, where Bradford advertised two sermons of Archibald Cummins at Christ Church on "the false and rash Reflections of Mr. Whitefield."
136. *Mercury* 1145.
137. *Mercury* 1176.
138. *Mercury* 1081, already cited, speaks of the books in its list as having been printed "for Daniel Brown, at the Black Swan, without Temple-Bar, London."

of medicine? In fact, in the twenty-five years between 1720 and 1745 almost every Philadelphian of importance must at one time or another have had business in Bradford's shop.

III

Though the *Mercury* and the store, not to mention other responsibilities, must have taken most of his time, Bradford never relinquished his original trade. Even after he had moved his printing office from their schoolhouse, he retained the patronage of the Friends. For instance, in 1724 he published at least two items for them,[139] in 1727 *Fruits of a Father's Love,* in 1732 a pamphlet entitled *Advice and Caution from Our Monthly Meeting At Philadelphia,* and in 1738 a treatise concerning the dangers of marrying "outside meeting." Indeed, says Nathan Kite, Bradford "did almost all the printing of the Society, until his death in 1742";[140] and Horatio Gates Jones considers it "a striking fact, and one indicative of the excellence, not to say the superiority, of Bradford's press, that, although Bradford was an active and devoted Churchman, and apparently in no respect specially sympathetic with the tastes or habits of the Society of Friends, . . . this Society . . . should have always supported him . . . ."[141] Their business relationship also included, apparently, a more or less permanent agreement about the Friends' press, which, even after his removal from the school, Bradford continued to rent. In 1732, for example, a bill between him and the Meeting mentioned among other items three years' rental of the press, from 1729 to 1732.[142] It is quite likely that the arrangement was made partly in lieu of cash payments for printing done by Bradford for the Society, for he continued in possession of the press to the day of his death.[143]

139. See Hildeburn.
140. Kite, 45.
141. Jones, 32.
142. Wallace quotes this bill with convincing accuracy and completeness, but without mentioning his source, in an article in the *Pennsylvania Magazine,* IV (1880), 442. The Historical Society of Pennsylvania does not, apparently, have the document. For other evidence of Bradford's continued business dealings with the Friends, see *Logan Papers,* XVII, 119, 130; *Minutes of the Yearly Meeting,* 349, 354, 359; and *Minutes of the Monthly Meeting,* 237.
143. In the spring of 1742, when news came to the Meeting that young William Bradford, recently returned from England, wanted to hire a press, it appointed a committee to get its equipment from Andrew in order to rent it to his nephew. We can only speculate about why the committee had difficulty in arranging the transfer; perhaps the delay was due to Andrew's ill health; perhaps family rivalry was involved. Whatever the cause, in June the committee reported that it had "got some part" of the press, but not all, and it was therefore urged "to get the remainder . . . & acquaint said Andrew that as he hath Kept it so long in use, its expected he should pay Rent for it . . . ." The matter, however, dragged on for

The Friends were also responsible for Bradford's first excursion into a foreign language. In 1721, at their instigation, appeared the first book printed in Welsh in America.[144] The Germans, like the Quakers, early made use of Bradford's press, and consequently the first German books of the colonies were also published by him, probably as early as 1728.[145] Between 1725 and 1728 Bradford and his father were joint printers for the Province of New Jersey.[146] In 1725 Bradford printed the Charter of Maryland and the proceedings of the Assembly of Maryland for 1722, 1723, and 1724. He retained his official position in Pennsylvania until 1730, when Franklin first printed the proceedings of the Assembly. Though within three years the newcomer had taken over most of the government publications of both New Jersey and Pennsylvania, Bradford continued to print the votes and proceedings of the New Jersey Assembly[147] and the whirligig of time brought back to him in 1740 the privilege of printing the New Jersey acts.[148]

Hildeburn expresses his opinion of Bradford's activity as a printer in uncompromising fashion. "Beyond establishing a newspaper," he says, "the issues of Andrew Bradford's press show no enterprise on his part as a publisher."[149] Though this criticism seems rather severe, it is true that Bradford was less prolific than his leading rivals, Keimer and Franklin. In 1724, the year after Keimer's coming to Philadelphia, Bradford published only three or four almanacs and two Quaker pamphlets, as opposed to a dozen publications of his opponent, including several moral dialogues (to which form of literature Keimer was much attached), some verse, and reprints of Thomas Woolston's *A Free Gift to the Clergy* and of *The Independent Whig*.[150] The following year

months, and it was not until the summer of 1743, eight months after Bradford's death, that the committee was able to report that the press was in its possession and the account with Andrew's estate settled. (See *Minutes of the Monthly Meeting*, 341, 356.)

144. This book was Ellis Pugh's *Annerch Ir Cymru, Iw Galw Oddiwrth Y Llawer O Bethau At Yr Un Peth Angenrheidiol Er Mwyn Cadwedigaeth Eu Heneidiau . . . .* Argraphedig yn Philadelphia, Ymhensilfania, gan Andrew Bradford, MDCCXXI. The charge for printing this item is included in the account between Bradford and the Meeting in the *Logan Papers*, XVII, 99, 100, 113. See also the *Minutes of the Yearly Meeting*, 228, 234.

145. Wroth, 262. The *Zionitischer Weyrauchs-Hügel* printed by Christopher Sower in 1739 was the first book in German type to be published in America.

146. Keimer took over the position in 1728, but in 1730, after Keimer's departure, the Bradfords again published the New Jersey acts. (See *Mercury* 564.) As early as 1725 Keimer shared with Bradford the publication of some of the Pennsylvania proceedings.

147. See Ethel Metzger, *Supplement to Hildeburn*, under date of 1732-1737. See also two items under 1740.

148. See *Mercury* 1090. In the same year Franklin printed the votes and proceedings of the Assembly. See Metzger.

149. Hildeburn, I, vi.

150. These and the following figures are compiled from Hildeburn and Metzger.

Bradford's publications numbered about a dozen, chiefly almanacs and political works, while Keimer not only maintained his numerical lead but also distinguished himself by reprinting *The Crisis,* Penn's Charter of Privileges of 1701, a dictionary of technical terms, and two histories — one that of Diodorus Siculus, and the other concerning the wars of Charles XII of Sweden. The challenge of this energetic rival seems to have had its effect on Bradford, for during the next three years he published fifty books and pamphlets, approximately double the output of Keimer's press, though the latter once again marked himself out for praise with his *Epictetus.* After the arrival of Franklin and the subsequent departure of Keimer in 1729, Bradford once more took second place, sometimes with only half as many publications as Franklin, sometimes with very nearly the same number, during a given year. When Christopher Sower joined the small group of Philadelphia printers in 1738, the work of the two major rivals was quite evenly divided, as it was also in 1739. In 1740, after William Bradford III had entered his uncle's firm, that press had its largest output since 1728, but Franklin that year almost doubled the previous publishing record by printing approximately forty works. During the last two years of his life, though he was no longer a serious competitor of Franklin, Bradford evidently continued to maintain his press without difficulty.

In 1737 Bradford lost the postmastership. During the period of more than nine years in which he had held the position, he must have gained from the many contacts it brought him considerable advantage for his paper. At first he had organized the work well and conducted it efficiently[151] but, according to Benjamin Franklin, Bradford's tardiness in later years in making up his accounts caused Colonel Spotswood, the postmaster-general, to transfer the office from Bradford to him.[152] Meanwhile Bradford had been growing affluent. Franklin in the *Autobiography* writes that, even when he was setting up his shop in Philadelphia in 1729, his rival "was rich and easy . . . not very anxious about the business."[153] Franklin's conception of wealth in 1729 may not be dependable as a criterion, and we know that in the *Autobiography* he delighted in disparaging the work of his competitor,[154] but other evidence leads us to believe that there was more than a grain of truth in the comment. The shop and the newspaper were obviously successful; the printing business, though by this time hardly more than a sideline, was firmly established; probably the Durham Iron Company brought in a comfortable sum. Moreover, we know beyond a doubt by his ventures into real

---

151. See mail routes, fees, etc., in *Mercury* 431 and 441; note in the *Mercury* of July 20, 1732, the excellent plan for extending postal connections southward.
152. See *Pennsylvania Gazette* of December 11, 1740.
153. *Autobiography,* 308-309.
154. *Ibid.,* 257, 302, 303, 308, 321.

estate that Andrew had money to spare.[155] William, his father, had long favored speculation in land as an investment; as far back as 1689, when he was a young man just come to Philadelphia, he had taken up land along the river front "in order to erect a wharf or key and to build houses thereon for the better improvement of the place as well as for his own particular profit."[156] Between 1717 and 1729, also, he bought and sold a considerable amount of land in the Eastern Division of New Jersey.[157] Andrew took up the tradition, it appears, in 1719/20, when he leased "A Square in ye City."[158] Later, he became the owner of two large lots in Philadelphia, both measuring 366 by 396 feet, one the "Twelfth Lott from Delaware" on the north side of Pine Street; the other the "Seventh Lott from Schuylkill," also on the north side of Pine.[159] Then on March 28, 1730, Bradford's aunt, Tacy Sowle Raylton, "in Consideration of the Love and Affection which the said Tace Raylton hath and beareth to the said Andrew Bradford and William Bradford her said Sisters Children and in Consideration of Five Shillings of lawful Money," granted to her two American nephews the thousand acres of land which had been bestowed by William Penn upon her father.[160] On December 7, 1732, Andrew purchased his brother's portion for £160.[161]

155. J. W. Wallace (*An Old Philadelphian*, 8) speaks of Andrew Bradford as "the most successful of our early Printers" and "one of the richest men of Philadelphia."
156. Wallace, *William Bradford*, 48. William Bradford continued to hold property in Philadelphia long after he had left the city, for on September 5, 1735, in describing the limits of Philip Howel's lot along the Delaware, the minutes of the Board of Property mention that it is bounded on the south by William Bradford's lot. (*Minutes of the Board of Property and Other References to Lands in Pennsylvania, Pennsylvania Archives*, Third Series, I, 59.) See also *Pennsylvania Archives*, Third Series, II, 667, 669, 674, 675, for other real-estate transactions of William Bradford, and note the advertisement in the New York *Gazette* of July 1, 1734, and thereafter.
157. See *New Jersey Deed Books*, Liber A-2, 164 (May 13, 1717) and 162 (May 30, 1717); Liber E-2, 315 (Jan. 4, 1728); Liber K, 282-283 (June 5 and 6, 1728), 115 (Dec. 3, 1729), and 265 (Aug. 7, 1730); Liber E-2, 318 (Aug. 9, 1732); and Liber F-2, 230-231 (May 16 and 17, 1737).
158. *Minutes of the Board of Property, Pennsylvania Archives*, Third Series, II, 665.
159. See *Deed-Books in the Office for the Recording of Deeds in Philadelphia*, F-10, 382-384. In 1858 Bradford's holdings in that part of the city were commemorated when "Pratt Street" became "Bradford Street." In 1897, however, in the interests of greater uniformity in the naming of city streets and against the protest of the Historical Society of Pennsylvania, "Bradford Street" was changed to the present "Smedley Street." See *Ordinances ... of Philadelphia* for 1858, 301; and for 1897, 173-174.
160. Philadelphia Deed Book F-5, 529-530. The deed further makes clear that Andrew Sowle, by his will of December 9, 1695, had left the land equally divided between his wife, Jane, and his daughter Tacy; Jane deeded her share to Tacy.
161. Philadelphia Deed Book G-6, 184-186. £160, though hardly comparable to five shillings, was still only a nominal sum, for after Andrew's death his widow sold the 500 acres acquired from William for £700. See Philadelphia Deed Book G-6, 186-191.

Andrew Bradford

Thus, chiefly by the generosity of two of his relatives, Andrew gained a large additional piece of property. Still his fortune increased, and in 1738 he moved from his long-established shop on Second Street to the more imposing and strategically located office on Front Street near Market.[162] He probably retained possession of the old place, however, for there William Bradford III installed himself in the summer of 1742.[163]

While he was amassing the wealth which, we suspect, aroused the envy of young Franklin, Bradford was still prominent in civic activities. In the autumn of 1737, probably because of his local eminence, he was invited to join the recently organized Union Fire Company.[164] Apparently he did not accept the offer, but when a second group of citizens established the Fellowship Fire Company on March 1, 1738, he was one of the charter members.[165] In 1739 he was one of the distinguished contributors to the fund for the completion of the interior of Christ Church.[166] A very different kind of evidence of Bradford's weight in local affairs is furnished by some obscure references in the *Mercury* in 1734 and again in 1738; they have to do with some ill treatment which Bradford apparently suffered as a result of the part played by his paper in a controversy over Andrew Hamilton, the famous lawyer. Though the story behind these references is not at all clear, there is no doubt that once again Bradford was engaged in a struggle which concerned the right of the printer to publish opinions, his own or other people's, on policies and officials of the government.[167]

Towards the end of his life Bradford was also involved in a family difficulty almost, if not quite, as obscure as the political conflict just mentioned. In or before 1734 he had taken into his shop either as a business partner or, more probably, by some less formal arrangement a young merchant named Reese Meredith,[168] who apparently used the Sign of the Bible as his headquarters until he could establish his own place of business. About the same time[169] Andrew's nephew, William Bradford III,[170] was apprenticed to him. Apparently the boy was an apt

---

162. See *Mercury* 951 and 955. The new store at 8 South Front remained the Bradford printing establishment for almost a century thereafter.

163. See *Mercury* 1176 and *Gazette* 708.

164. See *Minutes of the Union Fire Company* under date of November 28, 1737, and thereafter.

165. See *Articles of the Fellowship Fire Company*.

166. Benjamin Dorr, *A Historical Account of Christ Church, Philadelphia*, 72.

167. See especially *Mercury* 738, 954, and 962. A full discussion of the controversy over Hamilton appears below.

168. See the advertisement in *Mercury* 763 and many times thereafter.

169. Bullen (p. 166) gives the date as 1733; Wallace, *An Old Philadelphian*, gives no date.

170. William Bradford III, grandson of the first William by his son Wil-

pupil, for in 1739 he was admitted to partnership in the firm, as the imprint of the *Mercury* of December 13 shows. As we have seen, the output of Andrew's press increased considerably in the following year, possibly because of the younger man's initiative. Bradford's first wife — Dorcas Boels, sister of a well-to-do landowner, Thomas Boels, of Freehold, New Jersey[171] — died on December 20, 1739,[172] and within a year, it appears, Bradford married a New York woman named Cornelia Smith.[173] Isaiah Thomas, with a natural flair for gossip, tells us that the second Mrs. Bradford was the cause of a family disagreement and the breaking up of the business arrangement between Andrew and William.[174] His story is that Cornelia had a niece whom she wished to see inherit the Bradford fortune and therefore pushed in the direction of the eligible young man. William, however, stoutly resisted this attempt to force his affections, and when Cornelia in consequence made his life unpleasant, he left Philadelphia to visit a more sympathetic relative, his great-aunt Tacy Raylton of London. Andrew, who could not escape so easily, was compelled, Thomas continues, to change his

---

liam, was born in New York City on January 19, 1721/22 (Wallace, *An Old Philadelphian*, 7). The third William Bradford confusingly called himself "William Bradford, Junior."

171. Thomas Boels' will, dated May 14, 1735, and probated October 16, 1735 (*New Jersey Will Book* C, 45-47), solves the long unanswered question of the identity of Bradford's first wife. It establishes also the fact that Robert Ellis, the Philadelphia merchant (see, for example, his advertisement in *Mercury* 824) with whom Bradford was associated in the Durham Iron Company, was, like Bradford, a brother-in-law of Boels. Another brother-in-law of Boels was Richard Nixon, also of Philadelphia, husband of his sister Sarah. Beginning with the issue of October 27, 1736, Boels' three brothers-in-law advertised in the New York *Gazette* his 500-acre plantation to be sold. The inventory of Boels' estate included £2117, sixty-four bound books, seven Negroes and one Indian girl. (See *Archives of the State of New Jersey*, First Series, XXX, 51.) An advertisement in the *Mercury* of September 26, 1728, suggests that Boels was already connected with the Bradford family and with Ellis; two runaway servants are to be brought, if discovered, to Ellis or to Andrew Bradford in Philadelphia or to William Bradford in New York.

172. Obituary notice in the *Pennsylvania Gazette* of December 27. Dorcas was buried on December 22 in Christ Church yard. (See the burial records of the church.)

173. Thomas (I, 229) says that she was related to William Bradford, Senior's, second wife. There seems to be no extant record of the marriage of Andrew and Cornelia. Probably it took place in Trinity Church, New York, but the register of marriages between 1697 and 1748 appears to have been lost in the fire which destroyed the Trinity School on February 20, 1750/51. Cornelia was evidently a member of the Episcopal Church and her will, dated January 11, 1755, mentions her house and lot "in a Street called Smiths Street" and another house and lot in Beaver Street in New York City. The only evidence for the date of the marriage is Thomas's statement and the indirect testimony of his story, coupled with the fact that the partnership was dissolved before the end of 1740: William's name was dropped from the imprint of the *Mercury* with the issue of November 6.

174. Thomas, I, 241-242.

will in his wife's favor, and thus his attempt to provide himself with a suitable successor failed.[175]

The last important project of Andrew Bradford's life was the *American Magazine or a Monthly View of the Political State of the British Colonies,* which first appeared in February 1741, and ran for three numbers before its discontinuation.[176] It seems unlikely that Bradford — middle-aged, wealthy, and probably no longer ambitious — would have attempted a novel form of journalism had he not been spurred to it by John Webbe, who knew of Franklin's plan to start a magazine and wished to forestall him. In addition, it is not beyond conjecture that William, whose energetic contributions to Bradford's business have been suggested, was partly responsible for the original plan of the undertaking, even though he had left the firm before the project was announced. Whatever the reason, in the *Mercury* of November 6, 1740, appeared a lengthy prospectus; a week later the *Pennsylvania Gazette* bore a laconic advertisement of the proposed *General Magazine and Historical Chronicle* of Benjamin Franklin and a note accusing John Webbe of perfidy. The details of the paper war which followed will be considered later; while the quarrel raged, plans for the two magazines were pushed forward with all speed. Webbe and Bradford succeeded in winning by bringing out the *American Magazine* on February 13, three days before its rival. Thus Bradford won the right to call himself publisher of the first magazine in America.

When Bradford died, "after a lingering illness," on the night of November 24, 1742, even the editor of the *Gazette* thought it important

---

175. The whole story of this family upheaval is complicated by the fact that nothing is known of Bradford's son. In his will, dated October 10, 1741, he mentions "Andrew Sole Bradford," evidently his child, of whom no other record seems to exist. If the boy had been born before December 1739, it seems improbable that Bradford would have adopted William III as his son and heir, as Thomas says that he did (I, 241). On the other hand, if his first marriage was childless, it would be not unnatural for Bradford to consider his nephew as his partner and successor. Following his second marriage Bradford may have hoped to have a son of his own, and the departure of William may have been caused by this expectation or even by the boy's birth. It may or may not be significant that when William returned from London in the spring of 1742 with a stock of gloves, hosiery, caps, women's clogs, pewter, cutlery, and silver watches, he set up shop, not with his uncle, but with his aunt, Tacy Bradford Hyatt (Mrs. John Hyatt). (See William's advertisement in *Mercury* 1169.) Very soon, however, he leased or purchased the Second Street house where his uncle had formerly lived. John Hyatt, Andrew's brother-in-law, was a brass-founder; his shop was in Front Street, two doors from the Sign of the Bible, and he advertised his wares in the *Mercury,* for example, in Numbers 207 and 1065. Hyatt, Andrew, and William Bradford, Junior, were associated in the advertisement in *Mercury* 723 for the sale of five hundred acres of land in Chester County.

176. A full discussion of the magazine itself and the controversy it engendered appears below.

to print an obituary.[177] Bradford was buried on November 27[178] in Christ Church yard at Fifth and Arch Streets, where Franklin's body was later to lie.[179] For one week after his death the *Mercury* failed to appear. Then on December 2, Cornelia Bradford, having assumed the duties of publisher, brought out Number 1195, heavily lined in mourning columns and containing the notice of her intention to carry on both shop and newspaper to the satisfaction of her husband's customers.

    177. *Gazette* 728. *Mercury* 1195 also gives the date of Andrew's death.
    178. Burial records of Christ Church.
    179. After the purchase in 1719 of the lot at Fifth and Arch Streets most of the interments from Christ Church were made there (Clark, vii). Presumably Bradford and both his wives were buried there, though the evidence is only circumstantial.

PART II

The American Weekly Mercury

Chapter 1

History of the *Mercury*

The first issue of the *American Weekly Mercury*,[1] printed and sold by Andrew Bradford and his partner, John Copson, appeared on Tuesday, December 22, 1719, some fifteen years after the Boston *News Letter* had initiated the newspaper press in America. The title of the new journal — derived from Mercury, the messenger of the gods and the god of commerce — was popular for newspapers in the seventeenth and eighteenth centuries. Indeed, the term *mercury* was regularly applied to hawkers of pamphlets and news sheets and was often used as a general equivalent of "newspaper." Bradford may also have chosen the name as a good omen, for the *British Mercury,* an English commercial journal, had achieved considerable success shortly before the founding of his paper. Number 1

---

1. The only file of the *Mercury* which approaches completeness is in the possession of the Library Company of Philadelphia. It includes all the issues, with the exception of a few scattered numbers, between December 22, 1719, and January 1, 1746. A file of the remaining numbers of the paper, from January 1 to May 22, 1746, is owned by the American Antiquarian Society of Worcester, Massachusetts. In addition, scattered numbers of the paper are to be found in various other libraries, such as the Historical Society of Pennsylvania. A reproduction in facsimile of the newspaper was undertaken in 1897 by the Colonial Society of Pennsylvania; four volumes were brought out between 1898 and 1907, but there the project lapsed. Recently a microfilm of the paper has been made under the direction of the Library Company and the American Antiquarian Society. This film includes every issue of the *Mercury* from 1 to 1376 with the exception of five numbers and part of a sixth, which it is reasonable to suppose are no longer extant. (By errors in photographing Numbers 146 and 147 are reversed in order, the last page of Number 1000 and the first page of Number 1001 are missing, and occasional pages have been so photographed that they lack some words along one margin.)

The early history of the Library Company's file is not certain. Some of the issues, at least, seem to have belonged to Joseph Breintnall, for occasionally his name is written in the margins (for example, in Numbers 736 and 1192) and once (Number 1172) appears the phrase "Joseph Breintnall's Paper." The file, however, is said to have come into the possession of the Library Company not through Breintnall, who was its secretary, but from Francis Hopkinson, who had inherited the paper from his father, Judge Thomas Hopkinson. (See "The First Philadelphia Newspaper and its Republication by the Colonial Society," *Pennsylvania Magazine,* XXII, 219.)

of the *American Mercury* was printed on half a sheet[2] of pot paper[3] from the Rittenhouse mill, which William Bradford had helped to found nearly thirty years before.[4] The type was good and the lay-out conventional, the paper being in appearance and content much like its contemporaries, both British and Bostonian. Across the top of the sheet ran the title, with the date just below. Both pages were divided vertically into two columns, a pattern which remained standard for the *Mercury* throughout its history.[5] As in nearly all the colonial journals for many years to come, European news predominated over domestic and was given a more prominent place in the paper: Continental items under the heading "From the North"[6] took up three of the four columns; then followed a short paragraph from London; and finally came shipping news of

2. Lee (*History of American Journalism*, 62-63) says: "From 1704 to 1765 newspapers were generally printed on half-sheets. Shapes and sizes varied greatly, not only because of the scarcity of news of the various towns, but more frequently because of the scarcity of paper." The *Mercury* was unusually consistent among colonial journals in the size and shape of the sheets on which it was printed. Throughout its history its page measured $7\frac{1}{2}$ to $7\frac{3}{4}$ by $11\frac{3}{4}$ to $12\frac{1}{4}$ inches.

3. The term "pot paper" comes from the use of the water-mark of a jug or pot on paper of this size. (See Joel Munsell, *A Chronology of Paper and Papermaking*, 19.)

4. Wroth (p. 30) emphasizes the fact that the establishment of a paper mill in Philadelphia in 1690 gave Penn's colony "preëminence in the manufacture of a commodity essential to the printing trade." Though, as we have seen, Andrew Bradford imported considerable stationery from England for sale to his customers, the proximity of a paper mill must have greatly aided him, not only in general printing, but particularly in the regular publication of the *Mercury*. It seems certain that most, if not all, of the paper he used in printing his journal came from the Rittenhouse mill. We know, for instance, that much of Klaas (Nicholas) Rittenhouse's paper bore the watermark KR and a clover leaf, and this watermark appears again and again in the sheets on which the *Mercury* was printed, beginning with the first numbers and running through to the very close of the paper's history. (The paper of *Mercury* 1 in the Library Company file is watermarked KR; Number 2 is marked with the clover leaf. A sampling of the paper shows that the clover-leaf device appears more frequently than any other watermark and continues into 1746. According to Dard Hunter, *Papermaking*, 204, this symbol was taken from the seal of Germantown.)

A second watermark common to much of the paper used by the *Mercury* consists of a shield surmounted by a crown and enclosing a fleur-de-lis. This device appears first in Number 75 (May 25, 1721) and occurs quite frequently thereafter, especially in 1723 and 1724, and on paper exactly similar in appearance to the clover-leaf sheets. James F. Magee in *Watermarks of Early American Paper* (p. 63) reproduces a good many Rittenhouse marks, among them several variants of this shield, crown, and fleur-de-dis device, which Klaas Rittenhouse used at different times between about 1703 and 1734. These two marks account for a great part of the *Mercury's* paper and make clear that Bradford depended primarily, perhaps entirely, upon the Rittenhouse mill for his supply. William McCulloch ("Additions to Thomas's History of Printing," *American Antiquarian Society Proceedings*, n.s., XXXI, 114) notes that both Klaas Rittenhouse and his son William were said to have made paper solely for the Bradfords.

5. During the later years of the *Mercury's* existence some papers used a three-column arrangement, for example, the *Pennsylvania Gazette*, beginning on February 3, 1741/42, and the *South Carolina Gazette* in 1744.

6. Such a phrase as "From the North" was a usual heading in English papers

History of the "Mercury"

Philadelphia, New York, and Boston. That was all, except for the imprint at the bottom of the second page and the following advertisement:

> This Paper will be Publish'd Weekly, and shall contain an Impartial account of Transactions, in the Several States of Europe, America, etc. All Persons that are willing to Encourage so Useful an Undertaking at the Moderate rate of Ten Shillings, a Year for the City of Philadelphia[7] Fifteen Shillings, for New-Jersey, New-York and Maryland Twenty Shillings, for Virginia, Rhode-Island, and Boston Proclamation Money, (to be paid Quarterly) are Desired to send their Names, and places of abode, to any of the following Persons. Viz.
>
> Mr. William Bradford in New York, Mr. Evan Jones at the City of Annapolis Mr. Robinson, Post-Master at Williams-Burgh, Mr. Jacob Walker, at Hampton in Virginia Doctor Ryley at New-Castle, Mr. Thomas Hill, at Salem Mr. Campbell Post-master at Rhode-Island, Mr. John Barclay at Amboy. Mr. John Costard at Burlington and Mr. Andrew Bradford, at Philadelphia.

It is clear from this notice that Bradford did not leap unprepared into his new enterprise; he evidently considered that he was printing a paper not for Philadelphia and Pennsylvania alone, but for all the middle colonies and even for parts of the South and New England. With this in view he had made arrangements up and down the seaboard for the distribution of his weekly and very probably, though it is not mentioned, for the collection of news. In Number 9 he sought additional subscriptions and news items by an appeal directly to the public, especially to the business man:

> The Design of this Paper, being to Promote Trade it is hoped, that it will be Incouraged by the Merchants of this City, by Acquainting Us with the true price Current of the Several Good's inserted in it, which we presume may be Serviceable to All concern'd in Commerce, Especially to them, that have any of those Good's to Sell, who will find a quicker Sale, by Our Informing those persons that want them where they may be Supplied: We likewise Desire those Gentlemen that receive any Authentick Account of News from Europe, or other places,

at this time. See, for example, the London *Journal* of July 2, 1726, cited in *Mercury* 355: "From the North we have Advice . . . ."

7. Ten shillings a year was the usual cost of a newspaper in the colonies during the period covered by the *Mercury*. The *New England Weekly Journal*, which cost sixteen shillings, was exceptional.

which may be proper for this paper, that they will please to favour Us with a Copy.⁸

Whether because it fulfilled a positive need or because of Bradford's careful arrangements to create a demand, the *Mercury* prospered from the start. As early as Number 2 appeared the first regular advertisement — of a runaway slave, and by the end of the first year the advertising column was well patronized. Number 13 was the first paper to expand beyond the limits of a half-sheet; because of an unusually large amount of local and New York news it was four pages in length. Thereafter for several years, although it was usually only two pages, a whole-sheet paper was not infrequent and in later years four pages became the standard size.⁹ In Number 22 the usual format was elaborated by the addition of two cuts, one on either side of the title at the top of the first page: on the left was a postman riding a horse and blowing a horn;¹⁰ on the right was Mercury, winged and bearing his caduceus, but hastening afoot to some unspecified goal. Certain other expansions in the manner of the special sections of the modern paper also occurred; whereas shipping news began, as we have seen, with the first issue, Number 2 included the first prices-current list¹¹ and Number 65 contained the first genuine obituary, a type of news item which appeared very seldom in the early years of the *Mercury* but which became more frequent in the 'thirties. Number 108 presented another feature—a list of fatal accidents which had occurred in Philadelphia and the vicinity during the previous week and a second list, continued monthly for some time thereafter, of births and burials in the same area.¹² In spite of emphasis on Europe,

---

8. The Boston *Gazette*, like the *Mercury*, was intended to encourage trade. The notice in Number 1 of December 21, 1719, says that the paper has been published "in Compliance with the desires of several of the Merchants and others of this Town" and speaks of the plan to include a regular prices-current list. Number 3 (January 4) states that the chief purpose of the paper is "to endeavour to advance, but not prejudice Trade."

9. By actual count from year to year the two-page paper was more common than the four-page through 1728. Thereafter the four-page paper became the rule. Number 729 (December 22, 1733) was the first of approximately forty six-page papers which appeared occasionally in the last twelve or thirteen years of the *Mercury's* history. The six-page paper usually took the form of a four-page paper with a two-page "postscript."

10. The picture of a postrider was a common embellishment of British papers contemporary with the *Mercury*. See Stanley Morison, *The English Newspaper*.

11. The *Mercury* continued to include prices current throughout its history. Moreover, a comparison with the *Pennsylvania Gazette* shows that the *Mercury* was much more regular in printing this type of news item than Franklin's paper; indeed it is a major source of information about prices in Philadelphia in the early eighteenth century. See, for instance, Bezanson, Gray, and Hussey's *Prices in Colonial Pennsylvania*.

12. Vital statistics appeared intermittently in the paper and sometimes came out regularly for a considerable period, for instance, between January 1730 (*Mercury* 579) and December 1732 (*Mercury* 680). Sometimes special lists were

news of events nearer home promptly assumed an important place in the *Mercury*. Number 4, for example, presented the address of Governor Keith to the Assembly, and Number 44 devoted its news columns exclusively to Pennsylvania and New York items. Either by intention or in the natural course of its development the *Mercury* shortly became a means by which the local government might reach the public; for instance, on August 18, 1720, it published the proclamation in which Keith announced the opening of the Court of Equity for Pennsylvania, and beginning in 1726[13] election returns were regularly announced in the paper.

Unfortunately, since none of Bradford's account books are extant, it is impossible to determine the circulation of the *Mercury* for any period of its history. We can only infer its importance and popularity from certain facts — for example, that until 1725 it was the only paper published outside Boston, that Bradford's business contacts, as his original advertisement shows, were wide, and particularly that he had for six years the active co-operation of his father in New York. In addition, the general advertisements indicate that, even in its early years, the *Mercury* must have had a large audience, for there were not only many notices of local origin but also a considerable number referring to distant places. In Number 25, for instance, appeared an advertisement of a chocolate mill for sale by a man in New York, and in Number 52 a runaway from Maryland was sought for. Number 242 contained advertisements from or about "Statin-Island," Hackensack, "Packquenock," Bergen County, Hunterdon County, the "Pesayuck River," and Rhode Island. Number 244 listed a notice from Queen Anne's County, Maryland, and Number 290 included notices from Freehold, New Jersey, and "York-Town," Virginia. Even after the New York *Gazette* was established, Lewis Morris advertised in the *Mercury*[14] a meeting of the Council of Proprietors of the Eastern Division of New Jersey. Such advertisements, cited from only the first half-dozen years of the paper's existence, give some idea of the extent of its circulation in its pioneer days.[15] We know fur-

published, for example, the births and deaths in Christ Church parish from December 24, 1736, to December 24, 1737 (*Mercury* 942). All such lists included merely numbers, not names.

13. *Mercury* 354. Number 303 (1725) reported the election of the mayor of Philadelphia.

14. *Mercury* 341.

15. Later advertisements support the same view of the paper's wide audience: for instance, notices of farms for sale in West Chester County, New York, and on the James River in Virginia (Numbers 706 and 955); of letters being held at the post office in Perth Amboy for people in Monmouth, Essex, and Somerset Counties in New Jersey (Number 722); of runaways from Milton, Massachusetts, and from Westover, Virginia (Numbers 964 and 706); of a man from Roxbury, Massachusetts, resident in Maryland or Virginia, who was wanted at home (Number 847). Examples might be multiplied almost indefinitely.

ther that Bradford's acquisition of the postmastership in 1728 must have greatly increased the sale of his paper, for the colonial postmaster was not only in a peculiarly favorable position for accumulating news,[16] but was also permitted, or permitted himself, to send his own mail free. Accordingly, the postmaster-editor was able both to build up and to maintain a wide reputation and a correspondingly large circulation for his journal, so that there is no doubt that the *Mercury* profited substantially from Bradford's long tenure of the postmastership. Franklin grudgingly admitted his rival's advantage over him when he wrote in the *Autobiography:* "as he kept the post-office, it was imagined he had better opportunities of obtaining news; his paper was thought a better distributer of advertisements than mine, and therefore had many more, which was a profitable thing to him, and a disadvantage to me."[17]

The *Busy-Body* papers also accelerated the growth of the *Mercury,* for it was in 1729, the year in which that series of essays appeared, that the full-sheet paper superseded the half-sheet as the normal size, and it is reasonable to suppose that the change was both cause and effect of increased circulation.[18] Though we have few records, we can be sure that the *Mercury* was purchased regularly by many important Philadelphians; we know, for example, that Captain Edward Wright[19] was a subscriber at least from April 1737 to July 1742; we know that Thomas Penn purchased it between December 1732 and December 1742, and that John Penn also received it during his sojourn in Philadelphia in 1734-1735.[20] Moreover, it is significant that the proprietors regularly used the *Mercury* to give notice when the annual payment of quitrents fell due and to bring

16. Presumably all letters and other mail, whether carried by postrider or by ship captain, passed through the postmaster's hands. In addition, he had regular contact with the other colonial post offices, also focal points of news. It is noteworthy that several successful early papers were edited by postmasters: for instance, John Campbell's Boston *News Letter,* William Brooker's Boston *Gazette,* William Parks' *Maryland Gazette,* and Franklin's *Pennsylvania Gazette.*

17. *Autobiography,* 309.

18. A. H. Smyth (*The Writings of Benjamin Franklin,* II, 100 n.) says that the "cleverness and entertainment" of the *Busy-Body* "diverted newspaper readers from the drowsy numbers of Keimer's *Universal Instructor* to the sprightlier columns of the *Mercury.*"

19. Edward Wright was master of the *Constantine,* owned by James Logan and Thomas Lawrence and engaged particularly in the transportation of "Palatines." See "Ship Registers for the Port of Philadelphia, 1726-1775," *Pennsylvania Magazine,* XXIII, 261, and advertisements in *Mercury* 550, 668, 1081, 1116, 1183, etc. Captain Wright was the acknowledged source of some of the *Mercury's* European news; see, for example, Number 1008.

20. See "Mayors of Philadelphia," *Autograph Collection of Simon Gratz,* under Thomas Lawrence, concerning the estate of Wright; and *Penn Manuscripts,* II, 292, and I, 62. Note that Thomas Penn's subscription continued for more than a year after he had left America.

other business to the attention of the people.[21] In addition, as we shall see later, the *Mercury* was an important source of news for editors of papers in other colonies. It appears, therefore, that though we can quote no figures we are safe in assuming that the *Mercury* had a large circulation and considerable popularity even in places far from Philadelphia. Moreover, it had built up so well-satisfied a following that it was able to survive without noticeable ill effects the transfer of the postmastership from Bradford to Franklin in 1737.

Although American news was nearly always subordinated to European, the *Mercury* gradually increased the amount of space devoted to colonial, including local, events. After the acquisition of the postmastership Bradford found himself well and regularly supplied with news of the other provinces, and we have already glimpsed the part played by the *Mercury* in local politics in the affair of "the dying Credit of this Province" and in the famous case of the Busy-Body. In disseminating culture also the paper had some share, not only indirectly through its book advertisements, but in its own pages. The literary aspect of the *Mercury* was never of first importance, for the paper was always primarily a news journal and admittedly catered to the interests of the mercantile class. The slightness, almost the total lack, of literary content in the first years is easily apparent; indeed, the *Busy-Body* essays mark the first sustained literary endeavor in its history. Though their purpose was not belletristic, since they sprang from no loftier motive than Franklin's spite and desire for economic advantage, they nevertheless possessed the genuine flavor of the eighteenth-century periodical essay and unquestionably exerted a good influence upon the content of the *Mercury*. There appeared, following their discontinuation, more poetry and more essays than had been published previously. Bradford and his readers were obviously familiar with Pope, Addison, "the English Cato," and other eminent writers, and references to them or quotations from their work were not unusual. It became customary, indeed, for Bradford to put in first place in the paper, relegating pure news items to the bottom of page one or to page two, a piece with some literary interest — an essay borrowed from a British paper or an original essay, often in the form of a letter, dealing with a topic of current importance, or perhaps some verses. In fact, in later years, unless space was required for the speech of the governor to the Assembly or for another matter of special concern, issues of the paper regularly contained items of more than ephemeral interest and some literary merit. Like the other colonial papers, however, the *Mercury* was intended chiefly to purvey news; whatever it may have contributed to

21. See many numbers of the paper itself — for example, 478, 683, 719, 785, 841, etc. — and a bill between the proprietors and the estate of Andrew Bradford in *Penn Manuscripts*, I, 63.

make culture prevail was largely a by-product of its other aims. Still, it is worth noting that the amount and quality of literary material in the *Mercury* increased steadily as the paper became firmly established and that the total quantity is larger than a casual glance reveals.

Some of the technical aspects of the journal also deserve attention. To the Rittenhouse mill rather than to Bradford should go credit for the superior quality of the paper on which the *Mercury* was printed. After two hundred years, although they are discolored, the sheets remain tough and unfrayed. Also due mainly to Rittenhouse is the uniformity of size and shape of the *Mercury* throughout its history, especially noticeable in a period when such a detail of format was often disregarded by the hard-pressed editor.[22] The type — usually pica, small pica, or English, and from the beginning both roman and italic — was usually clear, for as the letters wore out they were replaced. As early as 1734 Bradford owned a font of German,[23] and as the paper expanded in size and importance he not only acquired a larger variety of type but also developed greater skill in displaying it. As was usual in colonial journals, typographical errors were common in the *Mercury*. For example, in an advertisement in Number 705 "SOLD" was mistakingly printed "SOSD" and continued uncorrected in four later issues of the paper.[24] On the other hand, a notice in Number 807 rectified two typesetting errors in 805; and when Number 600 was erroneously called 500, the following issue was correctly marked 601.[25] In Number 438, however, in the printing of a proclamation of Governor Gordon such serious errors occurred that Bradford reprinted the entire item in the next issue of the paper. The most interesting correction of an error appeared in Number 943; in that issue a note called attention to a news item in the previous paper, in which after mentioning that the Earl of Stirling had waited upon the king and queen at Hampton Court the report continued with a new paragraph beginning, "Their Majesties . . . . " Number 943 explained that a paragraph headed "Letters from Copenhagen" had inadvertently been omitted and that the "Majesties" referred to were the king and queen of Denmark. Then came the following comment:

22. The *Pennsylvania Gazette*, in contrast, shifted the size of its sheet at least twice during the lifetime of the *Mercury*. See Numbers 686 and 772.

23. *Mercury* 768 and regularly thereafter.

24. *Mercury* 707, 710, 712, 714.

25. Similar errors occurred elsewhere: Number 291 was marked 300, but the next issue was properly numbered 292; 359 was marked 358, but the following issue, 360. Not all colonial editors were so painstaking in correcting mistakes of numbering as Bradford; for example, when the Boston *Post Boy* of September 24, 1739, was wrongly marked 249 (instead of 258), the error was perpetuated in succeeding issues of the paper.

History of the "Mercury"

> Some small Mistakes in Printing are scarcely worth asking Excuse for, because 'tis next to impossible wholly to avoid 'em; but such an Omission as *this* well deserves an Apology: And the compiler of that *Mercury* hopes, by making one, to obtain the Reader's (as well as their Majesty's) Pardon. The reason of his being led into that Mistake, is greatly owing to the Transposition of those Paragraphs in his Copy, viz. *the Boston Post-Boy, N° 163.* and altho' this may not wholly excuse the Fault, yet he hopes it may be in some measure an Extenuation of it. Such is the Tendency of ill Example, or bad Copy, that we are thereby insensibly led into Error.　　　　　　　　J.G.[26]

Yet few of the *Mercury's* mistakes were serious, and the paper was certainly superior in printing and in general appearance to its earliest rival in Philadelphia, the *Universal Instructor*. Indeed, Thomas, who may be considered an informed as well as an unprejudiced witness, thought its typography equal to that of the *Pennsylvania Gazette*.[27]

In addition to employing a considerable variety of type, Bradford made more use of cuts than probably any other early colonial editor. Though all of them are crude and some are grotesquely inartistic, they doubtless served their purpose in catching the eye of the reader and they certainly indicate Bradford's enterprise and ingenuity. The first to appear were those in Number 22 already mentioned, and from that day the paper was never without its distinctive heading, although in Number 33 the postman and Mercury changed places and after 1724[28] two cuts of each appeared in various combinations. Late in the history of the paper, in September 1740,[29] the heading became a panel across the top, with Mercury on one side, the postman on the other, and in the center a picture of a city rising from the edge of a river, in which a ship or two rides at anchor — one of the earliest representations of the Philadelphia waterfront. Long before this elaborate and effective triptych was devised, however, cuts had come into general use in the *Mercury*. The first among the advertisements was a rude picture of a book beside the notice for the sale

---

26. "J.G." must have been one of Bradford's employees, possibly Jonas Green, who advertised in *Mercury* 954 and gave as his address Bradford's printing office. Green became editor of the second *Maryland Gazette* when it was established in 1745. The mistake in the news item may have been traced through the *Pennsylvania Gazette* of January 17, the same day on which the *Mercury* was printed, where the Copenhagen report appeared correctly.

27. Thomas, II, 133. When Franklin took over the *Instructor* its print was distinctly clearer than either Keimer's or Bradford's. After the type-faces had become worn, however (for example, in 1739), the *Gazette* was no better in appearance than the *Mercury*.

28. *Mercury* 239.

29. *Mercury* 1080.

of an almanac in 1721,[30] and later in the same year a cut illustrated the notice of an unclaimed bale of goods.[31] In 1723 Bradford first made use of a fac,[32] an unusually large variety of which he gradually built up, especially in the 'thirties,[33] and many of which were skillfully designed. In later years cuts became a regular part of the make-up of the paper: in Number 747, for example, appeared a curious allegorical picture of Liberty and Property;[34] frequently illustrations were attached to notices of the sale of Negroes, sometimes represented by crude little black figures with crowns and loincloths;[35] amateurish cuts emphasized the advertisements of houses or runaways or stolen horses;[36] a wigmaker's notice was appropriately illustrated,[37] and likewise various places of business such as "The Sign of the Black Boy" or "The Sign of the Paracelsus Head."[38] Most often, however, cuts were employed in advertisements of ship-sailings, frequently with different pictures for "Scooners," sloops, ships, and brigs.[39] And of special interest is the issue of October 17, 1734, in which the account of the battle of Philippsburg was supplemented by a diagram of the French lines.

During the later years of the *Mercury* other improvements in its format were also made. The advertisements, which increased constantly in number through the 'thirties, until by 1737 one-and-a-half to two pages were regularly given over to them, were set in varied type, boxed separately, and carefully spaced to catch the eye. Broken type was more often replaced and the print accordingly was more uniformly clear than in earlier days, and old cuts were superseded by better ones.[40] Rows of type ornaments divided one section of the paper from another — the "editorial" from the news, and the news from the advertisements.[41] Indeed, the *Mercury* of, let us say, 1740 compared most favorably in appearance and general make-up with other papers of its time; it was

30. *Mercury* 59.
31. *Mercury* 98.
32. *Mercury* 160. *Fac* (short for *factotum*) is a printer's term, now obsolete, for an ornamental border surrounding a letter. Any letter might be inserted and then removed, so that one fac might be used again and again.
33. See, for example, in the early years Numbers 168, 201, 243, 272, 741, 742; and later Numbers 1010, 1012, 1014, 1018, 1021, 1022, 1026, 1032, 1034, 1127, 1131, each of them different from the others. The list might be greatly extended.
34. The same illustration appeared also in Numbers 960 and 961.
35. *Mercury* 746, 766, 768, etc.
36. *Mercury* 767 and 769; 787, 789, and 821; 776 and 804; etc.
37. *Mercury* 1029, etc.
38. *Mercury* 832 and 766.
39. *Mercury* 705, 740, 742, 748, 751, 766, etc.
40. See, for example, the fine, clear type introduced in Number 1125, and note Number 1049, where a new post-rider takes the place of his much worn and broken predecessor.
41. See, for example, Numbers 528, 605, 676, 708, 804, 903, 973, 1009, 1094, 1141, 1209, 1296, 1340, etc.

well printed, its material was well arranged, its format as a whole was more than acceptable.

As we have seen, Andrew Bradford was aided in the early years of the *Mercury* by two business associates — first by John Copson, whose name remained in the imprint for seventeen months; later by William Bradford, Senior, whose name appeared first in June 1720 and remained until the close of 1725.[42] For fourteen years thereafter Andrew conducted the paper alone. Between December 1739 and the end of October 1740 his nephew was his partner, but after William's departure for London, Andrew once more was the sole editor. On November 25, 1742, the *Mercury* failed to appear with its accustomed promptness. It must soon have been known among the subscribers by word of mouth and by the notice in the *Gazette* that the lapse was caused by the death of the proprietor the night before the paper's scheduled appearance. On December 2, Number 1195 came out, each column marked off by heavy black lines, and with similar tokens of mourning surrounding the following notice:

> As Mr. Andrew Bradford departed this Life on the 24th of November last, I hope those who were pleased to be Customers for the *American Weekly Mercury*, (of which my deceased Husband was the first Publisher) will excuse the Omision of the last Weeks Paper at the usual Time; and for the future they shall be serv'd carefully: And all Persons who have any Printing Work to do, or have Occasion for Stationary Ware, shall be thankfully serv'd at the lowest Prices,
>
> By Cornelia Bradford.

Four months later Isaiah Warner — "a young Beginner," he called himself — assumed the editorship of the *Mercury*, though the paper was published jointly by him and Cornelia. In October of the following year Warner's name was dropped from the imprint and Mrs. Bradford carried on the paper alone. On May 22, 1746, appeared the last number of the *Mercury* of which we have knowledge. Thus came to an end after a notable history of twenty-six years Philadelphia's earliest newspaper.[43]

---

42. See the imprints of the paper for the source of these and the following details: December 22, 1719; June 9, 1720; May 25, 1721; December 21, 1725; December 13, 1739; November 6, 1740; December 2, 1742; March 1, 1743; October 18, 1744.

43. How long the paper continued after the last known issue of May 22, 1746, is problematical. Thomas (II, 134) says that it was carried on by Cornelia Bradford "till the end of 1746" but was "soon after discontinued." Peter Kalm, writing under date of December 12, 1749 (*Travels in North America*, II, 656), says that the *Mercury* "has continued up to the present time," though he can hardly mean this literally if another statement — that there were two English papers in Philadelphia at the time he wrote — is correct, the two papers being obvi-

ously Franklin's and William Bradford's. The Colonial Society in its prospectus announcing the republication of the paper spoke of "its last issue in 1752"; there seems, however, to be no reason whatever for believing that the *Mercury* existed until that date.

Three items from the *Pennsylvania Journal* in the summer of 1746 suggest the possibility that the *Mercury* came to an end even earlier than Thomas thought. (1) In Number 189 of July 3 appeared a letter beginning: "Five Months are now past since I publish'd, in the *American Weekly Mercury*, No. 1360 and 1361, *An Enquiry into the Cause of our present Animosities in Religion*." The writer explained that he had expected an answer from Whitefield's friends; finally a gentleman had sent him some "Remarks," which he now requested William Bradford to publish. (2) In Number 193 of July 31 Cornelia Bradford advertised various goods that were for sale in her shop. (3) In the following number of August 7 she repeated the advertisement and added the request that, since she intended "shortly to remove from this City to New-York, and there to settle," those indebted to Andrew Bradford's estate should pay their debts. This same notice appeared regularly until September 11 (Number 199). Although we cannot be sure, it seems unlikely that either the writer of the *Enquiry* or Cornelia Bradford would have used the *Journal* if the *Mercury* had been still in existence.

Cornelia, we know, did not move to New York as she intended. In the *Pennsylvania Journal* for October 23, 1746, and for eleven weeks thereafter she advertised Birkett's almanac for 1747, and in Number 263 (December 3, 1747) she advertised a lost horse. Hildeburn shows that she continued to publish until at least the end of 1751, since she issued Birkett's almanac for 1752. Moreover, her will was drawn up in Philadelphia and probated there, although it was also probated, nineteen months after her death, in New York City. She died in 1755 and was buried in Christ Church graveyard on August 21. (See the burial records of the church.)

Chapter 2

Sources of the *Mercury*

The main objective of the colonial paper was the same as that of the modern journal, that is, to present news. The problems of the eighteenth-century editor, however, were in many ways different from those of his counterpart today. For one thing, the limited size of the colonial newspaper[1] made the selection of news a serious task. The editor had to decide whether, like John Campbell in the Boston *News Letter*, he should aim at an orderly, dependable, and relatively complete record of contemporary events or at such timeliness as he might hope to achieve. If he imitated Campbell, his paper — like the *News Letter*, which in January 1718/19 was printing news of September and October 1717[2] — was sure to be outdated long before it appeared; if he tried to keep abreast of the times, he ran the risk of inaccuracies, inconsistencies, and frequent hiatuses in his news stories. A second problem faced by the colonial editor was whether he should emphasize local happenings or should pass on to his readers what he considered the choicest bits from distant places. The first question was usually settled by a compromise: the editor tried primarily to keep up-to-date, but he inserted occasionally a résumé or a commentary for the purpose of clarifying or supplementing the news. For example, the *Mercury* devoted parts of three numbers in 1724[3] to a "history" of Spain, interest in which had been aroused by news of the abdication of Philip V. The second question was almost invariably answered in favor of news from a distance. Except for addresses of the governor or the Assembly and other semi-official items, or a local sensation such as a murder trial, no early eighteenth-century colonial newspaper ordinarily gave more than a brief paragraph or two to events in and around the place of its publication, and frequently it contained no local news whatever. This characteristic neglect of what would seem a staple may be attributed in part to the fact that in the small communities of that day gossip not only spread the happenings of the vicinity, but often spread them more

---

1. In the period under consideration newspapers varied from one to three half-sheets a week.

2. On January 12, 1718/19, Campbell inserted a notice in the *News Letter* explaining that a half-sheet a week was too little to keep up with the news; accordingly, with that issue he began to print a whole sheet every other week. On August 10 of the same year he triumphantly announced the success of his scheme: he was less than five months behind!

3. *Mercury* 229-231.

quickly than could a weekly newspaper.[4] On the other hand, news from far-away places, especially from across the Atlantic, was less often talked about and what was said frequently lacked authority. In addition, colonials felt dependence, in manner as well as in degree different from ours, upon European, especially upon English, events; such a feeling caused a disproportionate interest in European affairs as opposed to colonial. Moreover, in the early period particularly, the editor must have been glad to encourage this public sentiment partly because the colonial governments practically prohibited the appearance in the journals of local politics and partly because, until an effective postal system and a considerable number of American newspapers were established, dependable news of other colonies was hard to come by.

Since most of the news which Bradford, like other colonial editors, wished to print originated in far places, we must consider first the question of how he obtained it. In general it came from two sources: from individuals, by letter or by word of mouth, and from other newspapers, European or American. From the advertisement in Number 1 already quoted, we can infer that in several colonies Bradford had allies who not only attended to the distribution of the *Mercury* but also, probably, kept their eyes and ears open for usable items of news. We have also evidence of definite aid to Bradford from various private sources, to whom he specifically appealed in Number 9. For instance, in Number 28, he acknowledged items obtained "By a Private Letter from St. Thomas," and in Number 17 mentioned "Private Letters from Paris."[5] Number 45 introduced an item with the comment: "By a Gally lately arrived from the Streights of Gibralter, we had the following News in a private Letter, writ to a Friend in these Parts," and Number 65 cited as the source of one of its notices "a Letter from the Roman Missionaries in China." Number 150 spoke of a "Private Letter from the Beaver" (a ship presumably) and Number 225 presented an "Extract of a Letter from Cadiz." In Number 156 the speech of George I to Parliament on October 11, 1722, was, Bradford said, "printed from a Manuscript Copy, brought by a Merchant from Maryland, who came there in a large Ship, and had a very quick passage from Holland, but last from England." Similarly there were such acknowledgments as: "Extract of a Letter from an Eminent Physician at Aix in Provence"; "An Extract from the

---

4. Some papers, for example the *Pennsylvania Gazette* (Numbers 43-55), tried semi-weekly publication, but evidently without success.

5. Quoting from private letters was common to European as well as to colonial papers. (See *Mercury* 144, 237, 248, 423, 424, 472, and many others.) Such letters, of course, were not necessarily addressed to the newspaper, but were frequently given to the editor for use in his journal by those who had originally received them.

Ship *Dorothy's* Journal"; "a private Letter from Annapolis Royal"; "an Express from Albany"; "By Letters from Boston"; "From on board the Hind, John Rogers Commander"; and "From on Board his Majesty's Ship the *Torbay*."⁶ The private letter, indeed, remained for many years an important, though irregular and perhaps undependable, source of news, for letters from Barbados, Jamaica, Boston, Annapolis, St. Kitts, Wales, London, and various other places appeared from time to time in the columns of the paper.⁷

Word-of-mouth news was also sometimes included in the *Mercury*, though generally Bradford seems to have avoided the inaccuracies necessarily attendant upon printing oral reports. In Number 171 he used a news item related in New York by a ship captain, and in 417 another by a shipmaster in Philadelphia.⁸ In Number 68 he mentioned a rumor that the French king had died, a piece of news, apparently recounted orally at some of its stages, which reached him from New York by way of a ship from Jamaica, which had picked the story up in Santo Domingo, where it had been brought by a French man-of-war. Not surprisingly, in view of its devious course, in Number 70 Bradford was forced to admit that the rumor was false. Once again in Number 122 he had to retract information, this time about the burning of a ship, offered him by an overconfident sea captain.

Though private letters and oral reports accounted for some of the news printed in the *Mercury*, by far the greater part of it, particularly that from Europe, came to the paper through other journals. In the first year these sources remained almost entirely unacknowledged, with but one mention each of the Lisbon *Gazette,* the London *Daily Courant,* and the Boston *Gazette;*⁹ but as the paper advanced in age and importance the sources were more diverse and the attributions were more complete and more accurate. Throughout the history of the *Mercury* most of its foreign news had English sources, quite naturally since the ties to England both of common interests and of language were strong. Up to 1727,

---

6. See the following numbers of the *Mercury:* 58, 29, 244, 248, 309, 316, 343.

7. See, for example, *Mercury* 397, 408, 417, 425, 474, 504, 606, 691. The phrase "a letter from" with the name of a place is frequently deceptive, especially in the later years of the paper, since the colonial printer might lift from another newspaper a letter printed by that paper. For example, when in Number 434 Bradford quoted a letter "from Mittau, the Seat of the Dukes of Courland" or in 575 a private letter from Dresden or in 601 one from "Algier" or in 305 "a Letter from Jamaica, to a Merchant in London" or in 1024 "a Letter from Ispahan," it appears likely that these were letters published in London papers which he borrowed along with other news items. On the other hand, many letters seem unmistakably genuine, for example, one quoted in 654 as a private letter from London, which began: "This comes to acquaint thee . . . ."

8. See also *Mercury* 369 and 486.

9. See *Mercury* 15, 18, and 24.

for example, news from the following British papers was requisitioned by Bradford: the London *Weekly Journal,* the *British Journal,* the *Political State of Great Britain,* the *Whitehall Evening Post,* the *Daily Courant,* the London *Gazette,* the London *Daily Journal,* the *Post Boy,* the *St. James Evening Post,* Mist's *Weekly Journal,* the *Flying Post,* and the *Daily Post.*[10] As the *Mercury* prospered and as other British journals were established, references to other titles, in addition to familiar ones, entered the paper: the *Political Mercury,* Read's *British Gazetteer,* the *Craftsman* (also called the *Country Journal*), the London *Evening Post,* the *Post Man,* the Cork *News Letter,* the *Kentish Post,* the *Weekly Medley,* Farley's Bristol *News Paper,* the Dublin *Journal,* the *Weekly Register,* the *Weekly Miscellany,* the *London Magazine,* the *General Evening Post,* the *Daily Advertiser,* the *Gentleman's Magazine,* the *Universal Spectator,* the *Daily Gazetteer, Common Sense,* the *Bee,* the *Grub Street Journal,* the *Corn Cutter's Journal,* the Dublin *Daily Post Boy,* the *Champion,* the Dublin *Evening Post,* the Bristol *Journal,* the *European Secretary of State,* the Edinburgh *Evening Post,* the Newcastle *Courant,* and the Portsmouth and Gosport *Gazette.*[11] The British

---

10. The London *Weekly Journal* was mentioned in Numbers 99, 112, 120, 123, 124, 130, 132, 133, 154, 199, 208, 209, 215, 235,* 239,* 244, 245, 246, 247, 248, 272, 274, 290, 305, 308, 333, 352, 355.
    British Journal: 229, 233, 235,* 237, 239,* 258, 259, 287, 312, 313, 335, 338, 362.
    Political State of Great Britain: 114, 118, 227, 276, 294, 296, 360.
    Whitehall Evening Post: 85, 102, 154, 275, 302, 318,* 328.
    Daily Courant: 18, 70, 99, 238, 287.
    London Gazette: 53, 82, 131, 279.
    Daily Journal: 113, 199, 285, 289.
    Post Boy: 333, 334, 338.
    St. James Evening Post: 101, 220, 318.*
    Mist's *Weekly Journal:* 340, 341.
    Flying Post: 254.
    Daily Post: 338.
**Mercury* 318 acknowledged simply the "Evening Post." *Mercury* 235 and 239 acknowledged simply the "Weekly Journal."

11. The first or an early reference to each of these papers may be located in the following numbers of the *Mercury:*

Political Mercury—406	*Grub Street Journal*—732
Read's *British Gazetteer*—408	*Corn Cutter's Journal*—753
Craftsman—422	*Gentleman's Magazine*—763
London *Evening Post*—460	*Universal Spectator*—789
Post Man—486	*London Magazine*—800
Cork *News Letter*—499	*Daily Advertiser*—829
Kentish Post—503	*General Evening Post*—841
Weekly Medley—523	*Daily Gazetteer*—900
Farley's Bristol *News Paper*—539	*Common Sense*—943
Dublin *Journal*—546	Dublin *Daily Post Boy*—965
Weekly Register—572	Dublin *Evening Post*—1013
Bee—708	*Champion*—1094
Weekly Miscellany—723	Bristol *Journal*—1188

belonging to the Library Company No. 1.

The AMERICAN
Weekly Mercury, 179 folio

December 22, 1719.

From the NORTH.

HAMBURGH August, 20. All Our Letters from Sweden, are full of the Dismall Ravages committed by the Muscovites there. Those Sent Christians have burnt the fine Towns of Nykoping, Nordkoping, North Telje, South Telje, Wall, Oftramar, Oregrund, Fortenas, Orcela, &c. with all the Castles and Gentlemens Seats near them; & ruined all the since, utterly Destroy'd the Copper and Salt Works, burnt the Woods and carried Thousands of the People on Board their Gallys in Order to Transport them into Russia, the Damage is computed at severall Millions, and a Hundred Years wont Retreive the Loss the Country has Sustained in their Woods and Mines.

Whatever the End propoded by the Muscovite in the present Ravage of Sweden, may be, we think they have neither pursued the Maxims of Christianity or Human Policy.

It was the Maxim of Augustus the greatest and mightiest Prince that ever reigned on the Earth, that Princes who would be truly great, should conquer for the Good of Mankind,

Stock, has brought the Company in such an immense Sum in Specie, that it is no Wonder they should be able to pay off the King's Debts of twelve hundred Millions, seeing they are Gainers by this particular Subscription, no less than four hundred and fifty Millions at one Blow in ready Money, and 'tis now said they Will still have Leave to advance and enlarge their Subscription for fifty Millions more, and so earn to fifty more, if they please, in which Case they may easily pay twelve hundred Millions; and it is said already from Paris, that they have eighteen hundred Millions in Cash now by them, in order to pay the publick Debts; if the People demand their Money, which it is thought no Body would do. They are now, it is talked there, to buy all the Plate with the old Species, and bring it into the Mint, and to oblige the People to part with it. Mr. Law, they say, has found out a miraculous Expedient for this, so advantageous that no Body will be able to resist it.

They write us further from Paris, that the Joy of the People there is not to be expressed; it is impossible to describe it; The poor find themselves all discharged at once from their Taxes and Provisions, which pinched them severely; and when the Turn-Pikes and Watch-Houses which were set up at all the Out-Parts of the City were taken down, as

No. 214

THE
AMERICAN
Weekly Mercury,

From TUESDAY January 14th, to TUESDAY January 21th, 172¾.

The Writer of the first Part of our Weekly Mercury will omit his Design of pursuing his Memoirs, for the sake of the young Lady, whose Condition is described in the following Letter. But Mr. B———— says, that if Lovina, by his means, acquires her Love, he shall expect a pair of Gloves.

Mr. B————
Sir,

 AS I always find, of late, the Front of your Paper employed in giving Lectures upon severall Subjects, which are not only often very diverting, but always very profitable. I hope you will not deny this Letter a Place in your Mercury, since it can be prejudicial to none, and may be the preserving me from Ruin. As you always avoid Scandal and Falsity's, I am the more desirous my Case should be seen in your Paper.

Know then, I am the Daughter, and only Child, of a Gentleman of ———— Pounds a Year, and being arrived at near Twenty Years of Age, severall have made their Ad-

to do but to spend it: And add, what else you think will lessen his over fond Opinion of Gentlemen, and encrease his Esteem for Tradesmen, which if you can do, you'll Oblige her who is,

Sir, Your Humble Servant, Lovina.

Madrid, (the Capital of Spain,) Sept. 21.

The Tempest we had here on the 25th was so dreadful, that we began to believe the World was at an end: The Lightning, Thunder, and furious Rain cannot be express'd; but tho' the Lightning fell on many Houses, it did no considerable Damage, except one Flash, which falling on the Church of our Lady of Constantinople, threw down a high Wall more than an Ell in Thickness, and tumbled down by its Fall a neighbouring House: The Impetuosity of its Torrent caused by the Rain that fell in Cataracts, made a most deplorable Havock in the Suburb of St. Barbara, where several Houses were thrown down, and four Persons buryed under the Ruins. All that Part of the City call'd the Old Guards was fill'd with Water to the second Story, and much mischief would have happen'd there, if

Early Nameplates of the *Mercury*
Courtesy of the Library Company of Philadelphia

papers used by Bradford make up a sizable list and include not only what we might call the standard London news sheets, but also a fair number of provincial papers, as well as such publications with a predominantly literary flavor as the *Universal Spectator* and the *Grub Street Journal*. In addition, the *Mercury* drew at least once upon the *Philosophical Transactions* of the Royal Society,[12] which came out periodically, and upon the *Essays* of the Royal Dublin Society.[13]

Of the foreign papers other than English from which Bradford quoted, it is difficult to say how many he used directly and how many came to him through the medium of British journals. We know, for instance, that the *Post Boy* neglected local news for foreign, especially Spanish,[14] and that the *Daily Courant* drew much material from the Haarlem *Courant*, the Amsterdam *Courant*, and the Paris *Gazette*.[15] Specific evidence of Bradford's indebtedness to a go-between is offered by *Mercury* 115, which included the heading, "London, Sept. 20. From the Amsterdam Gazette"; and Number 292 introduced an item as "Translated from the Amsterdam Gazette in French." Whether Bradford took this story from the French or from a further translation into English we do not know, probably the latter, but it illustrates in any case the indirect method by which he sometimes found news items. Although we should keep in mind, therefore, the possibilities of this roundabout transfer of information, it is notable that three non-English journals were frequently mentioned in Bradford's pages during a typical early period of the paper, from 1720 through 1727 — the Amsterdam *Gazette*, the Amsterdam *Courant*, and the Paris *A la Main*.[16] In later years,

European Secretary of State—1203
Edinburgh *Evening Post*—1272
(Bradford said that this item came to him by way of Boston.)
Newcastle *Courant*—1362
Portsmouth and Gosport *Gazette*—1364

12. A comparison of the *Mercury* (Number 1016) with the *Transactions* and with the *London Magazine* and the *Gentleman's Magazine*, in each of which the relevant part of the *Transactions* appeared in an abridged form, suggests that Bradford borrowed directly from the Royal Society's publication. The essay concerns a series of experiments conducted before members of the Society to demonstrate the efficacy of olive oil in curing the bite of a viper. The discussion occurs in the *Transactions* of October 1736.

13. The Royal Dublin Society was founded in 1683 to promote agriculture and the useful arts. The section of the *Essays* quoted in the *Mercury* (Number 1335) concerned the culture of flax.

14. H. R. Fox Bourne, *English Newspapers*, I, 56.

15. *Ibid.*, I, 66.

16. The Amsterdam *Gazette* was quoted in the following numbers of the *Mercury*: 109, 115, 121, 123, 125, 135, 292, 294, 318, 320; the Amsterdam *Courant* in 54, 102, 134, 170, 286, 300, 318, 323; the Paris *A la Main* in 125, 127, 135, 147, 318, 329, 359. In addition these other foreign journals were acknowledged: the Hague *Courant* in 54, 134, 170; the Haarlem *Courant* in 148, 151, 167; the Leyden *Courant* in 102; and the Lisbon *Gazette* in 15.

whereas Bradford's acknowledgments of British newspapers increased enormously, the references to Continental papers remained scattered and relatively infrequent. Both because of the language barrier and because of British restrictions on shipping between the colonies and Continental ports, it seems reasonable to assume that few foreign newspapers were direct sources of the *Mercury's* European news items.

On the other hand, Bradford's indebtedness to American journals steadily increased as more papers were established and as coastwise shipping and postal routes improved. In the first year of the *Mercury*, as we have seen, the Boston *Gazette* was referred to; in 1721 the *New England Courant* was once mentioned; in 1722 the Boston *Gazette* and the *Jamaica Courant* were cited; and in 1723 the *Gazette* was twice referred to and the *Courant* once.[17] A total of seven references in four years is certainly meagre, but we must remember that there were very few colonial papers in the early 'twenties and that access to them was not easy. In later years much more frequent citations of colonial journals occurred — in addition to those already mentioned, to the *Maryland Gazette*, the *South Carolina Gazette*, the New York *Gazette*, the New York *Weekly Journal*, the Boston *Weekly Rehearsal*, the *Barbadoes Gazette*, the *New England Weekly Journal*, the Boston *Weekly Post Boy*, the *Virginia Gazette*, the Boston (*Weekly*) *News Letter*, and the New York *Weekly Post Boy*, as well as to the Boston *American Magazine*.[18] Indeed, almost every colonial paper contemporary with the *Mercury* is mentioned in it at some time as a source of news, and several of them, notably the New York *Gazette* and the Boston *Gazette*, are cited repeatedly.

Even when we know what papers Bradford used, we cannot speak with finality about his sources. For one thing, he borrowed much more widely than he acknowledged; practically all of the European and much of the American news must have been lifted from other papers, yet only a small part of it was ascribed to its origin, and the same statement applies with equal justice to those parts of the *Mercury* which were not news — such as essays and verse. For another thing, it is impossible to trace all the items which he did acknowledge, especially since he frequently omitted the dates even when he mentioned the titles of the publications he referred to. In the third place, in the period when Bradford most systematically listed his sources — in the late 'thirties and the 'forties — the actual origin of an European item is often obscured by the

---

17. *Mercury* 24, 103, 139, 157, 184, 185, and 167.
18. The first or an early reference to each of these papers may be located in the following numbers of the *Mercury* in the order listed: 517, 699, 715, 729, 730, 620, 782, 804, 911, 1196, 1340, 1261. The reference to the *Maryland Gazette* in *Mercury* 1340 is obviously to the revived *Maryland Gazette* of 1745.

fact that it was reprinted, for example, in the *Gentleman's Magazine* or the *London Magazine*. For instance, in *Mercury* 733, Bradford published without mention of his source some verses called "Warbletta." References to St. Giles's, Wapping, Drury Lane, and so forth make it seem likely that the poem originally appeared in an English paper; and, indeed, upon investigation we find it in the *Grub Street Journal* of July 19, 1733, where the verses are accompanied by precisely the same introductory "letter" which the *Mercury* printed. But we find it also in the *Gentleman's Magazine* for 1733, and only the fact that the *Gentleman's* omits the letter makes it reasonably sure that the *Grub Street Journal* was Bradford's source. To cite another kind of example, when Bradford acknowledged that an essay "Of Punctilios among the Fair Sex" in *Mercury* 888 was taken from *Universal Spectator* 405, how can we know whether it came directly from that paper or from the *London Magazine*, where it was reprinted (with, of course, proper reference to *Universal Spectator* 405) in July 1736? Bradford, we know, was often either careless or addicted to mystification, since he quite often attributed items vaguely to a "late magazine" or to "the Magazine": for instance, "An odd Kind of Vanity exposed" in *Mercury* 889, which can be located in the *London Magazine* of June 1736, or "Of inoculating the Small-Pox" in *Mercury* 951, which apparently was derived from the *Gentleman's* of September 1737. Moreover, Bradford appears to have resurrected now and again a long-forgotten item; for example, in December 1739[19] the *Mercury* printed, without acknowledgment, a poem entitled "The Modern Goliah," an attack on free-thinkers, which had appeared at least as early as the *Grub Street Journal* of September 17, 1733. Yet in spite of such difficulties as these examples indicate, we can trace a sufficient amount of the *Mercury's* copy to be reasonably sure of two things: first, that Bradford plundered a large number — much larger than he admitted — of British and American papers in publishing the *Mercury;* and, second, that he nearly always borrowed verbatim. For a comparison of the *Mercury* and its sources, when we can find them, reveals that in reprinting not only poems and essays, but also news items, Bradford's compositors must regularly have set their type from clippings from other news sheets.[20]

19. *Mercury* 1041.
20. Bradford's practice in both of these matters was probably typical of the colonial editor. The reader who concentrates upon a brief period of a quarter of a century in the history of the colonial newspaper and who is especially interested in noting interrelations gets accustomed to seeing the same item appear in precisely the same words in several different places. Some of these identical items unquestionably go back to a common European source; some are the result of intercolonial borrowing. In either case they indicate that Bradford was not alone in preferring scissors to pen.

In pointing out where Bradford got the material published in his paper we have not, however, given any idea of the actual difficulties that beset him in procuring news. Obviously all European items were outdated by several months at the time they came from the colonial presses, but since everyone was equally uninformed about immediate happenings in Europe, staleness was not in itself a problem to the colonial editor. It was the infrequency of news or the unpredictable delay in its arrival that troubled him. Even at Philadelphia, a large town, in the 1720's few vessels from Europe put in. Franklin tells us in the *Autobiography*[21] that in 1724 there was but one ship which made a regular annual voyage between Philadelphia and London; and in the entire year of 1721, for instance, the *Mercury* listed six ships from London, three from Holland, seven from Bristol, and five others,[22] some of which arrived at Philadelphia only after a stop-over in the West Indies, so that whatever news they brought was even older than usual. Moreover, weather conditions frequently interrupted the transmission of news from Europe: again in 1721, seven consecutive issues of the *Mercury*[23] bore the notice that no vessel had entered the harbor during the previous week; winter after winter this sort of notice appeared, showing that the city was icebound nearly every year for a longer or shorter period.[24] By the 1730's, however, shipping in all the colonial ports had greatly increased; for example, between December 29, 1730, and March 7, 1731/32, 189 ships entered and the same number cleared from the port of Philadelphia.[25] Regular sailings to and from Great Britain were also established; for instance, in a single issue of the *Mercury* in 1734 advertisements appeared for two ships for London, one for Bristol, one for Cork or Dublin, as well as three for the coastwise trade.[26] It is clear, therefore, that whereas Bradford was seriously hampered in obtaining European news during the pioneer years of the *Mercury* by the paucity of trans-Atlantic ships, later he could count upon a certain degree of regularity in procuring it. In addition, whereas in the early years of the paper the dearth of news in mid-winter was severe and usually caused the *Mercury* to appear in its two-page form, in the late 'twenties and thereafter a seasonal variation in the size of the paper less frequently occurred; for even when ships did not come in for several weeks Bradford had an accumulated stock of foreign journals to draw upon. In later years,

21. *Autobiography*, 267.
22. One from Cowes, one from the Isle of May, one from Liverpool, and two from Londonderry. See the following issues of the *Mercury*: 55, 67, 69, 70, 71, 75, 78, 79, 80, 90, 92, 94, 97, 99, 101. (1721 was a typical year.)
23. From January 10 to March 2.
24. See, for example, *Mercury* 372, 421-422, 469, 683, 891, 1045, 1096.
25. *Mercury* 637.
26. *Mercury* 752.

moreover, river traffic quickly recommenced as soon as the harbor was free of ice; for instance, in 1741 twenty-four ships entered and cleared in the first week after the ice jam broke in mid-March.[27]

The transmission of news by land was also important to the colonial editor. The New York post brought to Philadelphia not only news from the northern colonies, but also reports of European events which perhaps had not come directly.[28] Bradford's marked dependence upon the New York post is illustrated by the fact that the *Mercury* regularly changed the day of its appearance as the post changed the day of its arrival in Philadelphia.[29] Yet even the overland method of acquiring news was not to be counted on; the *Mercury* occasionally had to make unannounced and unexpected alterations of date of publication, as with Number 154, which instead of coming out on Thursday was put off till Friday, when it appeared with an explanatory note: "Our Delay of this Paper hath been occasioned by the New-York Post coming in so late, who waited for the Eastern Post, but in vain." The paper not infrequently contained notices like the following: "The New-York Post is not yet come in, being hindred, we suppose, by the bad Weather," or "The New York Post designs to perform his Stage for this Winter-Quarter only once a Fortnight; so that now every other Paper, during that Time, will contain the material Advices he brings."[30] The importance of the post to Bradford was, in fact, so great that he sometimes held up an issue already in type, like *Mercury* 885, which is dated December 16, but which contains a note dated December 17, saying that the paper should have appeared the previous day but had been held for the New York post; since the post still had not arrived on December 17, Bradford decided to wait no longer.[31]

---

27. *Mercury* 1107. Number 1106 reported that no ships had entered the harbor from December 18 to March 12.

28. For instance, *Mercury* 841 printed news from New York, January 28, of England, November 4 and thereafter; *Mercury* 781 reprinted news from British papers down to October 8, which came to Philadelphia by way of Boston under date of November 25. A reversal of this procedure sometimes occurred; for example, *Mercury* 590 drew upon the *Political State of Great Britain* for November 1730 for news about Governor Belcher of Massachusetts—news which had traveled from New England to the West Indies and then to London before it crossed the ocean again and came to Bradford's ears.

29. From the middle of December to the middle of March ordinarily the paper came out on Tuesdays, throughout the remainder of the year on Thursdays. We might note, too, that Franklin and Keimer in publishing their papers, instead of issuing them on a different day from that of the appearance of the *Mercury*, were forced to accept direct competition because the post brought the news at that time and only then. The close connection between date of publication and postal arrangements is manifest in the history of all colonial newspapers.

30. *Mercury* 64, 158. For evidence of similar delays or changes in date of publication because of the New York post see, for example, *Mercury* 156, 408, 414, 517, 528, 532, 569, 582, 622, 983, 984.

31. An interesting and typical episode occurred in 1730. The *Pennsylvania*

Intercolonial intelligence, to be sure, travelled relatively fast; editorial lamentations should not blind us to the fact that Boston, New York, and Philadelphia were linked at an early period by post and were served with considerable efficiency. Moreover, for the obtaining of colonial news the *Mercury* was in a very favorable position, since Philadelphia was geographically mid-way between the northern and the southern colonies. Just before Bradford became postmaster in the winter of 1727-1728 there appeared an item from Boston which was about six weeks old when it reached Philadelphia,[32] but later news from Massachusetts came through more rapidly. In January 1730 a report from the Boston *Gazette* appeared in the *Mercury* three weeks after its original printing;[33] in November of the same year a speech of Governor Belcher was reprinted by Bradford ten days after it had appeared in Boston;[34] *Mercury* 804 and 1125 presented accounts from Boston two-and-a-half weeks old; and again in August 1736 an item reached the *Mercury* ten days after its publication in Massachusetts.[35] Whereas news from Boston was ordinarily from ten days to three weeks away from Philadelphia, in good weather New York was less than a week, as is shown, for instance, by the citation of a news report of September 10, 1733, in the *Mercury* of September 13, or in *Mercury* 978 of a three-days-old news story from the New York *Gazette*. In winter, delays sometimes stretched the interval to two weeks, as when Bradford borrowed on January 21 some verses from the *Weekly Journal* of January 6.[36] From the southern colonies and the West Indies news was slower than from the north. In 1728, when the Maryland post-route was set up, the stage went only once a fortnight in good weather and once a month in the winter; indeed, throughout the period we are considering, postal connections with the south were inferior to those with the north. From the West Indian colonies news came partly or entirely by sea and was subject to some of the vicissitudes of European intelligence. In terms of the speed with which news items reached Philadelphia from the south, Maryland was approximately one

---

Gazette and the *Mercury* were due to appear on Thursday, March 12; when the New York post did not arrive both papers were held back. A line below the imprint in the *Gazette* shows that Franklin waited until four o'clock on Friday afternoon before his paper went to press. Bradford waited until Saturday noon, although the date was allowed to stand as Thursday; then, when the post still did not come, he issued his paper. The southern post was never a determining factor in the schedule of the *Mercury's* appearance. (The southern post was established by Andrew Bradford on May 3, 1728, to go as far as Annapolis, and was extended in 1732 to Williamsburg. See the notices in *Mercury* 431, 441, and 655. Eventually, under the direction of Spotswood, it was extended to South Carolina.)

32. *Mercury* 424.
33. *Mercury* 524.
34. *Mercury* 567.
35. *Mercury* 869.
36. *Mercury* 786.

week to three weeks distant, Virginia from three weeks to two months, South Carolina seven or eight weeks or longer, and the West Indies from six to ten weeks.[37]

Colonial news, however, was only a minor worry to an early eighteenth-century American editor, for European intelligence was the backbone of his journal. Under favorable circumstances foreign news appeared in the *Mercury* not more than two or three months late.[38] Number 19, for example, of April 28, 1720, reported happenings in London of February 15 and in the Hague of February 20; and the issue of June 16 of the same year mentioned events in Warsaw of March 1 and in Paris of March 16 and 30. The *Mercury* of December 3, 1724, used material from the *British Journal* of September 19; that of June 30, 1726, cited Mist's *Weekly Journal* of May 7; that of October 17, 1734, referred to the *Whitehall Evening Post* of August 8; that of January 1, 1740/41, contained London news of October 14 and 18; and that of February 11, 1745/46, used material from the *Gentleman's Magazine* of the previous October.[39] Though these and innumerable other examples show that news of Europe could be expected under normal conditions to come through in three months or less, frequently the lag was much greater. In April 1731 Bradford used the *Political State of Great Britain* for November 1730;[40] in mid-August of 1734 he borrowed from the *Gentleman's Magazine* of March;[41] on April 5, 1739, he cited the *Daily Gazetteer* of November 22; on January 27, 1742/43, he made use of an item from the *European Secretary of State* of September 30; and early in January 1730/31 he referred to a letter from Dresden dated August 23.[42] At various times, moreover, news reports arrived six months late or even more, especially when they concerned far-distant places. The story of the destruction by an earthquake of Tauris, metropolis of the Persian empire, which occurred on April 26, 1721, was

---

37. These times are determined in the manner illustrated above: that is, by comparing the original dates and the dates of reprinting in the *Mercury* of typical items from southern papers.

38. Eight weeks seems to have been very good time for the crossing from England to continental American ports. See, for instance, *Mercury* 767, 921, and 1286. *Mercury* 1137 reported a voyage from Dover to New York of thirty-eight days; 1293 mentioned one from Newcastle to New York of forty days; and 1272 one from Glasgow to Boston of thirty-seven days. At the other extreme was the crossing mentioned in Number 144—twenty-eight weeks from Lisbon to Maryland.

39. It is important to remember in connection with such miscellanies as the *Gentleman's Magazine* that the issue for a particular month did not appear until the end of that month. In this example, therefore, the lapse was about three-and-a-half months, a relatively short time for mid-winter.

40. *Mercury* 590.
41. *Mercury* 763.
42. *Mercury* 575.

not presented to readers of the *Mercury* until November 30.[43] An account of an even more devastating earthquake, at Pekin in September 1730, in which 100,000 people were said to have lost their lives, reached the pages of the *Mercury* late in October of the following year.[44] The episode of the burning of a Jesuit Church in Paraguay by the Indians, in May 1736, appeared in the *Mercury* the next April.[45] And not until May 1732 did Philadelphians learn of the decisive battle of the Persian-Turkish war of the previous autumn.[46] Indeed, news of the Orient and of South America was both scant and very slow in reaching the British colonies, not only because it had to travel far, but also because it had to come the roundabout way of the ordinary European news channels.

Some of the results of these irregularities in obtaining foreign intelligence are both instructive and entertaining. For example, on January 10, 1721, one week after the announced arrival of a ship from London, much European news appeared in the *Mercury,* including an item dated London, September 29. For eight weeks thereafter no other foreign ships entered the port; yet during the entire period foreign news continued to come out in the paper, and a London story of September 20 appeared even as late as April 15. Obviously a great part of the European news which was retailed to Bradford's customers during two or three months was taken from the papers brought over on the vessel which arrived just before January 10 and was carefully chosen number by number to last through the lean winter season. On the other hand, in summer time and in later years Bradford could sometimes afford to be prodigal, as in the issue of July 24, 1729, in which he used items from six different numbers of the *Daily Post*. It is likely, indeed, that throughout the life of the *Mercury* the foreign journals on which it depended arrived either in batches or out of their proper order: for example, the Cork *News Letter* of April 26 was cited in *Mercury* 499, whereas *Mercury* 500 mentioned the same paper for April 15; *Mercury* 548 used the *Daily Journal* of April 7 and 23, and Number 549 the *Journal* of April 18; *Mercury* 891 borrowed from the *London Magazine* for July and Number 887 from that for August; Number 1188 cited the Bristol *Journal* of July 17, and 1191 the same paper for July 3. Moreover, the irregularity of the news and the limited size of the paper probably encouraged Bradford to use the same journal more than once as a news source: for instance, *Mercury* 879 and 882 both use the same issue of

43. The news came by way of London from Leghorn, thence from a French sea captain, who had heard the story in Smyrna.
44. *Mercury* 617.
45. *Mercury* 902. The news came by way of the Hague.
46. *Mercury* 644 and 647. Letters from Constantinople of November 1 were published in Amsterdam on February 12 and reached the *Mercury* on May 25.

SOURCES OF THE "MERCURY"

the *London Magazine,* Numbers 561 and 563 of the *Whitehall Evening Post,* and Numbers 1267 and 1270 of the *Gentleman's.*

The printing of news was constantly, but understandably, attended by delays and stop-gaps; in addition, it was sometimes inaccurate or contradictory. Some errors seem explicable only as carelessness. For example, *Mercury* 684 contained a lengthy account of the death of the Duke of Bedford; except for a few minor changes the identical item was repeated in Number 691, and it does not appear likely, although it is conceivable, that the second printing was intended to correct the errors of the first. Similarly, *Mercury* 450 and 452 contained exactly the same report concerning the opening of the Congress of Soissons. A more curious mistake occurred in Number 1001, where a speech of Governor Belcher was printed twice, first at the bottom of one page and again at the top of the next. Franklin was responsible for pointing out a particularly strange lapse in the editing of the *Mercury.* In the *Gazette* of November 9, 1732, "Memory" addressed to the printer a protest against Numbers 669 and 670, which, he said, had reported very stale news — an item under the heading of London, July 20, about the Congress of Soissons, and another of May 8 announcing the death of Admiral Hopson. To "Memory's" criticism the editor added a paragraph, pointing out that this letter should have been sent to the publisher of the *Mercury* — for the *Gazette* had reached only Number 206 — and ironically remarking: "I may however say something in his Excuse, viz. That 'tis not to be always expected there should happen just a full Sheet of New Occurrences for each Week; and that the oftener you are told a good Thing, the more likely you will be to remember it." "Memory" and Franklin (if they were not the same person) were both quite right: the items do appear in the *Mercury* in 1732, yet the Congress of Soissons dated from 1728 and Admiral Hopson had died on May 8 of that year. One can only conjecture that Bradford or one of his journeymen had inadvertently clipped the reports from old papers.[47]

Most mistakes, however, appear to have been unavoidable. We have already noticed some examples of inaccuracy in stories delivered to Bradford by word of mouth, but errors were bound to occur even when news came from reputable journals. Some may be attributed merely to the time-lag; when a single issue of the paper might contain two items from the same city relating to events separated in time by several weeks

---

47. Franklin's innuendo that Bradford deliberately padded his paper seems highly improbable, since reference to the Congress of Soissons especially was very likely to be detected. *Gazette* 297 also caught the *Mercury* in an error when it ridiculed Number 761 for stating that "the Dukes of Berwick and Savoy were both shot by a random shot from the Town of Philipsburg," since one was on the Rhine and the other in Italy. Franklin, however, was living in a glass house: *Gazette* 295 reported Berwick's death, while 296 told in the present tense of his activities at the siege.

— like *Mercury* 90, which had news from London of both April 29 and June 3, or *Mercury* 382, which had reports from December 14 to March 2 — it is not surprising that confusion and contradiction crept into the paper. Various inconsistencies occurred; for example, in the issue of May 5, 1720, under headings of three different places appeared three half-conflicting, half-corroborative pieces of information on the same matter: under date of Paris, February 7, was printed news of Philip V's acceptance of the treaty of 1718; under New York, May 2, was quoted the word of a ship captain that "a Peace with Spain was actually concluded"; and under "Portsmouth, New Hampshire April 22" was mentioned the report of another seaman "that the peace with Spain was near concluded." Sometimes, also, news stories were twisted quite out of logical order, as in this instance: in Number 280 from London appeared news of the death of the Czar of Russia and in Number 281 the statement was confirmed by a report from Berlin; but in Number 282 from St. Petersburg was printed the news of the Czar's arranging the marriage of his daughter, an event which took place some three weeks before he died. A similar confusion occurred in another episode: Number 358 announced the death of the Duchess of Orleans; the following issue spoke of the place of her interment and of the retirement of the Dowager Duchess upon the death of the younger woman; later in the same issue was the news, of earlier date, of her giving birth to a princess.

Nor was such confusion common only in the early years of the *Mercury*. In the autumn of 1745, Philadelphians, like other British subjects, were following with an interest scarcely diminished by the width of the Atlantic the Jacobite invasion of Scotland. For months the expedition of Prince Charles Edward absorbed more of the news columns of the *Mercury* than any other subject, often more than all other subjects combined. Mrs. Bradford's readers were unquestionably well informed about the invasion, but they must certainly have had to read attentively to keep the sequence of events in mind. For instance, Number 1344 reported under different headings, first, that the Pretender's eldest son had embarked from Brittany; second, from Paris, that the king had announced Charles's landing in Scotland; and third, from London, that a reward of £30,000 was offered to any who seized the Prince if he should land. Number 1346 reported from Newcastle, under date of August 28, that he had disembarked between Mull and Skye with 3000 men; Number 1347 reported as of July 24 that the Chevalier de St. George had acquainted the Pope that his eldest son was "preparing for a new Enterprize in Favour of his Family"; and in the same number, dated Glasgow, August 12, appeared the rumor that three hundred men had landed at Skye, though news from the same city of September 2, which appeared in

Sources of the "Mercury"

Mercury 1350, confirmed the earlier figure of 3000. Number 1352 contained the news that Charles had been defeated and taken prisoner by General Cope,[48] but 1354 more accurately reported that he had been proclaimed regent and had captured Edinburgh. And so the story went: Mrs. Bradford got the news, saw that it was good copy, printed it — and willy-nilly she made the episode exciting and the Prince a dramatic figure. But the exigencies of space and the everlasting irregularities in the transmission of news twisted and tangled the narrative. To edit, or even to read, a colonial newspaper must have required more than a little tolerance and flexibility of mind.

48. This news came in the familiar roundabout fashion: to Philadelphia from New York, where it had been brought by sloop from St. Kitts, which had received the report from a ship from Cork.

Chapter 3

Foreign and Colonial Affairs in the *Mercury*

The publication of the *Mercury* was manifestly no simple job merely because the paper was small in size and came out but once a week. Type was scarce and expensive;[1] for a regular supply of paper Bradford was dependent upon the Rittenhouse mill;[2] and the whole process of procuring news and presenting it intelligibly was beset with complications. Since we have now shown something of Bradford's delays and shifts and errors, we turn to the more constructive task of discovering to what extent he succeeded in bringing to his readers knowledge of the major events across the sea and in the American colonies.

J. M. Lee has asserted that "the colonial editor was often a master of his trade in 'boiling down' the news: he did not use three columns when three lines would tell the story."[3] As we have already noted, Bradford at least did very little "boiling down." Indeed, I should imagine that most of the concision which Lee praises is due to the British journals which the colonial editors plundered and imitated. Nevertheless, the fact remains that the colonial papers, including the *Mercury*, presented their news succinctly, if only because their limited space discouraged digression. Moreover, in the course, let us say, of a year the editor selected material from a sufficient number of different papers and treated so large a number of subjects that he gave his readers a fairly comprehensive idea of the events and issues of the time. In addition, by judicious apportioning of space, he was able to put emphasis over a period of time upon the really big news stories. The colonial paper was, in short, a sort of superior variety of tabloid; it presented in brief compass and unvarnished form, but quite reliably, the really important happenings of the day. The news columns of the *Mercury*, for example, on the whole are a surprisingly informative guide to the events of some twenty-five years of European history and supply also a more spotty but considerable knowledge of affairs in the American colonies.

During the first half-year of the *Mercury* much of the European news concerned the various phases of the complicated wars then in progress.[4] Through a mass of incident — such as Berwick's march into Catalonia, Russia's ravaging of Sweden's Baltic provinces, George I's intervention

---

1. Wroth, 93.
2. Bradford was, of course, fortunate among colonial printers in having a paper mill virtually at his disposal.
3. Lee, *History of American Journalism*, 67.
4. See chiefly Numbers 1 to 21.

to bring about a truce between Denmark and Sweden, Holland's clash with the Empire on the high seas, and Philip's acceptance of the Treaty of Paris — Bradford kept his readers well informed on the trends of conflict. The second big news event of the *Mercury's* early history was the South Sea Bubble. As Bradford presented the story, the soaring prices early in 1720, the towering profits and wild speculation, the sharp break in September, the futile attempts to bolster the stock, the flight of the treasurer and the death of Craggs and Stanhope, the fictitious names in the company's books "to conceal those who shared the Booty," and the ensuing parliamentary investigations and discoveries — all these make up a thoroughly convincing picture of the whole fantastic episode.[5] Nor did the *Mercury* leave out the element of human interest; Number 59 reported that "one of the Managers of the South Sea Company, was lamentably beaten by an Officer, who had sold his real and personal Estate, and lost all in the South Sea Stock, that if some good People had not step'd between he would have killed him on the Spot." Number 292 ran a typical story about the suicide of a man because of his losses in speculation. Two gayer tales also appeared:

> The prodigious Fall of South Sea Stock has ruined Thousands: several Gentlemen who kept their Coaches before they dipt into South Sea, are now forced to walk on Foot. By the same Turn of Fortunes Wheel, Footmen and Cook Maids loll in their gilded Chariots and smile at the Fate of their quondam Masters.[6]

> We hear that Mrs. Barbier, the famous Singer at the New Play House, having gained above 5000 *l*. by S. S. Stock, has sung her last Farewel to the Stage.[7]

A third news topic which figured largely in the early years of the paper was the plague which ravaged France and other parts of Europe from 1720 to 1722.[8] The *Mercury* not only reported its terrifying spread from place to place, but, even more interesting to present-day readers, pointed out some economic results of the epidemic: for instance, the Spanish blockade of French exports and the Dutch assumption of the woolen and silk trade with Spain which France had previously held.[9]

---

5. See especially Numbers 19, 30, 37, 41, 48, 52, 54, 71, 72, 74, 76, 77, 81-85. Almost twenty-one columns of small print concerning the South Sea Bubble appeared in Numbers 81 to 85 alone.
6. *Mercury* 55.
7. *Mercury* 65.
8. The most important issues of the *Mercury* for the story of the plague are 53, 54, 58, 59, 61, 65, 85, 88, 106, 112, 117, 165, 177.
9. *Mercury* 110 and 112.

In London, barracks were built to be used, if necessary, as infirmaries; the College of Physicians met to discuss precautions against the advance of the dread disease; and the government ordered a plague-ridden Dutch ship to be fired on to prevent it from putting into port.[10]

A little later the *Mercury* traced step by step the intricate negotiations preceding and at the Congress of Cambrai.[11] It told the story of the conspiracy to bring the Pretender into England in the summer of 1722 and of the wave of charges and recriminations which followed, including the dramatic episode of the trial and unfrocking of the Bishop of Rochester.[12] It recounted several cases of interference with freedom of the press which figured prominently in Whig policy in the early 1720's.[13] Scotland entered the news by way of the malt-tax riots in Glasgow in 1725;[14] and Ireland figured through the case, famous in literary history for its connection with *The Drapier's Letters,* of the patent granted to William Wood for coining copper halfpennies and farthings.[15] The persecution of the Protestants in France and Poland was excellent fodder for a colonial Protestant press,[16] and for a similar reason the reforming liberalism of Pope Benedict XIII received much attention.[17] The story of the coronation of Catherine I of Russia had its place;[18] Louis XV's assumption of active control of his government was announced;[19] and even the far-distant wars in Asia Minor, the outrages of the Persian rebel Mahmud,[20] and the invasion of Persia by Turkey[21] played a part in the pattern of foreign news which Bradford brought to his provincial readers.

In the late 'twenties and throughout the 'thirties the most frequent topic of political interest in the *Mercury* was the constant threat of a

10. *Mercury* 120.
11. See especially Numbers 86, 171, 184, 231, 245, 284.
12. See especially Numbers 148, 156, 163, 171, 174, 179, 208-209. Rochester's speech in defence of himself was presented completely by the *Mercury* in six numbers, from 199 to 205.
13. *Mercury* 98, 174, 229, 240.
14. *Mercury* 301, 345.
15. *Mercury* 213, 225, 321.
16. See, for instance, Numbers 153, 188, 254, 255-257, 269, 275-277, 280, 289, 327. The persecution of Protestants remained a lively topic in the *Mercury* for many years. See, for example, Numbers 455, 471-472, 585, 598, 624, 667, 674.
17. *Mercury* 251, 279, 287, 289, 291, 292.
18. *Mercury* 246, 253, 280, 281.
19. *Mercury* 352.
20. He is called "Meriweys" throughout the narrative in the *Mercury*. The rebel Mir Wa'iz, however, died in 1715; and it was his son, Mahmud, who at the head of an army of Afghans overran Persia in 1721. In March 1722 he defeated the Persian forces, and in September assumed the throne. Turkey and Russia took advantage of the disorder in the kingdom and seized parts of it for themselves. Mahmud, notorious for his inhuman cruelties and barbarism, died in 1725 at the early age of twenty-seven. (See *Encyclopaedia Britannica,* 11th edition, XXI, 233.) A long summary of the whole course of Mahmud's rebellion is contained in Numbers 406 to 414. Here Mahmud is given his correct name.
21. *Mercury* 149, 213, 215, 217, 219, 220, 222, 317, 323, 327, 355.

general European war and the protracted series of conferences, treaties, and international agreements[22] by which it was postponed from year to year even while the peace of Europe was interrupted by local strife. Bradford naturally reflected the British view, and in the early part of the period was loud in praise of Walpole's successful negotiations to preserve order and the balance of power.[23] Some of the important events which the paper high-lighted were the siege of Gibraltar, which almost precipitated war between England and Spain in 1727;[24] the death of George I and the accession of George II, and the appointment of Walpole as Chancellor of the Exchequer;[25] the opening of the Congress of Soissons in 1728,[26] the signing of the Treaty of Seville in 1729,[27] and the subsequent treaty of 1731 between Austria, Holland, and Great Britain;[28] the rebellion of Corsica against Genoa[29] followed by the rise of "King Theodore" and his successful attempt to enlist the aid of Britain;[30] the War of the Polish Succession, which again endangered the peace of all Europe;[31] the conflict between Russia and Turkey;[32] Walpole's last and short-lived victory over the war party in 1738;[33] and the final outbreak of hostilities between Spain and England in 1739.[34]

During the same period Bradford gave an important place in the *Mercury* to British domestic developments. The desperate poverty and unrest in Ireland,[35] including the food riots in Cork in 1729,[36] were vividly presented. The fierce opposition to Walpole's excise bill was

---

22. The *Mercury* frequently printed the terms of important treaties or extracts from the treaties themselves. See, for example, Numbers 533, 538-539, 600, 620, 841.

23. See, for example, the laudatory verses in *Mercury* 520, 782, 965, 989.

24. *Mercury* 380, 386, 390, 393, 394. Numbers 426-430 contained a retrospective account of the siege.

25. *Mercury* 399, 407.

26. *Mercury* 455.

27. *Mercury* 531.

28. *Mercury* 598, 600.

29. *Mercury* 563, 602, 606, 652, 663, 761, 877.

30. *Mercury* 880, 901, 957, 981.

31. *Mercury* 698, 704, 711, 723, 726, 739, 750, 787. Typically the *Mercury* devoted a considerable part of one issue (Number 730) to an account of the historical background of the Polish conflict, in order to make the news items more understandable to its readers. Throughout 1734 the Polish war figured constantly in the news.

32. *Mercury* 924, 932, 933, 939, 998, 1042, 1058.

33. *Mercury* 967. Number 1008 quoted George's address to Parliament in which he mentioned the Convention with Spain of January 14, 1739. Numbers 1009-1011 reprinted the Convention.

34. *Mercury* 1036, 1037, 1039, 1040, 1050. Number 1050 quoted in full the king's proclamation of war against Spain, dated October 19 and proclaimed on October 23. The quotation in the *Mercury* was accompanied by a description of the ceremony which attended the proclamation.

35. *Mercury* 476, 514, 516, 527, 870, 1092, 1113.

36. *Mercury* 491.

reported with effective detail;[37] on the other hand, the paper featured the eager co-operation of the country in putting itself into a position of defense while the Polish war raged.[38] The Gin Act of 1736 was reprinted in part in the *Mercury*,[39] an editorial on the bill appeared,[40] and some of its amusing or ironic accompaniments were reported: the protest of the coffin- and shroudmakers against an act which they considered a great detriment to their trade; the hold-up of a member of Parliament by a distiller who said that since he had been deprived of his business he was entitled by act of Parliament to follow any other calling necessary to support his family; and the celebration of obsequies for "Mother Gin" in Bristol.[41] The arguments for and against the continuing of twelve thousand Hessian troops in the pay of the English government were discussed;[42] the decline in woolen manufacturing and the threat to Irish economy from the establishment of linen manufacturing among the Irish immigrants to America were mentioned.[43] In April 1734, announced the *Mercury*, warrants were out for impressing men into the service of the king.[44] Shortly afterwards the Bank of England was reported moving into its "new House in Thread-Needle Street."[45] Number 904 contained a set of statistics for the year 1736: the deaths in the city of London and their causes, the number of ships entered into and cleared from the custom-house, and figures on the export trade. In 1738 news from Britain began to show clearly the mounting war fever; items concerning Spanish attacks on British shipping in the West Indies appeared, and a heated debate in Parliament encouraged by the demand for a declaration of war from "Mr. Pultney," with a long and persuasive rebuttal by Walpole, was reported.[46]

Important domestic occurrences in other countries than England received a much smaller place in the *Mercury;* still, the amount and variety of such news is very considerable. From Russia came the story of the split between Peter II and Prince Menshikov in the fall of 1727.[47] In 1732 it was reported that Spain, blessed by the Pope, had attacked the Moors and slaughtered eight thousand of them at Oran; there followed,

37. *Mercury* 699, 705, 709.
38. *Mercury* 747, 749, 750, 761, 776.
39. *Mercury* 867. As early as Numbers 341-342 the *Mercury* had featured the report of a committee of justices of the peace of Middlesex on the trade in Geneva and other "strong waters."
40. *Mercury* 895.
41. *Mercury* 856, 886, and 890 respectively.
42. *Mercury* 542.
43. *Mercury* 599 and 675 respectively.
44. *Mercury* 761.
45. *Mercury* 763.
46. *Mercury* 962, 963, 967.
47. *Mercury* 418, 421.

however, news of the withdrawal of the Spaniards from the siege of Algiers because of the scorched-earth policy instituted by their enemies.[48] In Holland, on the other hand, a thanksgiving day was proclaimed on March 11, 1733, to celebrate twenty years of peace,[49] and Amsterdam reported the cargoes of seven ships from the East Indies — pepper, nutmeg, saltpetre, shellack, dragon's blood, coffee, indigo, and silks.[50] The great fire in St. Petersburg in 1736 was followed by a proclamation of the Czarina exempting from all taxes for ten years those who would settle there and rebuild the city,[51] and in the bitter winter of 1739-1740 George of England ordered his own granaries opened for the people of his duchy of Hanover.[52]

After 1739, however, few incidental pieces of European news found their way into the *Mercury;* the foreign columns were almost exclusively concerned with the war between Spain and England, then with the War of the Austrian Succession into which it merged, and at the very close of the paper's history with that romantic by-product of the general conflict — the Jacobite invasion of Scotland in 1745. In much detail Bradford presented the different phases of the opening years of the war: the indecision of France,[53] the contradictory reports about Cartagena,[54] the death of the Emperor and the "Field of Contention" created by that event,[55] Prussia's march into Silesia and Maria Theresa's peril,[56] the rising tide against Walpole and his retirement,[57] the advance of 150,000 allied troops along the borders of France,[58] the threats of a French invasion of England,[59] and the belated declaration of war between France and Great Britain.[60] We learn of the death of Anne of Russia and the quarrel over the succession,[61] of the starvation of five thousand people during the siege of Prague,[62] of the death of Cardinal Fleury,[63] of Dettingen and Tournay,[64] of the capture of Ostend by the French and of Milan by the Spanish.[65] Indeed, we can follow in the *Mercury* week by week and in great detail the entire progress of the conflict and its many ramifications

48. *Mercury* 665, 666, 684.
49. *Mercury* 697.
50. *Mercury* 782.
51. *Mercury* 883.
52. *Mercury* 1068.
53. *Mercury* 1041, 1096, 1102.
54. *Mercury* 1066, 1081, 1115, 1127, 1132.
55. *Mercury* 1101, 1106.
56. *Mercury* 1108, 1118.
57. *Mercury* 1142, 1163, 1172, 1177, 1179.
58. *Mercury* 1241.
59. *Mercury* 1267-1269.
60. *Mercury* 1272.
61. *Mercury* 1105, 1106, 1160, 1161.
62. *Mercury* 1201.
63. *Mercury* 1213, 1216.
64. *Mercury* 1234, 1333, 1334.
65. *Mercury* 1347, 1357.

from the beginning to 1746. Already in 1743 the constantly increasing amount of European news, with more and more circumstantial reports of the war, had nearly crowded colonial items off the pages. By early in 1745 practically all the paper was taken up with events in Europe and with the repercussions in America of what was happening abroad. And from that time to the end of its existence the *Mercury's* presentation of European news continued to be comprehensive and substantial.

Whereas Bradford's presentation of foreign events between 1720 and 1746, particularly after 1740, was remarkably solid, orderly, and clear, the story of the American colonies was fragmentary and without focus. Most of the very large mass of news from Europe included in the *Mercury* can be seen in retrospect as part of a consistent and continuous narrative, perhaps because nearly all events were treated with Great Britain as their center and point of reference. On the contrary, it is difficult to see in the much smaller bulk of Bradford's colonial news more than several series of happenings, each one incomplete, largely isolated from one another even though contemporaneous.[66] Some of the colonial news reported in the *Mercury*, of course, had reference to America as a whole, but most of it related to one province or another as a separate entity. On the other hand, a considerable amount of news which purported to concern only Massachusetts or New York or Maryland was actually of interest and significance in all the colonies. For obvious reasons, especially in the early period of the paper, Bradford generally exploited uncontroversial subjects common to the provinces as a whole: the activities of the Spanish and the French, of Indians or pirates, human-interest stories, and accounts of earthquakes, eclipses, and floods. For example, we read in the early part of 1720 of the French settling of Louisiana, with its threat to the Spanish colonies of the Gulf,[67] of South Carolina's throwing herself upon the protection of the English king because of fear of attack by the Spaniards,[68] and of a running fight between an English and a Spanish ship off Hispaniola.[69] In October 1720, Governor Burnet of New York appealed to the province to safeguard itself against the French and Indians;[70] in the following month Governor Spotswood's address to the members of the Virginia Assembly warned them against a similar danger on their western frontier;[71] and

---

66. For reasons already made clear the reporting of colonial political events was much less complete and regular than that of similar happenings across the Atlantic. It is, therefore, quite impossible to trace in the pages of the *Mercury* any historical pattern.
67. *Mercury* 8, 9, 30, 32.
68. *Mercury* 13.
69. *Mercury* 33.
70. *Mercury* 44.
71. *Mercury* 60. Number 75 included some of the correspondence between Governors Keith and Spotswood concerning a joint treaty of Pennsylvania and

FOREIGN AND COLONIAL AFFAIRS IN THE "MERCURY"

Massachusetts was menaced repeatedly, the *Mercury* showed, by Indian warfare and was consequently engaged in frequent negotiations with various tribes.[72] Tales of piracy and privateering appeared in the paper many times,[73] and issue after issue included stories of epidemics, tempests, and hurricanes, of counterfeiting, robbery, and murder.[74]

Of political news about the colonies there was at first almost none. To be sure Bradford printed the speeches and proclamations of the governors and similar more or less routine matters: for example, Calvert's address to the Assembly of Maryland on the need of building up the tobacco trade,[75] the letters of Trinity Church and of the city of New York welcoming William Burnet upon his arrival as governor,[76] William Dummer's speech in the course of the perennial battle over the charter of Massachusetts asking for loyalty to George I and his proclamation concerning the treaty between the province and the Indians of July 1727,[77] the voting by the House of Burgesses of Virginia of a present of £500 to Governor William Gooch,[78] and the address of the officials of Perth Amboy to the new governor, John Montgomerie.[79] Moreover, he occasionally printed some account of the actions taken or the laws enacted by one of the provincial legislatures — for example, the New York Assembly in 1720[80] or the Assembly of Virginia in 1728.[81]

The first political problem, however, which the *Mercury* considered seriously and at length was the contest between Burnet and the Assembly of Massachusetts over the Governor's salary. The quarrel, of course, was a familiar element of the struggle which took place in nearly all the provinces in the eighteenth century between the colony on the one side and "prerogative" on the other.[82] Though the issue was not new, the

---

Virginia with the Indians. Number 141 announced the departure of the Governors of New York, Virginia, and Pennsylvania for Albany to treat with them.

72. *Mercury* 38, 136, 138, 139, 145, 192, 195, 247, 318, 351, 392.
73. *Mercury* 13, 21, 22, 53, 88, 108, 143, 339, 405.
74. *Mercury* 13, 23, 91, 96, 104, 157, 220, 221, 365, 374, 379, 381, 391, 406.
75. *Mercury* 351.
76. *Mercury* 42.
77. *Mercury* 317 and 400 respectively.
78. *Mercury* 429.
79. *Mercury* 435. For further examples of official addresses and similar items see Numbers 419, 430-431, 441, 450, 456, 459, 472, etc. This type of news was a staple of the colonial editor.
80. *Mercury* 46.
81. *Mercury* 437.
82. The point at issue in Massachusetts and elsewhere was whether the crown officials should have an established salary or whether the Assembly should have the right of voting what amount it saw fit from year to year. Obviously, if the latter situation obtained, the Assembly held a club over the head of the governor. The basic problem, then, was a constitutional one—whether the real governing power of the colony lay with the crown and the British Parliament or with the elected representatives of the people.

Mercury first mentioned it in 1729;[83] in all probability only the safe distance between Boston and Philadelphia made it possible for Bradford to devote so much print to it as he did in the months that followed. After an account of the hearing before the Privy Council in London on April 23 in which Burnet's position, naturally, was upheld, the *Mercury* reported his sudden death in September and the continuation of the quarrel by Governor Dummer.[84] Though Bradford thought it well to reprint the very eulogistic description of the late Governor which appeared in the Boston *Gazette*,[85] he printed also the extremely forthright answer of the House of Representatives of Massachusetts to Burnet's last message, including these vigorous sentences:[86]

> It is wonderful to this House, that you should argue so much from the Settlement of the Civil-List for the fixing of your Salary, when there is so great and obvious a difference between them! Can you expect such an Expression of Respect and Confidence from your Conduct ever since your Arrival? Can there be any pretence, that the Assembly have not shewn as great an Inclination for your Support, as your Excellency has for the Good of this Province.

When the salary issue flared up violently again after the arrival of Jonathan Belcher in 1730, once more the *Mercury* reported the conflict in considerable detail, if not with positive relish. In Number 560, for instance, Bradford stated that the post had brought him Belcher's speech to the Assembly, but that lack of space prevented his publishing it entire. "We shall therefore," the notice reads, "only give our Readers the most material Paragraph, concerning the so long disputed Point, the Setling of the fixed Salary." Number 561, however, printed the whole speech, as well as the Assembly's evasive reply; the next issue revealed that the Assembly still stubbornly refused to fix the amount of the salary; and for months afterwards Bradford continued to report the ups-and-downs of the quarrel,[87] even including in Number 590 an extract from the *Political State of Great Britain* on the controversy. In 1733[88] the *Mercury* reported that a petition of Massachusetts that the king withdraw his instructions to Belcher concerning money "as contrary to their Charter, and tending in their own Nature to distress, if not ruin them," was

---

83. *Mercury* 482.
84. *Mercury* 496, 506, 510. William Dummer was governor of Massachusetts both before and after William Burnet.
85. *Mercury* 509.
86. *Mercury* 511.
87. *Mercury* 567, 578, 579, 581, 585, 630, 695. Numbers 677, 678, and 686 are especially lively.
88. *Mercury* 713.

Foreign and Colonial Affairs in the "Mercury"

rejected by the House of Commons as "frivolous and groundless, an high insult upon his Majesty's Government, & tending to shake off the Dependency of the said Colony upon this Kingdom, to which by Law and Right they are and ought to be subject." Nevertheless, shortly thereafter Bradford was able to report[89] that the Assembly had passed a bill for the payment of public debts and that both Belcher and the representatives were presumably satisfied. From that time forward the *Mercury* contained only occasional references to the persistent financial disagreements in Massachusetts between the governor and the legislature.

Though few colonial problems absorbed so much of the *Mercury's* attention as the Massachusetts salary question and though few could have been so generally interesting to the colonial reader wherever he lived, in the late 'twenties and the early 'thirties Bradford now and again touched on other timely issues. For example, in the same number[90] in which he announced that Governor John Montgomerie of New York was visiting in Philadelphia in order to see the Governor of Pennsylvania, he printed Montgomerie's proclamation dissolving the House of Representatives of New Jersey because, he said, they "have Presumed to make some Resolves, in order, as they pretend, to obtain a Distinct Governour for said Province, without taking any proper Measures to know the King's Pleasure as to the subject Matter of them." Somewhat later the paper reported a proposal of the Council of New Hampshire to Governor Belcher that "discreet and indifferent Persons" be asked from neighboring colonies to settle the long-disputed boundary between New Hampshire and Massachusetts.[91] In 1731 the *Mercury* raised an issue of major importance to nearly every continental province when it published a report from New York that a bill was likely to be passed by the British Parliament prohibiting the northern colonies from exporting horses and lumber to "foreign plantations" and from importing thence sugar, rum, and molasses.[92] As the news account stated, such an act would be "a heavy Stroke to Trade" for the northern colonies; accordingly, the agents of Massachusetts, Rhode Island, Connecticut, New Jersey, and Carolina,

---

89. *Mercury* 725.

90. *Mercury* 472.

91. *Mercury* 560. This controversy was certainly of interest to Bradford's local customers because of the persistent boundary disputes between Maryland and Pennsylvania.

92. This attempt to restrict the commercial activities of the continental colonies was caused mainly by the protests of the sugar planters of the British West Indies, who found themselves, because of the flourishing trade between those colonies and the other West Indian islands, forced into direct competition with foreign sugar growers. The Board of Trade was the more willing to listen to such protests because it did not wish to encourage the strengthening of the French empire by supporting commerce between the continental colonies and the French West Indies.

the *Mercury* reported, had set up active opposition to it.[93] The bill itself was reprinted in the issues of July 29 and August 5, but in the second of these numbers came also the news that, though the act had been accepted by the Commons, it had not been passed by the Lords. For a time the matter was forgotten; then in July 1732 appeared the news that another sugar bill was before Parliament. In the same issue and the one following, as well as in two later numbers,[94] appeared discussions of the proposed restrictions on colonial trade. Finally in the spring of 1733 came word that an act imposing heavy duties on all rum, sugar, and molasses imported into the British colonies from foreign nations had been passed.[95] The bill was printed in the *Mercury* and the paper announced, no doubt with some bitterness, the rejoicing with which Antigua had received news of its enactment.[96] No other economic question of intercolonial importance won so much space in the *Mercury* as the Sugar Act, but the implications of that law were emphasized, perhaps intentionally, by Bradford when he allotted a place occasionally to other news of similar purport. One such item concerned an act to prevent the exportation of hats made in America, in order to encourage the manufacture of hats in Great Britain.[97] Another was a news story published in 1735 in which the Board of Trade was described as worried lest the North American colonies might raise sheep and manufacture goods and in other ways pursue a course detrimental to British economic interests.[98] Thirdly, several items in 1737 and 1738 dealt with the manufacture of iron in America; in Number 905 was mentioned a petition to be sent to Parliament to allow all American iron to be imported into England free, whereas in a later issue appeared the news that the British ironmongers had appealed to the government for protection against the competition of colonial iron manufacturing.[99]

About the same time that the quarrel between Belcher and the Assembly of Massachusetts reached something like a settlement and very shortly after the passing of the Sugar Act closed that subject to profitable discussion, the *Mercury* conveniently found a new controversy with which to fill its pages. In August 1732 William Cosby had arrived in New York to take up the position of governor left vacant by Montgomerie's death.

93. *Mercury* 599, 603.
94. *Mercury* 654-655, 657-658.
95. This piece of discriminatory legislation, the Sugar and Molasses Act of 1733, was notoriously disregarded and never seriously enforced.
96. *Mercury* 697, 714-715.
97. *Mercury* 659.
98. *Mercury* 804.
99. *Mercury* 905, 908, 965. Since Bradford had a business interest in an iron foundry, it is not surprising that this phase of the economic conflict between the colonies and Great Britain should have impressed him and been mentioned in his paper.

FOREIGN AND COLONIAL AFFAIRS IN THE "MERCURY"

Mercury 658 duly mentioned his coming and later numbers of the paper referred casually to him in connection with such routine matters as speeches to the Assembly and the enactment of laws.[100] Then in December 1733 appeared a letter addressed to Bradford with an opening paragraph to this effect:[101]

> Since your Mercury pretends to give an Account of Occurrences Foreign and Domestic, I admire you do not favour your Readers with some Transactions now on Foot in a Neighbouring Province, they being of a publick Nature, and such as every true Briton ought to know and understand, that they may take care to prevent any of our English Liberties and Priviledges from being invaded, and thereby we and our Posterity enslaved by base, corrupt and mercinary Men that hereafter may happen to rule and govern in these Parts of the World. The Occurrences I propose to you to make publick is a Controversie, now depending between his Excellency William Cosby, Esq; Governor of New-York, and Rip Van Dam, Esq; President of His Majesty's Council there, which Controversie is published in that Province by several Papers printed there, and one of them published by Lewis Morris, Esq; late Chief Justice of that Province, and the others by Mr. Van Dam aforesaid. Which printed Papers not being common in this Government, various Reports are spread amongst the People hereaway, some of them to the disadvantage and dishonour of that Governor. In order therefore that the Publick may be truly informed of the State of the Case there depending, I have collected out of said printed Papers a brief Relation of that Affair, which you are desired to give a place in your Mercury, which I am sure will be acceptable to many of your constant Readers, and will be a means to prevent falshoods being spread concerning the Transactions and Proceedings of his Excellency William Cosby, Esq; . . . .

After this introduction came a lengthy explanation — which would seem almost superfluous — of the origin of the quarrel.[102] In brief, for thirteen months between Montgomerie's death and Cosby's arrival the president of the Council, Rip Van Dam, according to custom had taken over the executive power of the province; the Council consequently had voted Van Dam the salary due the governor during that period. When

100. *Mercury* 657, 658, 660, 667, 676, 696, 698, 702.
101. *Mercury* 729. The writer seems in this introduction to blow hot and cold. Perhaps the apparent defense of Cosby at the end is a blind.
102. In almost every detail this account seems to be accurate, though it is, of course, favorable to Van Dam.

77

Cosby reached New York, however, he produced instructions from the king to the effect that he should be given half of Van Dam's salary. Van Dam agreed to pay him, but on the condition that Cosby in turn should pay him half of whatever amounts due during Van Dam's administration Cosby had received while abroad.

When Cosby refused this condition, Van Dam kept his salary. Cosby then set up a court of exchequer in order to sue Van Dam,[103] whereupon Van Dam alleged that the court was illegal because it had been established neither by act of Parliament nor by the New York Assembly. Lewis Morris, Chief Justice of New York, who "had served about Twenty Years without any charge or complaint against him," refused to act in support of Cosby and was consequently suspended,[104] his place being taken by James De Lancey.[105] At this point in the explanation there appeared in the *Mercury* a copy of Van Dam's third letter to Cosby, dated October 22, two earlier letters having failed, he said, to elicit an answer, and the courts being closed to him by Cosby's orders; in this he listed the amounts involved in the disagreement and threatened to take the matter to the king if Cosby continued to refuse to settle with him.[106] In the same issue of the *Mercury* was published with unmistakable intent the first borrowing from the New York *Weekly Journal*,[107] the paper founded a month earlier and printed by John Peter Zenger as a weapon against the Governor because the New York *Gazette* was controlled by the government.[108] Like many other items in the *Weekly Journal's* pages[109] the section reprinted in the *Mercury* was propaganda in disguise: it implied that Cosby was conniving with the French against the best interests of the colonies and warned New York against the danger of being "reduced to Slavery by Tyranny or Arbitrary Power."[110]

103. The writer in the *Mercury* does not explain, perhaps because the matter was familiar, the reason for Cosby's action. The Governor was forced either to give up his claim or else to start legal proceedings. As chancellor *ex officio* he could not bring his own suit into chancery; therefore, he empowered the judges of the Supreme Court to act as Barons of the Exchequer. Both this court, which had met occasionally before (though its legality had been disputed), and chancery were very unpopular. See *The Documentary History of the State of New-York*, IV, 1041. See also *Mercury* 831.

104. On August 21, 1733.

105. The third judge, raised to second rank by Cosby's suspension of Morris, was Frederick Philipse.

106. Van Dam's account stated that Cosby had received £8383/6/8 and he £1975/7/10. He therefore considered that Cosby owed him some £3200!

107. Of December 3, Number 5.

108. See New York *Weekly Journal* 7.

109. See, for example, the sham advertisements in Numbers 4, 8, and 9, and the equally fraudulent dialect letters in 19 and 20. Zenger and those who supported him, of course, did not wish really to deceive anyone; the counterfeits are, therefore, entirely transparent.

110. One of the most serious charges against Cosby was his refusal to allow a new Assembly to be elected. In 1734 leaders in the Assembly, seeing the tendency

Curiously, after this long and explicit discussion of what turned out to be a crucial episode in colonial history, the *Mercury* failed to take any positive stand on the Cosby case and did not follow its development with any regularity. In the *Pennsylvania Gazette* of February 20 appeared a letter, presumably from Burlington, which protested against the behavior towards their common Governor of those in a neighboring province, and which particularly insinuated that a recent uprising of Negroes in the Eastern Division of New Jersey had been occasioned by papers published in New York. In the *Mercury* of March 5 an anonymous writer ironically pointed out the extraordinary interest the correspondent of the *Gazette* seemed to have in supporting Cosby's reputation; but on the other hand a few months later[111] Bradford quoted at length an account from the New York *Gazette* attacking the Zenger propaganda story previously printed in the *Mercury*. Six months thereafter another reversal took place: the *Mercury* presented with evident approval two laudatory verses from the New York *Weekly Journal* on the departure of Lewis Morris for England to seek justice for himself and for New York,[112] and the following issue announced that the Pennsylvania Assembly had resolved to ask Morris to appear at court in behalf of Pennsylvania also. No reference was made by the *Mercury*, just as none was made by the New York *Gazette*, to the Zenger trial in August 1735, but when Governor Cosby died on March 10, 1736, the *Mercury* carried an account of his death and burial[113] and continued intermittently the story of Van Dam's conflict with the new governor, George Clarke.[114]

During the *Mercury's* existence no news story from the South was so dramatic in its historical implications as either the salary quarrel in Massachusetts or the case of the people *versus* Cosby in New York, but

---

to abuse of power in freeing representatives from responsibility to the people, succeeded in passing a bill limiting the life of each Assembly to three years. The bill was blocked by the Council and Cosby refused to dissolve the Assembly, as he did again in November 1735 (*Documentary History*, IV, 244).

111. *Mercury* 755, 756.

112. *Mercury* 786, from *Weekly Journal* 60 and 61. Morris sailed for England on Saturday, November 23, 1734 (*Weekly Journal* of November 25). The New York *Gazette* of December 2 accused Morris of having stolen off to England under false pretences and of having behaved in undutiful manner to his superiors. Zenger had been committed to jail on charges of libel on Sunday, November 17 (*Weekly Journal* 40, November 25).

113. *Mercury* 846 and 847, from the New York *Gazette* of March 15.

114. *Mercury* 847, 875, 876. The reason for Bradford's change of position, if there was any, on the Cosby affair is obscure. I am inclined to think that there was no change at all, that Bradford simply printed periodically whatever news of Cosby seemed to him likely to interest his readers. Since William Bradford supported the government, it is conceivable, of course, that Andrew felt it his duty, or was urged, not to join the hue and cry; but the *Mercury* certainly did not, like the New York *Gazette*, feel called on to defend Cosby. Moreover, Andrew Bradford's apparent animosity towards Hamilton (see below) is quite sufficient to explain his failure to report the Zenger trial.

Bradford had at least one long and interesting tale to tell. From London under date of July 30, 1730, first came the rumor that "there is a noble Settlement going to be made upon Savanna River in South-Carolina; and . . . Gentlemen of great Honour and Worth are at the Head of that Affair."[115] Nineteen months later appeared the further news that "his Majesty was graciously pleased to give his Royal Sanction to a Charter for incorporating Trustees for the Relief of the Poor, by settling a new Colony in the uncultivated Parts of Carolina, which is to be called Georgia."[116] Then came news of the meeting of the trustees in London on July 20, 1732, of the decision about the seal of the province, and of the plan to bring in not only Englishmen but also a group of Swiss Protestants.[117] Immediately thereafter appeared the statement that the king had "purchased South-Carolina" from the proprietors, and a description of the town sites and of the regulations for landholding and quit-rents.[118] Beginning in the spring of 1733 Bradford published an extended series of items about the new colony. First came an account of the progress of the undertaking from the embarkation from England on November 17, 1732, to Oglethorpe's departure from the newly established town of Savannah on May 1, 1733.[119] Then came news that the Massachusetts House of Representatives had appointed a committee to prepare a reception for Oglethorpe if he visited Boston during the summer.[120] Two items about the number of immigrants to Georgia prepared for the news that, in January 1733/34, nine hundred people were already in the colony.[121] Meanwhile the first intelligence directly from "Savanah (in Georgia)" appeared in the *Mercury*,[122] and the news of a parliamentary grant of £20,000 was quickly followed by the report of the trustees showing a favorable balance for the province of £6620.[123] In the summer of 1734 Oglethorpe sailed for London;[124] but within two years he had returned to the colony and had set about the impossible task of conciliating the Spanish.[125] Between that date and the outbreak of the War of Jenkins' Ear several items appeared, mostly indicative of the buffer-state aspect of the new colony;[126] then in the spring of 1740 came reports of Oglethorpe's expedition against St. Augustine, his proclama-

115. *Mercury* 563.
116. *Mercury* 645.
117. *Mercury* 667, 670.
118. *Mercury* 669.
119. *Mercury* 699, 705.
120. *Mercury* 706.
121. *Mercury* 712, 713, 741.
122. *Mercury* 719.
123. *Mercury* 748, 754.
124. *Mercury* 762.
125. *Mercury* 860, 882.
126. *Mercury* 941, 965, 969, 1029, 1046.

tion encouraging runaways to enlist, and the conflicting rumors about his success in Florida, followed by the news of the failure of the siege and his return to Georgia.[127] In the autumn of 1742 the *Mercury* printed news of the retaliatory expedition of the Spaniards against the new colony and of their failure to take Frederica,[128] and then came intermittent reports of raids and attacks,[129] coupled with occasional wild rumors such as that 5700 Spanish and Indians had taken Georgia and killed most of its inhabitants.[130] Indeed, Bradford gave a more complete and orderly account of Georgia than of any other colony, perhaps because the story was simple to tell and not much entangled with politics, as well as because the building of the new province must have been continuously interesting to his readers.[131]

In addition to the events that made big news in the *Mercury* a miscellany of smaller items on colonial affairs also appeared in its columns. For example, during the period when Maryland was without a newspaper,[132] the pages of the *Mercury* (and of the *Gazette*) were opened to one phase of the perennial problem of the Maryland tobacco trade. Beginning on January 14, 1729, the *Maryland Gazette* had devoted much space over a period of many weeks to the question of the profitable marketing of Maryland's "only Staple."[133] Among the participants in the discussion were Henry Darnell and Dr. Samuel Chew. In 1738 the *Pennsylvania Gazette* was used to make public and endorse a proposal of Philip Thomas that Maryland tobacco planters should sell directly to France, in order to save the cost of shipment to England and re-shipment to the continent.[134] The *Mercury* was employed by opponents of this suggestion, who claimed that the aim of the article in the *Gazette* was "to intice Ships from Philadelphia, upon the Credit of the French Scheme, without the hazard of actual Chartering."[135] The argument, at times heated, continued well into the summer, Darnell and Chew speaking in defense of the proposal, which was also supported by a man named Huber and by William Byrd of Virginia.[136]

127. *Mercury* 1056, 1065, 1076, 1077, 1080.
128. *Mercury* 1190, 1198.
129. *Mercury* 1210, 1213.
130. *Mercury* 1277. Number 1278 promptly contained a denial of this report.
131. There are many news items about Georgia in addition to those which I have cited.
132. The first *Maryland Gazette* ran from 1727 to 1734, with a break of nearly two years in 1731 and 1732. The second *Maryland Gazette* was not established until 1745.
133. *Maryland Gazette* 73, February 4.
134. *Pennsylvania Gazette* 477, January 31.
135. *Mercury* 949.
136. See the *Gazette* of March 7, April 13, June 22, and August 17, and the *Mercury* of April 13 and May 25.

From Massachusetts came reports in 1733 of financial difficulties caused by the circulation of Rhode Island paper money and private bills-of-credit,[137] and in 1738 of a serious money shortage.[138] From New York arrived news that the Governor of Canada demanded the demolition of a fort "in the Sennaca's Country," and threatened to have it destroyed by his order if New York refused to act;[139] later it was reported that the French had built a fort at Crown Point.[140] In 1729 the *Mercury* printed a portion of an act to preserve the woods of America, especially the white pines, which had been greatly reduced in number because of their use as ship-masts.[141] In Williamsburg disorders among the Negroes caused the calling out of the militia late in 1730,[142] and from the West Indies came periodic reports of Negro uprisings.[143] Governor Belcher of Massachusetts in 1731 invoked an old act to forbid the French to enter the colony without a license,[144] whereas the House refused to pay for the rebuilding of a fort at Pemaquid on the ground that it was an unnecessary expense in time of peace.[145] A custom-house report from Jamaica listed 11,421 hogsheads of sugar exported and 4631 Negroes imported between March 1729 and June 1730;[146] but from Barbados in 1734 came news of a devastating blight upon sugar cane, though later the flourishing state of the coffee plantations there was announced.[147] Massachusetts passed a bill for "preambulating" its boundary with Connecticut, and in 1735 the boundary between the Carolinas was established.[148] In Virginia the Quakers appealed to the Governor and Assembly for exemption from parish levies.[149] In 1738 the *Mercury* announced New Jersey's winning its long fight for an independent governor and the appointment of Lewis Morris, quondam protagonist in the Cosby affair, as its first chief executive.[150] In 1741 New York City was terrified by an outbreak of incendiarism and by the rumor of a Negro conspiracy to take over the province in anticipation of an invasion by the French and Spanish.[151] Although in

137. *Mercury* 727.
138. *Mercury* 992, 1001. Such a report was of interest because shortage of money was a constant perplexity in the colonies. Number 856 printed news of the approval by the king of £40,000 in New Jersey bills-of-credit. Early in 1742 the *Mercury* reported that Governor Shirley of Massachusetts had given his consent to the money bills which had been passed by the Assembly (Number 1154).
139. *Mercury* 397.
140. *Mercury* 615.
141. *Mercury* 514.
142. *Mercury* 568.
143. *Mercury* 798, 883, 895, 1009, 1359.
144. *Mercury* 609.
145. *Mercury* 715.
146. *Mercury* 571.
147. *Mercury* 758, 822.
148. *Mercury* 725, 818.
149. *Mercury* 990.
150. *Mercury* 978.
151. *Mercury* 1110, 1115, 1118, 1120, 1122, 1124, 1125, 1129, 1131, 1181.

1735, the *Mercury* reported, the Massachusetts House had voted that in case of war between England and France its governor should work with other colonial governors to preserve the neutrality of the American continent,[152] when the conflict actually came Massachusetts was deeply involved.

In the closing years of the paper, nearly all the colonial items referred to the American phase of the European war; from north and south came news of the mustering of the militia, the last-minute attempts to secure the neutrality of the Indians, the fitting out of privateers, and the voting of appropriations.[153] The fullest and most lively story of the American aspect of the struggle was the account of the expedition to Nova Scotia.[154] The *Mercury* did not live to see the end of the War of the Austrian Succession; by six weeks it missed the opportunity to report Culloden Moor.[155] But its story of the colonies, at least, came to a fitting and dramatic conclusion — with the episode of the siege of Louisburg and its successful culmination.

152. *Mercury* 789.
153. *Mercury* 1025, 1026, 1069, 1139, 1166, 1270, 1277, 1281, 1321, 1325, 1329, and many others.
154. *Mercury* 1249, 1274, 1276, 1277, 1278, 1280, 1287, 1297, 1318, 1320, 1322, 1325, 1331, 1332, 1334, 1338, 1339, 1341, 1343, 1346, 1357, 1363, 1365.
155. The last issue of the *Mercury* announced the success of the rebels in dislodging the British from Inverness on March 4. The climactic battle took place on April 16. On July 5 at eight o'clock in the morning the *Pennsylvania Gazette* published a postscript to announce the defeat of Charles Edward on "Culloden Mure."

Chapter 4

Politics in Philadelphia
and the Bradford-Hamilton Controversy

Thus far in the discussion of Bradford's reporting of major political developments, foreign and domestic, we have omitted the *Mercury's* treatment of local affairs. European events were considered by colonial newspapers with practically complete freedom, though seldom without bias; political questions relating to other colonies were sometimes given rather large space and represented in such a way that anyone could see their applicability to the colonies as a whole. But purely local problems were slow to find a place in the colonial paper, partly for reasons already discussed and partly because the printer-editor deemed it his privilege to deny the use of his paper to opinions, political or other, which ran counter to his own or to those of the party which chiefly supported him. The most striking example of the result of this restriction was the founding of the New York *Weekly Journal* by the anti-Cosby faction in order that it might have an instrument for the dissemination of its opinions. Similarly, as Mr. Wroth has pointed out, since the press of Annapolis was closed to it in 1732, "the unpopular cause of the established clergy of Maryland represented by the Reverend Jacob Henderson was forced to seek expression in Philadelphia in the columns of the *American Weekly Mercury* and in pamphlets printed in that city."[1] On the other hand, it is noticeable that colonial journals tended to become,

---

1. Wroth, 189. The paper war between "Portius" and "Marcus" conducted in the pages of the *Mercury* and the *Gazette* was evidently part of this quarrel. The argument concerned the conflict between conventional Christianity and the deistical beliefs which were common in the period. Portius, who wrote in the *Mercury*, supported the view that the "unhappy Way to all Revolutions and all Conquests has been paved by Atheistical Opinions and Dissolution of Manners . . ." (Number 638). Marcus, whose letters in defense of scepticism appeared in the *Gazette*, resorted to burlesque of what he considered Portius' feeble reasoning (*Gazette* 174). Other pseudonymous letter-writers carried the dispute further. Its connection with the episode of the Maryland clergy is suggested not only by its general subject matter but also by two specific facts: a letter from "T.E." in "New-Town, in Maryland" attacked both Marcus and an enemy of the Reverend Mr. Henderson (who was mentioned by name); a little later "Marcus Verus" referred to "T.E." (*Mercury* 641, 645). For a complete picture of the quarrel as it appeared in the two papers see the following issues: *Mercury* 638-641, 643, 645, 646, 648-650, and possibly 635 and 647; *Gazette* 174, 177, 179, 182, 183. The controversy is important evidence that the *Mercury* and the *Gazette* were likely to divide over religious questions. Since Andrew Hamilton and Franklin apparently held similar deistical views, this difference between the two papers is particularly significant.

if not always more tolerant of a diversity of opinion, at least bolder in the expression of opinion. Of this fact the *Mercury* is a good illustration.

The earliest local news reported by Bradford was by any standard unexceptionable: shipping news,[2] prices current,[3] accounts of a hold-up or a robbery, of piracy and fires,[4] the Governor's speeches to the Assemblies of Pennsylvania and the Lower Counties and his proclamation concerning the Court of Equity,[5] the report of the death of William Penn, eldest son of the first proprietor,[6] the arrival of Palatines "come here to settle,"[7] the sentencing of local malefactors,[8] floods along the Schuylkill,[9] the death of a popular clergyman[10] — such items are innocent not only of offending the authorities but also of throwing much light on Pennsylvania's political history between 1720 and 1722. The episode of "the dying Credit of this Province" was, indeed, the earliest evidence that the *Mercury* might become active or influential in local affairs. For several years thereafter, however, although it reported such significant news as the constant influx of Palatines and Irish[11] or the audacity of a pirate ship in sailing up Delaware Bay and stopping river traffic,[12] the *Mercury* did not presume to open its pages to controversial material. Then with an exemplary show of objectivity Bradford reported the recommendation of the proprietors that Patrick Gordon should replace Keith as governor, Keith's angry and bitter address to the Assembly, the petition to the Assembly in support of Keith, and the arrival of Gordon.[13] In the years that immediately followed Gordon's appointment an increasing amount of news of public affairs entered the paper, but very little reference was made to the actual working of the government. The

2. Beginning in Number 1.
3. Beginning in Number 2.
4. *Mercury* 10, 13, 14, 15, 101. Of one of the robberies the printer himself was evidently the victim (Number 10).
5. *Mercury* 4, 35, 44, 45.
6. *Mercury* 37.
7. *Mercury* 37, 92.
8. *Mercury* 44.
9. *Mercury* 80.
10. *Mercury* 95.
11. *Mercury* 150, 156, 297. Number 295 mentioned the desire of the Palatines for naturalization.
12. *Mercury* 136, 137. The secret of the pirate's boldness, of course, although Bradford would hardly have dared to mention it, was the well-known pacifism of Penn's colony.
13. *Mercury* 334, 336-339. It is an injustice to Keith's character that he is generally remembered by the incident of his deceiving with false hopes young Benjamin Franklin. Actually Keith was a quite successful and popular governor, with leanings towards democracy; indeed, Logan's disapproval of what he considered Keith's lukewarm attitude towards the interests of the Penn family was partly the cause of his being superseded by Gordon. After his removal from the governorship he was twice elected to the Pennsylvania Assembly before his return to England in 1728.

arrival of new immigrants was frequently mentioned;[14] Gordon's speech in the fall of 1726, in which he cited iron, hemp, and silk as Pennsylvania's chief products, was printed;[15] the agreement of a large group of Philadelphia merchants to accept in trade bills-of-credit of the Lower Counties appeared;[16] the loan office published its periodical demands for the payment of principal and interest;[17] James Logan inserted an advertisement asking that quitrents due to William Penn or his heirs should be paid;[18] for the especial benefit of Bradford's customers across the Delaware a notice was given of a new issue of New Jersey bills-of-credit;[19] and the Indian scare of 1728 was treated in detail: the news of the attack near Colebrook Iron Works northwest of Philadelphia, of Gordon's proclamation of May 16, of his successful journey to Conestoga to treat with the Indians and his return home, accompanied from the borders of the city by two hundred citizens, and finally his appeal to the people to avoid hysteria and to uphold the proclamation.[20]

In this same year Bradford showed the first new stirring of real independence; on October 3 he hazarded the equivocal remark that at the election two days earlier "there appeared the greatest Industry on all sides for gaining of Representatives for the County of Philadelphia, that ever was here before on such Occasion." The following spring he reprinted an address of the Assembly which also touched on a tender spot: the legislature asked the Governor to enforce the English laws against rioters, who, it contended, were taking advantage of the Quaker customs of the province "to Menace, and Threaten" both private individuals and the representatives.[21] Immediately afterwards, when Gordon and the Assembly were discussing with hardly a veneer of politeness the recurrent question of bills-of-credit, the *Mercury* printed both the Governor's speech and the answer of the representatives, the latter containing the tight-lipped statement:[22] " . . . we conceive it is the undoubted Privilege

14. *Mercury* 357, 412, etc.
15. *Mercury* 361.
16. *Mercury* 357. See also 535, etc.
17. *Mercury* 359, 420, etc.
18. *Mercury* 478. Later James Steel became the collector of the quitrents. See, for example, Numbers 582, 634, 683, etc.
19. *Mercury* 450, 509.
20. *Mercury* 437-440. The proclamation, an interesting document, stated that the Pennsylvania colonists and the Indians had always got along amicably and that the disorders had been caused by "strange Indians." The Governor charged all colonists in Pennsylvania and Delaware "that on no Pretence they abuse any Indian-Native of the Nations around us . . . or any other coming and demeaning themselves peaceably amongst us; but that on all Occasions, they treat all the said Indians, with the same civil Regard that they would an English Subject. . . ." He ordered, however, that all should be suitably armed "in Case of real Necessity."
21. *Mercury* 482.
22. *Mercury* 484. In connection with these two and other news accounts of

of this House, to judge of any Amendments made by the Governour, and only agree to them as they seem Just and Agreeable, to the true Interest of the People whom we represent." These three items, mild as they may seem to us today, suggest how it happened that by the fall of 1729 Bradford, braving the authorities, dared to allow the publication of *Busy-Body* 31 and to follow it with the yet more outspoken Number 32.[23]

During the next year or two no major issue was recorded in the *Mercury*, but the background against which a new controversy was eventually to be carried on was completed with the arrival in August 1732 of Thomas Penn, second surviving son of William and one of the three proprietors. What precipitated the fierce conflict that soon broke out in the *Mercury*, whether the paper was made the tool of the Governor's (and the Proprietor's) party or whether Bradford had some personal stake in the battle, what its exact course was, even the date of its beginning—these and a good many other questions are hard to answer. Apparently the issue was joined with the *Mercury* of September 27, 1733, four days before the annual election of members of the Assembly. In the place regularly occupied by editorials and letters, at the top of the first page, appeared an epistle signed "Cato Jun." and patently imitated from the familiar *Cato's Letters*, the point of which is shown by its opening sentences:

> To the Freemen &c.
> My Dear Countrymen,
> As the Time draws nigh of choosing our Representatives in the Legislative Capacity; let us duely Consider, that the Trust to be reposed in them, is of the greatest Importance and requires Persons of known Integrity, Ability, Discretion and Resolution to discharge it faithfully; for they are the Guard[i]ans of our valuable Liberties, which, as we are freeborn, it is our Interest and Duty to preserve, not only for our selves but also for the Benefit of Posterity....

In the following number three days after the election Cato, Jr. again spoke out, though more briefly, this time under the heading "When the Wicked Perish there is Shouting," and to this effect:

> Thanks to the kind Genius that watches over the Fate of Pennsylvania, and my hearty Thanks to You, my Dear Countrymen, and Fellow Citizens, for the brave stand You have made against lawless and arbitrary Power: A Power whose ghastly

important issues debated by the legislature, it is well to remember that in England during the same period public discussion, even straightforward reporting by the press, of parliamentary activities was severely restricted.
23. See above, pp. 16-19.

and pestilent Effects, are seldom fully understood, till they have been terribly felt.

Beside this expression of rejoicing Bradford printed the list of persons elected to the Assembly, a list ordinarily relegated to the third or fourth page of the paper, but in this circumstance conspicuously placed next to the victory letter. The Philadelphian who picked up the *Mercury* that Thursday, as well as many a reader far from Philadelphia, would instantly have got the point, even if Cato, Jr.'s generalities the week before had concealed from him what was happening: Andrew Hamilton had not been re-elected!

Hamilton had begun a distinguished career as lawyer and public servant with his appointment by Governor Keith as Attorney General of Pennsylvania in 1717, a position which he retained until 1724, when he resigned in order to make a trip to England, giving up at the same time the membership in the Council which he had held since 1721. In June 1727, shortly after his return from abroad, he was appointed to the position of recorder of Philadelphia[24] and in October of the same year he was first elected to the Pennsylvania Assembly as a representative of Bucks County.[25] The following year he was re-elected for Bucks and at the same time chosen a member of the Assembly of the Lower Counties; and in October 1729 he was elected speaker of both legislatures. In August 1730, when the Pennsylvania loan office was reorganized, Hamilton became one of the four new trustees and its virtual head.[26] In all of these and in other public offices, some of which he held for many years, Hamilton showed himself a vigorous and able man. When or how trouble began is difficult to say. In the Assembly of 1727 Hamilton had been an opponent of Keith and therefore, presumably, a friend of Gordon. Moreover, Hamilton was a close associate of James Logan and would be supposed for that reason to be sympathetic to the proprietary interests. However the change of alignment came about, two specific occurrences of 1732-1733 threw Hamilton and the Governor into opposite camps. One was a matter so petty as a quarrel between Gordon's daughters and Margaret, Hamilton's only daughter.[27] More important, let us hope, was the fact that in 1733 the proprietors were considering

---

24. He held this position until his death and was succeeded by his son-in-law, William Allen (*Mercury* 1128).

25. In eighteenth-century Pennsylvania and Delaware an assemblyman did not have to be resident in the county which he represented; Hamilton was a Philadelphian.

26. *Pennsylvania Gazette* 92, August 20.

27. So far as I can discover no one knows what this feminine battle-royal was about; there seems to be general agreement, however, that it was serious enough to cause bad blood between Gordon and Hamilton.

whether or not to reappoint Gordon as governor.²⁸ Accordingly, when the Assembly met in the summer of 1733, it either doubted or affected to doubt Gordon's authority and, after angry statements on both sides, permanently adjourned. Apparently Gordon considered Hamilton responsible for the Assembly's actions²⁹ and retaliated by attempting to bring about his defeat in the October elections. Three letters in the *Mercury* between August 9 and September 20 probably relate to the quarrel, the first two attacking in general terms those who are traitors and the third (apparently on the opposite side of the argument, signed by "C. Philop" and written in "plain language") objecting, as it said, to the lampoon of a gentleman universally esteemed.³⁰ As we have seen, Gordon's adherents were successful in keeping Hamilton out of the Assembly; but the battle did not end there, for the *Pennsylvania Gazette* had also entered the fray with a long poem published on September 28 and entitled "Against Party-Malice and Levity, usual at and near the Time of Electing Assembly-Men" and on October 11 with a satirical attack, "principally intended" for "my Friend Cato, jun.," asserting that Cato's "sacred Name . . . hath been subscribed to a weekly Paper, the unhappy Birth of a sickly Brain, born in Pennsylvania, and delivered into the World, by that most Sage Matron and accomplish'd Midwife A. ———— B. ————."³¹

The *Mercury* of October 18 contained not only a reprisal for these remarks, some verses signed "J.D." addressed to "the Gazeteers late Correspondent,"³² but also a very transparent letter discussing a certain lawyer: the fear that he would extend his power, the accusation that at the last election he had tried to keep away from the polls those who would not

28. Gordon's appointment had been made by Hannah Penn (William's second wife and the mother of the three proprietors), who had in effect held the proprietary authority until her death in 1727. John, Thomas, and Richard set up an agreement concerning their property in Pennsylvania in 1732, shortly before Thomas came to America.
29. Possibly Hamilton's active leadership in the Assembly, nearly always more or less at odds with proprietary officials, had gradually marked a difference between him and Gordon.
30. *Mercury* 710, 715, 716.
31. A note in the *Gazette* of October 18 stated that the printer had been absent for seven weeks and that he was therefore not responsible if during that time any "Personal Reflection" had been printed in his journal. This appears to be hocus-pocus, especially since Franklin was known to be a friend of Hamilton and was nearly always opposed to the proprietary party.
32. The verses began:
> I know thee Janus, both what thou art, and who;
> No Mask so dark, but Janus must shine thro'
> Big swelling Periods do the Author tell;
> Thy best Concealment had been writing well. . . .

It included also a threat of further warfare:
> The Printer too a Midwife! Horrid Stuff!
> His Types, if thou go on, may mark thy Buff.

vote for him, and the statement that, if he had been chosen by Bucks, matters would be in a sorry state. These were followed within three weeks by an essay, almost certainly aimed against Hamilton and perhaps against Franklin, entitled "Of Infidelity," borrowed from the *Weekly Miscellany* and attacking those who deny religion, especially on the ground that they hold an opinion which "cannot possibly be of Use, but infinitely pernicious." The *Gazette* countered on November 16 with "Half-hour's Conversation with a Friend," which explained that the present writer had seen the person attacked and now reproduced his sentiments, partly in his own words and partly in a paraphrase; the "Friend" admitted having had much power for seven years, but implied that he had used it not only justly but even in the service of the person who was assailing him; he spoke also of the writer in the *Mercury* of October 18 as "having got the Government on [his] side." This in turn was answered in *Mercury* 728 by a letter ironically stating that part of the "Friend's" remarks had been omitted in the *Gazette* and accordingly suggesting their inclusion; there followed a poem, in which the "Friend" is supposed to be speaking, of which the key lines, intended to indicate his conceit, were:

> 'Tis I, 'tis I, 'tis I alone,
> Can Mountains move, and reach the Moon,
> And see as well as Twenty-one . . . .

A new phase of the quarrel began with the *Mercury* of December 31.[33] In that issue appeared a letter addressed to the freemen of the colony by "Philo-Pennsylvania" asking that a protest be directed to the Assembly concerning the bad management of the loan office and specifically raising the question of whether trustees of that organization should be members of the Assembly.[34] Two events lay behind this letter; one was the confirmation of Gordon in the governorship, which had come through after the October election; the other was the death of one of the representatives of Bucks County, which left a vacancy which Hamilton naturally aspired to fill. The following week, two days after Hamilton had won the by-election — a fact to which the *Mercury* pointedly did not refer — appeared this statement:

> Mr. Bradford,
> This comes to Congratulate with you, on the Liberty allowed to the Press: Tho' your well-wishers were lately in pain for you, apprehending that you were to have been indicted and roughly

---

33. In the same issue the Cosby case was introduced to the *Mercury's* readers. The number was evidently very successful, for two different printings were made— one dated Friday, December 21, and the other Saturday, December 22.

34. Hamilton, as head of the loan office, was obviously the target of this double-barrelled attack.

handled for printing a Letter in your *Mercury* the 18th of October last; yet since the Gazetteer has been encouraged in a pretended Answer thereto, to publish something that mayn't please every body but may divert some body, 'tis plain enough that for the future you will be candidly indulged to take the like liberty of diverting your Customers; and therefore you may freely and safely insert the inclosed from

No-Body.

There followed a long effusion[35] addressed "To ———— some bodies particular Friend" with the salutation "Self-interested Sir," in which among other charges was raised the question of Somebody's irreligion. In Number 730 also appeared a letter by "Hezekiah Telltruth" pleading with someone, evidently a lawyer, to reform — because, since he was advanced in years,[36] the time approached when his "little Subtilties and Quirks" would stand him "in no stead." In the issue of January 22 came another variation on a now-familiar theme; headed "Venienti Occurrite Morbo,"[37] it declaimed:

> ... Religion, from whence Justice, Honesty, Fidelity, and every good of Society flow, has hitherto been a standing Maxim, and notwithstanding the many fertile Inventions and rediculous Sneers to undermine it, still remains the Basis of all Governments.
>
> What then must be expected from a Spinosa, Sejanus, or Protesilaus[38] at the Helm? truely, unless we can suppose we may gather Grapes from Thorns or Figs from Thistles, or that the accessary declines the Nature of its Principal, we must look upon a State thus Circumstanced to bear strong Symptoms of approaching Convulsions, if not a total Revolution, were there no other Overt Acts to precaution and prompt the use of the foregoing Motto.

This was succeeded in the papers of the next two weeks[39] by another poem and another answer to the *Gazette* of November 16. Then appeared on February 19 a letter which began:

35. Numbers 730 and 732.

36. According to most accounts Hamilton was about eighty when he defended Zenger in 1735. *The International Encyclopaedia* and B. A. Konkle (*The Life of Andrew Hamilton, 1676-1741*), however, date his birth from approximately 1676. Almost nothing is known of his early life.

37. Meet the disease at its first onset (Persius, *Sat.,* III, 64).

38. For a hundred years after his death the popular conception of Spinoza allowed his being put in the company of such men as Sejanus and Protesilaus. The Protesilaus referred to was not the Greek hero of the *Iliad,* but the wily and hypocritical favorite of Idomeneus who figures prominently in Book XI of *Télémaque.*

39. Numbers 735 and 736.

> Mr. Bradford,
> I am heartily sorry for the ill usage you lately met with, but equally glad that it prov'd of no worse Consequence; All that I have conversed with upon the Subject of the Remarks which your Aggressor took Offence at, could not imagine who was pointed at by them, and do still think he was too young to apply them to himself....

The writer then quoted the closing paragraphs of *Spectator* 568, upon "the difficulty of writing any thing in this censorious age, which a weak head may not construe into private satire and personal reflexion," and concluded:

> And who knows but this may be the very Case with your Paper, when I'm at leisure I intend to write fully, in the mean time, if you have been assaulted, and still threatened, as 'tis Reported, pray take care of your self, be upon your Guard, and appear resolutely for your own just and necessary Defence, against all private, irregular and illegal Attempts.[40]

In the next issue of the *Mercury* Bradford requested the indulgence of a gentleman who had written him a letter dated the previous Saturday. He explained (what may or may not have been true) that it had arrived too late to be published; but, he said, "the ill Usage I have lately met with, shall not deter me from Communicating his Sentiments to the Public, which have received the Approbation of better Judges than my self to whom I have shewn it." Two weeks later[41] another letter to Bradford began: "I am sorry to hear of the late Attack that has been made thro' your Sides on our English Liberty, I mean the Liberty of Speech, or which is the same Thing, the Liberty of the Press," after which introduction the writer went on to quote "our English Cato" upon free speech.[42] In Number 743 another letter, or essay, appeared, this time speaking of "a Set of Miscreants who talk aloud of putting the Press

---

40. The absurdity of the implication that the *Mercury* had been attacking merely the vices of the age is apparent, but to whom "your Aggressor" specifically refers I have no idea. The comment about his being "too young to apply them to himself" may be an ironical reference to Hamilton, or to Franklin or anyone else imagined to be a tool of Bradford's enemies. It is also not clear which of the *Mercury's* many "Remarks" over a period of several months caused this outburst of violence; it may be, however, that a reference in Number 736 to Vatinius, the buffoon who became a powerful and dangerous favorite of Nero, touched off the attack. The quotation concerning Vatinius came from Gordon's discourses upon Tacitus (vol. I, disc. IX, sect. IV, 110).

41. *Mercury* 741.

42. *Cato* 15 (February 4, 1720), "Of Freedom of Speech." Much of the quotation is practically verbatim.

under Restraints, of curbing the Licence of the Pen, and teaching the Rascals (that is the People) good Manners." In the succeeding issue came, first, a discussion of previous failures, mostly Roman, to check liberty, and then a curious, obviously ironical title, "An Alphabetical Key, explaining all the dark Innuendo's, Hyeroglyphicks, Magic and Conjuration of that Caitiff Mr. Bradford his late Papers." The "Key" itself, which is no key at all since it introduces new allusions and insinuations, began thus, its first line also being ironical:

> A, stands for *Andrew,* the *Saint* so renown'd,
> And B, denotes *Blunder* the Statesman profound.
> *Craft, Cruelty, Curses* begin with a C.
> The Devil and D——g——es are spelt with a D.
> E, Stands for a Name, I shall not speak out:
> But, Fool, Fop and Flatt'rer explain it no doubt.
> G, stands for GORDON, whom God long preserve,
> And H, for a *Halter* or *Hangman* may serve. . . .

There followed a long discourse, running through three numbers of the paper,[43] on the importance to the Polish nation of liberty of speech and on Poland's appeal to the monarchs of Austria, Russia, and Prussia to help maintain that freedom — a discourse which, we imagine, could hardly have come to Bradford's hands if, as the *Mercury* asserted, it had "not yet appeared any where in Print, except in Poland" and which bears a markedly greater relevance to Bradford's current obsession than to the affairs of Stanislaus. In the same issue in which this suspicious document was introduced appeared an equally curious advertisement:[44]

> There is now in the Press, and will be shortly published.
> The Lives and Characters of Sejanus and Protesilaus, Redivivus, with many other noted Politicions. 1 Giving an ample Account of their Political, Mataphysical, Sophystical, and above all their darling Baculine Arguments against that grand Enemy and betrayer of their Craft, Machinations, Intreagues, Avarice, Pride and Ambition, The Press. 2. Shewing how this Potent revealer of Politic Mysteries has rescued the Public from Slavery, and brought these Heroes into the lowest Degree of

---

43. *Mercury* 745-747.
44. If it is true, as I believe, that no copies of this book are extant or even known to have existed, is it too far-fetched to conjecture that no such book ever did exist and that the advertisement, like some of those in the New York *Weekly Journal,* was a hoax, intended only to cast aspersions upon Hamilton and his partisans?

Contempt. 3. Shewing that the Liberty of People, and that of the Press are inseperable.

To which is added some critical Remarks, on the subtil Practice of these Heroes, in Fomenting Differences between the Prince and People, that they may be thought useful to the One, and dreadful to the Other. Tho' in reality, Enemies to both.

printed by Subscription.

In the next issue, Number 746, appeared without acknowledgment of its source Gay's fable of "The Dog and the Fox."[45] Addressed to "a Lawyer," it first attacks the profession to which Hamilton belonged for avarice, hypocrisy, and sharp practice. Then in the fable itself the following generalization is illustrated, by which Bradford again implied his innocence of assailing Hamilton:

> I no man call or ape or ass;
> 'Tis his own conscience holds the glass.
> Thus void of all offence I write:
> Who claims the fable, knows his right.

Number 747 contained one of the most elaborate defenses in the whole series and the climax of the first act of the tragi-comedy. At the beginning of what purported to be a letter was a cut in which a standing figure, Liberty, was shown handing a pen to a seated figure (perhaps the Press?), who is evidently writing upon a table labeled Property, while another figure (perhaps License?) appears to reach for the pen. The essay began with Addison's lines:[46]

> O Liberty, thou Goddess heav'nly bright,
> Profuse of bliss, and pregnant with delight!
> Eternal pleasures in thy presence reign,
> And smiling Plenty leads thy wanton train;
> Eas'd of her load, Subjection grows more light,
> And Poverty looks cheerful in thy sight;
> Thou mak'st the gloomy face of Nature gay,
> Giv'st beauty to the sun, and pleasure to the day.

Then the writer mentioned having promised to discuss freedom of the press and praised the defense of it in Number 744, which, he said, had been reprinted in a neighboring colony.[47] The essay which followed

---

45. Second series, fable 1.
46. "A Letter from Italy, to the Right Honourable Charles Lord Halifax," ll. 119-126.
47. The statement is correct: both the letter and the "Key" were reprinted in New York *Weekly Journal* 24 (April 15, 1734), where the letter was spoken of as "an exellent Piece."

first distinguished between liberty and license; license, it said, consists in subverting religion or morality and traducing the conduct of "our lawful Governors," as well as attacking people for personal or family misfortunes or for deformities. Then it discussed the major point:

> But, by the Freedom of the Press, I mean a Liberty, within the Bounds of Law, for any Man to communicate to the Public, his Sentiments on the Important Points of Religion and Government; of proposing any Laws, which he apprehends may be for the Good of his Countrey, and of applying for the Repeal of such, as he Judges pernicious. I mean a Liberty of detecting the wicked and destructive Measures of certain Politicians; of dragging Villany out of it's obscure lurking Holes, and exposing it in it's full Deformity to open Day; of attacking Wickedness in high Places, of disentangling the intricate Folds of a wicked and corrupt Administration, and pleading freely for a Redress of Grievances: I mean a Liberty of examining the great Articles of our Faith, by the Lights of Scripture and Reason, a Privilege derived to us in it's fullest Latitude, from our most excellent Charter.
>
> This is the Liberty of the Press, the great Palladium of all our other Liberties, which I hope the good People of this Province, will forever enjoy; and that every Pennsylvanian, will resent with Scorn and Indignation, the least attempt to weaken or subvert it. . . .
>
> As therefore you love your Liberties, (my dear Countreymen) support and defend the Liberty of the Press.

Whether the anti-Hamilton faction had at last talked itself out, whether stringent measures were taken to silence Bradford, or whether the threat of a general European conflict proved a more marketable topic than further controversy, after this issue[48] the *Mercury* ceased its seven-months war against Hamilton, though there was only a truce and no treaty of peace.

During the next year and a half the *Mercury* concentrated its local attention chiefly upon the simple reporting of occurrences in the province, of which the most important was the arrival in September 1734 and the departure almost precisely a year later of John Penn, eldest and best liked of the proprietors.[49] Meanwhile Hamilton had been re-elected speaker of the Assembly in 1734 and had distinguished himself by his brilliant defense of Zenger in August 1735. It should not surprise us that Bradford failed to report the Zenger trial; Hamilton's triumph must

48. Of April 25.
49. *Mercury* 769, 821.

have been bitter, not only to Cosby and his adherents, but also to the lawyer's own enemies.[50] We cannot be certain, however, that hostilities were renewed at once. Possibly the untitled, unsigned essay in the *Mercury* of August 21 dealing with the success of bold pretensions was supposed to reflect on Hamilton's daring conduct of the trial.[51] A book advertisement in Number 817 seems to have referred to the trial. Possibly the essays in Numbers 819 and 820, both of which discussed patriotism, and the second of which contrasted a good man branded as wicked, and therefore condemned, with an evil man "extolled, caress'd, beloved by all," were disparagements of Hamilton's character and of the validity of popular acclaim. Possibly the "grandy Politician" who tried to keep Isaac Norris from being re-elected to the Pennsylvania Assembly, according to the *Mercury* of September 25, was Hamilton. Very probably the long letter to Bradford in the issue of October 16, which discussed once again the favorite subject of irreligion, especially the danger of youth's being led astray by "such Doctrines as flatter their Passions," and which quoted at length *Spectator* 441, referred to Hamilton. But without question the dispute had recommenced by December. In Number 831 Bradford printed, as part of an abstract of the votes and proceedings of the Assembly of New York in connection with the Cosby episode, the following item: "Resolved, That a Court of Chancery within this Colony, in the hands, or under the exercise of a Governour, without consent in General Assembly, is contrary to Law, unwarrantable, and of dangerous consequence to the Liberties and Properties of the People." Two weeks later appeared a letter to Bradford which began:

> I am so charitable as to believe when you inserted in your *Mercury* of the 4th Instant, the Resolve of the Lower House of Assembly of the Province of New-York, against their Governour's being entrusted with the Power of holding a Court of

---

50. Bradford's apparent animosity towards Hamilton may not have been the only reason for his omitting a report of the trial. The *Pennsylvania Gazette* also failed to mention it.

51. Hamilton's bold but successful strategy was to admit at the beginning of the trial that his client had printed the "libels" for which he was being tried. He then advanced the argument that what is true cannot be a libel; but the court upheld the opinion that the greater the truth, the greater the libel. When he was prevented from attempting to prove the truth of the alleged libel, Hamilton addressed the jury thus: "And as we are denied the Liberty of giving Evidence, to prove the Truth of what we have published, I will beg Leave to lay it down as a standing Rule in such Cases, *That the suppressing of Evidence ought always to be taken for the strongest Evidence;* and I hope it will have that Weight with you." The court tried to limit the jury to deciding whether or not Zenger had published the papers in question, leaving the court to decide whether they were libellous. Hamilton asserted that such a decision "in Effect renders Juries useless." In spite of the prosecuting attorney's last-minute efforts and the judge's charge, the jury returned a verdict of not guilty. See *A brief Narrative of the Case and Tryal of John Peter Zenger.*

Chancery within that Colony without Consent in General Assembly, you had no Design against the Peace of this Province. . . .

The writer went on to accuse "some Men" of "restless and unreasonable" tempers — one man in particular being aimed at — of arousing among the people of Pennsylvania fear of the governor's power. The essay that followed this introduction pointed out that, whereas in New York the governor was sole chancellor, in Pennsylvania the governor and Council[52] made up chancery and had the assent of the Assembly; it further defended the court of chancery in general as a "necessary and honourable" institution.

In 1720 Governor Keith had proclaimed the establishment of a permanent court of equity for the province of Pennsylvania;[53] his action had the approval of both Council and Assembly, and rules were set up by which the proceedings of the court might be regulated. Neither the existence nor the actions of this court appear to have been questioned until late in 1735; then, assisted or possibly even started by Hamilton, agitation against the court broke out in the Assembly. No doubt this agitation was encouraged by dislike of Gordon and the Council because of their adherence to the rights of the proprietors. In addition, the court of exchequer created by Cosby for the prosecution of Van Dam had received much and long publicity, and the popular tendency to revolt against "prerogative" had been fanned by the recent trial of Zenger. Moreover, it is conceivable that Hamilton's personal animosity towards Gordon was a factor in raising the issue.

The *Gazette* of December 24, in answering *Mercury* 833, not only spoke very disparagingly of "good Mr. Bradford," but — more important — in a long and well-written essay set forth the argument against the court: that in one significant way the government of Pennsylvania had departed from the founder's intention, since, although the original charter had established the principle that all justices, judges, sheriffs, and similar public officers should be elected, the court of chancery was constituted as such by the members themselves (the governor and some of the Council) and supported only by a resolution of the General Assembly. The writer, who signed himself "R. Freeman,"[54] went on to give examples — Cosby is suggested but not mentioned by name — of governors who had abused such power as the *Mercury* essay presumably allowed; he asked why Bradford was so indignant against those who

---

52. Actually, at least two of the six senior members of the Council, not the entire Council.
53. *Mercury* 35.
54. "R. Freeman" was also the signature of a person who wrote in the *Daily Gazetteer* and the London *Journal*.

stated that the court was illegal when it was clearly contrary to the Charter of 1701; and he insisted that such a court should be established by act of Assembly.[55] The *Mercury* countered on January 6 with a letter of "A Truman," which imitated the *Gazette* with slurring references to "pious Mr. F———" and "religious Mr. F———," and objected to his "running violently on the side of the Populace."[56] More seriously, it defended the court against the charge that it was "against Law and the Charter." The essay was not completed in this issue and was promised for a later one; in Number 838, however, Bradford announced that, since Mr. Truman had got the rest printed in another manner, he would not insert it in the *Mercury*. The point of this statement is made clear by an advertisement in the New York *Gazette* of February 3 to the effect that there had just been published "Mr. Truman's Observations on Mr. Freemans Performance against the Court of Chancery in Pennsilvania,"[57] and two weeks later William Bradford also announced: "We have received a letter from a Gentleman in Philadelphia (which he desires may be Published in our Gazette) to shew the Violent & Arbitrary Measures of a certain great Lawyer AH there, against the Liberty of the Press. But having not room in this, we delay it till our next."[58] Meanwhile the *Pennsylvania Gazette* presented a carefully reasoned essay on the history and jurisdiction of the British court of chancery and of the qualifications of the Lord Chancellor.[59]

On February 24 appeared in the *Mercury* a new and sensational attack upon Hamilton. In that number Bradford printed what purported to be a section, with a convincing-looking marginal gloss in French, of Le Vassor's history of Louis XIII,[60] in which a bitter political conflict between the Duke d'Épernon and the Marquis d'Ancre was the central event. A vulgar episode between d'Épernon's housekeeper and d'Ancre's

---

55. Later the crown lawyers upheld the legality of the court in Pennsylvania on the ground that it had been supported at its establishment by resolution of the Assembly and subsequently approved. Popular aversion, however, prevented its re-establishment (Shepherd, 394-395).

56. Shepherd (p. 85) remarks that Franklin "was not on good terms with the proprietary officers, while his dislike of the Penns and their cordial dislike of him are only too well known." He adduces a good many examples of Franklin's errors or deliberate misrepresentations concerning proprietary business.

57. See also the advertisement in the *Mercury* of March 2: "The Jurisdiction of the Court of Chancery in Pennsilvania, vindicated and asserted; with some Remarks upon Mr. Freeman's late Performance, in Franklin's Gazette."

58. There is nothing in the pages of the paper thereafter that answers the description of this letter. The New York *Weekly Journal* of March 1 referred to the *Gazette* of February 17 and expressed surprise, perhaps ironically, that the letter had not yet appeared.

59. *Gazette* 372-373.

60. The reference was to Michel Le Vassor (1646-1718), *Histoire du Règne de Louis XIII Roi de France et de Navarre. Contenant les Choses les Plus Remarquables Arrivées en France durant la Minorité de ce Prince.*

servant wench was introduced, in which d'Ancre was represented as using his servant in order to foment a quarrel and bring d'Épernon into discredit. There were other elements too: references to Galigai, "an old Gentlewoman," d'Ancre's supporter and confidante, and to a conference between Marie, regent of France, and "Madrid" at Alcantara. In the following issue of the *Mercury* — partly, no doubt, to deny the accusations of those who had succeeded in reading between the lines of the previous number and partly, we suspect, to encourage the slower-witted to do so — appeared a letter, headed by a quotation, to this effect:

> ———— Forbear you Things
> That stand upon the Pinacle of State
> To boast your slippery Height. When you do fall
> You dash yourselves in Pieces, ne'er to rise;
> And he that lends you Pity is not wise.
>
>   Ben Johnson.[61]

Sir.

It seems nothing can be Publish'd to the World so innocent in its Design and Tendency, that a Set of vile Libellers and Retailers of low Scandal, will not interpret into personal Invectives.

Thus it hath fared, I am told, with an Extract of matters of Fact, that happened in the seventeenth Century; which, by a visionary Tribe of Political Inquisitors, hath been most whimsically applied to the present Times. It would be doing them too much Honour, to take any further Notice of them: Giving them up therefore to the Contempt or Chastisement of those Gentlemen, whose Names and Characters by such an Application, themselves have most shamefully prostituted, and villainously stigmatized, I shall lay before you, for the Entertainment of your Readers, an Extract from a Pamphlet, Entituled, The Life of Ælius Sejanus.

After this pointed introduction came the promised essay on Sejanus, the gist of which was that, although Sejanus was a "wicked, bloody, rapacious, insolent, and most abominable Minister," he has been painted "in amiable Colours; which shews that the worst Men in Power will never want Flatterers."

A letter of James Logan to John Penn written months later, after the death of Gordon had made Logan acting governor of the colony, contains the clue to this extraordinary hoax.[62] The letter first referred to Logan's

---

61. Quoted with slight inaccuracies from the final speech of Arruntius in Jonson's *Sejanus*.
62. See *Penn Manuscripts: Official Correspondence*, III, 15, and *Logan Papers*,

regret at having to assume so heavy a responsibility as the governorship and to the difficulties occasioned by Robert Charles,[63] generally disliked because of "his haughty & imperious Carriage." He then went on:

> ... what gave a fresh occasion this year was Bradford's Print of ye 24th of febry last, wch I question whether thou hast ever seen. It was pretended to be taken out of Vassor's french history of Lewis ye 13th, but saving that 3 or 4 names are borrowed, 'tis wholly fictitious and designed to abuse A Ham: & me under the names of the Marq. d'Ancre & Galigai, (who was truly that Marquis's Wife) the Queen is thy brother, & the Duke d Epernon Govr Gordon. Barbin Dr Chew Alcantara Newcastle &c. I could not possibly procure one of the Prints to inclose, most I inquired of telling me theirs was stole or unaccountably lost, and being unwilling to part with my own, I therefore only send a transcript of the principal part of it. in wch thou wilt see somethings so nearly affecting thy brother, that we really thought it concerned his honr both in regard to himself and in justice to those who had most faithfully served you in that Affair with Maryl as well as others in public company at least to express his resentmt and detestation of it, but he himself, and as he said his friends, were of a different opinion and therefore he never took the least notice of it that I could learn. ...

Finally Logan stated that, though Charles was suspected of being the author, he had denied writing the article both to the Proprietor and to him; Logan himself thought Isaac Norris the author and Charles his accomplice. Taken as a whole, then, the hoax seems to have been intended to suggest that Logan and Hamilton had conspired to force Thomas Penn to break with Gordon, that Hamilton had deliberately encouraged his daughter to quarrel with Gordon's daughters for political motives, and that, in connection with the perennial boundary dispute between Maryland ("Madrid") and Pennsylvania, in some way or other Hamilton and Logan were betraying the proprietors and that Thomas Penn, though he had discovered Hamilton's duplicity, was afraid to cast him off.

This paper immediately precipitated another war with the *Gazette*,

IV, 413-416. The date of the letter is September 26. Logan became acting governor automatically because he was senior member and president of the Council.

63. Charles, who had come to Pennsylvania as Gordon's private secretary, had later become his son-in-law and secretary to the Council. According to C. P. Keith (*Chronicles of Pennsylvania*, II, 745, 756) Thomas Penn made Charles one of his close friends. The marriage of Charles and Miss Philadelphia Gordon, eldest daughter of the Governor, was announced in the *Gazette* of April 22, 1731.

which raged almost weekly and in which a person who signed himself "Z." (or sometimes "Z.Z.") was the *Mercury's* faithful opponent. Bradford printed essays on ambition and power, on sincerity, and on the difference between resentment and revenge,[64] while the *Gazette* cleverly suggested the errors into which a translation into English of a French book might fall, pointed out the desirability of considering the result, rather than the motives, of an action that tended to the public good, and in a vigorously argued essay of April 1 upon the virtues of a popular government made this broad statement:[65] ". . . a Body of People . . . cannot be supposed to judge amiss in any essential Points; for if they decide in Favour of themselves, which is extremely natural, their Decision is just; inasmuch as whatever contributes to their Benefit, advances the real publick Good." The *Mercury*[66] instantly pounced upon the *Gazette* for its "loose Republican scheme," which it considered "seditious" and destructive of the balance between the prerogative of the governor and the liberty of the people. On the same day the *Gazette* attacked the theory of absolutism and contrasted the government of Elizabeth with that of the Stuarts, unfavorably to the latter. *Mercury* 851 attempted rather feebly an answer to the essays of April 1 and 8, and harped once again on the supposedly intimate connection between "Apostacy from God" and "Disobedience to his Viceregents." At the same time "Z." continued in the *Gazette* to develop the diametrically different idea suggested earlier, the essence of which he thus expressed: "Now I define virtuous Actions to be those, which have a Tendency to promote the Happiness of Mankind; and by Consequence we have a Standard to distinguish good from bad. . . ."[67]

Curiously, the *Mercury's* next step in the quarrel was an essay in French, contemptuously dismissing both "Z." and his arguments as puerile, tutoyering him, and posing several rhetorical questions to this effect:

> . . . ne trouves tu point de différence entre la Tyrannie d'un grand Roy, qui vante son sang illustre et eclatant, et son droit hereditaire, et la Tyrannie d'un Esclave affranchi, d'un Fourbe, Vilain, et Fiefé, qui n'a point de droit, et qui n'en pretende rien? Eh! qu'aimerois tu mieux la domination superbe et hautaine d'un Louis le Grand, ou le Faste et la Tyrannie vilaine d'un Tigellene?[68]

64. *Mercury* 845, 846, 847. Two of these essays appeared also in the New York *Gazette*, of March 22 and 28.
65. *Pennsylvania Gazette* 378, 380, 382.
66. *Mercury* 849, of April 8.
67. *Gazette* 385.
68. Tigellinus was a favorite of Nero.

Ne se peut il faire (mon petit Enfant) q'une Constitution soit trés bonne, et le Gouvernement trés mauvais? ....

The *Gazette* of April 29 and May 6, meanwhile, attacked *Mercury* 851, partly by quibbling over a grammatical error in Bradford's paper: the application of the term *epithet* to the word *mob,* which, "Z." insisted, is a noun, whereas an epithet is always an adjective. More seriously, "Z." attacked the "Proconsuls" who "strut and king it away in the Provinces, and who usurp the Title appropriated to their royal Master, by calling themselves God's Viceregents, to which they have just as much Right as the Parish Constables, who as well as the others execute their Office in the King's Name."[69]

The next issue of the *Mercury* took up a well-rubbed theme: there is a natural transition from despising revealed religion to opposing government and there is no real difference between a deist and an atheist; on one point, however, the *Mercury* essayist agreed with "Z.": "That no Nation ever lost its Liberty, but by trusting too much Power in the hands of one Man."[70] But in the news section of the previous number Bradford had made a tactical error; in describing the disastrous loss of a West Indiaman he had used the worn and innocent phrase "not a Soul saved." *Gazette* 388, which appeared simultaneously with *Mercury* 854, leaped upon its victim. With dignified gravity it began by saying that, since men are governed by opinions, it is important that their beliefs be sound and reasonable and that the most detestable of opinions is that which pronounces uncharitably upon the salvation of souls. It went on to speak of prejudices against various kinds of people — Irishmen, Yorkshiremen, and so forth — prejudices such as

> that the Westindians are a People abominably vile, wicked and profane, for whom nothing can be expected but general Damnation. Of this latter Opinion the Author of the *Weekly Mercury* seems to be; when he tells us in his last Paper, that in a late Storm a West-India Ship with thirty-two Passengers on board, sank outright, *and not a Soul was saved.* Such strong Assertions should be supported by strong Evidence. He could not be inform'd of the Truth of so extraordinary an Article of News, by any other Means than by some Dispatches from the other World; which, if he has received he would do well to produce publickly, or otherwise it may be judg'd a Fiction of his own. If he does not clear up this Point, he will be thought extreamly ungrateful as well as uncharitable: For who that loves Good Punch, and esteems Sugar, Spirit, and fresh Fruit,

69. *Gazette* 387.
70. *Mercury* 854.

among the most valuable Enjoyments of Life, would, if he had the least Sense of Gratitude, invent a thing so injurious to the Reputation of those People from whose Industry he receives them.

Having delivered himself of this solemn mockery of Bradford's conventional views on religion, he went on to comment upon the letter in French and to answer it with another addressed "A Monsieur Chose," in which he attacked him for writing in a language he did not understand ("Votre dernier Essai est Mauvais Anglois traduit en plus mauvais Francois"), for using "tu," and for announcing himself by his talk of "Droit hereditaire" as a friend of the Pretender!

For several weeks after this quibbling retort the battle continued, partly in French and partly in English, though "Q.E.D." in the *Mercury* of May 27 ridiculed both "Z." and his opponent for their use of French and suggested that they stop writing since they had gained their point and proved themselves "Fools in Print." In the issue of June 10 the *Mercury* returned to direct attack upon Hamilton, by printing an account of the rise to power and subsequent assassination of the Marshal d'Ancre,[71] already identified with Bradford's chief enemy by the Le Vassor hoax. On July 15, "Z." presented his autobiography, claimed as his own all the papers previously marked with a "Z.," and exhorted the people "to act with Caution in the approaching Election." The following week the *Mercury*[72] asserted that "Z." was "at last discovered, and known to be a contemptible understrapper to the grand worker of In———y," and after some other uncomplimentary remarks wrote "Finis." So ended the second act of the Bradford-Hamilton controversy, two weeks before the death of Governor Gordon removed one of the major figures of the drama.

For about a year the *Mercury* apparently managed to avoid dispute. It paid fulsome tribute to Gordon;[73] it discussed an outbreak of horse stealing in the province;[74] it published the results of an agreement between the proprietors and the chiefs of the Six Nations confirming William Penn's purchase of lands along the Susquehanna northwards to "the blue Mountains" and westward to the place where "the Sun sets";[75] and it issued the proclamation of Acting Governor Logan enjoining Pennsylvanians not to furnish any supplies to the Spaniards that

---

71. This account must have been taken either from the *Gentleman's Magazine* (December 1735) or directly from *Fog's Weekly Journal* of December 27. The abstract in the *London Magazine* differs from Bradford's version.
72. *Mercury* 864.
73. *Mercury* 867, 868, 870.
74. *Mercury* 870.
75. *Mercury* 876.

might aid them in an attack on Georgia and South Carolina.[76] Then a letter in the *Gazette* of July 28, 1737, introduced a new phase of the quarrel. It began:

> Mr. Franklin,
> 'Tis now more than a Twelve-month, since I sent you some Speculations on Government, which you were pleased to give a Place to in your Gazette. As they were hasty Performances, without either Stile or Method to recommend them, and never design'd to raise any Reputation on, I could not think it proper to own them: Tho' the Subject-matter, I am still confident, can be fairly and legally defended in every Particular. . . .

The writer then went on to explain that he had acknowledged these "Speculations" only because another man had been caused embarrassment by having them attributed to him; his acknowledgment, however, had led to further difficulty, since the other man had then been accused of having paid the writer to acknowledge them. Therefore, the present writer — John Webbe — now publicly asserted his authorship of the articles signed "Z."

Webbe's attempt to protect the unnamed person (surely no other than Hamilton) laid him open to attack; it came in the very next *Mercury*[77] in the form of a poem:

> What silly Wretch would prostitute his Name,
> And bribe his Sense, to purchase worthless Fame!
> But thou, poor Slave, art venally beset,
> To own the Bastards thou did'st ne'er beget.
> The Traitor's known, and thou dost vainly aim
> To screen his Shame, or patronize his Claim.
> Retract, Friend W———, let Hirelings sound their Name,
> And for their imp'ous Scribblings bear the Blame.
>   B.L.

The *Gazette*[78] promptly countered in the only possible way, by mocking "B.L.'s" verses and asserting that the initials stood for "Blockhead."

---

76. *Mercury* 897. A striking omission in the *Mercury's* discussion of local affairs was its failure to report adequately the serious border warfare between Maryland and Pennsylvania which broke out on September 5, 1736, and continued intermittently for about a year. (See *Pennsylvania Gazette* of September 23, 1736; New York *Gazette* of January 4, February 17, 22, 1737, and January 31, 1738.) *Mercury* 892 (February 3, 1737) contained the letters between Charles Higinbotham and John Ross which the New York *Gazette* used on February 17 and 22. Except for the seven columns devoted to the conflict in this one issue, the *Mercury* did not appear interested in the episode. The neglect of such an important local problem was, however, characteristic of colonial journals.

77. *Mercury* 918.
78. *Gazette* 452.

A few weeks later when the annual election approached, the *Mercury* campaigned briefly against Hamilton: in Number 925 what was said to be a letter to Bradford contained veiled allusions against a certain candidate, including the rather transparent remark that in England officers concerned in managing the revenue and all foreigners, even though naturalized, were forbidden to take part in elections. In spite of the *Mercury's* efforts Hamilton was again re-elected, and apparently Bradford, perhaps because of his recent loss of the postmastership,[79] was willing to let well enough alone — at least publicly.

In the *Pennsylvania Gazette* from November 17 to December 8, however, appeared a long essay[80] on freedom of speech and of the press. The writer, having mentioned the Zenger trial and the fact that an account of it was in print,[81] set out to confute "a Gentleman of Barbadoes" who in a series of *Remarks* on Zenger's trial had attacked Hamilton's assertion that what is true cannot be a libel.[82] This able reiteration of the principles supported by Hamilton at the time of the trial elicited little or no response from the *Mercury*,[83] but a letter published in the *Gazette* in April[84] had greater effect. In that letter a New York man, presumably, spoke of the value of praise from disinterested people and quoted from an essay published in the *Craftsman* of January 21 a tribute to Hamilton's conduct of Zenger's defense.[85] The *Mercury* of the following week[86] contained a reply which began by stating that the writer could

---

79. So far as I know there is no reason to connect Bradford's loss of the postmastership with the quarrel over Hamilton. However, since the postmastership gave Franklin the opportunity to interfere with the distribution of Bradford's papers, the exchange of the position might have made Bradford more circumspect than usual in dealing with Franklin's friend Hamilton.

80. In the *Barbadoes Gazette* of the following January 21, in which it was reprinted, this essay was attributed to Hamilton himself. See *Caribbeana*, preface, vii.

81. The only first-hand account of the trial was prepared by Zenger himself and his supporters in New York. It was advertised as published in the New York *Weekly Journal* of June 21, 1736. It was published in Boston in 1738 and went through four editions in London in 1737-1738.

82. See *Caribbeana*, II, 198-221, 225-241. The *Remarks on Zenger's Tryal* by "Anglo-Americanus" were printed in Keimer's *Barbadoes Gazette* between June 25 and July 23, 1737, and specifically referred to the 1736 edition of the *Remarks*. A supplementary essay signed by "Indus Britannicus" appeared on August 10. The *Remarks* are attributed to Jonathan Blenman, King's Attorney in Barbados.

83. Possibly an article reprinted in *Mercury* 943, assailing the political custom of shielding the dishonesty of party men, might be construed as a reference to Hamilton. Bradford correctly acknowledged his source as *Common Sense* 24; the essay may be found in the *London Magazine* of July 1737.

84. *Gazette* 486.

85. Franklin may have included the essay partly as an advertisement, for at the end of the same issue came the announcement that he was selling copies of the *Remarks*.

86. *Mercury* 954.

not help smiling at "the notable Panegyrick" in the *Gazette*. He attacked as a hypocrite the person praised by the rival paper and implied that the people of Pennsylvania knew him too well to be beguiled by such a eulogy. Then in a passage the implications of which go back perhaps to 1734 he made a direct accusation:

> A Person that has cruelly harassed and imprisoned a Printer, and again caused him to be assaulted and knock'd down in the open Street, meerly for copying an English Print, or inserting in his News-Paper, some general Invectives against a particular Vice, which by a foreign Innuendo, or consciousness of Guilt, the Person applied to himself, can no more merit the Character of a sincere Advocate for the Liberty of the Press, than a venal Hireling for a fulsome Harangue does the Name of a Cato. . . .[87]

He added a further comment: "as well pretend to persuade us, that . . . Ben Lay is the tallest and straitest Man in America." In the same number appeared an account of the initiation ceremonies of the Masons,[88] attributed — like the *Gazette's* praise of Hamilton — to the *Craftsman* of January 21. The *Mercury,* however, had overreached itself, as the next issue of the *Gazette* showed.[89] In it was printed a letter in "plain language" addressed "To the Man that mentioned me in his idle Paper," beginning: "Thee has taken the Freedom to publish to the World, that I am neither tall nor strait in Body. . . ." Benjamin Lay had entered the battle.

Lay was perhaps as well known in the province as Hamilton himself;[90]

---

87. The reference to Hamilton's having "imprisoned" the printer is puzzling. The phraseology suggests that the imprisonment occurred at some time previous to the assault; that reference appears to concern the episode of 1734. Bradford seems also to suggest, if I read the parallels correctly, that the imprisonment was the result of his merely copying "an English print" as the assault was the result of his inserting "some general Invectives against a particular Vice." The second of these points Bradford had previously maintained. So far as we know, the only time that Bradford was imprisoned was in connection with the *Busy-Body* case in 1729, when he did — largely, if not "meerly" — copy *Cato's Letters*. If we knew that Bradford believed himself jailed in 1729 primarily at the instigation of Hamilton, we would have a plausible explanation, on personal as well as political grounds, of his long and bitter animosity. We know too that Hamilton was one of those who examined and presumably one of those who committed Bradford, since he was at that date the recorder and was specifically mentioned in the minutes of the Council. Why, however, even if we admit the general hypothesis, did Bradford hold Hamilton particularly responsible for his punishment? And, if he did so, why did he wait nine years to refer to what he considered his ill-treatment? The conjecture that the *Busy-Body* affair was the beginning of a decade of conflict between the *Mercury* and Hamilton is tempting, but dubious.

88. Interest in the Masons probably ran high because of the recent trial of Evan Jones. See below, pp. 138-139.

89. *Gazette* 488.

90. J. T. Scharf and T. Westcott, *History of Philadelphia,* II, 1249 n.

he was humpbacked, only four feet seven inches in height, with a large head and spindly legs. He wore odd clothes and a long white beard.[91] But his deformity of body and peculiarity of appearance were offset by a vigorous mind, as well as by a natural love of conflict which had been sharpened by preaching and pamphleteering. In his letter he asserted that every printer in the country was indebted to the defender of Zenger and that the evidence of his sincerity was so clear that it was impudent to call him a hypocrite. He accused the writer in the *Mercury* of having pilfered some lines of Greek in order to appear learned, and — which is more important — of having made a false *Craftsman* and dated it January 21 in order to cast doubt upon the validity of the quotations in praise of Hamilton in the previous *Gazette*. Moreover, he asserted that Bradford was responsible for spreading "silly Books, said to come from Barbadoes," against freedom of the press and Hamilton. Typically, he ended his letter in unequivocal fashion: "by thy spitting Venom round thee, by thy being swollen black with Envy, and by the low groveling dirty Malice that appears in all thy Papers, I do strongly suspect thee has eaten Toads lately." Lay was probably correct in all three of his specific accusations. As anyone could see, *Mercury* 954 had quoted Greek. In the second place, a publication without imprint of *Remarks on Zenger's Tryal, Taken out of the Barbadoes Gazette's. For the Benefit of the Students in Law and others in North America* contained a fac made of four coats of arms, which coat of arms Bradford began to use as a decoration in the *Mercury* of December 28, 1736.[92] As for the charge about the *Craftsman*, the issue of January 21, Number 602, did contain an account of the Zenger trial and a long quotation from Hamilton.[93]

The *Mercury*, possibly because Lay had raised questions which it could not answer, did not reply to the *Gazette;* but in three numbers between April 20 and May 25, Cato, Jr. — who had shouted prematurely when the wicked had *not* perished in 1733[94] — re-entered the lists against

---

91. See the drawing of him in Scharf and Westcott, II, 1120, and Fred Landon's article in *D.A.B.*
92. Since the *Remarks* was not printed in Barbados till the summer of 1737, it was probably printed in Philadelphia in the autumn. The New York *Gazette* of October 24 advertised a book entitled *Remarks upon Mr. Hamilton's Arguments in the Tryal of J. P. Zenger*. See also the *Pennsylvania Gazette* of May 18, Number 492, quoted below.
93. I have not been able to see this issue of the *Craftsman* itself. Both the *London Magazine* and the *Gentleman's Magazine* of January 1738, however, cite it and quote from it. It is improbable that another essay, such as the one on the Masons, appeared in the same issue. The fact that the New York *Gazette* (Number 650, April 24) printed the same article on the Masons and gave the same source proves little, since intercolonial borrowing was common and eleven days elapsed between the appearance of the essay in the *Mercury* and its reappearance in the *Gazette*.
94. I here assume, perhaps without sufficient reason, that the same person

Hamilton in a discussion of "Liberty, Property, Publick Justice, and the Duty of a Good Magistrate." Though these essays might appear to a casual reader to be abstract and theoretical, a knowledge of the background against which they were written and printed makes clear how many of the allusions were intended for a particular person; references to wicked magistrates who neither fear nor worship God,[95] to persons who seize power "by subtile Arts" and "for sinister Ends" and thus "creep into our Legislature, or our Courts of Justice,"[96] to the need of rotation of offices in order to maintain a free government,[97] to "Men of profligate Lives" who "for base Crimes fled their Native Country" and with small knowledge and much craft plus uncommon impudence "ride a good and free People"[98] — these and more suggest the *Mercury's* habitual attitude towards Hamilton.

While Cato, Jr. was thus dexterously keeping on the fair side of libel, the *Gazette* once again published a letter signed "Z."[99] It began with a long Latin motto;[100] then followed the letter:

> *Zenger's Trial* having been lately published in Great-Britain and Ireland, with an extraordinary Applause, I thought proper to send you the following abstracts, taken from several private letters here in town, which give a particular account of the reception It met with in London. Every true Lover of Pennsylvania will receive a sensible pleasure, when he is informed that Mr. Hamilton has acquired a high Reputation at home, on account of his learned and generous Defence of the Rights of Mankind at New-York: For nothing can reflect greater honour on this Government, than the Praises which our Mother-Country has so liberally bestowed on a Gentleman, who has annually presided in our Assemblies for above these Ten Years past. His Character is now raised much above the reach of

called himself "Cato, Jr." in 1733 and in 1738. The quotation is from the first essay.
 95. Third essay.
 96. First essay.
 97. Second essay. Compare *Busy-Body* 31, which sent Bradford to jail.
 98. Second essay. This seems to be a reference to Hamilton's dubious early history.
 99. *Gazette* 492. "Z." was probably again the pseudonym of Webbe.
 100. The same quotation was used earlier in the Hamilton controversy in the *Gazette* of June 3, 1736. The passage, attributed to Livy, ran as follows: "Homo certe mirabilis, quippe qui quum in Terra, peregrina tam procul ab domo ingenti consensu summum Imperium per multos annos tenuerit. Multitudinem mixtam ex colluvione omnium Gentium, quibus non Lex, non Mos, non Lingua communis, alius Habitus, alia Vestis, alij Ritus, alia Sacra, alij prope Dij, ita quodam uno vinculo copulaverit, ut ex tam varijs diversi Gentibus Respublica bene constituta exstiterit." The passage appears to be not an actual quotation from Livy, but rather an adaptation of the description of Hannibal in Book XXVIII, 12.

ignorance, envy or malice: Therefore Be It Known to all his Detractors, of whatever size or denomination they be, who have signalized themselves in the *Mercury,* and without daring to own their names have hitherto spit their poison in the dark, That they may from henceforth and at all times hereafter, peaceably and quietly crawl out of their holes even in open day, and Curse Him in their usual Jargon and Gibberish; Without the Let, Suit, Trouble, Molestation or Denial of any person or persons whatsoever. As it would be highly imprudent in any man of sense to descend so low, as to take the least notice of such scribling Reptiles, So it would be altogether impertinent to offer any thing in justification of a Character that stands in need of none; notwithstanding that it has been so often attacked by every infamous method, that Rage, or Spite, or Envy, or Cowardice could suggest: For The Defender Of The Liberty Of The Press, by the Strength of his own Genius, has, on the noblest Foundation, that of promoting the Good of Mankind, erected to himself a Monument, which will transmit his Memory with Honour, to latest Posterity.

Finally came the quotation:[101]

We have been lately amused with *Zenger's Trial,* which has become the common Topic of Conversation in all the Coffee-Houses, both at the Court-End of the Town and in the City. During my Observation, there has not been any piece, published here, so greedily read and so highly applauded. —————— The greatest Men at the Bar have openly declared, that the Subject of Libels was never so well treated in Westminster-Hall, as at New-York. —————— Our political Writers of different Factions, who never agreed in any thing else, have mentioned the Trial in their public Writings with an Air of Rapture and Triumph. —————— a Goliath in Learning and Politics gave his

---

101. An examination of the *London Magazine* and the *Gentleman's Magazine* for the period bears out "Z.'s" contention that the trial had much favorable publicity in London. The *Tryal* was listed in the register of books in both magazines for December 1737. *Common Sense* (December 10, 1736) discussed the trial and Hamilton's speech *(Gentleman's);* both magazines reprinted the *Craftsman* of January 21. *Common Sense* of January 7 *(Gentleman's)* contained an essay entitled "The Importance of the Liberty of the Press." The *Craftsman* of April 8, 22, 29 continued to discuss libels and specifically mentioned the *Remarks (Gentleman's). Common Sense* of April 29 praised Hamilton's arguments highly, "whose Tryal, therefore, no Printer ought to be without" *(Gentleman's).* Much later the *Old English Journal* of July 15, 1745, quoted Hamilton's speech at the trial *(Gentleman's).* The preface to *Caribbeana,* on the other hand, attacked Hamilton. It is worth noting that "Z." attributes the praises of Hamilton which he cites to "private letters," a fact which makes the comments almost impossible to trace.

> opinion of Mr. Hamilton's Argument in these terms, If It is not Law it is Better than Law, it Ought to be Law, and Will Always be Law wherever Justice prevails. —————— The Tryal has been reprinted four times in three months, and there has been a greater demand for it, by all ranks and degrees of People, than there has been known for any of the most celebrated Performances of our greatest Geniuses. —————— We look upon Zenger's Advocate, as a glorious Assertor of Public Liberty and of the Rights and Privileges of Britons. —————— I had almost forgot to tell you, that there has been also lately printed here some Remarks on Zenger's Defence. It is said (in the preface) that they were wrote by two eminent Lawyers in one of the Plantations. But (notwithstanding a good Book generally makes a bad Answer sell) It has so happened that the few Persons, who out of curiosity bought the Remarks, have been ill-natured enough to damn the piece as a stupid, senseless performance; so that the greater part of the impression remains unsold, to the no small mortification of the Bookseller, &c.

The following week, in the same number with the third essay of Cato, Jr., the *Mercury* replied with the following very outspoken criticism:

> When I perused some of our *Gazetts* stuff'd with Panegyricks on a famous Mock Patriot, I was Tempted to think the Author designed what he had Written not as a real Encomium, but rather as a Virulent Satyr and Pasquinade. But when I considered the real Z's Talents and Attachment to his Patron, I could no longer suspect but his praises were bestow'd in earnest. This not being Equal to the Task must be partly owing to what has been often observed, *viz.* that when those Men are to be praised, who are notoriously Corrupt and Guilty of very many vile and unworthy Actions, it requires a very nice and masterly Address to form a Panegyrick in such a manner, that the Generality of Readers shall not understand the Author in a Ironical Sense, and take his unjust Compliments for Banter, Grimace and Ridicule: But verily Z blunders egregiously in his way of Arguing, when he undertakes to Embellish and Defend a Character, which he tell's us, stands in need of no Justification, and erects a Monument to perpetuate his Hero's Memory on one single Attempt on the side of Liberty; and that too, however Applauded by some, yet sufficiently exposed by others, for its gross Absurdities. At this rate, the vilest Wretch that ever lived may suddenly be Metamorphosed into the greatest Saint, A devourer of Widows and Orphans, a Bl———r,

> M———r, B———r, a publick Pest, one that has been a Tyrant in, and a disgrace to a Government, let such an one at this rate make one feeble and feigned Effort for the Liberty of the Press, and he shall be Screened from the Infamy of many Crimes and Villanies that perhaps stain'd his Character both in publick and private Life, provided he find Sycophants to sound his Praises. Flattery thrives most among the Weakest and the most Wicked, hence the vilest among the Roman Emperor's such as Tiberius, Caligula, Nero, and Domitian had much finer things said of them, than the most Worthy and Virtuous Vespasian, Titus, and Trajan. . . .

The issue of June 1 continued the attack. It accused "Z." of breathing "Hyperbolical airs of applause" and of insulting common sense; it pointed out that the reprinting of the "famous Performance" meant nothing because scandalous and profane works were often popular; it asserted that not all London papers praised Hamilton and that neither New York nor Pennsylvania would be duped; and it attacked "Z." as a paid defender of his patron and accused certain nameless "mighty Friends" of denying "their right Name" and their parentage and country for forty years.[102] On June 8 appeared an ostensibly theoretical discussion of cowardice and courage, which contained, however, the following pointed sentences:

> The Courage assigned to Brutes regards only their Boldness to attack, and their Fierceness to destroy . . . . But rationals when of their own accord (much more when prompt'd by others) they attack and abuse their Fellow Creatures without due regard to that Virtue and right Reason, are so far from meriting the respect due to Men of Courage that they come thereby nearer the Brute, and consequently that they deserve to be banished from all civil Societies. Equally unworthy are they, who endeavour to eternize their Fame as advocates for Liberty, when at the same Time they exercise all acts of Violence against those they even but suppose to have made use of that Liberty, but more of that hereafter, and of the nature of stopping and Assaulting a Man upon the Highway, as a Caution to Travellers, &c.

And on June 15, two weeks after the announcement of the arrival of Governor George Thomas, appeared an essay on the qualities of a good

---

102. Another reference evidently to Hamilton's uncertain background. There was a persistent story that Hamilton's real name was Trent and that he had come from Ireland. See Konkle, 7 n.

governor, with special emphasis upon the dangers of irreligion and bad counsellors. From this date forward the controversy became irregular and obscure. Three sardonic letters from "A.B." to "Ned" which appeared in the *Gazette* on July 6 and October 13, 1738, and March 29 and April 5, 1739, certainly were directed against the proprietors and may well have related to the Hamilton episode. A curious advertisement in the *Mercury* of June and July 1738 and succeeding editorials[103] may also have concerned Hamilton; and the issue of September 21 printed the usual pre-election appeal to the voters of Pennsylvania to resist the encroachments of tyranny and "the influence of Men of corrupt and Irreligious Principles." One can speculate also on later items, such as the essay on hypocrisy in the *Mercury* of April 5, 1739; but apparently the long quarrel between Bradford's paper and Hamilton had about run its course, and after 1738 there appears to have been no serious recurrence of hostilities.

What happened to bring the controversy to an end is even more obscure than what caused it. Possibly the approach of war with Spain afforded the *Mercury* livelier material, and surely the arrival of Thomas and the subsequent conflict between him and the Assembly over paper money and provincial defense were more timely. Moreover, at the end of the session of 1738-1739 Hamilton voluntarily retired from the Assembly and thus removed a major cause of the *Mercury's* opposition. In addition, at some time in 1740 the paper's one-time enemy "Z." — John Webbe — became Bradford's ally in planning the *American Magazine;* and when the monthly appeared one of its features was Hamilton's farewell address to the Assembly of 1739. Whatever the reason, the anticlimax of the long warfare came at the death of Hamilton in 1741; in the issue of August 6 appeared the same elaborate and eulogistic obituary which was printed simultaneously in the *Gazette:*

> On the fourth Instant died Andrew Hamilton, Esq; and was the next Day interr'd at Bush-Hill, his Country Seat. His Corps was attended to the Grave by a great Number of his Friends, deeply affected with their own, but more with their Countrys Loss. He lived not without Enemies: For, as he was himself Open and Honest, he took pains to Unmask the Hypocrite, and boldly censured the Knave, without regard to Station, or Profession. Such therefore may Exult at His Death. He steadily maintained the cause of Liberty; and the Laws made during the time he was Speaker of the Assembly, which was many Years, will be a lasting Monument of his Affection to the People, and of his Concern for the Welfare of this Province.

103. *Mercury* 964, 965, 967.

He was no Friend to Power, as he had observed an ill use had been freequently made of it in the Colonys, and therefore was seldom upon good Terms with Governours. This prejudice, however, did not always determine his Conduct towards them; for, when he saw they meant well, he was for supporting them Honourably, and was indefatigable in endeavouring to remove the prejudices of others. He was long at the Top of his Profession here. And had he been as Griping, as he was Knowing and Active, he might have left a much greater Fortune to his Family than he has done. But he spent more time in hearing and reconciling Differences in private, to the loss of his Fees, than he did in pleading Causes at the Bar. He was Just where he sat as a Judge, and tho' he was Stern and Severe in his Manner, he was Compasionate in his Nature and very slow to punish. He was the Poor Mans Friend, and was never known to with-hold his Purse or Service from the Indigent or Oppressed. He was a tender Husband and a fond Parent. But ——— these are Virtues which Fools and Knaves have, sometimes, in common with the Wise and the Honest. His Free manner of treating Religious Subjects gave Offence to many, who, if a Man may Judge from their Actions, were not themselves much in Earnest. He feared God, loved Mercy, and did Justice. If he could not subscribe to the Creed of any particular Church, it was not for want of considering them all, for he had Read much on Religious Subjects. He went through a tedious Sickness with uncommon Chearfulness, Constancy and Courage. Nothing of affected Bravery or Ostentation appeared; but such a Composure and Tranquility of Mind as results from the Reflection of a Life spent agreeable to the best of a Mans Judgment. He preserved his Understanding and his Regard for his Friends, to the last Moment. What was given as a Rule, by a Poet, upon another Occasion, may be justly applied to Him, upon this

——————————— Servetur ad imum
Qualis ab incepto processerit, & sibi constet.[104]

With this strange reversal of nearly all that it had previously maintained about the character of Hamilton, the *Mercury* brought to an end the most dramatic conflict of its career.

The last eight years of the paper's history, as might be expected, reveal that it had won a remarkable degree of freedom in the discussion of

---

104. Horace, *Ars Poetica*, ll. 126-127. "Keep him to the very end as he was at the beginning, and make him consistent."

local problems. In 1738 Philadelphia was apparently disturbed by infringements upon the quiet and peacefulness of Sunday; accordingly barber shops were ordered closed, and a few months later an old act against the operation of alehouses on the first day of the week was put into effect.[105] More important, early in 1739 a new money bill was passed by the Assembly, the discussion of which between Thomas and the legislature was printed in the *Mercury* without any obvious restriction.[106] For a few weeks in the summer of 1739 the *Mercury* and the *Gazette* were again at war, this time over a petition to the Assembly from some of the citizens to remove the tanyards outside the city. The petition, asserting that stench and filth were caused by the industry, was supported by the *Gazette*, whereas the *Mercury* presented the point of view of the tanners, who in effect won their case.[107] At the same time that the question of the tanyards was being debated, Governor Thomas proclaimed the offer of commissions to those who would privateer against Spanish ships,[108] and early in 1740 he made a direct appeal to the Assembly for the defense of the province.[109] His request touched off a very serious collision between the interests of the proprietors and of many of the colonists and the convictions of the still-dominant group of Friends and their sympathizers. Whereas Thomas was willing to accord the Friends religious freedom, he failed to realize or preferred to disregard the practical implications of their theory of pacifism, as he clearly showed when he asked the Assembly "to act, as undoubtedly will be expected of you by his Majesty, for the Security of this Part of his Dominions, as becomes Protestants, and Lovers of your Liberties, your Country and your Families." The answer of the Assembly was a dignified explanation of the Quaker position, which in turn called forth a rather heated reply from Thomas.[110] To this the Assembly justly responded that it did not intend to restrain people from acting as they saw fit but that it would not "enact any Law, which should oblige the Inhabitants of this Province to bear Arms."[111]

On Monday, April 14, 1740, war against Spain was declared in Philadelphia, and Thomas issued a proclamation in English and in German calling for volunteers for an expedition against the West Indies.[112] While the Governor continued to rail against the backwardness of the

105. *Mercury* 966, 993.
106. *Mercury* 996, 999, 1015.
107. *Mercury* 1024, 1028; *Gazette* 559, 566.
108. *Mercury* 1025. The *Mercury* also reported similar proclamations by the Governors of New York and New Jersey in Numbers 1025 and 1026.
109. *Mercury* 1047.
110. *Mercury* 1047, 1048.
111. *Mercury* 1049.
112. *Mercury* 1059, 1060.

colony,[113] seven companies and part of an eighth were quickly raised;[114] but a new point of disagreement arose because of the serious difficulty caused farmers and tradesmen, the Assembly asserted, by the enlisting of their servants. Thomas's reply to this objection[115] was followed by an announcement from Thomas Penn that he would accept deferment of the payments due him in order to encourage the Assembly to vote money for defense; once more, however, to the consternation of Penn, the Assembly refused to act, and petitions from the Council and from some of the merchants of Philadelphia requested the legislature not to block the will of the majority. In the same number in which these developments were reported,[116] the *Mercury* also printed news that the Lower Counties had passed an act allocating £1000 for the victualling and transporting of their troops; and in the following issue appeared the news that the Pennsylvania Assembly had finally voted £3000 for the use of the king, though with various strings securely attached. The issue of September 18 contained the further intelligence that seven companies had embarked from Philadelphia for the West Indies, and paid an emphatic tribute to Governor Thomas.

For a time thereafter the problem of defense was less critical and other matters filled the local columns of the *Mercury*. The Council passed a regulation that no ship should be cleared until the master had given bond that his supplies would be landed in British territory;[117] the city prematurely celebrated the reported capture of Cartagena;[118] and Thomas Penn departed for England, leaving the colony once more without a member of the proprietary family.[119] A new and serious problem arose in 1741 in connection with the rapid spread of communicable diseases in Philadelphia, particularly among the immigrants from Europe.[120] In September the Council discussed the urgent need of a quarantine officer to examine "unhealthy Vessels" entering the port, the previous officer having been so ill paid by the Assembly that he had declined to carry on his duties.[121] In January, Thomas asked the legislature to set up a hospital in Philadelphia, primarily to care for immigrants, pointing out that he had recommended such an institution in 1738 without success

---

113. *Mercury* 1070.
114. *Mercury* 1073, 1075.
115. *Mercury* 1075-1076.
116. *Mercury* 1076.
117. *Mercury* 1106. Compare the action of the New York Council, reported in Number 1100.
118. *Mercury* 1115.
119. *Mercury* 1129, 1130. Thomas Penn never returned.
120. In *Mercury* 1149 the list of burials for Christ Church parish alone indicated that 206 "Palatines" and 94 "Strangers" had died within the year, approximately half of the total number of deaths recorded.
121. *Mercury* 1134.

since, he asserted, "some look with jealous Eyes upon the immigrant Germans, but . . . every industrious Labourer from Europe is a real Addition to the Wealth of this Province. . . . "[122] In addition, he said, it was the colony's Christian obligation to care for the newcomers. The Assembly relegated the problem to a committee, stubbornly insisting that "a due Execution of the Laws" might have prevented the spreading of disease and that it was unjustly accused by the Governor of discouraging the immigration of Palatines.[123] Then after a further exchange of angry remarks with the Governor, the Assembly adjourned for four months,[124] according to the *Mercury* with the deliberate intention of thwarting Thomas.

Before the legislature met again the paper forcibly reminded its readers of the war by printing a list of vessels bound to and from Philadelphia which had been captured by the Spanish since the outbreak of hostilities.[125] When the Assembly reconvened, Thomas's answer to its last message, in which he pointed out that as early as 1729 the Assembly had tried to discourage the immigration of foreigners by a duty of forty shillings a head, was promptly printed by the *Mercury*.[126] The Assembly, meanwhile, had addressed the proprietors concerning "the unhappy Conduct of our present Governor" and asked for his removal. In the issue of June 3, accordingly, Bradford printed this address and the reply to it, containing an unqualified defense of Thomas's actions, a recommendation that the Assembly restore harmony by taking proper steps for the safety of the colony, and a threat of interference from abroad if the legislature continued to prove recalcitrant.[127] Four months later the paper also printed the findings of a subcommittee appointed by the Privy Council to consider a petition from various citizens of Philadelphia protesting against the defenseless state of the province.[128] The *Mercury* reported the committee's encouraging Thomas to provide for the security of Pennsylvania and quoted, as part of the Governor's report, a passage which suggested again the paper's sympathy with the Governor's cause: ". . . the Navigation of Delaware River, formerly thought difficult, is now

---

122. *Mercury* 1151.
123. *Mercury* 1151. Thomas's views upon the desirability of the Palatine immigration are interestingly supported by a comment quoted in the *Mercury* of December 16, 1742, from Governor Shirley's address to the Massachusetts Assembly. Shirley, who wished his colony to encourage immigration, said: "Such an Accession of Numbers and Wealth to the Province, is particularly desireable . . . . And herein we have an Example from the Province of Pensilvania, who have, by this Method, within a few Years, most surprizingly increased and flourished beyond all other of His Majesty's Colonies in North-America."
124. *Mercury* 1152.
125. *Mercury* 1166.
126. *Mercury* 1169.
127. *Mercury* 1170.
128. *Mercury* 1188.

become so familiar that near three hundred Vessels come up, with safety, every Year, and yet, there is not one Battery, or even one Piece of Cannon upon it, to prevent a Privateer from Plundering and burning a City, consisting of near seventeen hundred Houses, and ten thousand Inhabitants. . . ." Meanwhile the Assembly was using the old trick of withholding the Governor's salary until he assented to its demands,[129] with the result that in February 1743 Thomas agreed to six new bills, received a payment of £1500, and brought the session of the legislature to a relatively harmonious close.[130]

The story, as it was told in the *Mercury,* came quickly to its conclusion. In the summer and autumn of 1744, after war between England and France had actually been declared, conflict between the Governor and the legislature again flared up. Thomas wanted to establish a militia law and — after four ships had been captured in the Delaware by a French privateer, obviously contemptuous of Philadelphia — he wished also to equip a vessel to protect the city's shipping. The Assembly, however, refused to pass a militia law and postponed discussion of Gordon's second request;[131] but the following summer when the Governor asked financial aid, the legislature granted £4000, with a comment that makes a fitting, though ironic, conclusion to the episode: ". . . altho' the peaceable Principles professed by divers Members of the present Assembly, do not permit them to join in raising of Men, or providing Arms and Ammunition, yet we have ever held it our Duty to render Tribute to Caesar. . . ."[132]

It is obvious that, just as no complete or coherent account of the happenings in America as a whole between 1720 and 1746 can be found in the *Mercury,* so no consistent narrative of political developments in Pennsylvania is to be discovered there. Instead, the paper touches intermittently on dozens of phases of local history, some of them of great importance — for example, the recurrent problem of insufficient money, the constant readjustment of the relation between whites and Indians, immigration, and the export trade. Sometimes events that one might expect to find covered by the paper are barely mentioned or altogether omitted, and for reasons which one can only guess — notably the Walking Purchase of 1737.[133] On the other hand, the *Mercury* gives a very

---

129. *Mercury* 1183. The *Mercury* omitted all discussion of the election of 1742, in which Thomas and the faction desiring a vigorous defense of the province was soundly defeated. Possibly the failure of his candidates also showed Thomas the necessity of cooperating with the Assembly.
130. *Mercury* 1206.
131. *Mercury* 1284, 1295.
132. *Mercury* 1334.
133. The *Pennsylvania Gazette* also failed to report this famous episode in the history of the province.

adequate impression of the basic political development of the time: the movement of the colony towards autonomy. Indeed, the increasing boldness with which the paper expressed its views on political questions may well be related to the tendency of the elected Assembly to assume constantly greater authority at the expense of governor, Council, and proprietors. To be sure, so far as we can judge, the *Mercury* seems ordinarily to have supported the vested interests; yet, however conservative its opinions may have been, in the course of twenty-six years it gained the privilege, which it did not possess inherently, of expressing those opinions. For example, if the generally accepted estimate of Hamilton is valid, the *Mercury's* long conflict with him was, to say the least, misguided if not occasionally libelous; nevertheless, that controversy shows us a significant occurrence: a colonial newspaper in the very process of winning the right which we call freedom of the press; and the tendency towards that freedom is, in turn, a symptom of the colony's progress towards independence and democracy. Thus, it seems to me, the *Mercury's* handling of local affairs must be evaluated by two different standards. As straight reporting it is meagre and fragmentary; but in total effect it throws much light upon certain main currents in eighteenth-century American thought.

NUM. 1098

THE AMERICAN
WEEKLY MERCURY.

From Thursday *January* 8, to Thursday *January* 15. 1740-1.

MR. BRADFORD,

It now being Winter and not much News stirring, I here send you a Paper taken from the Spectator, concerning the great Hoop Petticoats which are now wore, and take up so much Room in our Streets that we can scarce pass by, and in publishing the same in your next Mercury you'll oblige many of your Readers.

MR. SPECTATOR,

YOU have diverted the Town almost a whole Month at the Expence of the Country, it is now high time that you should give the Country their Revenge. Since your withdrawing from this Place, the fair Sex are run into great Extravagancies. Their Petticoats, which began to heave and swell before you left us, are now blown up into a most eroneous Concave, and rises every Day more and more...

Manner, in Circle within Circle, amidst such a variety of Out-Works, and Lines of Circumvallation. A Female who is thus invested in Whale-bone is sufficiently secured against the Approaches of an ill-bred Fellow, who might as well think of Sir George Etheridge's way of making Love in a Tub, as in the midst of so many Hoops.

AMONG these various Conjectures, there are Men of Superstitious Tempers, who look upon the Hoop Petticoat as a kind of Prodigy. Some will have it that it protends the Downfall of the French King, and observe that the Farthingale appeared in England a little before the Ruin of the Spanish Monarchy. Others are of Opinion that it foretells Battle and Bloodshed, and believe it of the same Prognostication as the Tail of a Blazing Star. For my Part, I am apt to think it is a Sign that Multitudes are

Nameplate of the *Mercury*, Showing an Early View of Philadelphia
Courtesy of the Library Company of Philadelphia

Chapter 5

The *Mercury* as a Mirror of the Times

When the first issue of the *Universal Instructor* appeared, Keimer introduced his news items with a characteristic remark:

> We have little News of Consequence at present, the English Prints being generally stufft with Robberies, Cheats, Fires, Murders, Bankrupcies, Promotions of some, and Hanging of others; nor can we expect much better till Vessels arrive in the Spring, when we hope to inform our Readers what has been doing in the Court and the Cabinet, in the Parliament-House as well as the Sessions-House . . . . In the mean Time we hope our Readers will be content for the present, with what we can give 'em, which if it does 'em no Good, shall do 'em no Hurt, 'Tis the best we have, and so take it.

Not all colonial editors were so humorously outspoken or so didactic as Keimer, but for all of them a major problem was how much space to allot to court, cabinet, and parliament-house and how much to cheats, fires, and hangings — or, to put it more broadly, how much to serious political news and how much to human-interest stories, to the celebrities of the hour, to the curious and the sensational, to the ideas, attitudes, and day-to-day activities of the times.

Bradford, we have seen, devoted a great part of his paper to the purveyance of political news; and although he was not averse to drama — for example, in the story of Walpole's rise and fall — in reporting political events he was seldom led astray by what was merely exciting. Basically he seems to have been more interested in Indian conferences than in Indian massacres, in treaties than in battles; in presenting political intelligence he appears rightly to have preferred the significant to the sensational. But after having satisfied his customers, or perhaps his conscience, with a reasonably complete and accurate picture of important events at home and abroad, Bradford's next objective seems to have been to amuse or harrow or inform them, possibly to cater to their prejudices, with a miscellany of news items on less urgent topics. No doubt his readers were especially eager to hear tidings of the great and near-great. Hence the names of eighteenth-century notables crowd the pages of the *Mercury*. Cardinals and popes, kings and prime ministers and colonial governors, military and naval heroes, actors and musicians, scientists and religious leaders, writers and highwaymen and beaux — all these and more jostle one another to claim the attention of Bradford's provincial audience.

The Stuarts furnish an admirable example of the news value that lay in a name; for curiosity about the Old Pretender as an individual, in addition to his political importance, must have accounted for the ever-popular rôle played by him and his family in the *Mercury's* news columns. Ordinarily Bradford referred to him by the romantic title of the Chevalier de St. George, and from beginning to end of the paper news about him lent drama or suspense to its pages.[1] In 1720 a project to make him ruler of the Moors in Africa was rumored, and it was said that by his touch he had cured of the evil a niece of one of the cardinals.[2] In September of the same year Bradford informed his readers that the Pope had "Order'd the blessed swadling cloths to be got ready against the Lying in of the Consort of the Chevalier de St. George."[3] On the birth of Charles Edward, the *Mercury* reported, there was rejoicing in Brussels, and a year later it announced that, though the prince was but a baby, his father insisted that he hear mass daily.[4] On his deathbed Clement XI was said to have recommended James's cause to his successor, and in 1725 the *Mercury* printed news that the Chevalier had received presents from Benedict XIII, as well as from English and Scottish Jacobites.[5] Meanwhile, the Stuart conspiracy of 1722 had given new prominence to the exiled family,[6] and in 1726 it was reported in rapid succession that the former Bishop of Rochester had become head of the Pretender's affairs in France, that James had given an explanation of his wife's retirement to a nunnery, and that he had accidentally dropped a paper telling of a new scheme for the invasion of Great Britain.[7] In 1731 he was reported in Naples, surrounded by Irish officers but passing under the inoffensive cognomen "Mr. Brown"; in contrast, by 1733 it was rumored that he might be elected king of Poland.[8] In 1739 he and the Pope were said to have quarreled violently over a game of backgammon; but two years later the papal physician attended the Chevalier when he was suffering from a severe throat infection, and early in 1744 the Pretender was reported made a cardinal.[9] Although in 1740 it had been announced that he was resigning himself to a peaceful, unambitious life,

    1. The items I mention are typical of the very large number of references to the Stuart family.
    2. *Mercury* 68, 47.
    3. *Mercury* 38.
    4. *Mercury* 77, 123.
    5. *Mercury* 80, 291.
    6. *Mercury* 148, 156, 163, 171, 179, etc.
    7. *Mercury* 330, 332, 337.
    8. *Mercury* 615, 703.
    9. *Mercury* 1026, 1121, 1253.

at the close of 1743 the contradictory news arrived that he was holding many conferences at his private palace and receiving much money.[10] Indeed, before two years were out, the Jacobite invasion was under way and, in consequence, the Stuarts held the spotlight in issue after issue of the *Mercury*. While from France came the report that miracles had been wrought in the name of James II and that he might be canonized,[11] from Scotland and the north of England came the story of the fabulous success of his grandson's "Don Quixote Enterprize"[12] — the taking of Edinburgh,[13] the march across the border and the fall of Carlisle,[14] the wild rumor that the rebels were but fifty miles from London[15] — and then the hardly less amazing story of the retreat towards Culloden Moor.[16]

So through the pages of the *Mercury,* at the cost of disentangling fiction from fact and straightening out here and there some chronological confusion, we can follow for a generation the fortunes of the Stuarts. More important, we come to realize how closely and with how strange a mixture of curiosity and apprehension England and its colonies watched the activities of the Pretender and his family. Especially interesting is the way in which the *Mercury* in 1745 put aside its dispassionate chronicling of gossip about the Stuarts. When they became once more a threat to the order established by the Glorious Revolution, the paper appealed no longer to idle curiosity or vague anxieties; instead, it devoted its columns to propaganda, merging the popular interest in the Pretender with a serious attempt to persuade its readers that his cause was infinitely pernicious. With horrid warning it reproduced what purported to be a letter of Charles's confessor, anticipating the restoration of abbey lands and containing the terrifying sentence: "Our Smithfield Fires shall again blaze."[17] It repeated stories which dramatized the supposed violence and cruelty of the rebels, especially of the Highlanders, who, one account said, even robbed and ravished a lady loyal to the Stuart cause.[18] With evident approval, on the other hand, it published news of the addresses of fidelity which poured in upon George in the moment of crisis, letters full of such phrases as "unnatural Rebellion," "Despotick Power," "Papal Tyranny," and such rousing sentiments as: "The Protestant Succession is our great Palladium; if this is lost, we are no more a Nation, at least not a Nation of free People";[19] "If ye set a Papish on the Coach-

10. *Mercury* 1083, 1248.
11. *Mercury* 1366.
12. *Mercury* 1348.
13. *Mercury* 1354, 1356, 1357.
14. *Mercury* 1363, 1366, 1367.
15. *Mercury* 1367.
16. *Mercury* 1371, 1372, 1375, 1376.
17. *Mercury* 1361.
18. *Mercury* 1363.
19. *Mercury* 1358.

Box, he will drive to the Devil";[20] or "The Alternative is short, to save all, or to lose all; to destroy, or be destroyed."[21] Again, the *Mercury* resorted to satire — in "The Chevalier Charles's Declaration," which mocked the principles for which the Prince was popularly believed to stand,[22] or in the description of the procession lampooning the invasion with which the town of Deptford celebrated George's birthday.[23] Sometimes Mrs. Bradford borrowed from an English journal a wry joke, such as: "The Punsters are of Opinion, that though we could not Cope with the Rebellion at first, we shall make shift to Wade thro' it at last."[24] More seriously, in parallel columns the paper drew a comparison between Charles and George, and listed a dozen reasons for rejecting the Pretender.[25] When from Antigua early in February 1746 came a rumor that the rebels were defeated, the item was printed with an editorial comment: "Tho' we wish this News may be true; yet . . . we are apt to think it stands in Need of Confirmation."[26] The *Mercury* also reprinted a letter originally directed to the Boston *Evening Post* deploring the indifference of people in North America to European events and insisting that the colonies, though far away, would be profoundly affected by the outcome of the struggle across the Atlantic.[27] Indeed, the attitude of the *Mercury* was fiercely partisan; a perfect illustration of its opinion on the Stuart invasion was a quotation from a letter, printed first in a London paper,[28] by "A Free-Born Englishman": "What wretch is there so abject, as to wish to live, to behold with his eyes this great city, the queen of Europe, this fair England, the land of liberty, a prey to Romish vermin, French dragoons, and highland cut throats?"

Like the Stuarts, though for very different reasons and for a briefer period, Marlborough offered good copy to a colonial newspaper. The *Mercury* reported, for example, that he was serving, as usual, on the regency commission during George's trip to Hanover in 1720, that in the summer of 1721 he was ill at Windsor, and that he had lodged an appeal in the House of Lords against the men working on Blenheim House.[29] Following his death, which was announced in the issue of September 13, 1722, news of Marlborough appeared very prominently

20. *Mercury* 1374.
21. *Mercury* 1365.
22. *Mercury* 1359.
23. *Mercury* 1363. This lively description appeared also in the *Pennsylvania Gazette* of February 25 and in the *Pennsylvania Journal* of February 18.
24. *Mercury* 1363. Neither Sir John Cope nor Field Marshal George Wade was successful in stemming the Jacobite invasion.
25. *Mercury* 1364.
26. *Mercury* 1369.
27. *Mercury* 1364.
28. *Mercury* 1362. The letter originally appeared in the *General Evening Post* of October 1. See the *Gentleman's Magazine* for 1745.
29. *Mercury* 37, 78, 79.

in the pages of the *Mercury:* the amount of his estate and the preparations for his funeral, the "noble Legacy" to Eugene of Savoy, the magnificent ceremony of interment in Henry VII's chapel, the settling of the title and the disposition of the enormous fortune.[30] For years, in fact, the spell of Marlborough's name remained potent. In 1724 the *Mercury* printed news of a Latin epitaph for his monument which supposedly had been submitted to the Dowager Duchess in competition for a prize of five hundred guineas, and it reported the completion of the family vault at Blenheim and plans for the removal of Marlborough's body there from Westminster.[31] Later came news of the purchase by the Dowager Duchess of an estate in Buckinghamshire and her subsequent offer to lend her establishment at St. James to Frederick, Prince of Wales.[32] An anecdote about Lord Spencer's tour in Switzerland must certainly have been inserted in the paper in 1727 primarily because of the fame of his grandfather.[33] In 1731 Bradford devoted parts of two issues to a eulogy of Marlborough and to quotation of the inscription on his monument at Blenheim.[34] Moreover, when the Dowager Duchess died in 1744,[35] the *Mercury* printed at length the provisions of her will, including her elaborate and explicit plan for the writing of her husband's biography.[36] Marlborough, unlike the Stuarts, was never a subject of propaganda in the *Mercury;* interest in him looked backward, not forward. But his frequent reappearance in the paper supplies an excellent example of the way in which the Bradfords capitalized on the human tendency to be curious about great men.

Dispossessed royalty and military heroes, however, did not absorb an undue share of the attention of the *Mercury's* readers. In a place and time when the church was still a preoccupation of many people, it is not surprising that several religious leaders appeared prominently in Bradford's pages. In general, the *Mercury* seems to have neglected the New England theocrats; it does not discuss Edwards and the Awakening and it contains but one important reference to Cotton Mather. That story, a famous one though it does not relate to his theological pursuits, was told originally by Mather himself and appeared in the *Mercury* under date of Boston, November 20, 1720:[37]

> At the House of Dr. Cotton Mather, there lodged his Kinsman, a worthy Minister, under the Small Pox, received and

30. *Mercury* 146, 148, 149, 152, 159, 163, 172.
31. *Mercury* 235, 236.
32. *Mercury* 330, 406.
33. *Mercury* 368.
34. *Mercury* 619-620.
35. *Mercury* 1307.
36. *Mercury* 1311.
37. *Mercury* 104. A note, obviously taken from Bradford's source, said: "The above Account we received from the Doctor's own hand."

managed in the successful Way of Inoculation.[38] Towards three of the Clock in the Night, as it grew towards the Morning of Tuesday, the 14th of this Instant November, some unknown Hand threw a fired Granado-Shell into the Chamber of the sick Gentleman, the Weight whereof alone, if it had fallen on the Head of the Patient (which it seemed aimed at) would have been enough to have done Part of the Business designed. But the Granado was charged with such Materials, and in such a Manner, that upon its going off, it must probably have killed the Persons in the Room, and would have certainly fired the Chamber, and soon have laid the House in Ashes; which has appeared incontestible to them that have since examined it. But the merciful Providence of God so ordered it, that the Granado passing through the Window, had, by the Iron in the Middle of the Casement, such a Turn given to it, that in falling on the Floor, the fired Wildfire in the Fuse, was violently shaken out into some Distance from the Shell, and burnt out upon the Floor, without firing the Granado. When the Granado was taken up, there was found a Paper, so tied with a Thread about the Fuse, that it might out-live the Breaking of the Shell; wherein were these Words, — *Cotton Mather, I was once one of your Meeting, but the cursed Lie you told of — you know who, made me leave you, you Dog: And, damn you, I'll inoculate you with this, with a Pox to you.* This is the Sum of the Matter, without any Remarks upon it; which no doubt will be various among the People, as they stand affected.

For Bradford's customers, it seems, Mather's religious convictions held no particular interest, but some other religious leaders received much notice in the *Mercury's* columns, notably George Whitefield and Count von Zinzendorf. Both were arresting personalities and centers of violent conflict, and both were for a time familiar figures in Philadelphia. The earliest news of Whitefield concerned chiefly his phenomenal success as a preacher in England: his enormous audiences, the large sums of money he collected, and the conversions which he brought about.[39] The *Mercury* of November 8, 1739, announced his arrival six days earlier in Philadelphia, and spoke of his daily sermons in Christ Church and their popularity among all sorts of people. From this date forward Whitefield's every move was apparently followed eagerly by the readers of the *Mercury,* for the paper not only devoted much print to his where-

---

38. Since Mather was one of the early advocates of inoculation, there was certainly an element of persuasion in the phrase "the successful Way."

39. *Mercury* 943, 1011, 1019, 1020, 1022, 1023, 1032.

abouts and activities, but also welcomed to its columns the controversy which sprang up around him as well as advertisements of pamphlets and books by him or about his teaching.[40] Typical news items,[41] for example, told of his arrival in Philadelphia on November 23 after a trip to New York. There he had preached eight times and on his return had stopped to address gatherings at Elizabethtown, Brunswick, Maidenhead, Trenton, "Neshamine," and Abington. In Philadelphia, the *Mercury* said, he preached regularly twice a day. Once, in Germantown, he spoke to a group of five thousand; and the church was so crowded for his farewell address in Philadelphia on November 28 that, in order to reach his audience of ten thousand, he took his place upon a balcony on Society Hill. The next day he set out southward, accompanied as far as Chester by one hundred fifty people. There he preached to five thousand, to five thousand more at "Willings Town" (Wilmington, Delaware), to two thousand in New Castle and three thousand at Christiana Bridge. On Sunday, December 2, he spoke twice at Whiteclay Creek, to eight thousand people, three thousand of whom came on horseback and stood outdoors in the rain in order to hear him. From the South came further news: of preaching in Maryland, of the beginning of the orphanage in Georgia,[42] of collecting seventy pounds at Charleston.[43] In the spring of 1740 Whitefield returned to Pennsylvania, New Jersey, and New York to appeal for funds to support the orphanage.[44] On April 15 he addressed at one service eight thousand people, within the next week fifteen thousand at one time, and at another farewell sermon twenty thousand.[45] In one day he collected £138 sterling, and the northern trip as a whole brought in £450.[46] During this sojourn in Philadelphia Whitefield also laid plans for another project, a Negro school to be established on a 5000-acre plot of land "on the Forks of Delaware."[47] Everywhere his success was spectacular, and the *Mercury* faithfully recorded the phenomenon. From the New York *Weekly Journal*

40. For examples of book advertisements in the *Mercury* relating to the Whitefield revival and controversy, see Numbers 976, 1034, 1039, 1041, 1045, 1046, 1049, 1050, 1053, 1058, 1065, 1071, 1073, 1078, 1081, 1082, 1088, 1091, 1099, 1104, 1108.
41. *Mercury* 1039, 1040.
42. Franklin, in the *Autobiography* (355-356), explains that the first settlers in Georgia, "unable to endure the hardships of a new settlement, perished in numbers, leaving many helpless children unprovided for. The sight of their miserable situation inspir'd the benevolent heart of Mr. Whitefield with the idea of building an Orphan House there, in which they might be supported and educated."
43. *Mercury* 1042, 1053, 1059.
44. *Mercury* 1059.
45. *Mercury* 1059, 1060, 1064.
46. *Mercury* 1060, 1064.
47. *Mercury* 1060. This land was located in the triangle formed by the Delaware and what is now called the Lehigh River.

and from the *Gentleman's Magazine* came verses in his praise;[48] the New York *Gazette* reported the experience of a sceptic who, having once heard Whitefield speak, defended in writing both his ability and his sincerity.[49] In curiously roundabout fashion from South Carolina came the report that in Philadelphia Whitefield had "given new Life to Religion";[50] and in Boston one of his sermons drew, it was said, twenty-five to thirty thousand people to the Common.[51]

Meanwhile disagreement over Whitefield had broken out in the columns of the *Mercury*. When Jonathan Arnold, an itinerant preacher, attacked him, Magnus Falconar[52] stoutly came to his defense;[53] William Smith, the eminent New York attorney, was drawn into the conflict as an opponent of Arnold,[54] whom various anonymous articles in the *Mercury* also censured.[55] In the spring of 1740 both the *Pennsylvania Gazette* and the *Mercury* were involved in a local dispute over Whitefield.[56] It began when Franklin, at the request of William Seward, one of the revivalist's companions and attendants,[57] printed a statement that Whitefield's preaching had caused the "Assembly and Concert Room" in Philadelphia to be deserted. In the following issue a letter accused Seward of attempting to create a false impression of the effect of Whitefield's preaching and asserted also that news reports were doubling or tripling the number of Whitefield's hearers. Franklin stated in the same issue that he printed this letter to counteract the rumor that Whitefield had engaged all the printers not to publish anything against him.[58] Two weeks later "Tom Trueman," through the *Mercury*, defended the group which frequented the Concert Room; and from that point the argument drifted into irrelevancies. Meanwhile in New York the Anglican and Dutch churches closed their doors to Whitefield, though great crowds congregated in the Presbyterian church and in the fields to hear him.[59] At Charleston he was impeached by the Commissary's Court for not using the liturgy of the Church of England; nonetheless people flocked to his

48. *Mercury* 1040, 1050.
49. *Mercury* 1043.
50. *Mercury* 1065.
51. *Mercury* 1086.
52. Falconar was a Scot, a former "mariner," and at the moment a Philadelphia schoolmaster.
53. *Mercury* 1039.
54. *Mercury* 1042, 1045, 1046.
55. *Mercury* 1040, 1041-1042, 1049.
56. *Gazette* 594-598; *Mercury* 1064-1066.
57. A letter of Seward to his brother, published in *Mercury* 1060, explained his conversion to Wesleyanism and the reasons for his joining Whitefield on his second trip to Georgia. *Mercury* 1101 reported the death of Seward in Wales during one of Whitefield's journeys.
58. Compare Franklin's various comments upon Whitefield in the *Autobiography*.
59. *Mercury* 1043.

sermons.⁶⁰ In fact, the *Mercury* gave so strong an impression of Whitefield's triumph over all odds and all opponents that a certain "W.W." in a letter openly accused Bradford of partiality towards Whitefield. In a six-line "epigram" he contemptuously attacked both the preacher and his followers:⁶¹

> To the Reverend Mr. Whitefield, on his Preaching Faith Alone.
> Whitefield to what End do you preach,
> Since you have no good Works to teach?
> No Man e'er preach'd so much as you;
> Yet, more Good, many Preachers do,
> None e'er such Crowds of Hearers had
> And none so Few, that were not Mad.

Whatever was said about him, however, Whitefield continued to be "big news." Even during his absence abroad from 1741 to 1744 the *Mercury's* readers were constantly informed of his activities: of his journeys through England, Wales, and Scotland, preaching and collecting money for the Georgia orphanage,⁶² and of the quarrel between him and John Wesley.⁶³ A particularly good story came from Bath, where, according to the *Mercury,* Whitefield for once met his match; for when news arrived that the preacher "design'd to disturb the Water-drinkers there, it was resolv'd by Mr Nash in Council, to order the City Musick to keep Time with him in his open-air'd Conventicle, the Churches being very justly refused him."⁶⁴ As we follow Whitefield's story in the *Mercury* it appears either that Bradford's attitude towards him changed or, more probably, that the paper reflected a change in the popular attitude, perhaps the dying out of the first wave of religious enthusiasm or the strengthening of the opposition. By 1742 the *Mercury* began to show unmistakably the reaction against revivalism; for example, the suicide of a boy in Connecticut was attributed to the sermons he had heard, and the account of his death concluded: "What will the end of these Things be?"⁶⁵ From Boston came most disparaging reports of the extravagant behavior of the revivalist James Davenport, whose followers, it was said, "look'd more like a Company of Bacchanalians after a mad Frolick than sober Christians who had been worshiping God."⁶⁶

60. *Mercury* 1077.
61. *Mercury* 1094.
62. *Mercury* 1115, 1118, 1146, 1230, 1236.
63. *Mercury* 1126.
64. *Mercury* 1283.
65. *Mercury* 1164.
66. *Mercury* 1177, 1178. The quotation is from 1178. Davenport was mentioned a good many times in the *Mercury.*

Gilbert Tennent,[67] anxious because of the split within the Presbyterian Church over the teachings of Whitefield, expressed his grief for "such enthusiastical Fooleries";[68] while Whitefield, in turn, protested against Tennent's warmth of temper in treating with the Moravians.[69]

In the meantime there were mutterings about the orphanage in Georgia — that it was a "scandalous Bubble" and "a Cloak for Whitefield to extort Money from ignorant and unthinking People."[70] In 1744 the Presbyterian minister at Christiana renounced Whitefield's "gross Errors";[71] six months later Davenport retracted his enthusiastic teachings.[72] Indeed, according to the *Mercury*, when Whitefield returned to America near the close of 1744,[73] he faced much hostility: he was accused of causing division within the churches he visited and of affronting Harvard College;[74] the congregation at Cambridge, Massachusetts, decided not to let him preach;[75] and the attack on the orphanage continued,[76] supplemented by the charge that Whitefield believed in the motto "Ignorance the Mother of Devotion." On the other hand, defenders of the orphan house also arose,[77] and once again Whitefield preached to huge audiences.[78] At the very end of the *Mercury's* history appeared a well-reasoned argument against Whitefield, written by a person who called himself appropriately "Disinteresse Spectateur."[79] This essay, entitled "An Enquiry into the Cause of our present Animosities in Religion," expressed belief in Whitefield's good intentions but cast doubt upon his methods. By 1746 many an honest and intelligent American must have held such an opinion.

Nothing else in the *Mercury* shows so well the religious currents of the 'thirties and 'forties as the intense and long-continued interest in

---

67. Gilbert Tennent was the most distinguished son of William Tennent, Senior, kinsman of James Logan and founder of the "log college" at Neshaminy from which Princeton University developed. William and his four sons, all of them Presbyterian ministers, anticipated many of the teachings of Whitefield. Gilbert, after experience at New Brunswick and as an itinerant preacher, became minister of the Second Presbyterian Church of Philadelphia, the outgrowth of Whitefield's "New Building" congregation.

68. *Mercury* 1180.
69. *Mercury* 1220.
70. *Mercury* 1219, 1253.
71. *Mercury* 1259.
72. *Mercury* 1286.
73. *Mercury* 1298.
74. *Mercury* 1298, 1300.
75. *Mercury* 1306.
76. *Mercury* 1233, 1295, 1309, 1368. See also *Gazette* 755. The quotation comes from *Mercury* 1233.
77. *Mercury* 1314. See also *Gazette* 756, 757. In *Gazette* 910 appeared an abstract of the whole account from the establishment of the orphanage to January 1746, with affidavits and the seal of Savannah.
78. *Mercury* 1301, 1338, 1340.
79. *Mercury* 1360.

the person and teachings of Whitefield. Compared to him, Zinzendorf seems a minor figure; but Zinzendorf's connection with the colony of Pennsylvania was particularly intimate and for a brief time Bradford gave him considerable space. His wide renown is indicated by the fact that, almost a year before his coming to America, Bradford printed an account of his life, especially emphasizing his conversion to Moravianism.[80] Then, on December 3, 1741, the *Mercury* announced his arrival in New York and his setting out for the tract of land at the forks of the Delaware which the Moravians had purchased from Whitefield.[81] The activities of Zinzendorf during his year in Pennsylvania were, however, hardly mentioned in the *Mercury,* perhaps because of the tremendous opposition to his attempt to unite the various German sects. He was assailed, it has been said, by Samuel Blair, Christopher Sower, Gilbert Tennent, "and everyone else who could afford to print a pamphlet."[82] But in the summer of 1742 Bradford printed a book on Zinzendorf and the Moravian doctrine, "Intended," the advertisement said, "for a Summary of that Controversy, which at present is a Matter of Universal Speculation in this part of America."[83] In the same number in which this book was announced appeared news, in the form of an advertisement, of the breaking into and the alleged robbery of Radnor Township Church. When in the *Gazette* of August 26, Zinzendorf answered, under fourteen heads, charges against him which had been spread by an anonymous pamphlet, he likewise explained that his congregation, which had an arrangement for the use of the church alternately with another religious group, had entered it by force only because the key had been withheld. In the *Mercury* of September 2, however, Zinzendorf's arguments were attacked one by one, and even his right to the use of the church was disputed. After his departure at the end of 1742 suspicion and bad feeling lingered. When in a notice in the *Gazette* Peter Boehler[84] protested against the publication of unauthorized German-English translations of "Pieces" concerning the Moravians ("whereby the Brethren . . . are . . . misrepresented and misunderstood") and announced that in the future all legitimate articles would be signed by him, Zinzendorf's enemies used the *Mercury* to answer Boehler. Unjustly they accused him of trying to restrain freedom of the press and published certain letters purporting to be Zinzendorf's in parallel columns of German and English — as a

80. *Mercury* 1102.
81. This was the same tract which had been taken up in 1740 by Whitefield. The town of Nazareth had been established there before Zinzendorf's arrival.
82. G. H. Genzmer, "Zinzendorf," *D.A.B.* Blair was an associate of the Tennents and for a time minister of the Presbyterian church at Fagg's Manor. The German sects also were stubbornly opposed to unification.
83. *Mercury* 1176.
84. Boehler was a friend of both Whitefield and Zinzendorf and a leader among the Moravians. His letter appeared in *Gazette* 747.

warning, they said, against the principles of the Moravians.[85] Whereas the *Gazette* continued the controversy into the spring and summer with an argument between Boehler and Tennent,[86] the *Mercury* seems quickly to have lost interest in the conflict. Thus, though at best it reflects very inadequately one of the major religious movements of the day,[87] the *Mercury* shows once again in its intermittent discussions of Zinzendorf the news value of a name as well as the lively interest in religion which was characteristic of the time.

Innumerable other men as famous as these figured with equal or almost equal prominence in the pages of the *Mercury*. Like the Pretender and Whitefield some of them were good subjects in themselves and representatives of important movements or ideas. It is possible, for example, to trace in the *Mercury* in much detail the political career of Robert Walpole from the South Sea Bubble to his fall from power and his death. More interesting, the paper reflected unmistakably his increasing popularity through the 'twenties and early 'thirties and the waning of his political strength in the later 'thirties. Typically also it reported bits of personal news about him: that he was keeping open house at Houghton at a cost of £1500 a week or that, while hunting a stag at Richmond, he had fallen from his horse but fortunately had escaped injury.[88] There was news too of his family: of the raising of his eldest son to the peerage in 1723;[89] of the presentation to the king of his "new married Lady," the former Maria Skerrett;[90] of the diplomatic missions of his brother, Horatio Walpole;[91] and of "the grand Tour of Europe" made by another, more famous Horatio, Sir Robert's son.[92] The continuing public interest in the family of William Penn, even in those who had no connection with Pennsylvania, also indicated a natural

---

85. *Mercury* 1214. The charge against Zinzendorf suggested by these letters seems hardly more than that he had encouraged several young women to leave their families for lives of religious devotion. It was probably hoped, however, that some scandalous inferences would be drawn from them. A. G. Spangenberg (*The Life of . . . Count Zinzendorf*, 313) says that slanderous stories were circulated about him—for instance, that he had been banished from Germany because of vicious conduct and that Benigna, who accompanied him, was not his daughter, but a young woman whom he had seduced.

86. *Gazette* 753, 759, 760.

87. Possibly the apparent lack of interest in Zinzendorf as compared with Whitefield was due to the fact that the reform he was seeking to effect particularly concerned the up-colony German-speaking group rather than the people likely to be Bradford's customers. Moreover, Zinzendorf spent much of his time while in Pennsylvania on missionary journeys into remote districts and, unlike Whitefield, never attracted a great popular following.

88. *Mercury* 581, 619.

89. *Mercury* 191. Walpole refused the honor for himself because he did not wish to be relegated to the House of Lords.

90. *Mercury* 968.

91. *Mercury* 139, 227, 238, 240, 265, 309, 360, 926, etc.

92. *Mercury* 974.

curiosity. We hear alike of the conversion of Penn's granddaughter to the Church of England and of the marriage of one of his grandsons at "the Quakers-Meeting-House in Devonshire Square."[93] Eminent Friends, it is not surprising to note, were frequently referred to in the *Mercury:* for example, Andrew Pitt, a retired merchant, who was active in support of the Quakers' Tithe Bill;[94] Mrs. Miller of Edinburgh, "famous for her Industry and Improvement in home Manufactures";[95] and particularly Mrs. Drummond, the renowned and popular Quaker preacher.[96] An excellent anecdote linked the Pennsylvanian's interest in Quakers with the more sensational concern for a famous highwayman, Dick Turpin; the unexpectedly Robin-Hood-like tale appeared thus in the *Mercury:*[97]

> ... as Mr. Loan of Bristol and another Quaker, were coming over Hou[n]slow-heath, a man join'd them, and told them his name was Turpin; he rode some time in company with them, and coming near some of the fellows hanging in chains, he pointed to one of them and said, that would be his Fate; for he could trust no Body nor make his escape; besides he would never rest till he was reveng'd on the man that took his companion. Just as he said these words, he espyed a Gentleman with laced cloaths, and pointing to him cry'd, you get your money easily, I must speak with you, and taking his leave in a Complaisant manner, rode a full trot after the Gentleman.

From far and near came a constant flow of news of men celebrated for a variety of reasons. From London late in 1721 it was reported that Sir Isaac Newton, president of the Royal Society, was to be consulted about a perpetual-motion machine, and in the summer of 1723 appeared news of the death at Kensington "in a good old Age" of "that profound Mathematician."[98] Another scientist, Edmund Halley, was mentioned in 1728, when a scheme for determining longitude by "some difficult Stars" was laid before him, and several times in 1731 also his name appeared in the *Mercury*.[99] The most eminent musician of the day was Handel: in 1724 it was reported that "Their Highnesses the Princess Anne and Princess Carolina came on Monday last to St. Paul's Cathedral, and heard the famous Mr. Handel (their Master) perform upon

93. *Mercury* 216, 692.
94. *Mercury* 862, 870.
95. *Mercury* 661.
96. *Mercury* 834, 838, 846, 869, 887, 1243.
97. *Mercury* 923. See also Numbers 927, 1009 for other items on Turpin.
98. *Mercury* 101, 389.
99. *Mercury* 460, 604, 608, 624. See also Number 792.

the Organ."[100] Ten years later in celebration of the marriage of the Princess Royal "Mr. Handell's new Serenata" was performed before the royal family and "received with the greatest Applause; the Piece containing the most exquisite Harmony ever furnished from the Stage, and the Disposition of the Performers being contrived in a very grand and magnificent Manner."[101] Bradford's readers were likewise informed of the triumphs of the incomparable Farinelli: "the first Voice in the World" entertained the English royal family in 1734; two years later the French court was enraptured by the great singer, the king presenting him with a gold snuff-box with the royal picture set in diamonds; and the following year it was reported that Farinelli was to go to Spain for the ensuing season.[102] Thence at the beginning of 1738 came the news that he had had knighthood bestowed upon him by Philip and been given the king's picture set around with diamonds, as well as other gifts from the queen and the crown prince.[103]

More briefly the *Mercury* mentioned various other celebrities, announcing that Dr. Tindal, the great deist, had willed to Eustace Budgell £2000 and the manuscript of *Christianity as Old as the Creation*,[104] that Dr. Chambers had dedicated to King George his *Universal Dictionary*,[105] that Mrs. Oldfield's life was "despaired of,"[106] that Laurence Eusden would probably be succeeded as poet laureate by Stephen Duck,[107] that Mr. Nash had entered Bath ahead of the Prince and Princess of Wales in order to give proper notice of their arrival,[108] that "the poet Voltaire" had left the Hague for Berlin on a diplomatic mission,[109] that Eustace Budgell had committed suicide by jumping out of a boat

100. *Mercury* 255.
101. *Mercury* 752.
102. *Mercury* 784, 884, 922.
103. *Mercury* 940. The last reference in the *Mercury* to Farinelli is an error. Number 1114 says that letters from Spain advise "that the famous Signior Farinelli has been executed there for the Murder of one of his Servants." There is no doubt whatsoever that Farinelli lived until 1782 and died in Bologna. There Dr. Burney made his acquaintance in 1770. (See *A General History of Music*, IV, 385 n.) Moreover, so far as I can discover, there is no evidence of his having been implicated in such a crime as the *Mercury* describes; on the contrary, he is generally spoken of as a man of irreproachable character.

In connection with Farinelli it is interesting to note that the *Mercury* at least once reflects the reaction against Italian opera in England. Number 1158 mentioned the opening of the opera season at the Haymarket at a cost of £16,000 for six months. There followed the remark: "Is not Britain then in a fine State, when, notwithstanding our Taxes, we can fling away such a Sum on a Parcel of squeaking, capering, fiddling Italian Eunuchs, and Foreign Buffoons?"

104. *Mercury* 724.
105. *Mercury* 431.
106. *Mercury* 574.
107. *Mercury* 582. The prophecy was incorrect; Colley Cibber became poet laureate.
108. *Mercury* 1004.
109. *Mercury* 1248.

under London Bridge and Nathaniel Mist's stormy career had come to an end at Boulogne,[110] and that Bartholomew Green, the pioneer printer of the Boston *News Letter,* was dead.[111] Others besides Lord Spencer and Penn's grandchildren probably made the pages of the *Mercury* chiefly because of an ancestor's fame; we hear, for example, that the daughter of "the late Mr. Secretary Addison, a young Lady of great Accomplishments, and 70000 l. Fortune," was about to marry; and that Mr. Richard Cromwell, grandson of the Protector, chose for his wedding the day on which Oliver was born and died, the anniversary of the battles of Dunbar and Worcester, and the place "from whence the Royal Martyr was forced out upon the Scaffold to lose his Head."[112] The paper reported the death of Sir Richard Steele, and Pope's appointment of Bolingbroke and Marchmont as his executors.[113] It reprinted also a famous anecdote of Pope's last illness:[114]

> It is reported of Mr. Pope, that (upon seeing his two Phycisians differ in opinion as to the Medicines proper to be prescrib'd for his Distemper) he burst out into this Exclamation, *How justly doth the Lord punish me for having satiriz'd Dunces, in condemning me to die by two?*

Jonathan Swift probably received more attention in the *Mercury* than any other literary man, but not because of his accomplishments as a writer. A news item from Dublin under date of August 7, 1736,[115] shows how genuine and lasting was his popularity in the country of his "exile":

> Last Tuesday the Society of Wooll Combers of this City walk'd in Procession thro' most of the principal Streets of the Town. They made a most beautiful Appearance, being every one dress'd in a handsome Tye-Wig made of the Whitest Wooll, with Sashes hung over their right Shoulders of fine comb'd Wooll, colour'd blue, purple, red and white; such Persons as wore their Hats on had Wool in them of various Colours, which look'd as well as Ostriches Feathers. They made a particular Procession to the House of the Rev. Dr. Swift, D.S.P.D. and desir'd they might have the Honour of seeing that glorious and worthy Patriot of his Country; As soon as he appeared, they cry'd out, *Long live the Draper, and*

110. *Mercury* 917, 934.
111. *Mercury* 683.
112. *Mercury* 913, 203.
113. *Mercury* 520, 1287.
114. *Mercury* 1302.
115. *Mercury* 883.

> *Prosperity to Ireland.* After many Huzzas they pass'd in Review before the Dean, two and two, making the profoundest Reverences to him as they march'd by, which the Dean was pleas'd to return. Then they proceeded to the Bull-Head in Fishamble-Street, where they had a most elegant Dinner, at which they drank several loyal Healths, the worthy Dean's, all disinterested Patriots, and Prosperity to the Manufactures of Ireland.

Enlightening also are two anecdotes of 1737 when Swift was engaged in fierce opposition to Archbishop Boulter's plans for the reform of the Irish currency:[116]

> Dublin, Sept. 13. We have received several Anonymous Letters, concerning the displaying of a Flag on St. Patrick's Steeple, the muffling the Bells, which rung mournfully all Day, the Sexton of St. Patricks being sent for by a Tipstaff, the hanging of the Linen-Hall with black Bays, and putting the Signs of the Streets in Mourning, with the retiring of the Merchants to a Tavern, and their drinking long Life to Dean Swift, and Confusion to the Enemies of Ireland and the burning of an Effigy at the Linen-Hall; but Yesterday being an Improper Day, we could not take Time to inquire into the Particulars. All that we can now say, is, that the Citizens were greatly alarmed when they saw the black Flag up, imagining that our Patriot, who had been ill, was dead; many of them ran in great Consternation to the Church, where they learned that the Dean lived, and to their great Consolation was happily recovered from his late Illness; the Occasion of these Signs of Mourning, we hear, was on account of the lowering of the Gold. . . .

> October 13. We hear from Dublin, that the Reduction of Money has occasion'd a general Dissatisfaction in the People, and several Mobs in the City, which, on a publick Occasion, at the Lord Mayor's, the Primate imputed to Dean Swift; to which the Dean reply'd with great Indignation, that the Reduction was an iniquitous Job; which he oppos'd with Argument and Reason, and not with Power and Violence; that if he had held up his Finger the People would have torn him (the Primate) to Pieces; but that he did not desire that a Person in his High Station should die a Violent Death.

Finally, just before the *Mercury's* close, came news of Swift's death:[117]

116. *Mercury* 935, 940.
117. *Mercury* 1358.

The "Mercury" as a Mirror of the Times

Dublin, October 22. Saturday last died, the Rev. Jonathan Swift, D.D. Dean of St. Patrick's Dublin; the greatest Genius that perhaps this or any other Age or Nation ever produced; but for some Years past, he has been entirely deprived of Memory, and by Degrees fell into a perfect Insensibility.

Another famous Irishman, Bishop Berkeley, won a place in the *Mercury*. Early in 1729 Bradford announced that the philosopher had sailed for Rhode Island with his bride and a library of 20,000 books; not quite four years later appeared the news that he had given his farm in Rhode Island, worth about £3000, to Yale College, and several months thereafter came the explanation that the income from the gift was intended to support two graduate students, the recipients to be determined by competitive examinations in Greek and Latin.[118] The notorious Tom Bell, the colonies' most accomplished swindler and impersonator, also appeared in the *Mercury;* perhaps he was preaching "in the New Way" in the neighborhood of Plymouth, Massachusetts,[119] or perhaps he was extricating himself from jail "without the Ceremony of the Law,"[120] the second of which activities he had developed to the point of extraordinary skill.[121] Along with the doings of philosophers and sharpers, the private affairs and unofficial acts of royalty had their timeless appeal. Number 327, for example, presented this tidbit: "The Dutchess of Orleans is not with Child as reported." When White's Coffee House was burned in 1733, King George and the Prince of Wales were there on foot for more than an hour and distributed twenty-five guineas among the firemen and guards;[122] when the Princess of Wales had the measles, the street in front of the royal residence was covered with straw to prevent unnecessary noise;[123] at the battle of Dettingen the Duke of Cumberland, having previously noticed the bravery of a wounded gendarme, refused to be treated until the other man had been taken care of.[124] From Paris came an attractive story about young Louis XV:[125]

> Our young Monarch playing at Ticktack lately with one of his Courtiers, there arose some Difference about a Cast, which after they had argued a while, without being able to agree about it, his Majesty was pleased to refer the Matter in Dispute

---

118. *Mercury* 474, 671, 692.
119. *Mercury* 1237.
120. *Mercury* 1223.
121. Other references to Tom Bell's ever-lively actions occur in Numbers 1205, 1227, 1228, 1246, 1252, 1254, 1265, 1279, 1289. As America's most sensational criminal, Bell figures in nearly every colonial newspaper.
122. *Mercury* 708.
123. *Mercury* 865.
124. *Mercury* 1239.
125. *Mercury* 153.

to the Judgment of the Standers by, but they all stood mute; whereupon the King said I find I am in the Wrong since no body speaks.

During the same year a similarly human anecdote about the King of Poland was published:[126]

> ... An Accident remarkable enough happen'd to his Majesty within a League of Gorlitz.... His Postillions to avoid a bad Road, turned into a Field, where the Farmer, who had been manuring it, stop'd them, laid hold of the Reins of the Horses, and threatened to hew the Coach Wheels in Pieces, with an Axe he had in his Hand, if they did not return into the Road; upon which two of his Majesty's Pages who followed the Coach began to abuse the poor Peasant, and the Postilions were going to knock him down, when the King, hearing the Noise, charged his Pages not to hurt a Hair of his Head, order'd him some Money, and bid his Postilions turn off into the High-Road, saying, That the poor Man was in the Right to defend his Property, and that a King had no more Authority than the meanest of his Subjects, to ruin any Body without Cause.

To indicate even in summary fashion all the notables whose names gave lustre to the columns of the *Mercury* would be a very lengthy task. In addition, the paper reflected other popular interests; for instance, accounts of sensational crimes must always have been acceptable to Bradford's readers. A particularly lurid type of story, of which a good many examples appeared in the course of the *Mercury's* history, is illustrated by the following item from Oporto:[127]

> A small English Man of War arrived at Lisbon, some Days ago, which met at Sea a Portugueze Vessel driving with only two Men in it, who relate, that being arrived at the Island of Madera from thence and steering toward another Island, they mis'd it, and wander'd for forty five Days in the Ocean, till their Provision being spent, they were reduced to the Necessity of eating six of their Fellow Sailors....

The Italian Count de la Torre also afforded Bradford's customers a chill of horror, first in the story of the murder of his wife to make room for a marriage to one of the several women he had seduced, and then in the following diabolical tale:[128]

126. *Mercury* 147.
127. *Mercury* 9. Tales of cannibalism also appear in Numbers 30, 913, 917, 936, 1141, 1320.
128. *Mercury* 134, 135.

The "Mercury" as a Mirror of the Times

> Riding out one Day in a Wood with a Friend, he met two Capuchin Fryars, upon which said the Count to his Friend, You shall see me send one of these Fryars to Paradice, the other to Hell: Upon which he set himself to Work in the Manner following; He clap'd his Dagger to the Brest of one, bidding him renounce the Trinity, or he would kill him. The Capuchin readily submitted; then the Count pierced him through and through. He made the like Proposition to the other Fryer, who (seeing the Fate of his Brother) would not consent to the Count's Proposition, and so was killed on the spot. The Count then turning to his Friend, Did I not tell you (said he) that I would send one of these Fryars to Heaven, the other to Hell?

From Ireland came news of the trial of a man who had killed his maid-servant for resisting his attempt to enforce the old custom of *droit du seigneur*;[129] and from England was reported the murder of Sir John Goodere by his brother, who had been cut off in the baronet's will with a meagre £700 a year.[130] The *Mercury* printed the usual ugly stories of the murders of bastard children by their mothers, and other sordid commonplaces.[131] Occasionally there was a tale in which pathos was the dominant note, as, for example, in the episode of the little Welsh girl of eight who was acquitted of the murder of her brother and sister.[132] The child lived on the coast in Carmarthenshire, where she had been nourished on stories of the cruelty of the Spaniards and the perpetual danger of their landing on that shore. One day when the children were alone a severe thunderstorm came up; frightened, imagining that the Spaniards had come, the child seized a hedging-bill to kill herself. When the other children cried to be killed first, the older girl did as they asked and then seriously wounded herself. Failing in strength or courage, however, she ran out of the cottage to throw herself into the river, but was saved from death by the neighbors.

Certainly the most famous of all the murder cases discussed by the *Mercury* was the episode of John Porteous, later immortalized in the opening chapters of *The Heart of Midlothian*. The paper's first account of it concerned the trial:[133]

> Edinburgh, July 6 Yesterday John Porteous, late one of the Captains of the City-Guard, was brought from Prison to the High Court of Justiciary, when the Indictment against him was

129. *Mercury* 453.
130. *Mercury* 1112, 1114, 1125. See also the book advertisement in Number 1149.
131. *Mercury* 127, 136, 264, etc.
132. *Mercury* 1181.
133. *Mercury* 876.

read, setting forth, *inter alia,* That on the 14th of April, he, in the Course of Rotation with the other Officers of the Corps, commanded a Body of about 70 Men, at the execution of Andrew Wilson; after the said Wilson had been hang'd 'till he was dead, he, without any just Cause or necessary Occasion, ordered his Men to fire among a Croud of People innocently and lawfully assembled; and some of his Guard having fired (as he apprehended) over the Heads of the Multitude, he with Threats and Imprecations, call'd, *Lower your Pieces and be damn'd!* That he, levelling his own Piece at Charles Husband, most wickedly and murderously fired at him, whereby he received four Wounds, of which he died on the Spot: That in the Street call'd the Bow, he ordered his Men to face about and fire, without any just Cause or Occasion, and also fired again himself there. To all which, and the other Facts therein set forth, he pleaded Not Guilty, and put himself upon Trial.

Then followed news of the sentencing of Porteous to hanging, the Queen's reprieve, the lynching, the search for the murderers, the threatened disgrace of Edinburgh, and the Duke of Argyll's sturdy defense — in all, a dramatic and well-told story.[134]

Probably even more interesting to Bradford's local customers, however, was the case of Evan Jones. In the *Mercury* of June 16, 1737, appeared news of the death three days earlier of a gullible apprentice at the hands of "some People pretending to be Free-masons," at what ostensibly was an initiation ceremony. In the same paper an advertisement, signed by the local Masonic lodge, disclaimed all connection with what it spoke of as a spurious group which had imposed upon several people's credulity. The following week Bradford printed the result of the coroner's inquest, which found that the young man's death had been caused by burning spirits accidentally thrown upon him in the course of the mock rites. In the same number, however, appeared the news that after the inquest further evidence, tending to show that the death was intentional, had been submitted to the magistrates. Six weeks later — whether to make capital of public interest or to express indirectly his own opinions we cannot be sure — Bradford printed a long article from the *London Magazine* for April attacking the Masons, particularly for their secrecy, and imagining them to be at the bottom of the Porteous affair.[135] On February 1 of the following year came the trial of Evan

---

134. *Mercury* 878, 879, 882, 886, 912, 915, 916, 935, 942. Because of Argyll's defense of the city Edinburgh celebrated his birthday. (See *Mercury* 998.)

135. *Mercury* 918. Bradford said that this article was inserted by request. Eleven days after it appeared in the *Mercury* it was reprinted also in the New York

Jones, a chemist, and two other men for their part in the alleged murder. "There was the greatest Throng of People to hear the Trial," the *Mercury* said, "which perhaps ever appear'd at any Trial in this Province."¹³⁶ Jones was found guilty of manslaughter and branded in the hand; one of the other men was found guilty but pardoned; the third was acquitted. The next week a letter to the *Mercury* cast doubt upon the evidence given at the trial by a man named Tackerbury and implied that Benjamin Franklin had encouraged, though he had not assisted at, the mock initiation. The *Gazette* of February 15 contained a lengthy self-defense by Franklin, which, however, avoided the main issues raised in the *Mercury* and was convincingly demolished in the succeeding number of Bradford's paper.¹³⁷ There the matter dropped, but hardly before Philadelphians in particular and the *Mercury's* readers in general had presumably enjoyed a thrill.

Stories of crime less violent than murder were also plentifully supplied to Bradford's customers. There were, for example, frequent tales of piracy and highway robbery.¹³⁸ Bradford seems to have preferred to the more conventional story, however, episodes with an ironic twist: for example, the account of some men who robbed a group which included a Jesuit, and who — since the Jesuit had no other valuables — compelled him to give them absolution for the crime they were committing.¹³⁹ Other stories illustrate the same tendency — for example, these:¹⁴⁰

> A Young Lady living at Blackheath, having frequently appeared in a Hat, plentifully set with Bristol Stones; it was observed by some Sharpers who taking it to be loaded with

Gazette (Number 615, August 15). As early as December 15, 1730, the *Mercury* published an unsympathetic article on the Masons; the paper appears consistently to have opposed the organization. Freemasonry was under fire in many parts of Europe and America in the 1730's.

136. *Mercury* 945.
137. In effect the writer in the *Mercury* disputed Franklin's assertion that he had protested against and tried to prevent the initiation. He asked (1) why, if Franklin so earnestly opposed the initiation as he insisted that he had, he kept and passed around among his acquaintances for several days before the fatal episode the mock oath which was to be used at the ceremony; and (2) why, if he wanted to warn the young man, he found no opportunity to do so between Saturday and Monday. These charges, of course, were not intended to imply that Franklin was involved in the actual crime, but they suggest unmistakably that he did not try, as he had asserted, to prevent the practical joke which led to the tragedy. In connection with this episode it is worth noting that only seven weeks after the *Mercury* had thus attacked Franklin appeared the *Craftsman* essay about the Masons which Benjamin Lay accused Bradford of having faked. (See above, p. 107.)
138. *Mercury* 13, 20, 53, 90, 108, 136, 143, 183, 221, 222, 233, 244, 339, 342, 348, 371, 444, 566, etc.
139. *Mercury* 882.
140. *Mercury* 98, 154.

more valuable Ornaments, found Means a few Days ago to steal it. But discovering upon Examination how they were deceived, they returned the Hat with all its Appurtenances a Night or two after down the Chimney.

Some Sharpers . . . contrived lately a new Way to get a Croud about them, two of them laid a sham Wager, pursuant to which one undertook to lie on his Back for the Space of three Hours, with his Eyes open towards the Sun, this Scene was acted in the Street called St. Andres des Artes, and in an Instant drew an immense Croud of Spectators, whose Pockets, it seems, were as open as the Eyes of the Imposter, for few escaped losing either Money, Watches, Snuff Boxes, &c.

Another story with a quirk in its ending concerned a Savoyard who bought a rope for six sols: when a friend told him that he had been overcharged, he claimed and got back from the merchant two sols; then he returned home with his rope and used it as he had intended — to hang himself.[141] And there was the entertaining story of the quick-witted Quaker riding a jade, who tricked a highwayman by throwing his purse over a hedge and then swapping horses and galloping off while the robber went after the money.[142]

Confessions and executions were occasionally featured in the *Mercury*. Most of the confessions make dull reading today,[143] since they consist of conventional moralizing and dying exhortations to repentance; but one at least was the remarkable, if specious, apologia of a certain George Manly, who was executed for murder at Wicklow, Ireland, and whose dying speech ran thus:[144]

My Friends,
You assemble to see — What? — A Man take a Leap into the the Abyss of Death. Look and you shall see me go with as much Courage as Curtius, when he leapt into the Gulph to save his Country from Destruction. — What then will you see of me? — You say that no Man without Virtue can be courageous. — You see I am courageous. — You'll say I have kill'd a Man. — Marlborough kill'd his Thousands, and Alexander his Milions. — Marlb. and Alex. and many others who have done the like, are famous in History for great Men. — But, I kill'd one solitary Man. — Ay, that's the Case. — One solitary Man. — I'm a little Murderer, and must be hang'd. Marlborough and

---

141. *Mercury* 564.
142. *Mercury* 886.
143. Examples occur in Numbers 49, 127, 141, 688-689.
144. *Mercury* 976.

Alexander plundered Countries. — They were great Men: I ran in Debt with the Ale-Wife, I must be hang'd.

Now, my Friends, I have drawn a Parallel between two of the greatest Men that ever liv'd, and my self; but these were Men of former Days. Now I'll speak a Word of some of the present Days: How many Men were lost in Italy and upon the Rhine during the last War, for settling a King in Poland. Both Sides could not be in the Right; they are great Men; but I kill'd a solitary Man, I'm a little Fellow. The King of Spain takes our Ships, plunders our Merchants, kills and tortures our Men; but what of all that; what he does is good; he's a great Man, he is cloathed in Purple, his Instruments of Murder are bright and shining, mine was but a rusty Gun; and so much for Comparison.

Now, I would fain know what Authority there is in Scripture for a rich Man to murder, to plunder, to torture and ravage whole Countries; and what Law it is that condemns a poor Man to Death for killing a solitary Man, or for stealing a solitary Sheep to feed his Family. But bring the Matter closer to our Country: What is the Difference between runing in a poor Man's Debt, and by the Power of Gold, or any other Priviledge, preventing him from obtaining his Right and clapping a Pistol to a Man's Breast and taking from him his Purse? Yet the one shall thereby obtain a Coach, and Honours, and Titles, &c. The other — What? — A Cart and a Rope.

From what I have said, my Brethren, you may, perhaps imagine I am harden'd. But believe me, I am fully convinced of my Follies, and acknowledge the just Judgment of God has overtaken me; I have no Hopes but from the Merits of my Redeemer, who I hope will have Mercy on me, as he knows that Murder was far from my Heart, and what I did was thro' Rage and Passion, being provok'd thereto by the Deceased.

Take Warning my dear Comrades: Think! O think! — What wou'd I now give that I had lived another Life.

Some items reported the savage punishments in vogue in the eighteenth century, such as burning at the stake or breaking on the wheel,[145] and there was a grim account of a presumed murderer who, since he would not speak, was crushed to death by the placing of more and more weight upon the board under which his body lay.[146] Several stories are reminders that executions were still public entertainment: for

145. *Mercury* 25, 184, 602.
146. *Mercury* 839.

example,[147] "... the same Day two persons Convicted of Blasphemy had their Hands cut off, their Tongues bored thro' and were afterwards burnt alive. This Execution was performed in the Place De Greve, and the like having not been seen for many Years, there was such a Concourse of people that three Persons were Crushed to Death in the Croud." Crimes of sexual perversion were often reported in the *Mercury,* especially a veritable epidemic of sodomy which broke out in the Netherlands in 1730 and led to many public executions.[148] A particularly unpleasant superstition was illustrated at one execution; several people requested that their necks might be stroked by the hand of the dying man as he swung in the noose so that the sweat of his death-agony might reduce the wens with which they were afflicted.[149]

The credulity of the age is fortunately, however, not always so disagreeably manifested. Though there are tales of witchcraft,[150] Bradford also printed more entertaining news of a servant girl who put a love-philtre into her sweetheart's ale,[151] of the discovery of a merman at Brest and of a mermaid near Exeter,[152] of a "Female Prophetess" at Torburgh who had taken neither food nor drink for nine months,[153] of an apparition in Perthshire and a vampire in a Hungarian village.[154] There were unbelievable or almost unbelievable stories of old age: of a woman born in the last year of Elizabeth's reign who lived until 1725 and of an Irishman who at the age of 119 took a girl a hundred years his junior as his wife.[155] An account, admittedly "of a very extraordinary Nature," concerned the death at 117 years of the very man who, he insisted, had been the executioner of Charles I.[156]

Monstrosities were also a staple among the sensational items in the paper: for example, an eagle with two heads, which was found in Mexico and sent as a present to the king of Spain, or a conglomerate animal — mouse, horse, ass, rabbit, camel, and heifer! — which John

---

147. *Mercury* 25. An even more grisly account of an execution—this one in England for treason—appeared in Number 1216. See also the sentence of Christopher Layer in Number 179. On the other hand, a very popular type of story concerned the person hanged for a crime who survived his "execution." Such stories appeared in Numbers 264, 367, 881, for example. There is also the tale of a woman whose husband was a prodigal who, with the aid of a confederate, extorted money by "hanging" herself (*Mercury* 650). Another grotesque tale concerned a tom-tit who built his nest and raised his family on the shoulder of a body hanging in chains (*Mercury* 871).
148. *Mercury* 134, 167, 297, 355, 559, 562, 567, 574, 585, 1007, 1208, 1212.
149. *Mercury* 887.
150. *Mercury* 345, 596.
151. *Mercury* 345.
152. *Mercury* 320, 965.
153. *Mercury* 348.
154. *Mercury* 591, 650.
155. *Mercury* 293, 878.
156. *Mercury* 1210.

Saunders exhibited in Philadelphia in 1743.[157] More often human monstrosities figured in the news, of which the following item is a typical example:[158]

> Letters from Lisbon give an Account of three monstrous Births which lately happen'd there the like of which perhaps was never heard of; the first was a beautiful young Lady, Rich, and the only Child of her Parents, who suffer'd a large Water Dog to lye with her, by which she conceived, and was delivered of 3 Monsters, which had Shoulders, Claws and Head like a Dog, and from the Middle downwards like a Man. Another Woman was also delivered of three Monsters, two dead, and one alive, their Heads and the fore parts of their Bodies like Monkeys with a long Bushy Tail; that which came alive was stifled in a Pan of hot Water, their Pictures were drawn and set up to Publick View. A third Woman was delivered of a dead Child, whose Back was gnaw'd by five Serpents, which came alive into the World with it, and leap'd up and down the Room, which so affrighted the Midwife and others present, as made them run out; but the Husband took Courage, and enter'd the Room with a Stick and destroyed them.

A similar interest in unusual, though not necessarily abnormal, natural phenomena was displayed in the *Mercury*. The paper reported, for instance, that a "Land Tortoise" supposed to have been there since the time of Laud lived in the Bishop of London's garden, and spoke of the arrival in London from the East Indies of "a most wonderful Creature call'd a Rhinoceros, or Unicorn, weighing at least twenty hundred weight, though not yet three Years old, loaded with a Coat of Mail that is by Nature Pistol-Ball Proof."[159] From Vienna came this story: "The court continues Heron-hunting at Laxenburg, where one was lately taken which had a Ring about the Foot, engrav'd with the Name of Ferdinand III. and the Year 1651. The Emperor let it fly again, after having put another Ring about its Foot, with the Name of Charles VI and the Year 1723."[160] In 1727 the *Mercury* advertised that "The Lyon King of Beasts" would shortly be taken away from Philadelphia and that those who were interested should make haste to see it — at a cost of one

---

157. *Mercury* 225, 1243.
158. *Mercury* 169. See also Numbers 211, 249, 441, 901, etc. Number 451 told of a living animal that popped out of a vein during bleeding. Stories of multiple births and similar infrequent occurrences also appeared — for example, in Numbers 367, 383, 571, 785, 874, 907, 912, 988, 1222.
159. *Mercury* 168, 1094.
160. *Mercury* 195.

shilling a person; almost five years later from Boston came news that the lion had died there, but that its body was still on view.[161] In 1744, another exotic animal was being shown in Philadelphia, a "Beautiful Creature, but surprizingly fierce, called a Leopard: His Extraction half a Lion and half a Pardeal."[162]

Flora as well as fauna evidently interested the *Mercury's* readers. It was reported, for instance, that an English gardener had gone to Holland to learn how the Dutch had naturalized "the Pine Apple (a famous West-India Fruit)" and from Leyden came news of a rare plant, supposed to be what tempted Eve, and so beautiful that "it ravishes the Sight, and raises the other Senses almost to an Extacy."[163] In 1729 several issues of the *Mercury* devoted space to "the great Aloe, which blossoms but once in an Hundred Years,"[164] of which one account is especially interesting:[165]

> On Thursday Night there was a great Meeting of Gardeners and other curious Persons again at Mr. Cowell's at Hoxton, for the farther Observation of that Curiosity in Nature, called the Cereus, or Torch Thistle: The Meeting, it seems, was occasioned by the extrodinary Observation made some time before, by some Learned Gentlemen, with their Microscopes and other Glasses, at which time such a strange Appearance was seen of the Working of Nature, in the Flower opening it self, as was most surprizing to those Gentlemen . . . .
>
> The Gentlemen that came at this time, were likewise furnished with several Kinds of Glasses, and some, as we hear, came prepared to be disappointed, nor fully believing that the Motion was possible to be so visible to the Eye as had been said in Publick.
>
> But on the contrary, the whole Company was surprized when the unaccountable Phœnomenon, or Apperance, shewed itself; for that about half an Hour after 6 in the Evening, the Bud on the Branch next adjoining to that Blossom which blow'd began apparently to swell, and in half an Hour more, the Twilight being wholly shut in, the outmost Leaves opened one by one; some time after that, the small Epices, or Capilary Leaves, (which are so many as not to be numbered) began to move like a little Army of Men, which being drawn up in a

---

161. *Mercury* 400, 631. In the report of the lion's death printed in the *Pennsylvania Gazette* (Number 165) it was said that the animal had been exhibited all over North America.
162. *Mercury* 1293.
163. *Mercury* 248, 925.
164. *Mercury* 508.
165. *Mercury* 515. See also Numbers 543, 565.

The "Mercury" as a Mirror of the Times

close Orb or Circle, had received the Word of Command to extend themselves every Way to a certain Distance.

These small Leaves compose the Body of the Flower when it is fully opened, and being of various Colours, place themselves in such good Order, as no Artist could imitate, for making or casting the Shades of the Flower, which by 10 o'Clock was fully blown out, and in the Morning shut itself up again in the same Order.

It is observable that the Flowers blow in their exact Order, one every Night, and duly sequent to one another as they grow upon the Stalks, There are about seven Flowers already blown, and are 6 more yet to blow; so that this Rarity will be seen for the most Part of the Season, but all the Artists in the World cannot make it hold any longer, unless more Branches should shoot out.

What Appearance of Fruit, or what Kind of Fruit it may yield, we have not yet heard; but if any Thing of that Kind shews itself, and should be very Curious, we are promised an Exact Account of it.

Bradford's customers were also made acquainted from time to time with new inventions and scientific investigations. Perpetual-motion machines seem particularly to have occupied the ingenious of the age,[166] but there were also experiments with a process for converting forged iron into steel, engines for pumping water, clocks that would run without winding, a machine to make ribbons (which Paris feared would ruin its weavers), a "Wind Gun" that fired thirty-seven times without reloading, a device "for preventing of House breaking," which "rings a Bell, fires a Pistol, and strikes a Light," a pair of boots on which a man might cross a river without boat or bridge, a mechanical music-box, a "Chaise that travels without Horses" and goes forty miles a day "with very little Trouble to the Rider," and a "flying Warlike Machine" that bears a heavy armament and is so strong that it can attack "the most complex Phalanx."[167] This last invention, the *Mercury* took pains to point out, was rejected by the British government because it could not "be long preserved from the Enemy; and . . . if it should become General, it would be of no Effect. . . . Several Princes having refused the like murderous Schemes, it may be concluded, that the present Way of making War being look'd upon sufficiently cruel, it would not be consistent with the Honour of any Prince to use Means for making it more destructive."[168] A few news items referred to medical or surgical experiments;

---

166. *Mercury* 101, 188, 243.
167. *Mercury* 175, 198, 245, 296, 319, 902, 959, 989, 1168, 1252.
168. *Mercury* 1258.

Mrs. Mapp, "the Bonesetter," and Dr. Chevalier Taylor, who was said to have cured many cases of cataract, were mentioned.[169] In the mid-'thirties Mrs. Mapp performed some cures in the presence of Sir Hans Sloane at the Grecian Coffee House, and both she and Dr. Taylor were made the subject of a play entitled *The Husband's Relief*, which was given before them at Lincoln's Inn Fields. There were constant references to inoculation for smallpox, nearly all of them favorable to it;[170] there was an account of a young Scottish woman who suffered from a mysterious illness which evidently resembled sleeping sickness;[171] and there were various allusions, often ironic, to the venereal diseases.[172] Though we read of a gravedigger who was indicted for exhuming and selling a body to an anatomist, we hear also of experiments made by a group of young scientists on the body of a malefactor hanged at Tyburn and of a series of wax figures made by a professor of anatomy and exhibited in the Strand to illustrate the muscular and circulatory systems and other features of the human body.[173]

The *Mercury* reminds us too that in the eighteenth century exploration still went forward. The paper told of an expedition sent out by the Royal Academy of Sciences at Paris to the North Pole "to discover the true Form of the Earth,"[174] and of another to Peru for the purpose of making astronomical and geographical discoveries.[175] In 1740 a Russian explorer was reported trying to find a passage to China and Japan along the northern coast of Siberia; much later, the arrival of Captain Behring's expedition at Kamchatka after perilous adventures was announced, and shortly thereafter the paper spoke of the anxiety felt by the Dutch merchants over Russia's interest in the Northeast Passage.[176] Nor was the wealth of the Indies a mere figure of speech to readers of the *Mercury;* we learn of the arrival at the Bank of England of gold from the West Indies, at Cadiz of five ships from the Caribbean bearing "Eight Millions of Dollars, Tobacco, Snuff, Brazil-Wood," and at Lisbon of a treasure fleet from South America bringing gold and diamonds, sugar and hides.[177]

The more intellectual readers of the *Mercury* must have been particularly impressed by other types of news. For them perhaps Bradford

169. *Mercury* 833, 878, 896, etc. These were two of the most famous quacks of the eighteenth century.
170. *Mercury* 152, 441, etc.
171. *Mercury* 276.
172. *Mercury* 709, 915. References to venereal disease and advertisements of alleged cures are noticeably fewer in the *Mercury* than in British papers of the period.
173. *Mercury* 176, 597, 997.
174. *Mercury* 873, 883. Possibly 905 referred to the same expedition.
175. *Mercury* 989.
176. *Mercury* 1074, 1258, 1274.
177. *Mercury* 940, 79, 707.

included such items as that Harvard College had received the gift of a double microscope, "a large and exquisite Armillary Sphere," and "a very costly Orrery," the last of these being at the time unique in America; that Yale College, not to be outdone, was receiving from London "Mathematical Instruments" valued at £55; or that the New York Assembly and the Governor had passed an act to encourage the establishment of a public school in New York City for instruction in Latin, Greek, and mathematics.[178] No doubt some readers were interested in the report that for the first time in three centuries a woman, Laura Maria Kathrina Barsi, was defending a "philosophical disputation" at Bologna to qualify for the doctor's degree.[179] In 1733 the *Mercury* announced that the Royal Academy of France would award an annual prize of four thousand livres for the best essay on a topic proposed each year by the Academy, and in 1737 it reported that Alexander Stuard, M.D., physician to the queen of England, had won that year's prize for an essay upon muscular motion.[180] There were many accounts of the unearthing in various parts of Europe of Roman antiquities — weapons, coins, statues, and pavements[181] — and of other archeological and literary finds as well, for example, some silver coins, presumably of the kingdom of Northumbria, found at York,[182] Danish urns and an ax dug up in County Tyrone, Ireland,[183] and some manuscripts said to be a thousand years old in the Arabic and Persian languages.[184] For what must have been a small group of his customers Bradford included a description of the alcazar of Segovia and a discussion of the ancient sepulchres near Lincoln Cathedral.[185] Probably few of the *Mercury's* readers realized the seriousness of the loss by fire of part of the Cottonian library in 1731, though more may have lamented the damage suffered by the cathedrals of Ely and Salisbury in the terrible storm of January 8, 1735,[186] and connoisseurs of the art of bell-ringing must have enjoyed reading this paragraph in the *Mercury:*[187]

> On Monday last the Society of London Youths rang at West-Ham in the County of Essex, a complete Peal of 11088 Bob-Major, or all eight in, which was completed by eight Men only,

178. *Mercury* 666, 781, 676.
179. *Mercury* 658.
180. *Mercury* 705, 938.
181. *Mercury* 123, 162, 169, 184, 194, 337, 349, 374, 398, 424, 479, 519, 683, 813, 962, 1273.
182. *Mercury* 927.
183. *Mercury* 1161.
184. *Mercury* 603.
185. *Mercury* 349, 608.
186. *Mercury* 638, 796.
187. *Mercury* 948. Number 998 told of installing a "new Tenor" at Bow Church.

in seven Hours and eleven Minutes, being the longest Peal that ever was rung, and is allow'd by all Judges to be the greatest Performance ever done in that Exercise, the Tenor weighing 2500 lb. The Bells were cast by Mr. Samuel Knight, and hung by the famous Mr. Robert Catlin, the most ingenious Man of his Age.

All sorts of items that resist classification also appeared in the *Mercury:* accounts of the return to Virginia of three ships from slaving on the coast of Madagascar,[188] the opening of a new amphitheatre for bullfighting in Lisbon,[189] George II's decision that English should be the language of the court,[190] a riot at Drury Lane Theatre when the footmen were excluded from their gallery,[191] a man who won a wager by eating 120 eggs, five pounds of bacon, and a twelve-penny loaf in an hour and a half at the George Inn at Glastonbury,[192] a man who sold his wife for a bowl of punch,[193] the return to his family in Portsmouth, New Hampshire, of a young man captured more than twenty years earlier by the Indians,[194] a football match at Bath between two teams of women,[195] a clash between town and gown at Oxford,[196] a girl of eighteen who for five years had followed the sea and become a dexterous sailor,[197] a New Englander, suspected of fornication, who was made to ride skimmington,[198] an eighteenth-century Houdini who escaped prison in spite of padlocks, bolts, and bars[199] — the list might be extended indefinitely. Some reports were evidently included in the *Mercury* purely to raise a laugh: for example, the not very delicate stories of the rabbi who could not afford a large family or of the lusty young man who was released from a charge of gross immorality when he claimed as an extenuating circumstance "the Richness of his Constitution," or of the "tempting Fruiteress" who conspired with her husband to trick an amorous young fellow out of all his money.[200] Perhaps the most genuinely entertaining of the *Mercury's* stories, however, was this one:[201]

188. *Mercury* 85.
189. *Mercury* 119.
190. *Mercury* 404.
191. *Mercury* 908, 913.
192. *Mercury* 375. See also Number 483 for another example of a phenomenal appetite.
193. *Mercury* 518. Compare here and below (footnote 198) *The Mayor of Casterbridge.*
194. *Mercury* 634.
195. *Mercury* 379.
196. *Mercury* 397.
197. *Mercury* 1231. See other examples of girls masquerading as men in Numbers 355, 396.
198. *Mercury* 1137.
199. *Mercury* 261.
200. *Mercury* 225, 554, 216.
201. *Mercury* 178.

The "Mercury" as a Mirror of the Times

An elderly Gentleman, who was accustomed to shave at a Barbers near the Royal Exchange, and who never found the Way thither but on a Sunday, had so tired the Barber's Boy with attending him on that Day, that the Youngster had contrived several Ways to lose that Customer, but to no purpose; however, about a Month since he fell on an Expedient that did it effectually; and when the old Gentelman came, and was under his Hands (there being none in the Room but those Two) the Boy on a sudden started, seem'd to be in a great Surprize, and looking towards the corner of the Room, cry'd out *I will not,* which he repeated several times: The Gentleman seeing him in such a Fright, asked him the Cause; the artful Youth reply'd, *Yonder stands the D———l and tempts me to cut your Throat for shaving on this Day.* At which the old Gentleman, who was somewhat credulous, was so frighten'd that he run away with half his Beard on. This has had such an Effict on him, that he can now find Time to shave on a Saturday.

In addition to what has already been discussed, the *Mercury* reflected many aspects of the day-to-day concerns and activities of the colonists as a whole but particularly of those who lived in or near Philadelphia. For example, it regularly reported any freak of the weather. On August 3, 1724, there was a tremendous storm in Philadelphia,[202] which lifted millstones and plows, uprooted trees and tore down houses, even picked up men and whirled them into the air;

> ... it made clear Work where it went, took up all as tho' it had been Grubed, and where it went a cross the Roades, it laid Trees so thick that it is very Difficult to Travel, it made a Road of about 40 Pole in Breadth, and in some Places it parted, and then met again about two Miles off.

This excitement was followed on August 6 by "a small Convulsion of the Earth . . . which lasted about half a Minute, and was felt by many People . . . ."[203] Earthquakes, in fact, were reported several times, notably the serious convulsion in New England in November 1727, and that of December 1737, which was felt up and down the coast from Philadelphia to New London.[204] Again and again we learn of very cold winters in Philadelphia; for example, "We have had very hard Weather here, for near this two weeks past, so that it has Frose our River up to

---

202. *Mercury* 243-245.
203. *Mercury* 242.
204. *Mercury* 412, 937.

such a Degree that People go over daily, and they have set up two Booths on the Ice, about the Middle of the said River."[205] Five years later, in the bitter January of 1733, a two-horse sleigh with four men in it crossed the river and back on a wager in two and a half minutes.[206] Almost yearly the *Mercury* reported the disruption of Philadelphia trade by the ice in the Delaware and sometimes acute suffering or even death from the cold.[207] In contrast the summers were often sweltering; for example, in 1727: "We have had such excessive Hot Weather here these four Days past, that two labouring men dropt down dead in the Fields, and several in this City, overcome by the violent Heat, have been taken ill, and dyed suddenly."[208] And in the spring, floods sometimes followed the thaw, or perhaps unexpected frost damaged the crops.[209]

In an age which was almost powerless against contagious disease, news of epidemics was frequent: we hear, for instance, of smallpox in Nova Scotia, Boston, New York, and South Carolina;[210] of a throat infection that swept over Marblehead, Massachusetts;[211] and of the outbreak of "Pluresy Fever" in Connecticut that caused the authorities of Yale College to send the students home.[212] In 1731 the mortality from smallpox in New York and Philadelphia was very high;[213] both Salem County and Burlington forbade the holding of their annual fairs;[214]

---

205. *Mercury* 421. Numbers 110 and 423 spoke of New Yorkers going across on the ice to Long Island. The winter of 1725 saw an unusually heavy snowfall in Philadelphia. (See *Mercury* 272.)

206. *Mercury* 683. In the winter of 1740-1741 it was reported that horses and sleds were crossing back and forth over the Delaware. (See Number 1096.) From New York came news of similar weather, so cold, said the letter from which the newspaper quoted, that "while I am Writing in a Room by a good Fire Side the Ink Freezes in the Pen." Two weeks later New York news items reported that wood was selling for fifty shillings a cord and that a collection for the poor was being made. (See Number 1098.)

207. *Mercury* 372, 422, 469, 684, 891, 1045. The most appealing of the several stories told in connection with the severity of colonial winters and the sufferings of the poor came from Newport, Rhode Island, where it was reported that, after a poor man in desperate need had robbed his neighbor's large woodpile, he received next day another load of wood from the neighbor and an invitation to come back for more when he needed it. (See Number 899.) The story is reminiscent of an episode in the life of John Winthrop as told by Cotton Mather in *Magnalia Christi Americana*.

208. *Mercury* 396. Number 758 also mentioned deaths from the heat.

209. *Mercury* 80, 686, 749.

210. *Mercury* 609, 613, 701, 971. Between April and October 1721, the *Mercury* reported, 2750 people in Boston had smallpox (Number 96).

211. *Mercury* 922. The medical naiveté of the period is illustrated by this comment on the epidemic: "And what seems remarkable in this Distemper, the meaner the Patients live, the worse they are: The Doctors, we hear, have left off the Use of Physick, and put their Patients upon a good generous Diet, which seems to have a better Effect than any other Remedy."

212. *Mercury* 749.

213. *Mercury* 587, 590.

214. *Mercury* 588, 590.

To be SOLD,

At Christiana-Bridge, within the County of New-Castle,

A Good Dwelling House, with two Brick Chimneys, a large Stone-wall'd Cellar, and a small Lot, lying convenient in the Town for a Store or a Tradesman to Live in: Together with Thirty Acres of good rough Land (joyning to the Town) two or three Acres of it is newly clear'd for Meadow; there may be made 10 or 12 more of Meadow-ing. Whoever inclines to Purchase the same may repair to *Lewis Howell* at the Place, or to Messrs. *White* and *Taylor*, Merchants, in *Philadelphia*, and know further.

THere was lately taken up and are now in *Burlington* Goal, Two Negro Men, who belong to *Baltimore* County, in *Maryland*. The right Owner is desired to pay the Charges and take them away.

For JAMAICA directly,

THe Sloop *Elizabeth* and *Mary*, *William Burrows* Master: For Freight or Passage agree with said Master at Mr. *Brown's* Wharfe, on very reasonable Terms. She will Sail for the above Port with all convenient Speed.

RAn-away from *William Rumsey* on the 26th of *September* past, an indented *Irish* Servant Lad named *Bernardo Mosley*, about 19 Years of Age, middle Stature, fair Complexion, large Nose, light brown hair pretty much Sun-burnt, he talks good English; had on an old yellowish colour'd Coat of Cotton Ribb (somewhat like Fustian) too long Wasted for him, and trimm'd with white Metal Buttons with wooden Moulds in them, and an old red Duffil Great Coat, Oznabrigs Breeches and Jacket, an old fine Hat, and old Jockey-boots, his Linen uncertain, had Oznabrige Shirts, but 'tis supposed he took one or more Garlick Holland Shirts with him ruffled at Bosom and Sleeves. Rode away on a fine large natural Pacing Bay Mare branded R S, shod Before, and one of her Hoofs being broke before Shoing is cut shorter than the other, had also an old Breasted Saddle and a Snaffle Bridle.

Whoever apprehends the said Servant and secures him, and the aforesaid Mare, so that their Master shall have them again, shall have *Fifty Shillings* Reward. And if either of them be brought Home to their Master living near the Head of *Bohemia* in *Cecil* County, *Maryland*, shall have a sufficient Reward and reasonable Charges, Paid by *William Rumsey*.

RAn-away on the 22d of *August* ast, from *Joseph County* of the Manner of *Moreland* in the County of *Philadelphia*, an *Irish* Servant Man named *Martin Farril*, a pretty lusty Man, of a sandy Complexion; he has large grey Eyes, no Hair but wears a Cap; he had on a light colour'd Kersey Coat without Cuffs, and has Pewter Buttons with a flap over the Button holes, a pair of Trowsers and Drawers, homespun Shirt, good Stockings and Shoes, and a Castor Hat.

Whoever takes up the said Servant and brings him to *Philadelphia* Goal, shall have *Six Pounds* Reward, and all reasonable Charges, paid by *Joseph County*.

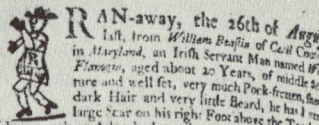
RAn-away, the 26th of *August* last, from *William Beaslin* of *Cecil* County in *Maryland*, an *Irish* Servant Man named *Will Flanegin*, aged about 20 Years, of middle Stature and well set, very much Pock-frozen, short dark Hair and very little Beard, he had very large Scar on his right Foot above the Toes lately cut with an Adz; had on when he went away a Felt Hat half worn, two Shirts one of Oznebrigs, an old Flannel Jacket, a linsey-woolsey Vest with large flat Metal Coat buttons down the Breast, a pair of half worn Buckskin Breeches with some white Metal and some Brass Buttons and three streight Seams down each Knee, two pair of old Trowsers one of Oznebrig the other striped Linen, one Yarn Stockings and old Leather-heel'd Shoes. He is by Trade a Miller, but may pretend to be a Sailor or Plaisterer. He speaks pretty good English, but can neither read nor write.

Whoever takes up and secures the said Servant, and gives Notice thereof to *Bohemia* Ferry in *Cecil* County aforesaid, so that his Master may have him again, shall have *Fifty Shillings* Reward and reasonable Charges, paid by *William Beaslin*.

To be Sold by *George M'Call*,

A Very likely Young Negro Woman; also Broad Cloaths, Kerseys, Druggets, Shalloons, plain and strip'd Calamincoes, Tammies, plain and strip'd Camblets, Ruggs, and Stockings, Worsted Caps, Muslins, Garlix and *Irish* Linens, Writing Paper, and *London* double Refin'd Sugar, Iron Pots, Nails, Short and Long Pipes, Hats, & sundry other sorts of Goods, on reasonable Terms.

To be Sold by *Humphrey Garland*,

AT the House late of Mr. *Shoemell*, in Second-Street near Arch-Street, Worsted Damasks, Silk and Worsted Crapes, Plain Calimincoes, Camblettees, Mantua Silks, Persians, Tickens; sundry Haberdashery, Cutlery and Iron Wares, at very reasonable Rates.

For BRISTOL directly,

THe Snow *Pompey*, *James Wyllie* Master, will Sail with all convenient Expedition: For Freight or Passage agree with *William Heller*, or the said Master.

N. B. She will have very good Accommodations for Passengers.

ALL Persons Indebted to *Reese Meredith*, are desired to come and Settle with him, and Pay their respective Balances, he designing to leave the Province by the first convenient Opportunity.

To be Sold by said *Meredith*, at his Store on *William Fishbourn's* Wharfe, Three quarter Garlicks, Plain and Corded Dimitys, Broad and Narrow Shalloons, Tammys, Worsted and Cotton Caps; Mens, Womens and Childrens Stockings, Stuffs, Calimincoes, Crapes, Sagathees, Mohair and Buttons, Metal Ditto, Fine Hats, Bohea and Green Tea, Coffee, Single and Double refin'd Sugar, Sail Duck, Cutlery and Iron Ware, Guns, Anchors, a set of Blocks and Pumps for a Ship and Sloop, Logwood, Short Pipes, Earthen Ware, and *Manchester* Goods: All very reasonably for Ready Money.

CHoice good LAMP-BLACK made and sold by the Printer hereof.

Philadelphia: Printed and Sold by Andrew Bradford, *Post-Master,* at the *Sign of the Bible* in *Second-Street,* where *Advertisements* are taken in, and all Persons in Town or Country may be supplied with this Paper.

Advertising Page of the Mercury, *October 9, 1735*
Courtesy of the Library Company of Philadelphia

advertisements of slaves and servants frequently concluded with the reassuring phrase, "and has had the Small-pox";[215] and the *Mercury* gave editorial space in six successive numbers to discussion of the scourge.[216] Again in the spring of 1737 Salem advertised that no fair would be held there or at Cohansey because of fear that Pennsylvanians might bring smallpox with them, though two months later the paper announced that Philadelphia was almost free of the disease and added the comment: "we hope very shortly to give our Readers an account of the great Success which attended the Practice of Innoculation."[217] In 1721 the *Mercury* reported a serious distemper among farm animals, especially horses, in New York; and in 1736, when a disease of the throat broke out in New Jersey, Bradford printed a recipe for a gargle made of honey, vinegar, and "allom."[218]

The advertisements in the *Mercury* indicate an ever-increasing number of chemists and physicians in the city: for example, "At the Corner Shop, over-against Nicholas Scull's, at the George Inn in the Second street, Philadelphia, are to be sold, all sorts of Useful Medecines and Druggs: where also all Masters of Trading Vessels may be Furnish'd with Boxes of Medecines, fitted for their respective Voyages, with ample Directions for their Use, at Reasonable Rates, by Patrick Baird Surgeon."[219] Later came an announcement that Hendrick van Bebber, a doctor of physic, was setting up practice in Philadelphia.[220] In 1736 appeared two testimonials in support of an elixir supposed to cure dropsy,[221] and in 1737 Evan Jones offered "a Specifick Medicine of his own preparing" for the cure of venereal disease.[222] Peter Sonmans, one of the Philadelphia doctors who practiced inoculation for smallpox, also sold drugs, whereas William Whitebread, "Operator for the Teeth," advertised a cure for "the Scurvey in the Gums," and Anthony Duchée, a dyer, made bandages and trusses and advertised himself as "a very good Artist at putting up of Ruptures."[223] Once at least in the history of the *Mercury* and the *Gazette* a quack was the subject of a paper war; for when Francis Torres printed almost two columns in the *Gazette* of October 17, 1745, to advertise his "Chinese Stone" and powders (which would cure, it would appear, practically anything, but sold at the very

215. *Mercury* 578, 590, etc.
216. *Mercury* 582-587.
217. *Mercury* 902, 914. The promised discussion of inoculation appeared in Number 923.
218. *Mercury* 90, 91; 839. The "disease of the throat" mentioned in colonial papers was sometimes diphtheria.
219. *Mercury* 329.
220. *Mercury* 650.
221. *Mercury* 840, 841.
222. *Mercury* 907.
223. *Mercury* 923, 963, 1232.

high price of twenty-five shillings), a writer in the *Mercury* attacked the panacea as grossly exaggerated in its claims and far too expensive, since it could be made by anyone at very little cost.[224] He explained how to make the stone and powder, how they produced their cures, and to what extent they were really helpful. Though Torres and his cure-all were lampooned also in the *Gazette* of the same date, both papers later carried advertisements of his medicine.[225] Then, as now, people liked to be fooled.

Like the weather and the state of the public health, accidents were a staple of local news. There were many reports of fires, including one in which Bradford's enemy Andrew Hamilton lost several buildings.[226] Probably the most serious fire in the colonies mentioned by the *Mercury* was the burning of Charleston, South Carolina, on November 18, 1740, with destruction of 334 houses and damage to the extent of £200,000, but fortunately with little loss of life.[227] In Philadelphia an enterprising tradesman named Abraham Cox followed up the news of a fire in Chestnut Street in December 1728 with an advertisement of leather buckets that might be useful in similar contingencies; and in 1734 the success of a new engine, which threw water much higher, it was said, than the one previously imported from London, was triumphantly announced.[228] News of hunting accidents and drownings inevitably appeared.[229] Local crimes and misdemeanors of various sorts were reported; from the number of advertisements it is obvious that runaway slaves and servants were a constant problem to the propertied class, and escapes from jail were frequent.[230] In 1736 came an outbreak of horse-stealing in Pennsylvania;[231] there were periodical warnings against passers of counterfeit bills;[232] occasionally someone was tried for larceny or piracy;[233] less often occurred an execution for murder.[234] Everyone in or near

224. *Mercury* 1347.
225. *Gazette* 903 and *Mercury* 1369. At this date there was a mad-dog scare in Philadelphia (*Gazette* 902); the "Chinese Stone" was supposed to cure, among other things, rabies. Torres was doubtless taking advantage of public hysteria.
226. *Mercury* 466, 987, 1057, 1301.
227. *Mercury* 1099, 1100, 1105.
228. *Mercury* 466, 734.
229. *Mercury* 835, 869, 1160, etc.
230. *Mercury* 18, 29, 31, 41, 450, 735, etc.
231. *Mercury* 870.
232. *Mercury* 777, 911, 964. From New York in 1744, in connection with the report of the execution of a counterfeiter, came this pointed remark: "If some of our neighbouring Governments would but act with equal Justice, it might be presumed, these Pests of Society would be something scarcer than they are" (Number 1286). Similar to the warning against counterfeit bills was the notice of the "New-Jersey Society" cautioning against the illegal sale or purchase of certain land in Salem County (Number 843).
233. *Mercury* 666-668, 733.
234. *Mercury* 391-393, 444-445, 1004-1005.

Philadelphia must have been interested in such matters as the establishment of legal weights and prices of loaves of bread,[235] or in the agreement of seventy-four Philadelphia merchants equating common gold and silver coins of English, French, Spanish, Dutch, German, Portuguese, and Arabian origin with Pennsylvania paper money.[236] Some of Bradford's customers must surely have been drawn to Charlestown, Maryland, or to the James valley in Virginia by the *Mercury's* advertisements of cheap land there;[237] probably even more were interested in the lottery in 1733 for the sale of 100,000 acres of Pennsylvania land.[238] No doubt many Philadelphians eagerly awaited the eclipse of the sun of February 18, 1737, or watched the aurora borealis of the following August.[239] Though a shark might be found in the Schuylkill or a grampus in Darby Creek,[240] not every day even in the eighteenth century could the inhabitants enjoy the sight of two whales spouting in the Delaware beside the city.[241] Many of the citizens must have turned out to cheer the *George* when it came in with a rich Spanish ship as a prize in the fall of 1743,[242] especially since some of them had certainly attended the auction of the vessels she had brought in earlier and some must have had friends and relatives who had answered her plea for "Gentleman Sailors and others."[243]

There was little commercial entertainment in Philadelphia in the early eighteenth century. The *Mercury*, of course, mentioned various inns and taverns — the Indian King,[244] the London Coffee House, the Pewter Platter — where, no doubt, good food and drink and lively company might be found. The Concert Room, involved in the Whitefield controversy, was evidently popular, and fairs combined business and entertainment for their visitors. In 1737 Roger Ellicott advertised in the *Mercury* as follows:[245] "The Bowling-Green (at the Center) is now kept in good Order, and fit for the Reception of all Gentlemen who would Divert themselves at Bowls: Who may depend upon having good Liquors, and ready Attendance . . . ." Occasionally some curiosity was exhibited in the city, not only animals, but also, for example, "a very curious and exact Modell of the Czar of Muscovia's Country seat" or a piece of clock-work which showed eight men ringing bells "truly round

---

235. *Mercury* 972.
236. *Mercury* 1185. See also Number 1121.
237. *Mercury* 955, 1215.
238. *Mercury* 814, 815, 831.
239. *Mercury* 894, 920.
240. *Mercury* 869, 1214.
241. *Mercury* 694.
242. *Mercury* 1239.
243. *Mercury* 1168.
244. Both the Lion King of Beasts and the leopard were exhibited at this inn.
245. *Mercury* 907.

Ringing and Changes, much in Imitation of Ringing in England.[246]

In 1724, however, appeared an advertisement of what must have been one of the earliest theatrical entertainments in Philadelphia; by permission of the Governor, it announced,[247]

> This is to give Notice to all Gentlemen, Ladies and others, That there is newly arrived to this place the famous Performance of Roap-Dancing, which is performed to the Admiration of all the Beholders,
>
> 1st, By a little Boy of seven Years old, who Dances and Capers upon the strait Roap, to the Wonder of all Spectators.
>
> 2dly, By a Woman, who dances a Corant and a Jigg upon the Roap, which she performs as well as any Dancing Master does it on the Ground.
>
> 3dly, She Dances with Baskets upon her Feet, and Iron Fetters upon her Legs.

246. *Mercury* 191, 1296.
247. *Mercury* 229. It is possible that "your Old Friend Pickle Herring" was the strolling player who had distressed James Logan the previous spring. In a letter dated April 9, 1723 (*Papers Relating to Provincial Affairs in Pennsylvania, 1682-1750*, 76-77) Logan wrote:

> . . . the Speaker, by appointment of the House, applied to the Govr to discourage a Player who had Strowled hither to act as a Comedian. The Govr excused himself from prohibiting it, but assured them that he would take care good ordrs should be kept, and so the man went on to publish his printed Bills, as thou wilt see by one of them inclosed, and to act accordingly.
>
> How grievous this proves to the sober people of the place, thou wilt easily judge, but it happens at p'sent to be more particularly so on me, for having, unfortunately, been chosen Mayor of Philada for this year, there is an expectation that I should exert that authority to suppress their acting. But as they have chose for their Stage a place just without the verge of the City, and ye Govr himself resorts thither, I can by no means think it advisable to embroil myself with the Governour to no purpose, or to raise a dispute between the Corporation and him in which nothing is to be gained.

The *Mercury*, it is interesting to note, also contains the earliest-known news report concerning the theatre at Williamsburg. The item (in Number 869) ran thus:

> Williamsburg in Virginia, May 3. 1736.
>
> This being the Time of our General Court, the Town was last Week filled with an extraordinary Concourse of Gentlemen and Ladies; who came hither to see our Governors Sister and Son,* in company with one Dr. Potter, Apothetary Gilmore, Abraham Nicholas, a Painter, and several others, put Plays on the Public Theatre: And in Acting the *Recruiting Officer,* and *Busy-Body,* they performed their Parts with so much applause, that they have already got about One hundred and fifty Pounds Subscriptions, to encourage their Entertaining the Country with the like Diversions at future Public Meetings of our General Court and Assembly.
>
> N.B. The Terms of Subscriptions are, that a Ticket will be delivered for every Twenty Shillings Subscribed.

*The Governor was William Gooch.

4thly, She walks upon the Roap with a Wheel-Barrow before her.
5thly, You will see various Performances upon the Slack Roap.
6thly, You are entertained with the Comicall Humour of your Old Friend Pickle Herring.[248]
The whole concluded with a Woman turning round in a swift Motion with seven or eight Swords Points at her Eys. Mouth and Breast, for a Quarter of an Hour together, to the Admiration of all that behold the Performance.
There will likewise be several other diverting Performances on the Stage, too large here to mention.

The above Performances are to be seen at the New Booth on Society Hill, To begin on Thursday next, being the last day of April, and to continue Acting, the Term of Twenty Days and no longer.
The Price upon the Stage is Three Shillings, in the Pit Two Shillings, and in the Gallery One Shilling and Six Pence.
To begin exactly at Seven a Clock in the Evening.

In addition, various societies, established in Philadelphia for social or intellectual purposes, used the *Mercury* as a means of advertisement: the English Society, which met on St. George's Day to honor its patron saint,[249] and the Society of Ancient Britons, which was "established in Honour of Her Majesty Queen Caroline's Birth-Day, and the Principality of Wales" and celebrated St. David's Day.[250] The Library Company, though its activities were ordinarily not discussed in the *Mercury*, figured on the important occasion when the directors of the association addressed their thanks to the proprietors for granting them a charter.[251]

The *Mercury* reflected too, chiefly in its advertising columns, the ever-increasing interest of Philadelphians in education of various sorts. George Brownell advertised in 1728 "A Boarding School, also Reading, Writing, Cyphering, Dancing, and several sorts of Needle-work."[252]

---

248. "Pickleherring" was a generic name for the clown in the performances of the "English comedians" in Germany in the early seventeenth century. See, for example, Albert Cohn's *Shakespeare in Germany in the Sixteenth and Seventeenth Centuries* (London, 1865).
249. *Mercury* 642, 745, 798, etc.
250. *Mercury* 633, 636, 739, 790, etc. Caroline's birthday and St. David's Day were March 1.
251. *Mercury* 1246.
252. *Mercury* 428. Brownell also advertised in other issues of the *Mercury*, for example, 585, 835. He taught also in Boston, New York, and Charleston. See advertisements in the Boston *Weekly Rehearsal* (151, August 19, 1734), the New York *Gazette* (294, June 14, 1731), and the *South Carolina Gazette* (546, September 10, 1744). His most famous pupil was Benjamin Franklin (*Autobiography*, 233).

John Walby at "the Free-School" in Strawberry Lane taught not only English and Latin, but also "Book-keeping, Gauging, Dialling, with some other Practical Parts of the Mathematicks"; and Samuel Perpoint, who had taught previously in Jamaica, gave instruction in dancing and the small sword.[253] Admittedly a specialist was G. Michael Weis, a minister, who notified Bradford's readers that since he wished to be as "Generally useful" as possible in a country where he was a stranger, he would teach "Logick, Natural Phylosophy, Metaphysicks, &c." to all who wanted to learn.[254] Likewise specialists were Daniel Duborn and Anthony Duchée, who taught French,[255] and Andrew Lamb,[256] Magnus Falconar,[257] and Theophilus Grew,[258] teachers primarily of accounting, navigation, and similar technical subjects. John Salomon, who showed his talents by including in the paper a long advertisement in Latin, taught French and Latin and was willing to go to the homes of his pupils,[259] and Theobald Hackett, a dancing master, also expressed his willingness to teach in private houses.[260] In the summer of 1742 Joseph Crellius opened a school for German, French, and Low Dutch, especially intending to teach the art of translation from these languages into English and the reverse.[261] Indeed, the surprising number of such advertisements indicates that early eighteenth-century Philadelphia must have been a promising place for schoolmasters;[262] there were evidently money, leisure, and the desire for instruction sufficient to encourage a large group of more or less talented young men to set up schools of various kinds in and near the city.

The *Mercury's* advertising columns throw light also on other aspects of life in and around Philadelphia, in particular upon the activities and

253. *Mercury* 465, 500.
254. *Mercury* 527.
255. *Mercury* 546, 734.
256. *Mercury* 692, 716, 748, 774.
257. *Mercury* 1029, 1042, 1054, 1118.
258. *Mercury* 771, 835. Grew was also a merchant.
259. *Mercury* 859.
260. *Mercury* 974.
261. *Mercury* 1173.
262. Other schools were also advertised, for example, in Numbers 480, 534, 838. Other schoolmasters mentioned in the paper were Richard Kyneall (or Lyneall), who taught the "true Art of Defence" (Numbers 1150, 1189); Thomas Phipps (Number 463), Ebenezer Wickes (Number 598), Alexander Mackenzie (Number 996), Thomas Edwards (Number 1007), John Shields (Number 290), John Stevens (Number 1013); Lewis Mulhallond, a dancing master (Number 1019); Andrew Lauder (Number 1020), Nathaniel Walton (Number 1190, 1338), Alexander Seaton (Number 1241), W. Hetherington (Number 1338). Note also such an item as that in Number 1016, where a servant man's time is advertised and he is spoken of as "well Qualified . . . to teach a School." In Number 1154 a runaway schoolmaster from Solebury Township was sought for. At least twice the *Mercury* carried advertisements of New York schoolmasters (Numbers 201 and 284).

customs of tradesmen and businessmen, who supported it liberally with their advertisements throughout its career. It goes without saying that Bradford's columns regularly announced a great quantity and variety of goods for sale: food and clothing, utensils and machinery, houses and land, ships and wagons and horses, books and musical instruments, jewelry and chinaware, drugs and spectacles — in short, almost anything that the eighteenth-century family might wish or require. Sometimes an entire business was advertised for sale, for example, a smithy in Maryland and Thomas Lloyd's chemist shop in Philadelphia.[263] The *Mercury* advertised also services of different sorts, not only the professional assistance of doctors, schoolteachers, and lawyers[264] and the increasing number of sailings to distant ports, but such things as a "most commodious Ferry" across the Potomac[265] and stage-wagon routes connecting Burlington, Amboy, Trenton, New Brunswick, and Bordentown.[266] Individuals as well offered their services to the public: George Plumley sharpened sickles; Elizabeth Horner made and mended gloves and mittens, and grafted and footed stockings; James Rogers offered to whiten brown linen at a cost of threepence a yard at the bleach-yard which he had erected seven miles from the city; William Goddard piloted ships up and down the Delaware and accepted in pay one-third in cash and two-thirds in goods; John Atkins did dry-cleaning and dyeing.[267]

Customarily, too, a person engaged in business announced in the paper, usually in advance, his removal from one part of the city to another or from Pennsylvania to another colony or to foreign shores, often accompanying the announcement with a request for the prompt settlement of any current account.[268] Reese Meredith, for instance, the young man who for a while shared Bradford's store, evidently left Philadelphia several times on business trips and regularly advertised his coming and going in the *Mercury*.[269] Tradesmen from other places frequently announced their establishing new businesses in Philadelphia — for example, Michael Brown, a silk-dyer from Bohemia, Maryland,[270] and Michael Cario, a jeweller from London.[271] On the other hand, when property owners in Chestertown, Maryland, being "obliged by Act of Assembly to build on their respective Lots within Eighteen

263. *Mercury* 405, 1070.
264. See, for example, John Webbe's advertisement in Number 1087.
265. *Mercury* 638.
266. *Mercury* 472, 689, 945, 1060, 1120.
267. *Mercury* 968, 1055, 1058, 1064, 1075.
268. *Mercury* 223, 395, 427, 463, 481, 513, 585, 716, 748, 834, 1145, etc.
269. *Mercury* 818, 873, 981, 1023.
270. *Mercury* 834. He had previously advertised in the *Mercury* (Number 704) his business in Bohemia.
271. *Mercury* 861.

Months," needed "Carpenters, Joyners, Bricklayers and other Tradesmen," as well as "Tanners, Curriers, Hatters," they advertised in the *Mercury* in the hope of attracting the assistance they required.[272] When George Lucas Osborne went to Antigua, his wife informed the public that she would continue to sell tea and sugar and that, since she had given up housekeeping, she had also for sale various household goods in excellent condition.[273] Mary Cowley and Eleanor Wormley, widows, gave notice that they expected to carry on their husbands' businesses, the one as a dresser of buckskin, the other as a baker;[274] and Barbara Lewis, announcing that she was giving up tavern keeping at the Crooked Billet, advertised that she expected to rent a large room where she would continue to sell liquor and that she wished to dispose of a good cook, especially fitted for work in a public-house.[275]

In addition to offering lively encouragement to nearly every kind of local business, the *Mercury* also served the personal ends of its readers, in lost-and-found and help-wanted advertisements and in weightier matters. While Samuel Farmer was languishing in the Philadelphia jail, he appealed to his creditors and debtors to bring him their accounts in the hope of straightening them out and escaping "his present Confinement."[276] Executors of estates frequently advertised in the *Mercury* in an effort to locate those with claims to be settled,[277] and creditors used its columns to appeal to those who owed them money.[278] Moreover, a considerable amount of private linen was washed — rather publicly, it would appear — in Bradford's pages: for example, when William Tyrrell inserted a mysterious little advertisement objecting to being called "an insolent Rascal";[279] when Jane Smith denied as "notoriously False" the report that John Jones was in prison in Philadelphia and there had offered to commit fornication with her;[280] or when Samuel Chew vigorously replied to "a certain scurrilous abusive Paper" directed against him and attributed, he believed incorrectly, to a Quaker.[281] Frequently an aggrieved husband announced in the *Mercury* that he would

272. *Mercury* 574.
273. *Mercury* 868.
274. *Mercury* 1135, 1137.
275. *Mercury* 1135. The number of women who conducted businesses in Philadelphia was surprisingly large; it was quite customary for widows to carry on their husbands' occupations. The Crooked Billet is famous as Franklin's first lodging in Philadelphia (*Autobiography*, 255).
276. *Mercury* 1176.
277. *Mercury* 379, 481, 1020, 1209, etc.
278. *Mercury* 759, 1111, 1125, 1139, 1192, etc.
279. *Mercury* 1166.
280. *Mercury* 391. Jane Smith and John Jones look suspiciously like fictitious names, though the advertisement itself does not suggest undue modesty.
281. *Mercury* 1157.

not assume responsibility for debts incurred by his eloped wife;[282] once or twice this statement brought an indignant reply, for example, when Elizabeth Dunlap followed her husband's accusation[283] with advertisements in both the *Mercury* and the *Gazette* stating that she had fled her home in terror of her life, but had gone only to her father's house in the same county, and that prospective purchasers of land from her husband should beware, since she expected to assert her full legal claim to their joint property.[284] John Ryan, a Philadelphia merchant who was reduced by ill luck to poverty and the debtor's prison, aired his grievances against a certain Thomas Campbell, the world, and the fates in a lengthy series of announcements in Bradford's paper.[285] And a personal quarrel between John Robinson, a lawyer, and his client Prudence Grinaway over the recovery of her estate spread itself for several weeks over the pages of both the *Mercury* and the *Gazette*.[286]

In innumerable ways, then, the *Mercury* aimed to serve its readers, reflecting and perhaps guiding their religious and political convictions, satisfying their curiosity about notable people and events, reporting sensational stories to give them vicarious excitement, encouraging their public enterprises, and giving space to their personal whims and grudges. The paper's news columns were largely solid and informative; its advertisements also — in contrast to many of ours today — were sober and factual. Many of the *Mercury's* pages, therefore, make pedestrian reading; but the total effect of the paper is anything but dull. Both news items and advertisements cut in a hundred ways across the customs, habits, interests, ways of living and thinking of their time; both are constantly tinged with humor or drama or irony, sometimes bestowed gratuitously by the passing of two centuries. They constantly reveal the unchangeableness of human nature in general and of the newspaper reader in particular, and at the same time illustrate those quirks of the eighteenth-century mind which we imagine ourselves to have outgrown.

282. *Mercury* 413, 427, 1139, 1223, etc.
283. *Mercury* 1160.
284. *Mercury* 1172 and the *Gazette* of the same date. *Mercury* 1180 contained her husband's rejoinder.
285. *Mercury* 1262, 1269, 1274, 1280, 1281, 1310, 1322, 1348. Ryan was one of the victims of the fire described in *Mercury* 1201. See *Gazette* 735 of the same date.
286. *Gazette* 537, 539, 541; *Mercury* 1005, 1007, 1009.

Chapter 6

Editorials and Features in the *Mercury*

A very brief acquaintance with colonial newspapers makes clear why none of them had an editorial policy in the sense in which we apply the term to a modern paper. Since the eighteenth-century journal was restricted in its expression of opinions on matters of public concern and since both the acquisition and the publication of news were attended with many difficulties, the colonial editor's policy was to a large extent involuntary. On foreign questions he could not choose but reflect the attitudes of the British papers from which he borrowed; on many domestic problems he dared to state his convictions only obliquely if at all. Further, since the colonial paper had no regular section devoted to editorial opinion, it is especially difficult to determine what principles any particular journal really supported. Though it is clear that James Franklin's *Courant* opposed Mather's campaign for inoculation against smallpox, or that Zenger's *Weekly Journal* attacked Cosby and his party, or that the *Mercury* fought Hamilton, it is not at all certain, especially in the Hamilton controversy, that any editorial principle was involved. We do not know, for instance, whether the struggle against Hamilton was primarily a political conflict or the result of a personal quarrel. We do not know whether Bradford or a member of his staff wrote the various "letters" against Hamilton or whether Hamilton's political enemies used the columns of the paper for their propaganda. Indeed, so vague are the *Mercury's* references to Hamilton even at the height of the controversy that we today might very well miss the fact that the conflict was in progress. Hamilton is not mentioned by name; his specific acts as city recorder, speaker of the Assembly, or attorney for the defense at the Zenger trial are cautiously avoided. Only by a process of putting together piece by piece an allusion in the *Mercury,* a fact from the colonial records, a remark in the *Gazette* do we see the framework take shape — and even then, as we have already observed, the picture cannot be completely filled in. Granted that Bradford's original readers must have been quicker than we to grasp the point of the *Mercury's* innuendoes, still we question whether the eighteenth-century man-in-the-street would have known Le Vassor, for example, well enough to have spotted the hoax. And if we may assume that the point of such an "editorial" escaped the understanding of many of Bradford's readers, especially of those at a distance from Philadelphia who were cut off from the aid of local gossip, can we, from a modern point of view, consider the Le Vassor article an editorial at all? In other words, we must dispose at the start of the idea that the *Mercury,* or probably any colonial paper contemporary with it, represented significantly any consistent political attitude. The *Mercury* was pro-British and anti-Catholic on European questions; it was pro-American on colonial questions; and — if the Hamilton episode represents any political theory (which is debatable) — it appears to have been rather proprietarian than democratic on local issues. But if we can speak with little assurance about Bradford's basic policy as a newspaper editor, we should remember that he shared with other colonial "authors" the unsophisticated aim of informing his readers rather than moulding their opinions. Moreover, since the newspaper was in its infancy, neither he nor any of his fellows on either side of the ocean probably dreamed of the power of the press which makes editorial policy today a strong and subtle weapon.

Though he cannot, therefore, be said to have had a genuine policy, within the limits imposed by the circumstances of his time and the novelties of his profession, Bradford included a considerable amount of editorial material in his journal. The conception of the editorial as something distinct from the news item had not fully emerged; in addition, commentary upon news was obviously considered a poor substitute for news itself. Hence the earliest editorials in the *Mercury* appear either as corporate parts of news reports or else are offered apologetically to the reader because of a scarcity of regular intelligence. For example, as part of the first news item in the first issue of the *Mercury* the following discussion of Russia's policy in conquered Sweden was printed:

> If it be not reckoned prudence to make a private Enemy or Army desperate, much less is it to make a Nation desperate. The Sweeds, left in Possession of their Estates and Land, Houses and Towns, though reduced and brought low, nay, though even conquered, had been a Nation of Christians still; and being brought low by their Misfortunes, would, as it is most natural, to all People, have been the more humble and apt to submit to the Conqueror; but the Sweeds ruined, starved, beggar'd, Irretrievably impoverish'd, stript of all, their Houses, Towns, and Ships burnt and destroyed, the whole Country laid waste, and themselves exposed to Hunger, Want, Nakedness, and all the Horrors of an approaching Lapland Winter; what will this make them, but an enraged Nation of meer desperate distracted Men? and that is, in plain English, a Nation of wild Beasts; for without any Reproach upon the Swedes, who are a brave and gallant as well as generous and Christian Nation, a Man made desperate is more raging, more

> furious, more fierce than a Lyon; a Man stript naked, injured, starved, oppressed, as a Bear robbed of her Whelps, and the braver and more daring he is, the more furious raging he grows, made mad by Oppression.

Without much doubt this paragraph was lifted, with the report of which it was a part, from some British paper; in both places, of course, it was essentially an editorial interpolation.

Similarly disguised as news appeared a year later a vigorous attack on the British policy of banishing felons to the American colonies; inserted among the regular intelligence under the heading of "Philadelphia, February 14," it ran thus:[1]

> Those Malefactors mentioned in our last as sent from New-gate and the Marshalsea to be transported into the Plantations, are now arrived in Maryland, to the Number of above 180.
>
> The Punishment of hard Service these Criminals are sentenced to in the Plantations, is now cunningly eluded, if they can muster a small Parcel of Money, as a Gratuity or —— to the Merchant, for Trouble and their Passage, they are set at Liberty as soon as they set their Feet on this Shore, and are made equal with Freemen in these Parts, to settle and traffick, and may in a small time claim a Liberty above 'em.
>
> Instances of this are in this last transported Gang, among whom is a Person[2] we particularly mentioned with a Cargo, who is come over in Pomp, instead of the abject Condition of a Slave for some time. He brought his Mistress too along with him, who wears, 'tis said, rich Silk Cloaths and a Gold striking Watch. He lives in great Splendor at Annapolis, jollily carrousing with some of his Associates, who have had equal Fortune with him of getting Money to buy off their Servitude. There is now with them only this Part of their Sentence to be answered, that they must not return to England in so many Years.
>
> We may expect some of these wild Creatures, who were untamable and not to be brought to any civil Manners in England, to take their Traverses into our Province, and strive perhaps to settle here, and so we could do no less than give this publick Notice of them; nay, we have positive Advice that some intend to be here in a short time.
>
> When the flourishing Condition of his Majesties Planta-

---

1. *Mercury* 61.
2. *Mercury* 60: "among them is William Wrigglesden, the Person that formerly robbed the Kings Chappel at Whitehall, who has carried with him a great Cargo of Cutlers Ware to Traffick."

tions in America is considered, it is a sad Case that they cannot be ordered to be better peopled than by such absolute Villains and loose Women, as these are proved to be by their wretched Lives and criminal Actions; and if they settle any where in these Parts can only by a natural Consequence have bad Seeds amongst us; for never doubt the Proverb, *What's bred in the Bone will never out of the Flesh.* Our only Hope must be, that those who are not likely to be reclaimed, are very likely to be tip'd off here, and find their *Ne plus* with us, though they have escaped Tyburn.

Spain and other Kingdoms have their particular Islands for the Banishment of Criminals, which they reserve on purpose for such, in which small Confines and Spots of Land they are obliged to get a living by painful and forced Industry: Or else they find a safe Lymbo and Purgatory in the Gallies, where they are always chained and drove to servile Business by Force. In which Places they may be sure of getting no better Company than themselves, and so are unable to debauch the honest Natures and Manners of Mankind; and its a great Pity England has no such Islands, Gallies or Mines to dispose of and confine such untameable Persons in.

In these Western Parts, as it is the Desire of our Legislators, so all possible Care is taken to cultivate and encourage Morality and Industry, that our Sovereign King George may find a plentiful Territory and ample Strength and Happiness from our Colonies, and He or his Successors by these Parts may have a noble Addition to Great Britain for Empire, when our Lands shall be improved and accounted rich in Competition with very ancient inhabited Kingdoms. But by these Ways of transporting Villains amongst such a flourishing People, is to lessen our Improvements and Industry, by filling the Vacancies of honest Men with tricking, thieving, and designing Rogues, who will hardly be brought to get their Livelihood by such labourious and settled Means; the ill Consequences of which would without doubt be remedied in Great Britain, were they as sensible of 'em as we who are made so by living amongst them.

Such examples as these suggest that the eighteenth-century editor on either side of the Atlantic was not always aware of the distinction between reporting news and commenting upon it.

On the other hand, Bradford and many another colonial editor were acutely conscious of the factor which was probably most responsible for the development of the editorial column of the colonial newspaper — that is, the irregularity or the dearth of genuine news. Probably the confession of a man about to be hanged for counterfeiting, which was printed at length in late November of the *Mercury's* first year, was not only a sop to lovers of the sensational but also a practicable means of stretching a meagre supply of news.³ The first "filler" worthy to be considered an editorial, however, appeared later in the same winter. It began with the sort of apology to which the reader of colonial newspapers soon becomes habituated:⁴

> This being a dead Time for News, no Vessel having arrived here since our last. Our Readers must not expect Impossibilities, or that we can entertain them with fresher Advices from England, Spain, France, &c. than those already published by us in our preceeding Papers: We shall therefore beg leave to recapitulate on those Heads, with some modest Reflections on the present mysterious Conduct of the European Powers.

There followed the promised commentary (an intelligent criticism of foreign, chiefly Spanish, affairs), borrowed no doubt from an English journal. Then Bradford continued the column with some remarks on the fact that American merchants, unlike the English, did not recompense their sailors for loss of limb or for wounds sustained in battle. Later numbers of the paper included in much the same way what Bradford evidently considered makeshifts: for example, a summary of Marcus Varro's treatise on the proper conduct of "an Elegant Supper," introduced with the hesitant remark: "In this Scarcity of News, I here present to my Readers a small Essay on Entertainments."⁵ Another typical item was given the preamble: "In this scarcity of News I here present my Readers with a Journal of the Siege of Gibralter, which I hope will be acceptable;"⁶ and still a third ran thus: "Having but few remarkable Occurrences to fill up this our Paper with at present, We believe it will not be unacceptable to our Readers, to Incert the following Letter from a Gentleman to his Friend, upon the loss of his only Daughter . . . which seems to have something Elegant and Refined both in the Sentiments and Reasoning."⁷ Unquestionably Bradford's defensive attitude towards what he published in place of ordinary news tended to become a convention rather than a genuine expression of regret. As the paper flourished, moreover, he obviously assumed the privilege of printing what he saw fit without, in effect, asking his readers'

3. *Mercury* 49.
4. *Mercury* 57.
5. *Mercury* 224.
6. *Mercury* 426. The account ran for five numbers.
7. *Mercury* 374.

permission. Still, at almost any point in the *Mercury's* history, we may come upon the device of the editorial by-your-leave.

For the same reason that there was no sharp distinction between news item and commentary, the *Mercury* sometimes revealed in its early numbers a curious didacticism in the reporting of news. From the London *Journal,* for instance, came word of restrictions imposed by the Czar upon the number of monks and monasteries in Russia, an item capped by the characteristic remark: "A wise Regulation! pity but it was copied after in the Roman Catholick Countries, where so many useless Mouths devour the Fat of the Land."[8] In more homely fashion, after an account of the burning of a house with three children in it during the absence of their parents, Bradford volunteered the admonition that homes should not be left in charge of a careless servant.[9] Following a similar story of a disastrous fire, he added the comment: "Such Tragical Instances as these ought to Stir up diligence in every Person, of what Station soever, to do their utmost Endeavours in their respective Places to prevent such terrible calamitys as these poor miserable Objects are plung'd into."[10] Sometimes Bradford's moralizing appears to have had a flavor of malicious humor, as in this account: "Last Week the Wife of a Mechanick . . . died in a Fit of Scolding, being the first Instance we can give of this kind, but may be deem'd a dreadful Warning and Example to all Women, who give their Tongues too much Liberty in this way, to beware lest they share the same unlamented Fate."[11] As the *Mercury* became more mature, however, this naive, paternalistic style of reporting became less frequent.[12] Instead, the front page, or part of it, came to be more and more often set aside for an essay, a letter, or a commentary upon current events, or for some other feature article essentially the equivalent of an editorial. The subject might be almost anything: religion, fashions, education; a remedy for bedbugs or the culture of flax; a discussion of Cromwell's instructions to Admiral Venables or a dialect letter from a man in New York giving advice to a friend emigrating to America; an essay on hypocrisy or a criticism of matches made by parents for their children.[13] Appropriately, nearly all the many letters and essays of the Hamilton controversy appeared as first-page features, and no doubt other "editorials" have still-undiscovered connections with local politics.

8. *Mercury* 272.
9. *Mercury* 101.
10. *Mercury* 343. The identical account with the identical comment was borrowed by the New York *Gazette* 39.
11. *Mercury* 106.
12. The tendency to moralize upon news events was not a peculiarity of the *Mercury,* but of the times. See, for example, the report of a hunting accident in *Pennsylvania Gazette* 256, which was copied by New York *Gazette* 421.
13. *Mercury* 709, 1335, 1141, 980, 1005, 789.

The greater number of Bradford's essay-editorials concerned politics or religion and were taken from British papers, often without acknowledgment. Nearly all were written anonymously, frequently by men whose identity was obscured by Greek or Latin pseudonyms, and most of them probably expressed more or less accurately Bradford's own views. Of these borrowings by far the most important came from *Cato's Letters*.[14] The popularity of these essays was enormous; the monthly *Political State of Great Britain*, for example, gave them much space,[15] and on both sides of the Atlantic the *Letters*, together with *The Independent Whig*[16] and, later, Gordon's *Discourses upon Tacitus*, were constantly read.[17] Cato first appeared in the *Mercury* on February 20, 1722, with the following introduction by Bradford: "The Political Letters of Cato meeting with great Applause in England, the following is inserted here." The essay was an accurate reprint of the article published on July 22, 1721, entitled "The Right and Capacity of the People to judge of Government."[18] Four weeks later *Cato* 40, of August 5, 1721, "Considerations on the restless and selfish spirit of Man," came out.[19] In two weeks, "An Abstract of one of Cato's Letters, sent to the Author of the London Journal" was printed — the abstract consisting of the greater part of the essay "Of Flattery," of June 24, 1721.[20] Three weeks thereafter Cato again appeared, in a portion of the article entitled "Of publick Spirit."[21]

The *Mercury* of May 31 and that of June 21 printed letters addressed to Bradford by "Americo-Britannus," enclosing, first, a letter of "Plato" and, second, another letter of Cato, for which he requested and was accorded places in the paper. The Plato essay was also probably taken from the London *Journal*;[22] the other was the article of June 17, 1721, entitled "Cautions against the natural Encroachments of Power." This

14. See above, p. 16 n.
15. Note that Bradford's first two Cato letters were attributed to the *Political State*.
16. We have already seen that Keimer reprinted this book in 1724.
17. Note, for instance, in the New York *Weekly Journal* (Number 6) the phrase: ". . . the following Sentiments of (I had almost said, the Divine) English Cato . . . ." In *Mercury* 1182 a letter to Bradford referred to Cato as "that incomperable Lay Author." Note also the frequency with which *Cato's Letters* appeared among Bradford's book advertisements, and consider the significance of the fact that, when an unknown Philadelphian wished to address the public on matters which he deemed of utmost seriousness, he called himself Cato, Jr.
18. *Mercury* 114; *Cato* 38. (All references to *Cato* are to the sixth edition.) It should be understood that Bradford seldom gives number, date, or original title for any of these essays.
19. *Mercury* 118. This *Cato* essay was also used in *Busy-Body* 31.
20. *Mercury* 120; *Cato* 34. Two cuts — one of 22 lines, the other of about a page and a half — were made.
21. *Mercury* 123; *Cato* 35, with a cut of about two and a half pages.
22. Essays by "Plato" appeared in the London *Journal*, for example, on September 30 and October 7, 1721.

is a particularly interesting essay and, though in the *Mercury's* reprint there are several long cuts and some changes in the last two paragraphs, the crux of the argument is clear: "Government ... was the mutual Contract of a Number of Men, agreeing upon certain Terms of Union and Society, and putting themselves under Penalties, if they violated these Terms, which were called Laws, and put into the Hands of one or more Men to execute. And thus Men quitted Part of their Natural Liberty to acquire Civil Security." Meanwhile, on June 7, Bradford had printed still another Cato letter, "Of Loyalty," with a long cut and the omission of the four concluding lines which, since they referred to Europe and England, were not appropriate.[23] Several of these letters appeared in the spring and early summer, when news from abroad was not especially difficult to obtain, and each of them came out in a four-page paper during the early period of the *Mercury* when a half-sheet was the rule. Their inclusion suggests, therefore, that perhaps as early as 1722 Bradford had glimpsed the advantage of printing other kinds of material from abroad than news items, not simply to mollify his customers when intelligence was scarce, but, more positively, to make the *Mercury* livelier and more varied in its content, to expand simultaneously its size and its popular appeal.

For some time, however, the Cato letters were not followed by anything of comparable importance. During the following winter a "Britannicus" letter was introduced,[24] and in the autumn of 1723 in seven successive numbers the Bishop of Rochester's defense against the charge of treason appeared.[25] At the close of the same year Cato made his second bow in the pages of the *Mercury* with two essays called by Bradford "Of the Facility of dividing the People into Parties" and "On False Reverence."[26] A month later four consecutive issues of the paper published what was entitled "The British Cato's Lucabrations on the Conspiracy address'd, by Way of Letter, to the Disaffected Laity,"[27] in

23. *Cato* 36. The cut was about three and a half pages.
24. *Mercury* 154. "Britannicus" was another writer for the London *Journal;* Cato did not appear every week.
25. *Mercury* 199-205. The Bishop was the central figure in the conspiracy to bring the Pretender back to England in 1722.
26. *Cato* 134, "What small and foolish Causes often misguide and animate the Multitude," and *Cato* 131, "Of Reverence true and false." The first, which appeared in *Mercury* 211, was considerably cut. The second was printed completely in *Mercury* 212-213.
27. Between May 11 and 25, 1723, Cato published three letters under the common title "Address to such of the Laity as are Followers of the Disaffected Clergy, and of their Accomplices." Bradford reprinted the first of these three letters in *Mercury* 217 and down to the top of the second column of page one in Number 218; without any mark of transition he then continued with the third letter, which went through Numbers 219 and 220. The reprinting was accurate except for a few words and some awkward paragraph divisions. John Webbe, masquerading as "Z.," quoted from these same essays in the *Pennsylvania Gazette* of June 10, 1736, during his controversy with the *Mercury* over Hamilton.

which Cato discussed the dangers to England of the Pretender and the Roman Catholic Church and the serious threat to the laity of a powerful clerical group. Thereafter for several years Cato did not figure in the *Mercury*, although Bradford continued to import features from other sources — for example, in 1724 and 1725 much material supplementary to the ordinary news stories on the persecution of Protestants in France and Poland.[28]

Joseph Breintnall was responsible for re-introducing the *Mercury's* readers to Cato, for in several of the *Busy-Body* essays, sometimes without acknowledgment, he made use of the letters, which by 1729 were available in book form. *Busy-Body* 7 reproduced almost verbatim Cato's "Discourse upon Libels";[29] Number 10 spoke of Cato as "an Author who has acquir'd an immortal Fame in the Memory of all honest Men, by his Exposing the Nonsense, as well as vigorously opposing the Knavery, of overgrown Power and unlimited Ambition," and then reprinted the greater part of "The Contemptibleness of Grandeur without Virtue."[30] Number 11 presented "from a late famous political Writer in England" the complete Cato letter entitled "Of Plantations and Colonies."[31] Number 31, it has already been pointed out, was a patchwork of ideas and quotations from various Cato articles. And the final *Busy-Body*, in exhorting the people to inquire into the conduct and opinions of their representatives, was strongly reminiscent in theme and phrase of Cato's addresses to the freeholders of England.[32]

In the spring of 1730 another group of Cato letters appeared in the *Mercury* at the request of a person who signed himself "L.T." The first of these, printed completely in the issue of April 9, was a powerful discussion "Of the Equality and Inequality of Men," which began with the arresting sentence: "Men are naturally equal, and none ever rose above the rest but by Force or Consent . . . ."[33] The second made use of one of two essays entitled "Of Liberty and Necessity";[34] the third was an attack upon religious fanaticism, an "Inquiry concerning Madness, especially religious Madness, called Enthusiasm";[35] and the fourth carried the same discussion further and among other matters gave high

---

28. *Mercury* 255-257, 290, 294, 296, 297.

29. *Mercury* 480; *Cato* 100. The only important change is the omission in the *Mercury* of the fourteen concluding lines which form a transition in the original to the next essay.

30. *Mercury* 484; *Cato* 102. The stars in the *Mercury's* reprint indicate a cut of about a page.

31. *Mercury* 486; *Cato* 106. Why the Busy-Body was suddenly so disingenuous about admitting his source is hard to say.

32. *Mercury* 507; *Cato* 69, 70.

33. *Cato* 45.

34. *Cato* 111, reprinted in *Mercury* 537 and 539.

35. *Cato* 123, reprinted in *Mercury* 541-542.

praise to the Quakers[36] — which, no doubt, made the essay especially acceptable in Philadelphia. In 1732, without either introduction or explanation, there appeared in the *Mercury* an article defending freedom of speech but expressing abhorrence of those who publish attacks upon religion. Towards the bottom of the first column the anonymous writer began to quote without acknowledgment from the first of Cato's remarkable series of essays on liberty,[37] which he continued verbatim to the end of his article. The theme of this Cato letter was that all governments exist for the sake of the governed and that when they cease to be administered for the common good they become usurpers; its most striking passage reads thus: "All Men are born free; Liberty is a Gift which they receive from God himself; nor can they alienate the same by Consent, though possibly they may forfeit it by Crimes." Two years later in connection with the mysterious attack on Bradford a letter printed in the *Mercury* quoted at length, as the writer admitted, from "our English Cato"; the essay "Of Freedom of Speech"[38] was well chosen to support Bradford's rôle as indignant victim of the machinations of those who had threatened the liberty of the province.

In 1738 came the three letters of Cato, Jr.[39] introduced with a spurious claim to philosophical detachment and with an admission of indebtedness to "those celebrated Authors and Champions for Liberty, who published several admirable Letters on this Subject, and subscribed them with the Name of that famous Roman, Cato; which Letters being full of noble and generous Sentiments, I shall blend some of them with my own in this Publication." The blending turned out to reflect more credit upon Cato the First than upon the offspring he unconsciously fathered, for the essays are far less cogent and necessarily more scrappy than their original. Still the method of their concoction is interesting: in Number 1, for example, the four opening sentences were quoted almost verbatim from one of the Cato series on liberty already mentioned.[40] Then the writer discussed liberty as the "distinguishing Character of this flourishing Colony." At the point where he introduced Cicero's letter to Lentulus he paraphrased a section from another Cato essay;[41] and the remainder of the article, asserting that those who violate the liberty of a country should feel its vengeance, came from still another.[42] The

---

36. *Cato* 124, entitled "Further Reasonings upon Enthusiasm," reprinted in *Mercury* 543-544.
37. *Cato* 59; *Mercury* 640. The Cato series ran from December 30, 1721, to April 21, 1722, and discussed liberty in all its aspects: political, social, industrial, and cultural.
38. *Cato* 15; *Mercury* 741.
39. *Mercury* 955, 957, 960.
40. *Cato* 62.
41. *Cato* 27.
42. *Cato* 35. The quotation is cut, but accurate.

second essay, largely concerned with the right of the people to judge their leaders, began with an argument reminiscent of *Cato* 38, already printed in the *Mercury* on January 20, 1722. In the fourth paragraph came the sentence, "A Rotation of Power and Magistracy are essentially necessary to a free Government," also taken from Cato[43] and previously used in *Busy-Body* 31. The conclusion was quoted almost verbatim — though with changes of phraseology and in its new context less effectively — from the final paragraph of Cato's series on liberty:

Cato 73	*Cato, Jr.* 2
And here I conclude this noble Subject of Liberty; having made some weak Attempts to shew its glorious Advantages, and to set off the opposite Mischiefs of raging, relentless, and consuming Tyranny: — A Talk to which no human Mind is equal. For neither the sublimest Wits of Antiquity, nor the brightest Genius's of late or modern Time, assisted with all the Powers of Rhetorick and all the Stimulations of poetick Fire, with the warmest and boldest Figures in Language, ever did, or ever could, or ever can, describe and heighten sufficiently the Beauty of the one, or the Deformity of the other: Language fails in it, and Words are too weak.	Justice and Injustice are Opposite as Light is to Darkness, so is a wicked and good Magistrate: And it has not been in the power of the Sublimest wits of Antiquity, nor the brightest Genius of late and modern Times, assisted with all the powers of Rhetorick, and with the warmest and boldest figures in Language ever sufficiently to describe and heighten the Beauty of the one or the Deformity of the other; Language fails in it, and Words are too Weak.

The third essay, something of an anticlimax, drew extensively upon one of the finest of the Cato letters[44] — the same one which had been reprinted in *Mercury* 132 — and borrowed as its topic sentence the following statement: "Some have said, that Magistrates being accountable to none but God, ought to know no other Restraint,"[45] an assertion which both Cato and his imitator, of course, refute. Very probably, in addition to those just discussed, other editorials in the *Mercury* are at least partly taken or imitated from *Cato's Letters*,[46] but the score of essays which I have traced is sufficient evidence of Bradford's indebtedness to them. Certainly no other piece of writing was so frequently pressed into service for the benefit of Bradford's readers.

Many other writers besides Cato, however, contributed editorials to the paper on the ever-pressing topics of religion and politics. For example, in 1725 the *Political State of Great Britain* furnished material for three of the several numbers of the *Mercury* which discussed the

43. *Cato* 61.
44. *Cato* 33.
45. Cato, Jr. began: "It has been said that . . . ."
46. In *Mercury* 736 in the letter "To some Bodies particular Friend" appeared a quotation from Gordon's Tacitus.

persecution of Protestants.[47] What purported to be a letter from "Philalethes" considered absolute morality;[48] an essay of "Pythagoras" argued against the belief that good is only possible in a world where there is evil;[49] an anonymous writer who originally published in *Fog's Weekly Journal* attacked the basic principles of deism;[50] and still another article controverted Lucretius' belief that the gods take no active or interested part in the world.[51] From Farley's Bristol *News Letter* came an essay on the decline of woolen manufacturing in Great Britain;[52] somewhat later appeared articles on Sweden, on the logwood industry in Yucatan, on the revolution in Persia,[53] and at the time of the rumor concerning the repeal of the Septennial Act an essay on the frequency of parliamentary elections.[54] From the *Bee* in 1735 came reflections on the Marshals de Villars and Berwick,[55] and about the same time appeared three letters written by Monsieur de Catte just before he was executed for treason.[56] Further editorials reflected the continuing interest in religion and moral problems: "Advice, by Madam Guyon, to a young Ecclesiastick who was about to Commence Preacher,"[57] an essay written by Bishop Burnet shortly before his death which showed his belief in the need of further reformation in religion,[58] "Of the Divine Providence" from the *London Magazine*,[59] a part of one of Mrs. Drummond's sermons,[60] and an anonymous essay in defense of the proposition that our own consciences tell us that goodness is productive of happiness,[61] including a passage the irony of which would not have been apparent in the eighteenth century: "As well may it be supposed, that the Structure of the Universe, was formed as Epicurus Dreamed, by the accidental Concourse of Atoms, after having undergone numberless Revolutions in the immense Spaces, and that it can

---

47. *Mercury* 294, 296, 297.
48. *Mercury* 312. By "absolute morality" is meant morality independent of belief in God or personal immortality.
49. *Mercury* 519.
50. *Mercury* 521-523.
51. *Mercury* 534.
52. *Mercury* 595.
53. *Mercury* 626, 670, 707 respectively.
54. *Mercury* 763, 764, 766. The essay was taken without acknowledgment from the *Craftsman* of March 2, 1734.
55. *Mercury* 788.
56. *Mercury* 790-791. Though Bradford gave no source, this item probably came, directly or indirectly, from the *St. James Evening Post* of October 12, 1734.
57. *Mercury* 793. In Number 893 appeared her "Address to the Inhabitants of Great Britain" from Fénelon's *Dissertation on Pure Love* and in Number 898 "An Account of the Lady Guion."
58. *Mercury* 835.
59. *Mercury* 840, from the *London Magazine* of August 1735, originally from the *Grub Street Journal* of August 14.
60. *Mercury* 838.
61. *Mercury* 817.

support and govern itself, by I know not what Energy originally imprest, as that Decency and Order can result from Vice...."

Early in 1737 a letter from the *Daily Gazetteer* of the previous November 5 was published, in which the forty-eight years since the Glorious Revolution were summarized and the Hanoverian kings praised;[62] in the following year came an article entitled "Of managing a War with Spain to the best Advantage";[63] and in 1741 appeared an explanation of the method by which the emperor was elected.[64] At the request of "M.T." an extract from Bishop Hall's sermon on "the Character of Man" was inserted,[65] and another reader was gratified by the publication of a summary of Tillotson's sermon on John 1:47.[66] From the *Universal Spectator* came an essay on man's inconsistency in desiring others to obey him but being unwilling himself to obey God.[67] In its last half-dozen years the *Mercury* occasionally borrowed from the *Gentleman's Magazine* its monthly summary of the state of affairs in Europe;[68] descriptive accounts of the various places important in the war were included — for example, of Prague, Alsace, Cape Breton, Tournay, and Brussels;[69] and there were many articles such as "Reflections on the Loss of Ostend" or an eye-witness account of the fall of Carlisle,[70] "The Character of Cardinal Tencin" or "Case of a Corrupt Minister," the last an attack upon Robert Walpole.[71] The ever-important question of colonial finance was represented by an extract from a treatise "intended to be published" on "the Nature and Advantages of a Paper-Currency."[72]

Rather uncharacteristically Bradford published an essay "Of Superstition,"[73] in which it was asserted that superstition is much more dangerous than atheism since it involves the passions and leads to irrational fears, and another[74] in which the belief in the resurrection of the body was condemned as absurd since "the greatest Part of a Mans Body ... has been Part of several other Mens Bodies," and since the body has nothing to do anyhow with good or bad actions. An essay entitled "Mirth and

62. *Mercury* 900.
63. *Mercury* 979. Bradford gave as his source "the Magazine"; the article appeared in both the *London Magazine* and the *Gentleman's* of June 1738, originally in the *Craftsman*.
64. *Mercury* 1109.
65. *Mercury* 1055-1056.
66. *Mercury* 1104.
67. *Mercury* 1100.
68. *Mercury* 1146, 1197, 1300, 1304.
69. *Mercury* 1207, 1324, 1249, 1342, 1376.
70. *Mercury* 1353, 1369.
71. *Mercury* 1276, 1179. The article on Walpole was evidently taken from the *London Magazine* of March 1742. It does not mention him by name but was obviously directed against him.
72. *Mercury* 1155.
73. *Mercury* 1197.
74. *Mercury* 1153 and 1156.

Chearfulness consistent with Religion"[75] supported the comfortable belief that, since man has as natural a tendency to mirth as to food, those who have no reason to be repentant and uneasy should look on God as a friend and be happy; therefore, it ended, "Be merry and wise." A reader who deplored the giving way of religious tolerance in Philadelphia to the conflict engendered by "Enthusiasm and Superstition" requested the inclusion of the passage from Sir William Temple's *Observations upon the . . . Netherlands* which begins, "The great and general End of all Religion, next to Man's Happiness hereafter, is their Happiness here,"[76] and which supports the idea that, since man can no more govern his belief than the color of his eyes, complete freedom of religion should be everywhere allowed. More conventionally religious, however, were "Distant Thunder," an essay contrasting the security of the virtuous and the precarious position of sinners,[77] some passages from Gilbert Tennent's "The Necessity of holding fast the Truth,"[78] and "Principles of a Consistent Protestant."[79] Especially striking is an article published in the *Mercury* during the Jacobite invasion, the heading of which read thus: "To shew what Detestation all true Protestants ought to have of the Popish Religion, we here insert the following Account of the Proceedings of the Court of Inquisition at Lisbon, against . . . an Englishwoman."[80] Such a list, although it mentions but a fraction of the total number of "editorials" on political and religious subjects, gives some idea of their nature and variety. When we add to these such recurrent features of the *Mercury* as the addresses of the colonial governors, the reprinting of provisions of treaties or acts of Parliament especially interesting to the colonists, in addition to the great numbers of essays which were published as part of the Hamilton controversy but which had a general applicability, we gain some idea of the amount of space which Bradford devoted over a period of years to the colonial equivalent of the editorial.

In addition, the *Mercury* supplemented its news items with features other than straightforward discussions of religion and politics. For example, "Socrates" — who, like Cato, wrote for the London *Journal*[81] — contributed to the *Mercury* two discourses on human nature, an essay

---

75. *Mercury* 939. The essay was originally published in the *Weekly Miscellany* of July 1, 1737, and was republished in the *London Magazine*.

76. *Mercury* 1209. The passage quoted comes from Chapter V, "Of their religion," and is quoted accurately, but somewhat cut.

77. *Mercury* 1340.

78. *Mercury* 1211.

79. *Mercury* 1263. From the *American Magazine* of Boston, January 1744.

80. *Mercury* 1370.

81. "Socrates" was also the pseudonym of a local writer; see *Mercury* 630.

on charity, and a eulogistic account of Dr. Samuel Clarke.[82] Francis Osborne, who carried on the English paper after it became a ministerial instrument, was responsible for "A Discourse on Wisdom," of which the key sentence was: "Wisdom consists in proposing worthy Ends, and pursuing those Ends by worthy Means."[83] Occasionally, there was such a *tour de force* as "Political Quadrilla," in which each of the European powers was represented in turn as speaking a sentence which might refer either to the popular game of cards or to the situation in Europe in 1734;[84] or the curious dream-vision of Liberty, Justice, Pecunia, Usury, and other allegorical figures which appeared early in 1738.[85] Similarly from Paris came a clever satire "Logemens des Puissances de l'Europe, & d'autre Particuliers, pour l'annee 1744," in which the Queen of Bohemia was described as living at the Fortune in Victory Square, Cardinal Tencin at the Chimera in Fox Street, and so on.[86] A few months later appeared another satire, less entertaining and more vicious, called "The French King's Catechism" with the ironical note "licensed by Cardinal Tencin."[87] Several times the *Mercury* devoted space to education: one essay,[88] entitled "Some Thoughts of Education, To render the Education of Youth more Easy and Effectual in respect to their Studies at School," quoted Locke in support of its attack on Latin schools, and insisted that parents should try to decide whether their children were best fitted to be scholars, clerks, or tradesmen and should educate them accordingly; that all children should learn English before Latin; and that only would-be scholars should learn Latin at all. Compared to this essay, "Philanthropos' " advice to parents to support their precepts by the example of right-living was familiarly dull,[89] whereas another letter — from "Carissimi," who had recently been reading a translation of Horace into French — encouraged parents to see that their children learned both French and Latin.[90]

From the *Political State* came a story to illustrate the contention that the lower classes of people were being led astray by the examples of their

---

82. *Mercury* 525, 527, 546, 510. Samuel Clarke was an English philosopher and divine; not original, but of considerable logical power, he defended Christianity against deism, determinism, rationalism. *Mercury* 511 contained a long poem in heroic couplets on his death.
83. *Mercury* 696. The essay appeared in the London *Journal* of January 20, 1733; Bradford acknowledged its source correctly.
84. *Mercury* 758. Compare "The political Auction," also a satire, in Number 839.
85. *Mercury* 949. This essay may have something to do with the Hamilton controversy.
86. *Mercury* 1274.
87. *Mercury* 1294.
88. *Mercury* 784-785.
89. *Mercury* 840.
90. *Mercury* 875.

superiors, and by request Bradford inserted an attack on fencing and dancing as dangerous to the morals of youth.[91] Parts of two numbers were given over to the will of a certain Richard Norton of Southwick, England, "so Remarkable, we have thought it might oblige our Readers by publishing it";[92] and another will, "a very extraordinary Instance of Drollery," also appeared, in which the testator bequeathed his body to the worms, to lawyers the proverb that honesty is the best policy, to married women cleanliness, to prudes virginity and wrinkles, and to the London *Journal* and the *Free Briton* "one ounce of modesty, to be divided equally between them."[93] From the *London Magazine* was borrowed an article on Peter Kolbe's *The Natural History of the Cape of Good Hope* which illustrates the eighteenth-century conception of the noble savage in its emphasis upon the innocence, honesty, and simplicity of the Hottentots;[94] and from a later issue of the same magazine were reprinted two letters from a man on an expedition to discover a northwest passage, which commented upon the Indian natives encountered by the party and especially upon the "Usquemays."[95] The Bristol *Journal* supplied a readable account of how Gustavus Adolphus had acquired his motto and emblem;[96] whereas several satires in Biblical style lampooned such notables as Whitefield, Walpole, and the Marshals "Broglio" and Noailles.[97] In 1745 appeared "An Explanation, and short History, of Tontines,"[98] and at the beginning of the *Mercury's* final year, "An essay on the British computations of time, coin, weights, and measures," which proposed a new calendar of thirteen months and changes in the coinage and measuring standards to eliminate illogicalities.[99] Finally might be mentioned a curious numerological "prophecy" from France, printed in the *Maryland Gazette* and borrowed by Bradford in the early autumn of 1745, which was alleged to prove that peace would come before the end of the year.[100]

91. *Mercury* 865, 869.
92. *Mercury* 700-701. It appeared in England in the *Weekly Miscellany* of February 3, 1733, and in the first issue of the *Bee* (February 1733), from one of which Bradford may have taken it. It was remarkable chiefly in that Norton, being childless, left his estate to the poor with the legislature of England as his executors.
93. *Mercury* 777. The same will appeared in the *Pennsylvania Gazette* the week before Bradford published it. He gave as his source the *St. James Evening Post;* Franklin gave none. The *Gentleman's Magazine* of August 1734, which reprinted it, referred it to the *Grub Street Journal* of August 1.
94. *Mercury* 1157-1158. The article was taken from *Common Sense*, September 12, 1741. The title of the two-volume translation from the German, published in London in 1731, was *The Present State of the Cape of Good-Hope or, A Particular Account of the Several Nations of the Hottentots*.
95. *Mercury* 1229.
96. *Mercury* 1241.
97. *Mercury* 1214, 1222, 1243, 1244, 1245.
98. *Mercury* 1317.
99. *Mercury* 1356-1358.
100. *Mercury* 1340.

A special aspect of Bradford's use of "features" was the frequent inclusion of letters presumably sent to him by his subscribers. It was, of course, a convention of journalism on both sides of the ocean to mark as "letters" what were really products of the editor's pen — for example, in the *Tatler* and the *Spectator*. Moreover, a considerable number of the essays and articles already mentioned were called letters by Bradford, the introductory phrase having usually been lifted along with the essay itself from his source. A large number of the *Mercury's* contributions to the Hamilton controversy, also, were styled letters, though for all we know Bradford or someone hired by him may have written them. Still, some of the letters bear marks of genuineness, and others, whether hoaxes or not, add a special flavor to the *Mercury*. Some dealt with serious matters not very different from the sort we have previously illustrated; for example, immediately following the inclusion in the *Mercury* of a report on the evil effects of strong liquor in England[101] appeared a letter signed "Telemachus"[102] which pointed out a similar condition in Pennsylvania and spoke gloomily of "the Entire waste of above one half of the Labour, Industry, and Produce of this Province." Again, late in the history of the paper, a reader requested Cornelia Bradford to include a letter published originally in the *Barbadoes Gazette* and more recently republished in the *Virginia Gazette* about the masters' neglect of the religious training of the Negro slaves and their failure to set them a sound example in religion.[103]

Sometimes, if we can trust the *Mercury's* headings, a reader not only made a suggestion about an item to be included, but criticized the paper's policy in general. For instance, in July 1722 a letter concerning the discovery of a mineral spring near Philadelphia began uncompromisingly:[104]

> As I conceive our homeward News would be acceptable, and have a Place in your Mercury, as well as the Accounts of foreign Transactions, Leagues, Alliances, and the Course of the Politics of Nations, which perhaps will never affect us in these far distant, rough and woody Parts of the World: So I take this Time to give you a Piece of News, the publication whereof may be beneficial to us all at one Time or other.

In midwinter of 1724, when news was skimpy, someone suggested the inclusion of "some Pieces of Morality or other Instructive Animadversions out of Books which may not be in every Body's Hands," and

---

101. *Mercury* 341-342.
102. *Mercury* 343.
103. *Mercury* 1302. Keimer was evidently still riding one of his old hobbies.
104. *Mercury* 136.

politely told Bradford where he might obtain a second-hand, seven-volume set of the *Spectator* to aid him in carrying out this idea. On February 19, 1730, appeared the following unsigned letter, which may or may not be genuine:

> Mr. Bradford, You have ask'd my Assistance, at a Time when fresh Advices from Abroad cannot be had. I am not able to send you anything of my own so good, and useful, as the following Discourse, taken out of Mr. Crousaz's System of Reflection, concerning the Conduct and Improvement of the Mind. If you have not the Books, I may hereafter send you the remaining Parts of this Chapter.[105]

In addition, the *Mercury* gave space to the airing of criticisms of local fashions — for example, the following letter.[106]

> Having lately read a Letter, that in my Opinion very justly exposed a New fangled Custom, which of late Years has been introduced by our Young Fellows who have travelled abroad: It has often given me great Offence to see two lubberly Fellows run into one another's Arms, and hug and kiss, which I think an indecent kind of Rapture. I have also frequently observ'd one of these Demi Britons put a plain honest Englishman into a Confusion, by falling a Kissing him when he only expected a hearty Shake by the Hand. There was indeed a Custom among the Primitive Christians of Saluting with the Kiss of Charity; but I believe Religion has nothing of inducement in this Affair; nor are these Raptures founded on Friendship; for this Kiss of a common Friend is like that of a common Woman, bestow'd on any Fool who would accept of it. I wish you could by your Paper, abolish so foolish a Ceremony; as for my Part, if the Coxcombs must in their Greetings make a kiss, I would advise pretty Masters, to kiss their own Hands to one another, and cry, Your Taa which would be more in Character and less Offensive.
>
> John Downright.

Some letters suggest that Bradford, like other colonial "authors," either actually tried or pretended to fulfill the responsibilities of the "ethical problem" column of today's newspaper. The following epistle,[107] for instance, no doubt offered amusement to the sophisticated

---

105. Jean Pierre de Crousaz was a Swiss writer and philosopher whose numerous works on a variety of subjects were popular in his own day but have been largely forgotten.
106. *Mercury* 1179.
107. *Mercury* 214.

and human interest to everyone, and Bradford himself added a note of humor by closing his brief introduction with the remark, "The Writer of the first Part of our Weekly Mercury will omit his Design of pursuing his Memoirs, for the sake of the Young Lady, whose Condition is described in the following Letter. But Mr. B—— says, that if Lovina, by his means, acquires her Love, he shall expect a pair of Gloves." The letter itself ran thus:

Mr. B——
Sir,

As I always find, of late, the Front of your Paper employed in giving Lectures upon several Subjects, which are not only very diverting, but always very profitable. I hope you will not deny this Letter a Place in your Mercury, since it can be prejudicial to none, and may be the preserving me from Ruin. As you always avoid Scandal and Falsity's, I am the more desirous my Case should be seen in your Paper.

Know then, I am the Daughter, and only Child, of a Gentleman of —— Pounds a Year, and being arrived at near Twenty Years of Age, several have made their Addresses to me, but none so successful as the only Son of a Wealthy Tradesman: As he is entirely pleasing to me, I have return'd his agreeableness with a modest Civility; but my Father being biggotted to the very Name of Gentleman, and having an innate Aversion for Traders, opposes my Choice, and declares his Blood shall never be tainted by my Wedding a Machanick. This is his Principal Argument, together with his saying, If I Disobey I shall not Inherit. He recommends to my Bosom an aged Gentleman of Sixty, but of a superior Fortune and ancient Family. Alas! Mr. B——, he little knows the Sweetness of the young Traders or Mechanicks Conversation, or the melting Musick of his Voice! How dull will be the Day, if I Marry the old Sire! the light of the Sun will be tedious to me. When we are with a Person we like, the most trifling Objects can afford delight, but with him we hate the Groves have no Pleasure, and the gentle voice of Birds is nothing agreeable. Oh! that I could give my Father my Eyes, or else see with his! 'Tis Shocking to my Nature to disoblige my Parent, but I must affront him or Injure my self. If Self-Murder is as Criminal as the Murder of another, then an Injury done to one's self is as great a Fault as one done to another. Tell him, Sir, that Riches are not essential to Happiness; That a Person may be no Gentleman, tho' descended from Lords, and the Tradesman have the Soul of a Gentleman, with the Birth of a Mechanick. Grandure and Insignificence are not incompatible, any more than Meaness and Virtue. Oh let me rather Dye than Marry my Avertion! Therefore it is, Sir, that I call you to my Assistance. Tell my Father, That Tradesmen are not only advantageous to themselves, but Serviceable to the Nation in General; That there's not only profit but real Pleasure attending Business. Also advise him, how dull it is only to be a Gentleman; and ask him which is best, To get Money, or to have nothing to do but to spend it: And add, what else you think will lessen his over fond Opinion of Gentlemen, and encrease his Esteem for Tradesmen, which if you can do, you'll Oblige her who is,

Sir, Your Humble Servant, Lovina.

Whether the young lady was a real person or a fiction, her problem must have been far from unique in eighteenth-century Pennsylvania. Even though we cannot be sure that Bradford won his gloves, we know that he had tapped a good vein. Later, for example, he printed the plaint of a wife against a husband who was ruining his family by drink, bad company, and debt.[108] And an essay on the kind of woman a man should marry and a letter to Bradford on the evils that result from habitual tea-drinking[109] may have been the cause of "Generosa's" objections to what she considered the satirical tone of the *Mercury's* comments on ladies.[110] She insisted that not all women like fools and coxcombs, but that "Men of Sense are scarce, Sir, very scarce indeed," thereby stirring up — surely fictitiously — several lively replies. One came from "Generosus," who praised the lady for her wisdom and invitingly described himself as "a Batchelor (advanced beyond the Years of spritely Youth, but not beyond those of Health and Love)."[111] Another, from "Ignavus," was a defense of fops,[112] though in the issue of the next week he wrote to say that he had fallen in love with Generosa and now asked Bradford to insert a poem in her honor — in which, however, he used the name "Cælia" instead of "Generosa" because of the meter — and which ended with the following endorsement of marriage:

> Then Choose to Live while Health and Youth Invite,
> And taste the Raptures of a new Delight;
> Lest, lonely Hours by late Repentance driven,
> Should dedicate th' unwilling Saint to Heaven.

108. *Mercury* 532.
109. *Mercury* 559, 568 respectively.
110. *Mercury* 575.
111. *Mercury* 576.
112. *Mercury* 577.

Another fictitious letter[113] on a not uncommon problem appeared early in 1732 when "an Unfortunate Girl" addressed herself to "Mr. Mercury"; her difficulty was that, though she and a young man were very much in love, she wanted to marry him, whereas he wanted only to "ruin" her; her appeal ended with mock pathos thus:

> Now if you are an Oracle, if you have any Witchcraft, any Knowledge beyond what is common to other Scriblers, let me have some Tryal of your Skill; and tell me by what Method, how, and in what manner shall I learn to hate what I always lov'd, learn to forget what I Night and Day remember, learn to contemn what I think of with the utmost Tenderness: Do this speedily, Sir, or confess you cannot to your Importunate Servant,
>
> Eleanor.

Nor can there be much doubt that "E.W." of the "Female Sex" but "a constant Reader of News-Papers," was a product of somebody's, perhaps Bradford's, imagination, for she wrote to the *Mercury*[114] to protest against a remark in the *Pennsylvania Gazette*[115] to the effect that, since man is a sociable creature, he is unable to pass through the world happily without the assistance of his fellowmen — which statement, E.W. quibblingly contended, was a slight to women!

Under only a few circumstances did Bradford directly address his customers: occasionally, as we have seen, to announce an irregularity in the arrival of the post and a consequent delay in the appearance of the paper, and sometimes to introduce a news item or a feature. Once a year, however, he bowed to his readers when he appealed for the payment of subscriptions.[116] Usually the note read very much like this:[117] "N.B. Those Gentlemen, and others that have been pleased to encourage this Weekly Paper are desired to take Notice, that this No. 52 ends the Fourth Quarter thereof, and are desired to pay their Subscription-Money at the several Places where they entered their Names, in order to enable the Printer to continue the Undertaking the ensuing Year."

---

113. *Mercury* 628. "Socrates" in Number 630 admitted having sent Eleanor's letter, "knowing that such Performances are generally pretty well received when little Foreign News can be had . . . ."

114. *Mercury* 850.

115. *Gazette* 383. This "letter" appeared in the midst of one of the perennial quarrels between the two papers.

116. The first of such appeals appeared on September 15, 1720, and read thus: "This Paper No. 39 Ends the third Quarter those Gentlemen that have promoted it, are desired to send in their Payments to the Printer." Thereafter, Bradford ordinarily included such notices only at the end of the year.

117. *Mercury* 52.

Editorials and Features in the "Mercury"

Sometimes he had to take a firmer tone with his customers, as in these words:[118]

> N.B. This Paper No. 156 is the last Paper of the 3d Year. Those who are in Arrear are desired to make a speedy Payment at the Place of their first Subscription. If the Subscription for this Paper is not paid more punctually, it will oblige the Printer hereof to drop this Undertaking in a short Time; some Persons not having paid one Farthing since the first.

At the end of 1730 we know that Bradford had begun to feel Franklin's competition when he asked those in arrears to pay him, "especially those who have left off taking this Paper and gone to others";[119] and at the beginning of 1734 he announced, quite justly, that those who were more than a year behind in their payments would not receive further papers until they had paid, singling out particularly those who owed him money for the fourteen years since the paper's start, and requesting those who were interested in continuing their subscriptions to pay every six months or at least annually.[120] Two years later, still bolder, he said that those who owed for the paper or for advertisements in it should pay him or "expect Trouble."[121] Thus, now and again, Bradford wrote in his own character — not, however, as editor of the *Mercury*, but as its publisher. Such "editorial policy" as the paper had is implied only by the variety of its news, feature articles, and essays.

---

118. *Mercury* 156. Compare Numbers 208, 521. This sort of appeal was common in nearly all the colonial newspapers. Apparently the printers, at a time when ten shillings (the usual subscription rate) was a large sum, had great difficulty in collecting their debts. Compare also the long-standing bills for newspapers run up by Edward Wright and Thomas Penn. See above, p. 44 n.
119. *Mercury* 575.
120. *Mercury* 730.
121. *Mercury* 835.

Chapter 7

Literature in the *Mercury*

The intrinsic literary value of the *Mercury* we can dismiss with little more than a word. Largely because of the patchwork manner in which it was composed, its style was no better or worse than that of the other newspapers of its day. News items, whether foreign or local, were written in acceptable eighteenth-century prose. Some — for instance, the description of the plague in Marseilles — succeeded in being rather graphic; others — for example, the account of Marlborough's funeral — borrowed a certain dignity from their subject. The feature articles differed widely; whereas many of them, especially some of the letters from Bradford's correspondents, were written in slipshod language, others remain models of clear and vigorous style. Cato, for example, comes close to Swift's criterion of proper words in proper places. Since Bradford himself probably wrote very little for his paper, he deserves neither credit for its good writing nor blame for its frequent mediocrity. Doubtless he had little time to worry about the amenities of composition; perhaps he was not aware of them. But in any case his journal was not inferior in style to its contemporaries; even the *Pennsylvania Gazette* reflected very little, if any, of its editor's undoubted skill with the pen. Although we cannot, therefore, even by the farthest stretch of critical tolerance allow the *Mercury* inherent literary merit, it is not without literary interest. It contains many references to well-known writers and works, frequent borrowings from the popular essayists of the day and from the versifiers, as well as experiments in prose and poetry, serious and trivial, made by local dilettanti.

As we have already discovered, literary notables appeared from time to time in the *Mercury's* news columns along with those who had other claims to renown. Often, however, they were mentioned for reasons quite apart from their belletristic accomplishments; for example, Dr. Arbuthnot figured at least twice in the paper,[1] but as a physician; and Swift, we have seen, was a great Irish patriot rather than a famous satirist. Matthew Prior, one of the first and most important of the writers to be honored by mention in the *Mercury*, was the subject of several news items. Shortly after the report of his death,[2] appeared the three-line epitaph he himself, it was said, had designed for his tombstone:[3]

1. *Mercury* 120, 351.
2. *Mercury* 106.
3. *Mercury* 113.

> To me 'twas given to die: To thee 'tis given
> To live: Alas, one Moment sets us even.
> Mark! How impartial is the Hand of Heaven.

Later, however, came the report that a different epitaph was to be inscribed by Prior's order; this too was printed in the *Mercury:*[4]

> Here lies the Bones of Matthew Prior,
> A son of Adam and of Eve
> Let Bourbon or Nassau go higher.

This second epitaph occasioned an answer, "wrote by a Gentleman," which was also quoted by Bradford:[5]

> Hold Matthew Prior, by your leave:
>   Your Epitaph is something odd,
> Bourbon and You are Sons of Eve,
>   But Nassau is a Son of God.

Epitaphs and monument inscriptions seem to have had a special fascination either for Bradford or for his readers, for in addition to the three verses connected with Prior and two references to inscriptions for Marlborough,[6] several other items of the same kind appeared in the paper. For example, the inscription on the bust of Samuel Butler in Westminster Abbey was reported:[7]

> Th' Immortal Man serv'd Church and Court,
> Yet nothing got but Starving for 't.
> To After times be it recorded,
> How generously he was rewarded.

Similarly the *Mercury* discussed the setting up of a monument to James Craggs and quoted the six lines written by Pope which were inscribed upon it, correctly pointing out that they had originally been a part of the "Epistle to Mr. Addison on his Dialogue on Medals."[8] Later Bradford devoted space to the report that the monument in the Abbey to Sir Godfrey Kneller, also with an epitaph by Pope, was almost completed.[9]

Practically no English verse by well-known writers was reprinted in the *Mercury* except in the incidental fashion just illustrated, and nearly all of it was fragmentary. Gay's fable of "The Dog and the Fox" was

---

4. *Mercury* 214.
5. *Mercury* 229. The reference to Nassau as a "Son of God" may be an excess of patriotism or it may be irony.
6. *Mercury* 235, 619-620.
7. *Mercury* 96.
8. *Mercury* 433. The last line was slightly changed by Pope to fit its use as an inscription.
9. *Mercury* 549.

a rare exception; it appeared twice, both times in uncut form, though at least once for the very practical purpose of casting aspersions upon Andrew Hamilton.[10] Charles Wesley was represented in 1740 by his poem to George Whitefield beginning "Servant of God, the Summons hear" and by "Where shall my wond'ring Soul begin?" and "Come hither All, whose grov'ling Taste," printed in connection with the advertisement of the proposed publication of a hundred and fifty of the Wesleys' hymns.[11] The inclusion of both these citations, of course, was obviously dictated by the current enthusiasm for Whitefield rather than by their worth as religious poetry. Ordinarily only scraps from famous poets or poems were printed; for example, in Number 1305 nine lines from Garth's *The Dispensary* were quoted:[12]

> Auspicious Health appear'd on Zephir's Wings;
> She seem'd a Cherub most divinely bright,
> More soft than Air, more gay than Morning Light.
> Hail blooming Goddess; thou propitious Power.
>   Whose Blessings Mortals next to Life implore;
> With so much Lustre your bright Looks endear,
> That Cottages are Courts, when those appear,
> Mankind, as you vouchsafe to smile or frown,
> Find Ease in Chains, or Anguish in a Crown.

An epitaph on a young lady by "R.S." appropriated, somewhat inaccurately, two lines of the *Essay on Criticism*;[13] an article attacking the bogus lawyers in the province and one of the letters in the controversy over the Maryland clergy contained quotations from *Hudibras*;[14] an essay on man's thirst for knowledge, particularly on speech and writing as means to knowledge, began with two lines from Pope's "Eloisa to Abelard":[15]

> Speed the soft Intercourse from Soul to Soul,
> And waft a Sigh from Indus to the Pole.

Still another ended with four lines from *The Dunciad*, attacking

---

10. *Mercury* 594, 746; from the second series, the first fable. Bradford's first printing may have been innocent of any purpose except to entertain his readers; the second printing unquestionably was part of the Hamilton quarrel. Neither time was there any acknowledgment of source or authorship. Even the second printing antedated by four years the publication of the second series of fables as a book (in 1738, after Gay's death).
11. *Mercury* 1066, 1045.
12. The lines are from canto VI, 2-4, 305-310. There are slight changes. The author's name was given, but not the work.
13. *Mercury* 547. The lines are 466-467.
14. *Mercury* 632, 641.
15. *Mercury* 668. The lines (57-58) are quoted accurately.

Leonard Welsted,[16] and yet another, entitled "On Love and Marriage," was headed by Milton's famous passage beginning:[17]

> Hail, wedded Love, mysterious Law, true Source
> Of human Offspring. . . .

Addison, better known as a poet in the eighteenth century than he is today, was occasionally quoted — for example, thus:[18]

> The following beautiful Lines of Mr. Addison to Sir Godfrey Kneller, on his seeing His Majesty's Picture, are what we cannot omit giving Room to, since his Majesty's late Progress.

> O may I live to hail the Day
> When the glad Nation shall survey
> Their Sov'reign (through his wide Command)
> Passing in Progress o'er the Land!
> Each Heart shall bend, and ev'ry Voice
> In loud applauding Shouts rejoice,
> Whilst all his gracious Aspect praise,
> And Crowds grow Loyal as they gaze.

We have already noted that one of the essays on liberty of the press published at the height of the Hamilton conflict in 1734 began with lines from Addison's "Letter from Italy."[19] Much later, in 1739, a letter to Bradford, intended to remind the people of the "Blessings of a Free Government" and the consequences of arbitrary rule, ended by quoting from the same poem:[20]

> But what avail her unexhausted stores,
> Her blooming mountains, and her sunny shores,
> With all the gifts that heav'n and earth impart,
> The smiles of nature, and the charms of art,
> While proud Oppression in her valleys reigns,
> And Tyranny usurps her happy plains?
> The poor inhabitant beholds in vain
> The redd'ning orange and the swelling grain:
> Joyless he sees the growing oils and wines,
> And in the myrtle's fragrant shade repines:
> Starves, in the midst of nature's bounty curst,
> And in the loaden vineyard dies for thirst.

16. *Mercury* 669; *Dunciad*, III, 169-172.
17. *Mercury* 688; *Paradise Lost*, IV, 750 ff.
18. *Mercury* 162. The poem is entitled "To Sir Godfrey Kneller, On His Picture of the King"; the lines quoted are the third stanza.
19. *Mercury* 747.
20. *Mercury* 1057. The lines quoted, with slight inaccuracies, are 107-118.

Still another letter, connected with the Hamilton affair, quoted four lines from Addison's *Cato:*[21]

> Remember, O my friends, the laws, the rights,
> The generous plan of power delivered down,
> From age to age, by your renowned forefathers,
> (So dearly bought, the price of so much blood)....

A news story from London offers a final illustration of the most common kind of use of literary quotation in the *Mercury*.[22] The episode concerned the failure of a man to become a common councilman of the city because his supporters lingered too long over breakfast in the Boar's Head Tavern in Eastcheap and missed the election. The account concluded:

> This has created a great deal of Mirth in the Ward, which is likely to continue for some time. —— The Boar's Head is said to be the Tavern so often mentioned by Shakespear, in his Play of *Henry the Fourth;* which occasion'd a Gentleman, who heard the Circumstances of the Election, to repeat the following Lines from that Play.
> "Falst. Now Hall, what Time of Day is it Lad?
> "P. Hen. —— What a Devil hast thou to do with the Time of the Day? unless Hours were Cups of Sack, and Minutes Capons, &c."

Writers of prose, particularly of essays, were much more adequately represented in the *Mercury* than poets. Once again, some literary figures appeared only in the news columns; for instance, Bradford printed a report that the first edition of Eustace Budgell's pamphlet "Liberty and Property," containing "a great deal of Secret History," had been bought up in five days.[23] Defoe also appeared in a news item, but not by name, for the following paragraph was obviously printed because of its value as a sensation story and Bradford could hardly have known whose work he was celebrating:[24]

> This Day a Book has been published here called, The Fortunes and Misfortunes of the famous Moll Flanders, &c. who was born in Newgate, and during a Life of continued Variety for Three Years besides her Childhood, was Twelve Years a Whore, five times a Wife, (whereof once to her own Brother)

21. *Mercury* 820, from *Cato*, III, 5, 73-76.
22. *Mercury* 910. The quotation is from *Henry IV, Part 1*, I, 2, the opening lines, with a cut in Hal's speech.
23. *Mercury* 673.
24. *Mercury* 126. The title is quoted with slight inaccuracy.

Twelve Years a Thief, eight Years a transported Felon in Virginia, at last grew rich, lived honest and died a Penitent. Written from her own Memorandums.

Other well-known prose works or writers were referred to incidentally or perhaps quoted — to mention a few, Mather's *Magnalia,* Bacon, Sir William Temple, Swift's *Gulliver,* and Shaftesbury.[25] The established books and authors, however, were not so often or so extensively used in the *Mercury* as we should expect. For example, in spite of the recommendation of the person who had found the seven volumes of the *Spectator* for sale, Bradford did not borrow heavily from Addison and Steele. Perhaps the very popularity of these essayists deterred him from reprinting their work; at any rate they appear in the *Mercury* very much as the poets already discussed appeared, casually and often in mere snatches. The person who encouraged the use of the *Spectator* submitted as a sample part of Number 352[26] — the end of the introductory paragraph and the greater part of the quotation from Tillotson. Twice, both times in connection with a controversy, the *Mercury* printed the conclusion of Addison's essay "On True and False Humour": ". . . every honest Man ought to look upon himself as in a Natural State of War with the Libeller and Lampooner."[27] In the letter containing the first of the three references in 1734 to Bradford's "ill usage," a long passage from *Spectator* 568 appeared.[28] In the lengthy attack upon deism, probably Hamilton's, in the following year was printed *Spectator* 441,[29] including the translation into verse of the Twenty-third Psalm; and six years later, presumably at the request of a reader, Bradford printed from the *Spectator* a satirical discussion of "the great Hoop Petticoats which are now wore."[30] "Casettier" in his "History of the Cases"[31] practically admitted his indebtedness to "Chatterbox," who in the *Pennsylvania Gazette*[32] had presented the Box family as a parallel to Steele's family of the Staffs;[33] hence "Casettier" was indirectly an imitator of the *Tatler.* And a few months later, when "Mack" introduced the "Make" family,[34]

---

25. See, for example, *Mercury* 1196, 824, 1319, 669 and 734, 854 respectively. References to the Bible, of course, were common throughout the *Mercury's* history.
26. *Mercury* 215. This essay was written by Steele.
27. *Mercury* 645, 716; *Spectator* 35.
28. *Mercury* 738; "Coffee-house Discussion on the Mysterious Letter," by Addison. The passage quoted runs from "I could not forbear reflecting . . . ." to the end of the essay.
29. *Mercury* 824; *Spectator* essay by Addison entitled "Trust in God."
30. *Mercury* 1098. *Spectator* 127 by Addison; only the second paragraph was omitted in the reprinting.
31. *Mercury* 682.
32. *Gazette* 215.
33. *Tatler* 11.
34. *Mercury* 693.

referring to both the Cases and the Boxes, he quoted Sir Roger de Coverley's famous remark: "Much may be said on both sides."[35]

For the literary features of his paper, however, Bradford depended mainly on two sources, both strictly contemporary: on the familiar essays and the verse printed in the same British papers from which he drew his news, and on the products of local dabblers in literature. If such a choice condemned him generally to mediocrity, it supported what seems to have been in every phase of his newspaper policy a primary objective — timeliness. Moreover, not all of the periodical literature that was available to him was as inferior as its neglect today might suggest. For example, Bradford drew frequently, though not always admittedly, upon the *Universal Spectator,* one of the most successful as well as popular imitators of Addison and Steele.[36] Obviously in the manner of the earlier writers and almost equally readable is an essay on the shortness of human life, particularly on the foolish waste of time that makes it seem shorter than it really is. After some appropriate generalizations — the opening sentence is very much like the beginning of *Spectator* 93 — the writer satirizes those who pursue trifles: Mr. Flutterville, who collects butterflies; Mr. Plumage, who collects birds; Mr. Canker, who collects medals; and Mr. Vellum, who collects books but does not read them.[37] "A Censure on the usual Method of Disputes" is full of good sense and is well written;[38] so also are "Of Punctilios among the Fair Sex, and their obstinate Resolutions in maintaining them,"[39] and an essay explaining why neither wealth nor poverty, but "the middle Condition," is most conducive to virtue.[40] Particularly effective is a brief essay entitled "Of the Power of Custom," which reads as follows:[41]

> Custom is not ill defin'd to be another Nature, and certainly there is not any Thing so much Mistress of our Inclinations and Manners, or that hath so long a Being with Mankind. Therefore it is with so much Difficulty Persons change their Notions of Policy or Religion, which have been establish'd in their Minds from their early Infancy; their Opinions however wrong

35. *Spectator* 122, "Sir Roger at the Assizes," by Addison.
36. Walter Graham (*English Literary Periodicals,* 105) points out that the "Henry Stonecastle" who was editor of the *Universal Spectator* was in reality Henry Baker, a son-in-law of Defoe. Baker was assisted by several notable eighteenth-century writers (pp. 105-106).
37. *Mercury* 636. The source, not acknowledged by Bradford, was *Universal Spectator* 150. The similarity of Mr. Vellum to Tom Folio is obvious.
38. *Mercury* 840. The source, not acknowledged, was *Universal Spectator* 357.
39. *Mercury* 888. The source, acknowledged, was *Universal Spectator* 405.
40. *Mercury* 1084. The source, acknowledged, was *Universal Spectator* 464.
41. *Mercury* 894. Bradford gave as his source the *London Magazine,* which attributes the essay to *Universal Spectator* 412.

seem true, and the pleasing Familiarity with them takes off all those Deformities which another may behold. From hence it is that almost every Nation censures the Laws, Customs and Doctrines of every other as strange and unjust; but are confirm'd in their own Follies beyond a Possibility of Conviction. The Difference of Customs and Laws of Nations is so prodigious, that it may not be unpleasant to instance some, which are esteem'd by those who are educated in them as intirely consistent with Justice, Humanity and Politeness. There are a People who account it the greatest Act of Tenderness, Piety and Religion, to kill their Parents when they come to such an Age, and then eat them. There are Kingdoms where Children have no right to Inheritance, and Brothers and Nephews are accounted the next Heirs; where Chastity in unmarried Women is in no Esteem; they may lawfully, and without Loss of Reputation, be Prostitutes, yet, when married, they are Miracles of Chastity and Fidelity to their Husbands: Where they never have any Marriages, and therefore Children only own their Mothers, not being able to guess at the Father: Where Women are look'd on with such Contempt, that they kill all the native Women and purchase Wives of their Neighbours to supply their Use: Where it is the Fashion to turn their Backs to him they salute, and never look upon the Man they intend to honour: Where the greatest Beaus stink most, and instead of a Ribband they wear cross their Shoulders as a Badge of Honour, the Guts of a Sheep. It wou'd be endless to quote all the Absurdities which Custom in different Places warrants to be reasonable. By these Instances we see the grossest Follies are accounted sacred if customary, and the Fashion handsome and agreeable, tho' never so shocking to an unbias'd Spectator.

As Custom and Education have such strong Prevalency over the Minds of Men, how careful shou'd Parents be in giving their Children not a narrow and confin'd Method, but a generous and noble Way of Thinking; to teach them even from their Youth, that there are Errors, and that when, with an impartial Enquiry, they find them, they shou'd know how to retract them, and not let the false Step they made at their first Setting out keep them in a wrong Path thro' the whole Journey of Life afterwards; for too often, as Mr. Dryden tells us,

> By education most men are misled,
> We so believe, because we so were bred;

> The priest continues what the nurse began,
> And thus the child imposes on the man.[42]

Still another good essay was "The Use and Abuse of Riches," which began, "Seek not proud Riches, says the great Lord Bacon, but such as thou may'st get justly, use soberly, distribute chearfully, and leave contentedly. Yet have no abstract, nor friarly Contempt of them";[43] and which quoted from "Mr. Pope to Lord Bathurst" the ten lines beginning, "Wise Peter sees the World's respect for Gold,"[44] and other passages from the same poem, such as the section on the Man of Ross.

In like manner the *Mercury* borrowed literary essays from contemporary periodicals other than the *Universal Spectator*. From *Common Sense* came "Of the pernicious Custom of telling Lies in Conversation" by "Tom Tell-Truth,"[45] an essay in the style of the *Spectator*. From the *Craftsman* came a letter proposing that instead of taxing dogs, taxes should be put upon asses, though the writer admitted that he did not want to "make Asses of all Mankind,"[46] as well as an essay entitled "The Universal Ballance," a mild satire on the state of the times enlivened by the self-mockery of its conclusion.[47] The *Weekly Register* supplied "A general Review of Female Fashions address'd to the Ladies," which after a few introductory observations discussed in turn such objects as the farthingale, the stay, the tippet, or the riding-habit;[48] and the *Prompter* furnished "An odd Kind of Vanity exposed," that is, the curious tendency of people to claim to have known something or to have had some ability "formerly" and to value themselves accordingly.[49]

"Hercules Vinegar" of the *Champion* in an amusing essay supported the naturalization of the Dutch word *skellum*, which implied everything bad, for use against those who attacked patriots or engaged in similar

---

42. *The Hind and the Panther*, ll. 1683-1687. The first two lines are not accurate.
43. *Mercury* 1323. The source, unacknowledged, was *Universal Spectator* 822. The passage from Bacon appears in "Of Riches." Other essays from the *Universal Spectator* appeared in Numbers 789, 1096, and 1100. Doubtless there are also others which I have not found.
44. *Moral Essays*, Epistle III, 123-132.
45. *Mercury* 1199. Mrs. Bradford gave as her source only a "late magazine." This would appear to be the *London Magazine* of June 1742, which reprinted the essay from *Common Sense* 280. The same essay appeared also in the *American Magazine* of Boston of August 1744.
46. *Mercury* 879. Bradford gave the *London Magazine* of June 1736 as his source, which makes acknowledgment to *Craftsman* 520.
47. *Mercury* 1324. Bradford gave the *Craftsman* as his source, but without number or date. The correct date was April 14, 1744.
48. *Mercury* 621. The source, unacknowledged, was *Weekly Register* 66.
49. *Mercury* 889. Bradford gave as his source a "late magazine," probably the *London Magazine* of June 1736, which quotes the essay under the heading of *Prompter* 665.

objectionable activities. He likewise upheld the right of the woman "to wear the Breeches" under certain circumstances — for example, if she reads Latin and her husband does not or if she is young and he is a dotard.[50] In a more serious vein the *Champion* discussed marriage:[51] the differences between the attitude towards marriage at different periods of life, the two things upon which matrimonial success hinges — inclination and interest, and the importance of good manners within marriage. From *Fog's Journal* came the satirical "A Wizard's Harangue in praise of Poverty"[52] and "An Essay on the Fashions";[53] and from the *Grub Street Journal* came an entertaining bit on punctuation:[54]

> To exact writing true pointing either gives beauty, or marrs the sence, more than is commonly observed by the generality of readers; an admiration or interrogation point, or even a comma, wrong placed, may be of very ill consequence: and no pointing at all, may be as bad; and is a sure indication either of ignorance, or design, in the scribe. Thus when king Edward II was dethroned he was afterwards murdered, whilst a Prisoner, by the wicked contrivance of Adam, bishop of Hereford, who wrote these six words to his keepers, without any stops, or pointing between, *Edvardum occidere nolite timere bonum est:*[55] by which there was room left for a double construction to be put upon the same words, and by which the poor king lost his life; and the wicked prelate excused him-

---

50. *Mercury* 1094. The date of the *Champion* was given as June 24, 1740. The essay was probably not by Fielding. (See Wilbur L. Cross, *The Life and Times of Henry Fielding*, I, 251-259.) Cross points out that, though the articles reprinted in the Henley edition by no means comprise Fielding's entire contribution to the *Champion*, "since Ralph adopted more and more the technique of Fielding's style," one must be cautious about what one assigns to Fielding after June 17, 1740. In his analysis of articles after June 21, in which he discovers several "with Fielding's specific marks," Cross does not mention this one; nor does it bear the marks he uses for identification. In June 1741, Cross says, Fielding ceased altogether to write for the *Champion*.

Skellum appears to have become naturalized in Scottish; a famous example of its use occurs in "Tam o' Shanter."

51. *Mercury* 1321.
52. *Mercury* 842. Bradford acknowledged the *London Magazine* as his source. The essay originally appeared in *Fog's Weekly Journal* of September 28, 1734.
53. *Mercury* 891. Bradford cited the *London Magazine* of July 1736; this quotes from *Fog's* of July 10, which states that the essay was "Extracted from the *Holland Spectator*."
54. *Mercury* 732. Bradford gave no date or number, but the original may be found in Number 186 of July 19, 1733, in the form of a letter to "Mr. Bavius," editor of the paper, in the regular column called "From the Pegasus in Grub-street." The original included at the end a few lines omitted by Bradford.
55. Marlowe (*Edward II*, ll. 2341 and 2344) translates the sentence: "Feare not to kill the king, tis good he die" or "Kill not the king, tis good to feare the worst."

self, and all for want of a semi-colon, or comma, rightly placed.

But what I principally intend by this remark, is, to give your readers the copy of a very remarkable jury, taken at the assizes held at Huntington before judge Dodderill, in July 1619. Now one would think, that the whole county must be pick'd on purpose to find out names to range in this whimsical order: but that so it was, is a most certain truth, several copies of them being to be seen hung up in divers families there at this day. And it is self-evident, that a comma, placed after either the christian, or surname of these men, gives a very different idea of their persons: for with a comma (for example) after the name *Maximilian,* an ignorant reader might fancy him King of Toesland; whereas, if the comma was placed after his surname it would appear that Toesland was only the town at which Maximilian King lived; and so of the rest, (viz.)

> Maximilian King of Toesland.
> Henry Prince of Godmanchester.
> George Duke of Sommersham.
> William Marquis of Stukeley.
> Edmond Earl of Harford.
> Richard Baron of Bythorne.
> Stephen Pope of Newton.
> Stephen Cardinal of Kimbolton.
> Humphry Bishop of Bugden.
> Robert Lord of Wazely.
> Robert Knight of Winwick.
> William Abbott of Stukeley.
> Robert Baron of St. Neots.
> William Dean of Old Weston. . . .

Many other essays and articles of a literary nature appeared in the *Mercury:* "The Folly of Passion expos'd,"[56] "An Essay on Conversation,"[57] a piece which satirically interpreted the Prometheus-Pandora story to mean "that all sorts of Diseases own their Origin to the Use of Fire and Woman,"[58] an essay in praise of philanthropy,[59] "On the Spleen,"[60] an article attacking those fashions which try to change the form of the human body, such as the binding of Chinese women's feet or dieting in order to achieve "a slender Waste,"[61] a long discussion of

56. *Mercury* 1319.
57. *Mercury* 551.
58. *Mercury* 633, from the *Political State* of September 1731.
59. *Mercury* 676 and 678.
60. *Mercury* 837.
61. *Mercury* 948. Bradford gave as his source Boston *Weekly Post Boy* 169; the same essay appeared in the New York *Gazette* of August 21, 1738.

ill nature and good nature,[62] and a very readable essay against hypocrisy, containing the following anecdote:[63]

> A celebrated Historian tells us, that in a little City of Italy, there was a certain Man ... who lent Money upon Pledges at an exhorbitant Interest, but who did it however very privately, affecting in Publick an Air of extraordinary Austerity, and pretending to have a Conscience so scrupulous, as to be offended with the bare Appearance of an evil Action, This Man once offer'd a Parish Priest (who was perfectly acquainted with his Manner of Life) a very considerable Sum to preach a Course of Sermons against Avarice and Usury. The Priest was amazed at the Proposition. "My Friend, said he, are you in Earnest? Or do you think to add me to the Number of those whom you deceive? Let me intreat you to deal candidly with me, and declare for once what your true Meaning is? Why replied the Man, I really mean what I say. You must know that my Trade falls off, and if you can't fright some People from Usury, I shall not be able to live by it."

Particularly worth noting also is an excellent example of a literary type that had flourished in the seventeenth century but was already outmoded — the character. "Description of a Lover" began thus:[64]

> A Lover is a Planet stricken Wretch: He, like a Dog to a blind Beggar, is the Cur that leads blind Cupid; when he is at the greatest Value, the Fashion of his Clothes exceeds the intrinsic Worth of his Wit: He is never without soft Verses in his Pocket, and Sweet Powder in his Wig; and his Poetry, like his Scent, is sufficient of itself to make him nauseous. He fixes one Proposition, that Nature never made or afforded but one compleat Production, and that is, Cloe, or Amaryllis, or Jenny, or Sukey, or ——— ... Like Hamlet in the mad Scene, he is ungarter'd, quite negligent, yet thro' Affectation, he takes great Pains to shew that he takes none; he never writes but upon the best Paper; he sighs ... he is neat in the folding of his Letter, and in the Choice of his well flavour'd Wax; he is one of that Philosopher's Pupils who were enjoin'd five Years Silence; he never answers, at least never to the Purpose; he becomes an Optician, and studies Colours, and a Knot, the agreeable flowers on a Mantua, or a Night Gown is his peculiar

---

62. *Mercury* 971 and 973.
63. *Mercury* 1005. Bradford acknowledged his source as the *Daily Gazetteer* of November 22, 1738.
64. *Mercury* 983. Compare "the Character of a Good Man" in Number 974.

Talent to judge of; he loves, now swears, now forswears, now languishes; is a Paradox of Paradoxes and what no one could yet account for, above Description, Definition, or Emblem. . . .

As the only unified group of literary essays in the *Mercury* and as the product, in part, of Franklin's wit and skill, the *Busy-Body* has attained special eminence. For the same reasons this section of the paper has been previously studied (for example, by Elizabeth Christine Cook), but some comment on the essays not yet discussed here should perhaps be included. In his opening letter to "Mr. Andrew Bradford" Franklin entertainingly paved the way, not only for specific attack on Keimer,[65] but also for whatever subjects might later present themselves to his imagination. As "a kind of Censor Morum" he assumed the privilege, for himself and for those who carried on the series, of talking about anything he wished. The second essay, somewhat hypocritically, condemned those who are witty or satirical at the expense of others, and in the fictitious characters of Ridentius and Eugenius presented contrasting types. Similarly the third essay offered a contrast of characters, much of it praising "Cato," an honest, simple, virtuous man, but the end commenting upon "Cretico," a "sowre Philosopher," who lived "in a neighbouring Province" and was advised to "Neglect those musty Authors" and apply himself "to a Study much more profitable, The Knowledge of Mankind" and of himself. An ironical footnote asserted: " 'Tis to be observ'd that if any bad Characters happen to be drawn in the Course of these Papers, they mean no particular Person, if they are not particularly apply'd." Number 4 contained a letter from "Patience," represented as a single woman and a shopkeeper, who is continually annoyed by a neighbor whose children mix up her stock and whose constant presence keeps off a handsome suitor. Number 5 consisted, first, of a letter supposedly written by a great-grandson of Bunyan, who, the Busy-Body said, by a wonderful faculty of discovering the "most secret Iniquity" was capable of giving him much assistance in his "Work of Reformation," and, second, of an answer to a charge in the *Instructor* of February 25 that the Busy-Body was blasting reputations. The following essay, attributed to Breintnall, pointed out the error of

---

65. Actually the attack on Keimer had begun the week before *Busy-Body* 1 (that is, on January 28, 1729) with the letters of "Martha Careful" and "Cælia Shortface," who complained that "S.K." had printed in *Instructor* 5 of the previous week "such Things . . . as wou'd make all the Modest and Virtuous Women in Pennsylvania ashamed." In that issue Keimer had reached in Chambers' *Universal Dictionary*, which he was laboriously reprinting, "ABO" and had conscientiously published a column on abortion. Franklin was quick to seize the opportunity inadvertently offered him, and the scheme to oust Keimer from control of the *Instructor* was under way. In *Busy-Body* 1 he made specific reference to the "Fair Sex" and to his intention of "Brightning . . . their Understandings, without offending their Modesty."

attacking political and religious misconceptions by petulant and satiric criticisms; number 7 was the Cato letter already discussed; and Number 8, one of the best of the series and typical of the Poor-Richard side of Franklin's personality, was an essay condemning those who waste time in digging for pirates' treasure "while the rational and almost certain Methods of acquiring Riches by Industry or Frugality are neglected or forgotten."

Of the score of essays contributed to the series by others than Franklin several are borrowed — not only the letters of Cato, but also an article on the "Political Lion" from the *Guardian*,[66] as well as an anecdote from Plutarch's life of Timoleon.[67] Some deal with conventional topics of religion or morality: for example, in Number 19 a letter protesting against ridicule of Christianity, Number 21 on the nature of the deity and the reasonableness of the Christian religion, in Number 28 a letter on infidels, and in Number 26 a satirical attack on freethinking. Some deal with problems of conduct; Number 12, for example, discussed the proper bearing and manners of men both rich and poor in order to win a good reputation; a letter in Number 15 attacked the gallant who thinks it no wrong to seduce the wife or daughter of a friend; Number 23 lamented the "vicious Treatment" of one social class by another, especially of inferiors by their social betters, and Number 25 was a rambling discourse on the importance of people's doing the work in society for which they are best fitted. Number 30 was an appeal for greater understanding and intercourse between youth and age, and offered much advice on the proper handling of young people, and Number 29 assailed "Riddle Pedants," charlatans who in the absence of proper schoolmasters muddle the heads of the unlearned.

The device of the fictitious letter and character continued. Mathilda, for example, protested to the Busy-Body that her gallant, Florio, had made love to her childhood friend Flavia; she ended her appeal: "Dear Mr. Censor, revenge me of this perfidious Man, and name your own Conditions: Nay, I don't care if I make a Promise to you of my Person and Fortune, tho' I know not if you are young or old, handsome or ugly."[68] To this the Busy-Body chivalrously but noncommittally replied that he would defend the fair sex "to the last Drop of Blood and Ink." Florio, in turn, asked the Busy-Body's advice, pointing out that he had pursued Mathilda without success for two years before he turned to Flavia; now that Mathilda admitted her love, he wanted to return to her, but what could he do?[69] A realistic bit is the portrait of Octavio, an idle

66. *Busy-Body* 9.
67. *Ibid.*
68. *Busy-Body* 14.
69. *Busy-Body* 16.

young fellow, who wrote to say that he wished to be "a sort of an Under Busy-Body" because he had nothing to do but saunter up and down the city "swinging [his] Cane in [his] Hand, and counting the Pillars in the Market-House."[70] Likewise vivid is the petition of some young tradesmen of Philadelphia asking that the Censor appeal to women of their social class not to put on the airs of the upper classes and acquire an extravagant taste for "the Tea-Table and appertenances," both of which make them unattainable to the young men who would like to marry them.[71] Amy Prudent also directed a protest to the Busy-Body, this on behalf of wives against the "Twelve a-Clock Punch-Drinkers" of the Meridional Club who, she said, invaded various homes for their activities, disrupting the households they visited as well as neglecting their businesses.[72] Lucy Widowless, complaining that her husband, once loving and attentive, now considered her dowdy and slighted and abused her, boldly suggested: "And pray tell me, if my Husband looks out for a handsomer Woman, whether I may not look out for an honester Man ——."[73]

Some of the other items in the *Busy-Body* are decidedly inferior to these thumb-nail sketches, especially the catalogue of the vices supposedly prepared by Bunyan's great-grandson.[74] The "Canterbury" in Number 16 is a mildly amusing satire of the empty-headed conversationalist whose mind and tongue run from one idea to another without aim or coherence. Twice Keimer's project of reprinting the entire *Universal Dictionary* piecemeal in the *Instructor* was lampooned,[75] the first time entertainingly in a letter about "a Differunce amung Us pure cuntry Fokes": a quarrel has arisen between "my Cuzzin" and "our Skool-Mastur" about the spelling of three words; the schoolmaster says that the question will be decided by the *Instructor,* but the cousin "laffs" because "he fynds that theze Wards Woant wun off um be printed in the Struckter, In less Tyme then Sevvinti fyve Yeers, and twelv Wekes...." In addition to prose Breintnall included in the *Busy-Body* a good deal of verse, mostly submitted by "Damon," who contributed among other things a coarsely humorous verse on the marriage of a couple who had already "had a Bitt to taste."[76] More interesting than Damon's work, however, was a character sketch in poetic form which appeared in Number 13. The point of it was that its entire twenty-two lines were written

70. *Busy-Body* 14.
71. *Busy-Body* 15.
72. *Busy-Body* 20. A "reply" from the Meridional Club appeared in Number 22.
73. *Busy-Body* 28.
74. *Busy-Body* 24.
75. *Busy-Body* 16, 26.
76. *Busy-Body* 18. Damon also appeared in Numbers 17, 19, and 20.

in monosyllables, and the experiment was defended by a prose comment on Pope's famous objection to the monosyllabic line[77] and by the quotation of the opening monosyllables of Dryden's translation of the *Aeneid*.[78] Interesting for a different reason was the poem on High Street in Philadelphia, not good verse certainly, but a valuable descriptive piece.[79]

Just as the poetry contained in the *Busy-Body* papers was less skillful than the prose, so nearly all of the verse published in the *Mercury*, except for occasional quotations such as we have already mentioned, was inferior to the prose essays. Most of it was anonymous and was drawn, like the news items and the essays, from contemporary British journals, though local poetasters also contributed to the paper. Of the longer poems the greater number were occasional, most frequently suggested by political events or by the death of an eminent person; as literature most of these are pedestrian exercises in the conventional phraseology of the day, almost always written in the heroic or the octosyllabic couplet. A poem celebrating the arrival of Thomas Penn in Philadelphia, lines commemorating the passing of the Act of Succession and praising George I, "An Elegy upon Mrs. Burnet," "To Sir Robert Walpole. On Seeing the United Squadron of Great Britain and Holland," "On the Marriage of the Prince of Orange and the Princess Royal," "A Poem on the Spanish Depredations," a pseudo-Pindaric ode on the marriage of the Prince of Wales, "Verses, to the Memory of Henry Brooke," "On Whitefield's Preaching," "Hymn to Victory, on the taking of Cape Breton," a verse "By a loyal Tar" on the Scottish rebellion[80] — these and innumerable others had little to recommend them, even when they were printed, but their timeliness. Some of the satiric verse was livelier, even if not better written, than the other occasional poetry: for example, "Dialogue between the Pope and Cardinal Ottoboni," which mocked the Pretender's supposed request for 100,000 crowns to help him gain the throne of England,[81] or the ironical congratulation to Whitefield upon his preaching sixty-eight sermons in forty days and collecting large amounts of meat and money.[82] Typical of this occasional verse and interesting because of their subject-matter are some of the pieces which reflected the popular attitude towards Walpole. In 1734, for instance,

---

77. *Essay on Criticism*, II, 347: "And ten low words oft creep in one dull line."
78. "Arms, and the man I sing, who, forc'd by fate . . . ."
79. *Busy-Body* 18.
80. *Mercury* 659, 210, 418 (Mrs. Burnet was the wife of Governor Burnet), 520, 753, 968, 873, 850 (Henry Brooke was a local poet), 1057, 1345, 1358 respectively.
81. *Mercury* 412.
82. *Mercury* 1077.

Bradford printed some verses entitled "Written Extempore, on Reading the News," which ran thus:[83]

> In vain th' Indulgence of the warmer Sun,
> On Italy hath with such Vigour shone,
> Since Foreign Armies have her Soil undone.
>
> In Poland, Golden Harvests rise in vain,
> While hostile Troops destroy the ripen'd Grain,
> That neither Party may the Crop obtain.
>
> On Rhine's fair Banks in vain the Vines appear,
> Big with th' generous Juice which crowns the Year,
> While the contending Hosts distribute Fear.
>
> War, hideous War, defeats the Suns kind Ray,
> Vain is the fertile Soil, the lengthen'd Day,
> If Peace be absent, ev'ry Joys away.
>
> In Brittain's beauteous ever charming Isle
> Warm is the Sun, and fruitful is the Soil,
> And thanks to Walpole's Care, Success attends their Toil.
>
> Our yellow Fields the Farmer's Wealth increase
> Acquir'd with Labour, 'tis enjoy'd in Ease,
> The Statesmans Wisdom still preserving Peace.
>
> Such is our State, and let it be our Care,
> That none on us may this Reflection spare,
> All things but Gratitude can prosper there.

Later an ode "To the People of Great Britain" ended with this quatrain:[84]

> Who fears the Schemes of Gallic Art?
> Who shall of Philip's Arms complain?
> While Walpole Council shall impart,
> And George shall live and rule the Main?

In similar laudatory fashion some lines on Walpole's recovery from an illness concluded:[85]

---

83. *Mercury* 782. Bradford correctly attributed these lines to the *New England Weekly Journal*, which in turn (Number 401) acknowledged its indebtedness to the *Whitehall Evening Post*. Number 520 also contained a poem which stressed Walpole's peace policy.

84. *Mercury* 965. The source was the *Daily Gazetteer*, reprinted in the *London Magazine* of March 1738.

85. *Mercury* 989.

Custom-House, Philadelphia, *Entred Inwards.*
Sloop Joseph & Ann, Geo. Blair from Leverpoole.
Scooner Mary & Hannah, W. Fielding from Bolton.
Sloop Speedwell, Benj. Weaver from Virginia.
Sloop Prosperity, Tho. Carmell from New-York.
Sloop Charming Sally, David Hall from Virginia.
Entred Out.
Ship Surprize, Joseph Redmond for Antigua.
Sloop Speedwell, William Child for No. Carolina.
Brigg Revolution, John Houghton for Barbados.
Cleared Out.
Scooner Sea-Flower, Ja. Haselton to Coracoa.
Snow Warren, John Meas to Antigua.
Brigg Dolphin, John Evans to South-Carolina.
Ship Speedwell, Wm. Bell, jun. to Lisbon.
Billinder Lucy, John Lindfay to Georgia.
Snow Sarah, Ninian Boggs to Londonderry.
Sloop John & William, J. Gais to No. Carolina.
Ship New Sufannah, Tho. Landon to Jamaica.
Brigg Globe, Daniel Rees to Antigua.

Prices of Goods, &c. in Philadelphia

By the Hundred
Flour, 9 f 6
Biskett, White, 18 f 0
  Middling, 15 f 0
  Brown, 10 f 0.
  Ship, 10 f 6
Muse. Sug. 45 to 50 s
Rice, 14 s
Ginger, 25 s
Tobacco, 17 to 20.
Turpentine, 5 s.
By the Pound
London Loaf Sugar, 1 f 8.
Pennsylvania Do. 1 f 4
Allspice, 12 d
Cotton, 3 f 0.
Indico, 8 s
By the Gallon
West India Rum, 3 f 8.
New-England, ditto 2 f 8.
Mollasses, 2 s 4

By the Barrel
Beef, 27 10.39 s
Pork, 55 to 60 s.
Pitch, 15
Tar, 12 f 6.
Powder, 10 l 0 s
By the Bushel
Wheat 3 f 0 to 6 s.
Ind. Corn, 2 f 2.
Salt, Fine, 3 f 4
  Coarse, 2 f 4
Flax Seed, 6 f. 4
By the Thousand
Staves, Pipe, 7 l. 00 t 0
  Hogshd. 3 l. 15 s.
  Barrel, 2 l. 10 f 0.
By the Pipe
Madeira Wine 23 to 30

STolen from the House of Doctor *William Nichols*, in *Freehold* in *Monmouth* County, on Saturday the 6th or *November* Instant, a white Horse somewhat Fleabitten, no Earmark nor Brand, about thirteen Hands and a half high, goes a travelling Pace and thence to a Hand-Gallop, with a Ruffet colour'd Saddle and Bridle. Any Person bringing the said Horse, Saddle and Bridle to the said Doctor *Nichols*'s, or to *Job Throckmerton*'s in *Freehold*, shall have *Thirty Shillings* Reward with reasonable Charges.
Philadelphia, the 10th of the 9th Month, 1742.

LOST, the 5th of this Instant (*November*) a Leather Letter-Case (commonly called a Pocket Book) with a Leather String sewed to it to fasten it, containing several Notes and Accounts, and some Paper Currency. Whoever finds the same and brings it to *James Parrock* of this City, shall be well Rewarded for so doing.

NOTICE is hereby given to all Persons indebted to Mess. WHITE and TAYLOR, that if they do not immediately make Payment of their respective Debts, or give Security to *William Peters* their Attorney, they will be summoned to the next County Court.
Philadelphia, November 3. 1742. WILLIAM PETERS.

To be Sold,

A House and Lot of Ground in *Walnut-street*. Inquire of *John Snowden* in *Philadelphia.*

To be Sold,

ELeven Hundred and Fifty Acres of good Land, lying on a Branch of *Delaware* called *Pohatcong*, in *West-New-Jersey*. Inquire of *Abraham Bickley* in *Philadelphia.*

Just Published, and Sold by the Printer hereof,

W. BIRKETT's
& T. LEEDS's } Almanacks, for 1743.

For *Antigua* directly,
The Ship SURPRIZE,
Joseph Redmond Master,
Borthen 400 Tons, 20 Guns 6 Pounders, and 80 Men, now lying at Mr. *Plumsted*'s Wharf.
For Passage or Freight agree with the said Master, or Mr. *William Plumsted*. *October* 15. 1742.

THese are to give NOTICE to all Gentlemen who desire to learn the right METHOD and true ART of DEFENCE, and Pursuit of the SMALL-SWORD in its greatest Perfection, and extraordinary quick and speedy, with all the Guards, Parades, Thrusts and Lessons thereunto belonging, fully described, and the best Rule for Playing against Artists or Others with Blunts or Sharps; That they may be taught the same by Mr. RICHARD LYNEALL, Practitor and Master of the said Art, who is to be spoke with at Mr. *Fredrick Smith*'s, Hatter, at the Corner of *Market-street* and *Front-street.*

N. B. As he intends to continue in this Place no longer than *March* next, he humbly desires all Gentlemen who are acquainted with his Method of Teaching, and the Performance of those whom he had the Honour to Instruct, to give him a Character accordingly.

To be Sold by SAMUEL PERRY,
At his Store the Corner of *Carpenter's Wharf*, in *Water-street, viz.*

BRoad Cloths fine and coarse, Kerseys, striped Flannels, Cambletts, Cambletteens, striped and plain Callamancoes, tib'd Fustians, worsted Damask, Flower of Egypt, Lowestowns, striped Turketts, Prunelloes, Starretts, striped Holland, Linnen and Cotton Handketcheiffs, Shirt and Jacket Buttons, draw Boys, Mens and Boys Felt and Castor Hats, Mens white Lamb Gloves, Womens Ditto and Mittons, Broadcloth *London* broad and narrow Shalloon, worsted Shagg, Mens and Womens worsted Hose, worsted and Cotton Caps, Scotch Snuff, Egings of sundry Prizes, Hat Linings, Loops and Buttons sundry forts of Ironmongery and Cutlery Ware, Sadlers Ironmongery, Sadlers Tacks, 2 and 3 Nails, Joyners Brads, Hobb Nils, Sparrow Bills, Sprigs, clout Nails, 2, 3, 4, 6, 8, 10, and 20 penny Nails.

☞ The above Goods to be sold Cheap for ready Money or short Credit. The said *Samuel Perry* designing for *England* in the Spring.

AS Mr. *Andrew Bradford departed this Life on the 23th of November last, I hope those who were pleased to be Customers for the* AMERICAN WEEKLY MERCURY, *(of which my deceased Husband was the first Publisher) will excuse the Omission of the last Weeks Paper at the usual Time; and for the future they shall be serv'd carefully: And all Persons who have any Printing Work to do, or have Occasion for Stationary Ware, shall be thankfully serv'd at the lowest Prices,*

By CORNELIA BRADFORD.

JOSEPH GRAY is removed from the *Horse and Groom* in *Strawberry-Alley*, to his House at the Sign of *The Conestoga Stage-Waggon*, in *Market-street*, where he sells good Wine, Rum, Brandy, Sugar, Salt, and other Liquors, by the great or small Measures, at reasonable Rates, and keeps good Entertainment for Man and Horse.

To be Sold,

A Plantation in *Brandywine* Hundred in *New-Castle* County, containing 300 Acres, well situated, with a good Dwelling House and Orchard, a good Barn and Stabling, good Meadowing and well Water'd, with other Conveniencies. Whoever inclines to purchase the same may apply to *William Cloud* living on the Premises, and be further inform'd.

PHILADELPHIA: Printed and Sold by the Widow BRADFORD at the Sign of the BIBLE in *Front-street*, where Advertisements are taken in, and all Persons in Town or Country may be supplied with this Paper.

Advertising Page of the *Mercury*, December 9, 1742
Courtesy of the Library Company of Philadelphia

LITERATURE IN THE "MERCURY"

So W———s dangerous Illness being o're,
Again he glads Britannia as before.

But in 1740 appeared "Thales and Sir R——— W———," an attack on Walpole's attempts to avoid war, which began:[86]

Thales to take a Wife persuaded long,
Reply'd, for such great cares I'm yet too young,
Some time o'er past, to marry he was told
Was best, but Ah! Cry'd he, I'm now too old.

Whereas the verses on Walpole are characteristic, from a literary point of view, of the occasional poetry devoted to politics, two long pseudo-classical poems on the death of Aquila Rose[87] adequately represent the nature of much of the *Mercury's* elegiac verse. One was a pastoral dialogue by a certain Elias Bockett of London; the other was written, apparently in Philadelphia, "by an intimate Friend of A.R."; and a very few lines of each will be ample evidence of their florid mediocrity.[88]

A Poem to the Memory of Aquila Rose

Damon.
Marino! — welcome from the Western Shore.
Welcome to Britain! to thy Friend once more:
Why silent thus? —— Why this dejected Air?
The melancholy Cause let Damon hear.
By some fair Tyrant has my Friend been crost?
Or was his Cargo in a Tempest lost?
Or to what more disastrous Accident,
Must I impute these Signs of Discontent?

Marino.
Impute 'em to a Loss that human Pow'r
Can ne'er retrieve —— Amintas is no more!

Damon.
Forbid it Heav'n ——

Marino.
—— Yes, 'tis a fatal Truth ——
Cold in the Earth, lies the lamented Youth. . . .

86. *Mercury* 1092. A poem in Number 1169 also appears to attack Walpole.
87. Rose was a Philadelphia poet; his poems were published posthumously by his son.
88. *Mercury* 237 and 272.

On sight of Myris Tomb; An Elegy.

> Stream on my Eyes, with generous Grief o'erflow
> At this most solemn Spectacle of Woe:
> 'Tis Myris Tomb, this little Spot contains,
> Of that once active Youth the Dead remains:
> His mouldring Dust in silent Darkness lies,
> Dumb his sweet Tongue and clos'd his chearful Eyes.
> Lamented Friend! Thy Glass too swiftly Run,
> Too swift the Life, thou hadst so well begun:
> Oh why wert thou so early Snatch'd away?
> So quickly banish'd from the Realms of Day?
> And e'er we knew thy Merit mixt with Common Clay. . . .

Epigrammatic verse on various topics was popular with the *Mercury* — for example, lines on the Triple Alliance, on the coronation of George II, "On little Cleora," on the death of a lady's lap dog, a couplet on George's return from the European campaign of 1743,[89] or the "Epitaph" for a local poet, John Dommett, which read:[90]

> Wealthy while Rum he had, was John, yet Poor,
> Cause worth but little, Rich cause crav'd no more.
> Him England Birth, Heav'n Wit, this Province gave
> Food, Indies Drink, Rhymes Pence, White-Marsh a Grave.

Poems about love and tributes to fair ladies, usually very conventional, appeared quite frequently in the paper. Representative of this group are "Cupid Wounded"; a dialogue between "the Widow R——lt" and "a Lady"; a verse telling how Sampson wooed and won "our Nanny"; "To the Fair Camilla"; a curious pair of poems entitled "On a Negro Girl making her Court to a Fair Youth" and "The Youth's Answer" — a negative; "On the Departure of a Lady to a Foreign Country"; and "Sylvia to Philander," on the separation of lovers in time of war.[91] "On Woman," written in praise of the female sex by an Irish gentleman, showed more than usual skill in the use of the couplet, and "To my absent Chloe" by "Ruris Amator" was written in singable, if conventional, quatrains.[92] "The Journal of a Modern Lady" and "On the

---

89. *Mercury* 814, 427, 688, 814, 1259 respectively.

90. *Mercury* 1022. These were the closing lines of a longer poem styled an elegy.

91. *Mercury* 482, 284, 536, 805, 793, 1002, 1103 respectively. "To the fair Camilla" is interesting as one of the few poems in the *Mercury* written in blank verse. It was composed, presumably, by someone in Chester County and has footnotes referring to Homer and to Thomson's *The Seasons*.

92. *Mercury* 991, 876.

Fashion among the Ladies wearing White Stockings"[93] showed facility and a faint sparkle distantly derived from Pope. The second runs:

> Woman will ever find some roguish Fashion,
> To strike and tickle loose Imagination;
> Hence the white Leg most wantonly they show,
> To make with luscious Thoughts our Bosoms glow;
> What dire Disasters ought we not to dread,
> Were they all Killing made from Feet to Head:
> But oft white taper Legs can do no Harm,
> For the view'd Face can all the Powers disarm,
> Nature still kind our safety thus assures,
> And tho' one Part may wound, another cures.

Several of the *Mercury's* poems dealt with religion or religious figures; in addition to those already cited, there were other lines on Whitefield,[94] a tribute to the Reverend John Kearsley for his leadership in completing the building of Christ Church,[95] some verses in praise of Mrs. Drummond,[96] and a conventional poem entitled "On God's Omnipotency."[97] Moreover, one of the most effective of the *Mercury's* many attacks upon rationalism was "The Modern Goliah: Or Hero of Heroes. A Panegyric, humbly address'd to the venerable and worthy set of Free-Thinkers," which galloped along with a carefree disregard of both truth and the niceties of meter as follows:[98]

> Sing the Hero in strains so sublime, O my Muse.
> That my patrons the song may, attentive, peruse;
> The Hero, who, fir'd with a generous disdain,
> Of a mind that's enslaved, bravely shakes off the chain:
> So elate are his thoughts, and so high his desires,
> He abhors the low hopes, which Christ's Gospel inspires;
> Yea so high, that he scorns to have ought in his whole
> Composition so abject and mean as a soul;
> And himself, with his friends, always greatly suggests
> The glory of living and dying like beasts:

---

93. *Mercury* 554, 983. The first is a long poem reminiscent in subject matter of Addison's "Clarinda's Journal" and parts of "The Rape of the Lock."
94. *Mercury* 1040, 1090, 1094, 1309.
95. *Mercury* 1296.
96. *Mercury* 846. In "Verses on several of the Quakers Teachers" (*Mercury* 887) Mrs. Drummond was flattered by a line paraphrased from the *Essay on Criticism:* "She bids alternate passions fall and rise!" (Pope, 1. 375, "And bid....").
97. *Mercury* 847.
98. *Mercury* 1041. The form — anapestic tetrameter couplets — was most unusual. Though Bradford gave no source, the verses probably came from the *Grub Street Journal* of September 17, 1733.

To which lofty conceits he does proselytes win
By the wonderful powers of a sneer and a grin;
And when these allies fail him, calls in to's relief
The aid of rhetorical mutton and Beef;
The disputants slyly engages to dine,
When his thoughts to each guest appear noble and fine,
— For what can resist a persuasive surloin?
Through mazes they wander, and often in vain,
Who endeavour to come at the heart by the brain;
Whereas to that place, cunning fox! has in truth,
Always found the way easier by far from the mouth.
When in logical forms, mens assent we demand,
Some won't be convinc'd, and some can't understand;
But doctrines bid fair for engaging of hearts,
When prov'd by syllogestical chickens and tarts.
Thus to conquests we see they've but slender pretence,
Who trust such dull weapons as reason and sense:
But on him, oh! what triumph, what victory waits,
Who is aided by advocate dishes and plates!
And whose punch-bowl too is such a notable elf,
That it reasons and argues, as well as — himself!
    I should now, to conclude my detail of his merit,
Chant forth his most wonderful courage and spirit,
Who in war with his maker dares fearless engage,
And undauntedly sneers at omnipotent rage;
Who adventures (stout heroe!) to call God a liar,
And smiles at the thoughts of unquenchable fire;
Who mocks at such fools as with fears are possess'd,
And thinks to be damn'd, a most excellent jest.
And whereas it on searching the scriptures appears,
That Christians are styl'd there God's children and heirs;
He gallantly chooses for ever to die,
Before he'll commence a relation so nigh
(Oh! stinging dishonour!) unto the most High.
And since benefits conferr'd, tho' excluding the givers,
Denote imperfection and want in receivers;
He scorns, since the donor esteems it a favour,
T' accept the mean present of living for ever.
And tho' kingdoms and crowns t' engage him unite,
And glory, and honour, and bliss do invite;
He a constancy firm and unshaken will boast,
And prefers his old friend and acquaintance, the dust.
    But here I resign, and the subject dismiss,

Unable to celebrate merit like this:
Such inverted heroics suit ill with my pen,
And the task is more proper for devils than men.

Several poems referred to Philadelphia or Pennsylvania. A long piece published in 1740[99] discussed rather incoherently the province's tolerance and fertility; its snakes, plants, and birds; and, hopefully, the inevitable defeat of Spain. A typical passage ran:

Not gain'd by Blood, nor took by conq'ring Bands,
Healthy and Prosp'rous Philadelphia stands,
Design'd for Empire, fittest for Command,
Built in the Center of a fruitful Land.
Thou great Asylum, safe from lawless Foes,
Where Liberty in full Perfection flows:
As long as Winds may blow or Oceans rowl,
Safe may'st thou Stand, and Trade from Pole to Pole.

"The Wits and Poets of Pennsylvania" celebrated the fame and ability of Joseph Breintnall, Jacob Taylor, George Webb, Henry Brooke, and another unidentified versifier.[100] The following lines are characteristic:

For choice of Diction, I would B—ret—nl choose,
For just Conceptions, and a ready Muse;
Yet is that Muse too labour'd and prolix,
And seldom, on the Wing, knows where to fix. . . .
With Years opprest, and compass'd round with Woes,
A Muse with Fire fraught yet T—y—lr shoes.
His fancy's bold, Harmonious are his Lays,
And were He more correct, He'd reach the Bays . . . .
In Br——ks Capacious Breast the Muses sit
Enrob'd with Sense polite, and poignant Wit;
His Lines run smoothly, tho' the Current strong;
He forms with Ease, with Judgment sings the Song.
As th' Awful Elm Supports the Purpling Vine,
So round his Sense his sprightly Wit Entwines:
Oh! would he oftner write, so should the Town
Or mend their Tasts, or lay the Muses down . . . .

In the winter of 1733, one of the very severe winters previously mentioned, appeared "On the instant cold Weather,"[101] an interesting, if amateurish, poem — partly descriptive and partly didactic.

99. *Mercury* 1051-1052.
100. *Mercury* 592.
101. *Mercury* 684.

Cold as the Arctick Pole in Winter time
This seems to be a further Northern Clime,
When all the frozen Land and Water too
Lie cover'd long with Ice and heaps of Snow,
The River seems as a long open Plain;
For now no Waves thereon to rise are seen,
Nor foaming Billows breaking on the Shore
And multiply the Riches more and more,
All quiet now, but rugh before; tho'[102]
For tho' high stormy Winds may often blow
The silent Streams still calmly Ebb and Flow
By ponderous weight of solid Ice supprest,
Ships are confin'd, and the Harbour rest
And Seamen now enjoy a long *Quietus est*.
Highways are safely now pass'd on
Where boats with Sail and Ores did lately run.
Young Men now on their Skeetes to play delight,
As swift in Motion as some Birds in flight:
The Sturgeons now their wonted Sport forbear
To raise themselves up in the open Air;
And other Fishes are content to keep
Themselves there where the Waters are most deep
Yet Anglers here the Ice do often cut.
And take with Line and Hook Pike, Chub and Trout,
Cold and long Winters here before have been;
Carts loaden drawn from shore [to] shore I've seen.
Some Years but little Ice is in the River,
But Ships sail in and out as ever.
For two Foot in thickness, and six Inches more
The Ice was lately Measur'd near the Shore.
The price of Wood was never known before
So high as now, 'cause from the Jersey Shore,
None is convey'd, yet here's no want of it;
Wood must be had, before good Fires to sit,
And other Uses, as to boil the Pot:
But what must poor Folk do, who have it not,
Nor Cloathes enough to keep their Bodies warm?
To these cold Winter sounds a dire Alarm
Whose daily Commons too are very scant.
Who fast all Day sometimes for very Want.
These O ye Rich remember to relieve,
And unto them what's necessary give,

---

102. There appears to be an error, probably in typography, in line 9 or 10.

And they with Thanks and Joy shall it receive.
Remembring what ye give unto the Poor
The giver of all Good will it to you Restore,
For it is left upon divine Record,
(Who gives unto the Poor, does lend unto the Lord)
Rich Men can Winter into Summer turn,
In whose warm Rooms good Fires do always burn:
Who having many Cloathes, not thin and old[103]
Who every Day may Feast and make good Cheer;
Drink when they please good Wine, strong Ale and Beer,
Who have good Bed at Night to lye upon,
Prepared for them with the warming Pan:
If these Complain of Cold, what must the Poor,
Who all contrary Hardships do endure?

Though all these poems were anonymous, the *Mercury* contained a very few of which the authorship is known. Joseph Breintnall, for example, wrote the poetic tribute to the noted Quaker John Salkeld which accompanied the prose obituary in the paper.[104] Samuel Keimer, an inveterate scribbler, at the end of an advertisement which he inserted in Bradford's journal shortly after coming to Philadelphia offering his services to teach Negroes to read the Bible, included a rimed injunction against those who might "condemn this Undertaking"; and Jacob Taylor, protesting against the spurious almanac for 1726 put out in his name by Keimer, assailed "S.K." in a long and vigorous piece of rime.[105] Two poems on the Quakers, although only one referred specifically to Pennsylvania, must also have been of special interest to Bradford's local customers. One was reprinted from the New York *Weekly Journal* early in 1742[106] as a criticism of "my Neighbour Gravelook," who will seize a thief and have him hanged but will not resort to force in order to aid "his injur'd Country," though he will applaud those who protect him.[107] The verse ended with a question:

Say, prudent Reader, 'tis referr'd to thee,
What sort of Conscience must my Neighbours be?

The second came from Britain and was said to have been spoken extemporaneously by an English soldier the day after he had received a flan-

---

103. A line appears to be omitted here.
104. *Mercury* 1044. This attribution is based on the assertion in *Friends' Miscellany*, III, 69-70, and *A Descriptive Catalogue of Friends' Books*, I, 316. The poem on High Street in the *Busy-Body* also is usually attributed to Breintnall.
105. *Mercury* 165, 318. Keimer's authorship of the advertisement in the *Mercury* is established by the references in Taylor's attack.
106. *Weekly Journal* 426, January 25. The poem was answered with reason and moderation in the issue of the following week.
107. *Mercury* 1154.

nel waistcoat through the bounty of the Quakers.[108] One other poem deserves mention — an answer to an attack on Andrew Hamilton in a pamphlet called "The Life and Character of a Strange He Monster"[109] published in 1726, written in workmanlike couplets, which opened the poem thus:[110]

> Would you Attempt to lash a guilty Age,
> And rail at Vice, upon the publick Stage?
> To ev'ry Crime a conscious Mirror hold,
> And Arm your self with Satyr bravely bold,
> Expose the private Hypocrite to view,
> Bent to reclaim — or praise the vertuous few?
> Tho' it perhaps no Reformation cause
> Thy just Intent would Merit our Applause.
> So Persius wrote, with no design to wrong,
> And 'gainst his Country's Vices, arm'd his Tongue;
> Then Juvenal and Horace full of wit,
> Whose Manly Sence appears in all he writ,
> The publick good was still the Poet's Aim,
> Not spurr'd by Envy, that infernal flame. . . .

A few miscellaneous pieces illustrate the humorous verse which occasionally appeared in the *Mercury*. For example, in connection with a news item which must be quoted to make the lines intelligible, Bradford printed a deft burlesque of the heroic style employed in the elegies on Rose:[111]

> Several Bears were seen Yesterday near this Place, and one killed at German-Town, and another near Derby. Last Night a very large Bear, being spied by two Amazons, as he was eating his last Supper of Acorns up in a Tree; they calling some Inhabitants of this Place to their Assistance, he was soon fetch'd down from thence, and entirely dispatched by em. Afterwards finding no more Sport with Bears, they quarrel'd with one another for the Body, as madly as the Centaurs upon a like Occasion. The following Lines were writ in Praise of the Notable Heroine, who spied him first and attended him to his Execution.

---

108. *Mercury* 1376. The *Gentleman's Magazine* of November 1745 (p. 614) contained a news item about the Quakers' sending ten thousand woolen waistcoats to the army.
109. See Hildeburn, no. 282.
110. *Mercury* 344. This was written during Hamilton's absence in England. It suggests that the *Mercury's* animosity towards Hamilton must have begun after his return to Philadelphia.
111. *Mercury* 93.

Literature in the "Mercury"

    Fair P———r, sure 'twas wisely, bravely done,
To shew thy self a modern Amazon,
Unus'd to hunt, or draw the strenuous Bow,
To poize the Lance, or fatal Dart to throw;
Yet Atalanta's Courage shone in thee,
That durst approach the monster-bearing Tree:
For R———r's Arm you mark'd the destin'd Prey,
Nor fearful turn'd your Virgin Face away,
And merited with him the Honour of the Day.

From London came a punning epitaph on Mr. Presgrave, "an eminent Surgeon."[112] A lament for a dead damsel named Fanny became burlesque in the last line where it was made clear that Fanny was "a harmless Fawn."[113] "The Gardners Curse for such Visiters as leave his Gate open" and "On the Sign of the Black-Horse in Black-Horse-Lane. Written by a Jockey" (in which it was pointed out that the sign-painting was so abominable that one could not distinguish the mane of the horse from its tail) are both entertaining.[114] From Boston, in connection with the death of a young boy at play, came the following sally against writers of doggerel:[115]

    I cannot in this Place avoid devoting a Couplet to the Memory of this unfortunate Lad. Upon a like melancholy Occasion the immortal Tom Law, who was for a long Time the reigning Poetical Genius of New-England thus beautifully sings,
        He got his Death-stroke at the Dam,
        And in an Hour or two he died slam.
Now tho' the Beauty of the Word Slam does yet, and for ever will remain unrivall'd, yet we hope a faint Imitation may be no illaudable Ambition,
        He got his Death-stroke at the Sled,
        And in a Minute or two he died dead.

And "On the Comet," said to have been composed extempore, expressed effectively the writer's blithe cynicism:[116]

---

112. *Mercury* 155.
113. *Mercury* 939. The source was probably the *London Magazine* of October 1737.
114. *Mercury* 1110, 1134.
115. *Mercury* 576.
116. *Mercury* 935. The source was probably the *London Magazine* of September 1737.

> When a Comet presumes
> To sweep Heaven's Rooms,
> With a Tail as long as a Beesom;
> Astrologers shew,
> And Mortals all know,
> Some strange Thing will vex, or else please 'em.
>
> But fear not my Friends,
> What this Comet portends;
> For if any Wonder befall,
> They will be for the best,
> It must be confest,
> Or no Wonder can happen at all.

A word should be added about foreign languages and literature in the *Mercury*. From an early date advertisements in German were published in the paper; in connection with Zinzendorf some passages in German were printed; otherwise, however, German did not appear. References to the Latin classics and quotations from them — often in the original, sometimes in translation, and not always accurate — occurred frequently, quotations being used especially as headings for essays and "editorials"; Greek appeared less often. There were, for example, quotations from Tacitus, Juvenal, Ovid, Seneca, Plutarch, Persius, Cicero, Claudian, Virgil, Terence, and Horace,[117] as well as references to Aristophanes, Pliny, Socrates, Lucian, Lucretius, and Julius Caesar.[118] A curious essay entitled "A Criticism upon the Word *Woman*," reprinted from the *London Magazine*, contained among less unusual evidences of learning a reference to Trevisa, the quotation of a Spanish proverb, and footnotes in Greek and Hebrew.[119] Once at least a line of Greek appeared in a letter, and, though Spanish literature seems generally to have been outside the ken of writers and readers of the day, there was at least one reference to Don Quixote.[120] Occasionally the paper printed a piece of original Latin: for example, the proposed epitaph for Marlborough and John Salomon's advertisement;[121] or, immediately after Maria Theresa's consort had been elected emperor, an epigram, with two English translations below it, as follows:[122]

---

117. *Mercury* 211, 213 and 846 and 1096, 528, 66, 1197, 535 and 1199, 948, 859, 532 and 949, 820, 960 and 1127, for example. Many of these quotations were not acknowledged.

118. *Mercury* 1084, 535, 1319, 948, 535, 1319, for example.

119. *Mercury* 942.

120. *Mercury* 954 and 820 respectively.

121. *Mercury* 235, 859.

122. *Mercury* 1351.

Literature in the "Mercury"

Filia quae fueras, fies nunc Caesaris Uxor,
Caesaris Augusti tu quoque Mater eris.

Thou Caesar's Daughter wer't, but now the Wife,
And give hereafter future Caesar's Life.

Thou was't the Daughter, now thou art the Spouse,
And shall be Mother, of the Imperial House.

Moreover, a poem "presented to the brave and worthy Commodore Warren" was an admitted imitation of Horace,[123] and a transcription into serious verse of the dialect letter of a girl at Deal deserted by her sailor sweetheart was reminiscent of Ovid's *Heroides*.[124]

French was the foreign language used most freely in the *Mercury*. The extent of local interest in it is suggested by the large number of advertisements of teachers of French which regularly appeared in the paper, and part of the Hamilton controversy, we have seen, was conducted in French. A few feature articles, such as the jeu d'esprit on the lodgings of eminent Europeans and some verses on the death of Charles VI and the problems of the succession, were written in it.[125] Most surprisingly, one of the several tributes printed by the *Mercury* on the death of Governor Gordon was a sonnet in French by John Salomon, the language teacher, which read thus:[126]

Le Ciel, grand Gouverneur, ne vous avoit fait naitre
Avec tant de Vertu, que pour notre support;
Mais dans notre besoin, pourquoi cruelle Mort,
A jamais de ces lieux l'as tu fait disparoitre?

Malgré toi cependant, il ne cessera d'etre,
L'honneur qu'il s'est acquis triomphe de son sort,
Quel que fut son pouvoir il ne fit rien a tort,
Et par de beaux Exploits scent se faire connoitre.

Heureux, si nous eussions encor eu son secours,
Et qu'il n'eut point fini si tot son noble cours!
N'importe, pour parler dignement de sa Gloire,

Quoiqu'il soit ici bas au nombre des Mortels,
Un Merite si rare, au Temple de Memoire
Unanimement, va lui dresser des Autels.

---

123. *Mercury* 1339.
124. *Mercury* 882. The acknowledged source was the *London Magazine* of June 1736.
125. *Mercury* 1274, 1157.
126. *Mercury* 868.

In comparison with the amount of space in the *Mercury* devoted to news and advertisements not a great deal was given over to what we might call literature. Even among the feature articles certainly less than half had any literary interest and still fewer had literary worth. Bradford, it seems obvious, whether or not he had any personal inclinations toward bookishness, thought of the essay or the poem as no more than an embellishment of his paper. In so thinking, however, he was not out of step with his time. The difference between the *Mercury* and, let us say, the *Virginia Gazette,* one of the most literate of the early colonial journals, is a matter of degree — and a small degree at that. Similarly the differences between, for example, the Dublin *Evening Post* and the *Grub Street Journal* are not so many, from the perspective of two hundred years, as their likenesses. Although the *Mercury* has less belletristic value than the *Universal Spectator,* it has more than the *Daily Advertiser.* Nor does it particularly signify lack of taste or judgment in its editor that the *Mercury* printed, for instance, the essays of Henry Stonecastle in preference to those of Isaac Bickerstaff, for, like other weeklies and magazines, it drew upon contemporary periodicals, seldom — except incidentally or upon request — upon books, and seldom too upon works which, whatever their merit, were from the point of view of a newspaper publisher outdated. Indeed, when we take into account all the circumstances of its publication — place and time and the limitations of the folio sheet — the *Mercury* may very well surprise us with the quantity of literary and semi-literary material it printed and with the respectable, if not remarkable, quality of a considerable part of that material.

Chapter 8
Popularity and Influence of the *Mercury*

Though the *Mercury* contains not infrequent references to other papers and printers in addition to the acknowledgment of news items, there is no evidence that Bradford had any regular business arrangement with any of them except his father and John Copson in the early years of the paper and his nephew at the close of the 'thirties. With his father he apparently continued to have business dealings long after their formal partnership in the publication of the *Mercury* terminated. Sometimes William advertised his runaways in his son's journal — for example, a workman at his paper mill at Elizabethtown, New Jersey, and James Parker, an apprentice in his printing establishment.[1] William and Andrew together occasionally continued to print, to sell, or to take subscriptions for books.[2] And they appear to have made free use of each other's papers. For instance, in the following comment and the reprint which accompanied it Andrew at once defended his father and perhaps cast doubt upon a rival journal: "The following is a Copy of a Letter sent by Alexander Cumming, Bart. to South-Carolina, relating to a Paragraph inserted in the New-York *Gazette,* Dated July 13. Wherefore the Author of the New-York Paper desires hereby to inform the Reader, that he took the said Paragraph from the Pennsylvania *Gazette,* dated July 2."[3] In 1740, after war had broken out, Andrew — whose sympathies, the *Mercury* repeatedly suggests, were with the war party but who probably hesitated to speak out — published a very illiterate letter originally directed to the New York *Gazette* asking advice about enlistment.[4] Then came William Bradford's spread-eagle reply, promising the volunteer plunder in the form of jewels and plate, plantations and slaves, in addition to fame and glory (without cost!), and ending dramatically: "Go Volunteers in this Expedition, and take the Island of Cuba." Again, after the *Mercury* had reported the experiments conducted before members of the Royal Society to prove the efficacy of hot olive oil as a cure for snake bites, Andrew followed up the account with a letter written to the New York *Gazette* confirming this cure.[5]

1. *Mercury* 496, 703. Parker became—like another of Bradford's apprentices, Zenger, and like another runaway printer's devil, Benjamin Franklin—a well-known printer in his own right.
2. For example, see *Mercury* 131, 289, 564, 569, 1041, 1067.
3. *Mercury* 573. Sir Alexander felt that the paragraph damaged his reputation.
4. *Mercury* 1063. The letter, of course, may have been a fiction, a mere excuse for Bradford's patriotic appeal.
5. *Mercury* 1016, 1029.

With and without his father Bradford had business arrangements with other printers. One of Magnus Falconar's books, for example, was advertised in the *Mercury* as sold by Andrew Bradford in Philadelphia, William Bradford in New York, and Kneeland and Green in Boston; and the same list of printers supplemented by Benjamin Franklin appeared in an appeal for subscriptions for another of Falconar's projects.[6] William Parks, printer of the *Maryland Gazette* and the *Virginia Gazette*, was often mentioned in the *Mercury*.[7] For example, an advertisement for a runaway was published simultaneously in the *Mercury* and the *Maryland Gazette*;[8] when a servant ran off with one of Parks' horses, the *Mercury* requested that the stolen animal be brought to Andrew Bradford;[9] and when Parks proposed to print *The Virginia Miscellany* he advertised his intention in Bradford's paper.[10] On the other hand, Bradford used the *Virginia Gazette* to advertise for a roan horse, stolen from his pasture and "seen on the Road to Virginia."[11] References to Parks in the *Mercury's* columns were so common, in fact, that they suggest regular co-operation over a period of several years between him and Andrew Bradford.[12]

With Keimer and Franklin, Bradford must necessarily have had many contacts, probably personal as well as professional; yet his actual relation to them is difficult to determine. Certainly both used the advertising columns of the *Mercury* before their own papers were established. Keimer advertised not only his school for Negroes but also some of his publications and the stock of his shop;[13] and Franklin inserted a notice of his "A Modest Enquiry into the Nature and Necessity of a Paper Currency."[14] On the other hand, at least three times before he founded the *Universal Instructor* Keimer was attacked in Bradford's pages: by Jacob Taylor over the matter of the spurious almanac,[15] by "Aaron Goforth, Senior" on the ground that Keimer had robbed an honest man of his reputation and branded a minister of the Church of England, and by Bradford himself when Keimer printed Titan Leeds' almanac for 1727, which Bradford considered a piracy of Felix Leeds'.[16] Whether

6. *Mercury* 1016, 1037.
7. *Mercury* 441, 507, 543, 746, for instance, in addition to those specifically cited.
8. *Mercury* 514 ff. and 551.
9. *Mercury* 723.
10. *Mercury* 602.
11. *Virginia Gazette* 9, October 1, 1736.
12. Parks was postmaster at Annapolis while Bradford was postmaster in Philadelphia. (See advertisements in *Mercury* 431, 441, etc.) Their joint responsibility for the mails may have encouraged their co-operation.
13. *Mercury* 165, 213, 252.
14. *Mercury* 485.
15. See above, p. 205.
16. *Mercury* 318, 315, 348 and 349.

or not Bradford was privy to the real purpose of the *Busy-Body* we do not know; if he was, he must have been shrewd enough to see that Franklin would be a more dangerous rival than Keimer. He may have felt secure, however, in the established success of the *Mercury* and in his hold on the postmastership; or he may have hoped to gain — as he certainly did — more than he lost by the publication of the essays. In addition to planning the ouster of Keimer, Franklin also, more justly, used the *Mercury* to censure his misrepresenting "A Touch of the Times" as a product of Franklin's press;[17] further, a mock news item about Keimer in the *Mercury* of March 27, 1729, may well have been instigated by Franklin. Moreover, if Keimer is to be believed, Bradford was responsible — simultaneously with the inception of the *Busy-Body* — for what Keimer considered a libel;[18] and several of the numbers of the *Instructor* attempted fruitlessly to stem the effect of the *Busy-Body*.[19]

In the years after Keimer's departure Franklin's and Bradford's papers were often at odds, or at least on opposite sides of a question. A good many of these controversies we have already mentioned: the long warfare over Hamilton, the Maryland tobacco scheme, the Evan Jones trial, the episode of the tanyard, the quarrel between lawyer Robinson and his client, and several more. Others flared up occasionally — for instance, the conflict between Ebenezer Kinnersley and the Reverend Jenkin Jones of Christ Church,[20] and especially the paper war over the magazines. Once the *Mercury* issued an extra half-sheet to make room for an attack on Franklin's conduct as printer of the votes and proceedings and as clerk of the Assembly.[21] In spite of these evidences of conflict between their papers it appears, however, that in matters of business Bradford and Franklin often co-operated successfully. Indeed, it is possible that, though the *Mercury* and the *Gazette* sometimes espoused different views,

17. *Mercury* 485.
18. *Instructor* 7.
19. *Instructor* 10, 12, 13, 16, 24.
20. *Gazette* 606, 609, 613, 615; *Mercury* 1078, 1080, 1085.
21. *Mercury* 1050. The background of this episode is supplied by the *Minutes of the Provincial Council*, IV, 384-386. The Assembly had presented a bill for raising money for public purposes and repealing a former act with the same aim. The Council and Governor felt that it would remove from the control of the mayor and commonalty the streets, docks, wharves, and bridges, which presumably were managed for the benefit of all the inhabitants. In Franklin's printing of the votes, however (the letter in the *Mercury* pointed out), he mentioned the Governor's rejecting the bill and the Assembly's protest against the rejection, but omitted the Governor's message to the Assembly in which the reasons for his veto were set forth. The *Mercury* now printed the Governor's message. Some of the remarks about Franklin hit close: for example, "we know you can, upon some Occasions, strike a bold Stroke, and then depend upon your Wit to bring you off," or "you're never at a Loss for something to say, nor for some Body to say it for you, when you don't care to appear yourself." The *Gazette* did not reply to this attack.

their editors were on amicable terms. The imprint of the 1733 edition of Brady and Tate's *Psalms of David* shows that, although it was printed by Franklin, it was sold by both him and Bradford,[22] and Bradford announced the publication and sale by Franklin of the poems of Aquila Rose.[23] In the summer of 1738, on the very heels of Cato, Jr., strangely enough the *Mercury* advertised a book written by Benjamin Lay and published by Franklin.[24] On the other hand, the *Gazette* advertised the publication by Bradford of Kinnersley's letter on his controversy with Mr. Jones.[25] Both Bradford and Franklin were agents for the sale of "A Letter from the Reverend Mr. Whitefield to the Religious Societies lately form'd in England and Wales"[26] and Franklin, Warner and Bradford, and William Bradford III all sold the report of the investigation by the Assembly of South Carolina into the failure of the expedition against Saint Augustine.[27] Each paper also a few times devoted space to its editor's rival. The *Gazette,* we have noted, included obituaries of Dorcas Bradford and of Andrew; whereas at least three times, in addition to its implicit defense of the *New England Courant* in 1723, the *Mercury* mentioned the Franklins in its news columns: once to announce the death of James Franklin at Newport in 1735, again in 1735 to report that at a meeting in Boston of the Masonic Order Benjamin had been appointed Grand Master for the Province of Pennsylvania, and ten years later to announce the death of Josiah Franklin, Benjamin's father, and to eulogize his character.[28] A peculiarity in the reporting of local news suggests the possibility of regular co-operation between Franklin and Bradford, for it is noticeable that occasionally, even when the two papers came out on the same day, local items were printed in identical words in the *Gazette* and the *Mercury*.[29] The similarity of items from a distance or of "set pieces" like the speech of the governor

22. Hildeburn, no. 467. Bernard Faÿ (*Franklin, The Apostle of Modern Times,* 174) says that Bradford, "hard pressed by too much work, . . . confided to Franklin the care of publishing" this book.
23. *Mercury* 1128.
24. *Mercury* 973. In Number 982 John Kinsey, clerk of the Yearly Meeting, inserted a protest against the book, especially against the implication that the author was a Friend or spoke for the Friends; he asserted that the work abused particular Friends and the entire Society.
25. *Gazette* 613.
26. *Mercury* 1065.
27. *Mercury* 1256.
28. *Mercury* 793, 795, 1310. These items did not appear in the *Gazette.* The omission is especially noticeable in the third example, for *Gazette* 844 used two of the three items from Boston printed in *Mercury* 1310, but left out the middle one about the death of Franklin's father. Perhaps this kind of omission was considered a gesture of modesty. The address of the directors of the Library Company, which had Franklin's name at the top of the list, was also, as was mentioned above, published in the *Mercury* (Number 1246), but not in the *Gazette.*
29. See, for example, *Gazette* 65 and *Mercury* 527, 243 and 708, 347 and 813, 445 and 912, 453 and 920, 485 and 952, 572 and 1039, 660 and 1127.

to the Assembly or even of local news printed at different times suggest nothing except what is already abundantly clear — that colonial papers had common sources and that they depended on one another. But the likeness of accounts of local events published simultaneously may indicate either that Bradford and Franklin used the same "reporters" or that they had an arrangement for the exchange of local news.

Although we know very little about Bradford's actual business relation with other printers, the newspapers published in colonies other than Pennsylvania give us evidence of the extent to which the *Mercury* was used by his fellow editors. It would be difficult, perhaps impossible, to trace in all the papers contemporary with the *Mercury* borrowings or possible borrowings, but a sampling of various journals in different localities and in different years will give a basis for sufficiently accurate generalization on the *Mercury's* value to Bradford's compatriots.[30] Let us look first at some of the Boston papers. It is clear almost at once that the *News Letter* was not dependent upon the existence of a paper for its news of the Philadelphia area. In its first issue in 1704, indeed, appeared an item from Philadelphia, and during the year 1720, the *Mercury's* first year, several of the scant half-dozen pieces marked "Philadelphia" were definitely not from Bradford's sheet. On the other hand, two items may very possibly have been taken from the *Mercury*.[31] Beginning in 1721, the *News Letter* apparently drew regularly upon the Philadelphia paper; the account of the earthquake in China on July 19, 1718, came to the Boston weekly by a letter from Philadelphia which mentioned the *Mercury* as its source.[32] Several other items — such as the exchange of letters between Spotswood and Keith[33] — probably came directly; in fact it seems likely that nearly all, possibly every one,

---

30. The basic difficulty is that the colonial papers in general are even less conscientious in acknowledging the sources of their domestic than of their foreign news; indeed they practically never mention them. The second major difficulty is that few of the papers can be brought together, even in photostat or microfilm, for collation. In the third place, even when an article is identical in two papers, there is always the possibility that a third paper was involved in the process of transmittal from the first to the second. Fourthly, when (as sometimes happens) a Boston paper, for example, has an item which is printed in identical form in the *Mercury* and the *Pennsylvania Gazette,* one cannot tell whether it came from Bradford or Franklin. I should further explain that in order to bring my examination within workable limits and to avoid the impossible intricacies of tracing the paths of foreign news, I have studied in each paper the items marked "Philadelphia" (or places in the vicinity of Philadelphia) or those which in some other way suggest the likelihood of Bradford's paper as a source. For obvious reasons, therefore, I cannot guarantee accuracy for every illustration of indebtedness; I believe, however, that my general conclusions are sufficiently well supported to be valid.

31. N.L. 823 and *Merc.* 2; N.L. 833 and *Merc.* 13.
32. N.L. 890 and *Merc.* 65.
33. N.L. 902 and *Merc.* 75.

of the few reports from Philadelphia came from Bradford.[34] The *News Letter*, however, had very little intercolonial news of any sort until well into the 'twenties; for months in 1724, for example, there was not a single report from Philadelphia, though after 1725 a small but steady series of items from the *Mercury* appeared.[35] The *Gazette*, the second successful Boston paper, drew upon the *Mercury* almost from the start, although it also included news from Philadelphia not taken from any public print.[36] In its first year, 1720, it borrowed from more than twenty issues of Bradford's journal,[37] chiefly appropriating, since it was established expressly at the desires of the merchant class,[38] shipping reports and prices-current lists. Five years later, in 1725, the *Gazette* again took news from more than a score of the Bradford sheets, with the emphasis still upon commercial items.[39]

The *New England Courant,* the liveliest and most literary of the early colonial papers, lasted less than five years, from August 1721 to June 1726. During its first months so much space was absorbed by its attacks on inoculation that intercolonial news was scant, and for many weeks in 1723 and again in 1724 and 1725 there was no news whatever from Philadelphia and very little colonial news except from New England. There is no doubt, however, that James Franklin made use of the *Mercury*, since in approximately ten out of thirteen issues reporting news

---

34. *N.L.* 891 and *Merc.* 66, *N.L.* 898 and *Merc.* 72, *N.L.* 911 and *Merc.* 80, *N.L.* 916 and *Merc.* 85.

35. *N.L.* 1127 and *Merc.* 295, *N.L.* 1128 and *Merc.* 297, *N.L.* 1171 and *Merc.* 339, *N.L.* 1175 and *Merc.* 343, *N.L.* 1179 and *Merc.* 347, *N.L.* 24 (the *News Letter* began a new numbering with Jan. 5 1726/27) and *Merc.* 387, *N.L.* 60 and *Merc.* 421, *N.L.* 65 and *Merc.* 428, *N.L.* 79 and *Merc.* 441, *N.L.* 81 and *Merc.* 444, *N.L.* 109 and *Merc.* 469, *N.L.* 186 and *Merc.* 549, *N.L.* 187 and *Merc.* 550, *N.L.* 181 and *Merc.* 542. The last four citations overlapped the first eighteen months of the *Universal Instructor (Pennsylvania Gazette)*; during that period at least three items are traceable to that paper: *N.L.* 165 and *Gaz.* 60, *N.L.* 166 and *Gaz.* 63, *N.L.* 169 and *Gaz.* 66.

36. For example, shipping news in Numbers 1 and 3.

37. *B.G.* 6 and *Merc.* 2, *B.G.* 13 and *Merc.* 6, *B.G.* 17 and *Merc.* 14 & 15, *B.G.* 19 and *Merc.* 17, *B.G.* 21 and *Merc.* 19, *B.G.* 22 and *Merc.* 20, *B.G.* 23 and *Merc.* 21, *B.G.* 27 and *Merc.* 24 & 25, *B.G.* 30 and *Merc.* 28, *B.G.* 33 and *Merc.* 31, *B.G.* 36 and *Merc.* 24, *B.G.* 37 and *Merc.* 25, *B.G.* 38 and *Merc.* 36, *B.G.* 39 and *Merc.* 35 & 37, *B.G.* 41 and *Merc.* 29, *B.G.* 42 and *Merc.* 40, *B.G.* 43 and *Merc.* 41, *B.G.* 44 and *Merc.* 42, *B.G.* 46 and *Merc.* 44, *B.G.* 53 and *Merc.* 50.

38. See Number 1.

39. *B.G.* 269 and *Merc.* 263 & 262, *B.G.* 280 and *Merc.* 275, *B.G.* 281 and *Merc.* 276, *B.G.* 283 and *Merc.* 278, *B.G.* 286 and *Merc.* 281, *B.G.* 294 and *Merc.* 290, *B.G.* 295 and *Merc.* 291, *B.G.* 296 and *Merc.* 292, *B.G.* 297 and *Merc.* 293, *B.G.* 300 and *Merc.* 295 & 296, *B.G.* 301 and *Merc.* 297, *B.G.* 303 and *Merc.* 299, *B.G.* 304 and *Merc.* 300, *B.G.* 305 and *Merc.* 301, *B.G.* 306 and *Merc.* 302, *B.G.* 307 and *Merc.* 303, *B.G.* 308 and *Merc.* 304, *B.G.* 309 & 310 and *Merc.* 305, *B.G.* 315 and *Merc.* 310, *B.G.* 317 and *Merc.* 311.

from Philadelphia the items are traceable to Bradford's paper.[40] The *Weekly Rehearsal* of Boston, begun on September 27, 1731, offers evidence from a somewhat later period, when the New England editor had two well-established Philadelphia papers to draw upon. Like the *Courant* it contained little intercolonial news, but during its first year[41] it made much greater use of the *Mercury* than of the *Pennsylvania Gazette,* borrowing in at least ten issues from the former and but once or twice from the latter.[42] The Boston *Weekly Post Boy,* established in 1734, patronized the two Philadelphia papers more equally, in a period of a little more than four years[43] drawing at least fourteen times on the *Mercury* and at least seventeen on the *Gazette.*[44] Finally among Boston papers let us look at some of the issues of the *Evening Post.* Once again it is clear that Bradford's journal was used; in seventeen issues of the Boston paper during 1736[45] approximately twelve issues of the *Mercury* and seven of the *Gazette* were called upon for items,[46] and in the years

40. *N.E.C.* 5 and *Merc.* 88, *N.E.C.* 13 and *Merc.* 95, *N.E.C.* 16 and *Merc.* 104, *N.E.C.* 42 and *Merc.* 126, *N.E.C.* 53 and *Merc.* 137, *N.E.C.* 55 and *Merc.* 139, *N.E.C.* 56 and *Merc.* 140, *N.E.C.* 65 and *Merc.* 147, *N.E.C.* 192 and *Merc.* 270, *N.E.C.* 215 and *Merc.* 297.

41. The file in the Massachusetts Historical Society, which is the most nearly complete, is very scrappy from the end of the first year until the close of the paper in 1735.

42. *W.R.* 14 and *Gaz.* 158, *W.R.* 38 and *Merc.* 648, *W.R.* 39 and *Merc.* 649, *W.R.* 42 and *Merc.* 652, *W.R.* 43 and *Merc.* 653, *W.R.* 44 and *Merc.* 654, *W.R.* 45 and *Merc.* 655, *W.R.* 46 and *Merc.* 656, *W.R.* 47 and *Merc.* 657, *W.R.* 47 (another issue) and *Merc.* 658, *W.R.* 48 and *Merc.* 659.

43. The issues of this paper are scattered. I base my statements upon the file in the Massachusetts Historical Society between May 12, 1735, and December 10, 1739.

44. *P.B.* 62 and *Merc.* 835, *P.B.* 73 and *Gaz.* 379 & 380 and *Merc.* 847, *P.B.* 75 and *Gaz.* 383, *P.B.* 93 and *Merc.* 867, *P.B.* 94 and *Gaz.* 401 and *Merc.* 868, *P.B.* 96 and *Merc.* 870, *P.B.* 223 and *Merc.* 990, *P.B.* 227 and *Gaz.* 526 & 528, *P.B.* 234 and *Gaz.* 536 and *Merc.* 1004, *P.B.* 237 and *Gaz.* 539, *P.B.* 241 and *Gaz.* 544 and *Merc.* 1011, *P.B.* 243 and *Gaz.* 546, *P.B.* 244 and *Merc.* 1014, *P.B.* 245 and *Gaz.* 548, *P.B.* 246 and *Merc.* 1016, *P.B.* 247 and *Merc.* 1017, *P.B.* 248 and *Gaz.* 551, *P.B.* 252 and *Merc.* 1022, *P.B.* 254 and *Gaz.* 556, *P.B.* 256 and *Merc.* 1026, *P.B.* 257 and *Gaz.* 560, *P.B.* 251 and *Gaz.* 563, *P.B.* 252 and *Gaz.* 564, *P.B.* 255 and *Merc.* 1033 & 1034 and *Gaz.* 566 & 567, *P.B.* 256 and *Gaz.* 566. (The numbering of the *Post Boy* went astray in the summer of 1739. The numbers given above, however erratic they may appear, are in chronological order.)

45. A scattering between January 19, 1736, and January 3, 1737.

46. The reason for the apparent discrepancy in number is worth explaining since it indicates a common procedure of the colonial editor. In making up the items under, let us say, "Philadelphia," he would frequently use, if he had space and materials, several different papers — not only more than one issue of one paper, but perhaps an issue or two of another. Though colonial editors almost always, it appears, borrowed single items verbatim or nearly verbatim, several items under a single heading often represent an editorial selection. A particularly good example is the *South Carolina Gazette* of August 27, 1744, which had items from *Mercury* 1270 and 1271 and from *Pennsylvania Gazette* 809, 810, 811, and 812.

E.P. 23 and *Merc.* 835, *E.P.* 27 and *Merc.* 839, *E.P.* 29 and *Gaz.* 373 & 374 and *Merc.* 841, *E.P.* 31 and *Merc.* 843, *E.P.* 33 and *Merc.* 845, *E.P.* 36 and

1742 and 1743 borrowings from the *Mercury* continued,[47] even though by this date the paper had two competitors in Philadelphia. On the basis of these samplings from six important Boston newspapers it is plain that the *Mercury* was well known among New England editors and was frequently employed by them as a source of intelligence.[48] Moreover, although there is not sufficient evidence to make a valid comparison between the influence of the *Gazette* and that of the *Mercury*, it is certain that Bradford's columns were requisitioned by New England newspapers even after the establishment and success of Franklin's rival journal.

Much the same conclusion develops from the study of several New York papers. Family ties, in addition to the fact that for its first three years the only other paper printed within easy distance of the New York *Gazette* was the *Mercury*, no doubt encouraged William Bradford to make use of his son's weekly. Unlike several of the New England papers the *Gazette* included a large amount of Philadelphia intelligence; in issue after issue from the beginning of the paper[49] to the founding of the *Universal Instructor*, items from the *Mercury* were reprinted.[50] After the second Philadelphia paper was established, especially after Franklin became its editor, William Bradford evidently subscribed to both papers, using them regularly and often, and frequently bringing together items from each in making up his Philadelphia report.[51] Though Bradford certainly employed both papers, he probably continued to depend particularly upon his son's, for a sampling of the Philadelphia items in the New York *Gazette* as late as 1737, 1738, and 1739 shows several times

Gaz. 383, *E.P.* 38 and *Merc*. 851, *E.P.* 40 and *Gaz*. 386 and *Merc*. 853, *E.P.* 55 and *Gaz*. 401 and *Merc*. 868, *E.P.* 56 and *Merc*. 869, *E.P.* 57 and *Merc*. 870, *E.P.* 60 and *Merc*. 873, *E.P.* 63 and *Gaz*. 408, *E.P.* 64 and *Merc*. 877, *E.P.* 66 and *Gaz*. 441, *E.P.* 72 and *Merc*. 883.

47. For example, *E.P.* 368 and *Merc*. 1179, *E.P.* 370 and *Merc*. 1182, *E.P.* 394 and *Merc*. 1203, *E.P.* 395 and *Merc*. 1204, *E.P.* 401 and *Merc*. 1204, *E.P.* 421 and *Merc*. 1232, *E.P.* 427 and *Merc*. 1239.

48. Of three Philadelphia items in the short-lived *Rhode Island Gazette* two appear to come from the *Mercury*, one from the *Gazette: R.I.G.* 2 and *Merc*. 664, *R.I.G.* 3 and *Merc*. 665, *R.I.G.* 6 and *Gaz*. 203.

49. The earliest extant issue is Number 18 of March 7, 1726.

50. For example, *N.Y.G.* 34 (June 27, 1726) and *Merc*. 339, *N.Y.G.* 48 and *Merc*. 353, *N.Y.G.* 52 and *Merc*. 357, *N.Y.G.* 58 and *Merc*. 361, *N.Y.G.* 68 and *Merc*. 372, *N.Y.G.* 71 and *Merc*. 376, *N.Y.G.* 88 and *Merc*. 392, *N.Y.G.* 105 and *Merc*. 409, *N.Y.G.* 118 and *Merc*. 421, *N.Y.G.* 127 and *Merc*. 431, *N.Y.G.* 133 and *Merc*. 437, *N.Y.G.* 137 (June 17, 1728) and *Merc*. 439, 440, & 441.

51. For example, *N.Y.G.* 163 (December 17, 1728) and *Merc*. 467, *N.Y.G.* 181 and *Merc*. 484, *N.Y.G.* 185 and *Inst*. 21, *N.Y.G.* 241 and *Gaz*. 81, *N.Y.G.* 246 and *Merc*. 549, *N.Y.G.* 247 and *Merc*. 550, *N.Y.G.* 251 and *Merc*. 553 and *Gaz*. 90, *N.Y.G.* 252 and *Merc*. 555, *N.Y.G.* 268 and *Merc*. 570, *N.Y.G.* 274 and *Gaz*. 112, *N.Y.G.* 277 and *Merc*. 579, *N.Y.G.* 280 and *Gaz*. 114, *N.Y.G.* 282 and *Merc*. 582 & 585, *N.Y.G.* 284 and *Merc*. 587, *N.Y.G.* 288 and *Gaz*. 127 and *Merc*. 590, *N.Y.G.* 298 and *Gaz*. 136, *N.Y.G.* 306 and *Merc*. 609, *N.Y.G.* 311 and *Gaz*. 148 and *Merc*. 612, *N.Y.G.* 314 and *Gaz*. 152, *N.Y.G.*

as many pieces from the *Mercury* as from the *Gazette*.⁵² Whereas William Bradford, good business man though he was, may have been moved by partiality in his devotion to the *Mercury*, John Peter Zenger could have had little reason to use Andrew's paper except its actual value as a news sheet; yet he also apparently considered it a reliable source of material. The first twenty issues of the *Weekly Journal* were so thoroughly occupied with propaganda against Cosby that very little colonial news appeared. Between March 1734 and November 1735, however, a moderate number of reports from Philadelphia were included, nearly all of them traceable to the *Mercury*;⁵³ twice, in fact, Zenger violated the usual custom of the colonial editor by specifically citing Andrew Bradford's journal as his source.⁵⁴ For a typical period of three years from early in 1736 through 1738, however, Zenger obviously used both the *Mercury* and the *Pennsylvania Gazette* regularly and, so far as the relevant items can be traced, almost equally.⁵⁵

James Parker's *Weekly Post Boy*, like the New York *Gazette*, included a rather large amount of Philadelphia news; in the five months between January 7 and June 10, 1745, for instance, at least fifteen numbers con-

321 and *Merc*. 623, N.Y.G. 352 and *Merc*. 654, N.Y.G. 353 and *Merc*. 656, N.Y.G. 356 and *Gaz*. 194 and *Merc*. 659, N.Y.G. 364 and *Merc*. 666, N.Y.G. 405 and *Gaz*. 243 and *Merc*. 708, N.Y.G. 413 and *Merc*. 716, N.Y.G. 421 and *Gaz*. 256, N.Y.G. 425 and *Merc*. 727, N.Y.G. 439 and *Merc*. 740, N.Y.G. 453 and *Merc*. 758, N.Y.G. 460 and *Merc*. 762, N.Y.G. 486 and *Gaz*. 322, N.Y.G. 494 and *Merc*. 795 and *Gaz*. 329, N.Y.G. 520 and *Merc*. 822, N.Y.G. 532 and *Merc*. 835, N.Y.G. 534 and *Merc*. 837, N.Y.G. 541 and *Merc*. 845, N.Y.G. 547 and *Merc*. 851, N.Y.G. 548 and *Merc*. 852, N.Y.G. 562 and *Merc*. 866 and *Gaz*. 399, N.Y.G. 566 (September 6, 1736) and *Merc*. 870.

52. For example, N.Y.G. 588 (February 17, 1737) and *Merc*. 891, N.Y.G. 598 and *Merc*. 900, 901, & 902, N.Y.G. 635 and *Merc*. 938, N.Y.G. 638 and *Gaz*. 474, N.Y.G. 642 and *Merc*. 945, N.Y.G. 644 and *Merc*. 941, N.Y.G. 673 and *Merc*. 976 & 978, N.Y.G. 690 and *Gaz*. 526, N.Y.G. 711 (June 25, 1739) and *Merc*. 1015.

53. *W.J.* 21 and *Merc*. 741, *W.J.* 24 and *Merc*. 744, *W.J.* 28 and *Merc*. 749, *W.J.* 37 and *Merc*. 758, *W.J.* 38 and *Merc*. 759, *W.J.* 45 and *Merc*. 763, *W.J.* 65 and *Merc*. 787, *W.J.* 75 and *Merc*. 796, *W.J.* 100 and *Merc*. 822, *W.J.* 105 and *Merc*. 827 and *Gaz*. 361, *W.J.* 106 and *Gaz*. 361.

54. Numbers 24 and 45. Later, in Numbers 136 and 145, he specifically cited the *Pennsylvania Gazette*. Number 186 again acknowledged indebtedness to the *Mercury*.

55. *W.J.* 118 (February 9, 1736) and *Merc*. 839, *W.J.* 131 and *Gaz*. 386, *W.J.* 136 and *Gaz*. (acknowledged), *W.J.* 144 and *Gaz*. 399 and *Merc*. 866, *W.J.* 145 and *Gaz*. (acknowledged), *W.J.* 146 and *Gaz*. 400 & 401, *W.J.* 170 and *Merc*. 891, *W.J.* 179 and *Merc*. 901, *W.J.* 183 and *Merc*. 907, *W.J.* 186 and *Merc*. (acknowledged), *W.J.* 194 and *Merc*. 449, *W.J.* 197 and *Merc*. 919, *W.J.* 203 and *Gaz*. 458, *W.J.* 205 and *Gaz*. 460 and *Merc*. 927, *W.J.* 214 and *Merc*. 936, *W.J.* 215-219 and *Merc*. 466-469, *W.J.* 222 and *Merc*. 944, *W.J.* 239 and *Gaz*. 494 and *Merc*. 961, *W.J.* 240 and *Gaz*. 496, *W.J.* 242 and *Gaz*. 498, *W.J.* 244 and *Gaz*. 499 and *Merc*. 966, *W.J.* 250 and *Gaz*. 506, *W.J.* 254 (September 25, 1738) and *Merc*. 976.

tained reports about or by way of Philadelphia.[56] Unlike the New York papers already discussed, however, the *Post Boy* did not depend heavily upon the *Mercury*. In 1744,[57] for example, approximately half as many items were borrowed from the *Mercury* as from the *Pennsylvania Gazette*,[58] and from the beginning of 1745 until the *Mercury's* conclusion in 1746 Parker apparently used very little of the Bradford paper. The *Evening Post* of Henry de Foreest overlapped the *Mercury* by only eighteen months. Like the *Post Boy* it contained much news of Philadelphia; in fact, nearly every week several items were printed, sometimes to the length of a column. Like the *Post Boy* also the *Evening Post* appears to have drawn very little upon the *Mercury*, by far the greater number of its reports in the period under discussion not being traceable to Bradford's paper. Since by the time the *Post Boy* and the *Evening Post* were founded the *Mercury's* two energetic rivals were well established, its failure to gain a place of importance in Parker's and de Foreest's selection of news items is not surprising. Indeed, these two papers may well throw light upon the *Mercury's* decline, since they suggest both a cause and an effect of its increasing weakness against the combined competition of the *Pennsylvania Gazette* and the *Pennsylvania Journal*.

Of the three important southern papers contemporary with the *Mercury*, the *Maryland Gazette* was the earliest. It was founded in September 1727, but no issues of the paper dated before December 10, 1738, now exist.[59] The total number of Philadelphia headings is very small indeed, but it is probable that, though Parks used both the *Mercury* and the *Instructor-Pennsylvania Gazette,* he drew more frequently upon the Bradford paper, several items being traceable only to it.[60] The *South Carolina Gazette* apparently had very little intercolonial news; even as

---

56. Numbers 103, 105, 107, 109, 111, 113, 115, 117, 118, 119, 121, 122, 123, 124, 125.

57. The *Post Boy* began in January 1743, but few issues are extant until the beginning of the following year.

58. For example, *P.B.* 50 (January 2, 1744) and *Merc.* 1250, *P.B.* 51 and *Gaz.* 785, *P.B.* 53 and *Gaz.* 787, *P.B.* 56 and *Merc.* 1256, *P.B.* 66 and *Merc.* 1267, *P.B.* 69 and *Gaz.* 804, *P.B.* 71 and *Merc.* 1271, *P.B.* 81 and *Merc.* 1282, *P.B.* 82 and *Gaz.* 817, *P.B.* 89 and *Merc.* 1290, *P.B.* 95 and *Gaz.* 830, *P.B.* 96 and *Gaz.* 831, *P.B.* 97 and *Gaz.* 832, *P.B.* 98 and *Gaz.* 833, *P.B.* 99 and *Gaz.* 834, *P.B.* 101 (December 24, 1744) and *Gaz.* 835. Since Parker had a business connection with Franklin (McMurtrie, p. 50, speaks of him as "probably Franklin's most important partner outside of Philadelphia"), it is natural that he depended especially upon the *Gazette*.

59. Number 65. The paper was evidently discontinued after December 22, 1730, and revived about two years later. The last known number is dated November 29, 1734. Only fifty-seven issues are extant.

60. *M.G.* 67 (December 24, 1728) and *Merc.* 466, *M.G.* 81 and *Inst.* 11, *M.G.* 89 and *Merc.* 484, *M.G.* 94 and *Merc.* 492 & 493, *M.G.* 131 and *Gaz.* 66, *M.G.* 73 (new numbering) and *Merc.* 760, *M.G.* 81 and *Merc.* 768, *M.G.* 86 (November 1, 1734) and *Merc.* 773.

late as 1744, for example, the Philadelphia heading occurred but half-a-dozen times. Like the *Maryland Gazette* many years earlier, however, the South Carolina paper borrowed from the *Mercury,* though the *Pennsylvania Gazette* may well have been a more regular source of news.[61] The *Virginia Gazette* allows more opportunities of comparison than the two earlier papers. From the beginning there was intermittent news from Philadelphia, and between September 1736 and January 1740 Parks drew constantly upon the *Mercury*.[62] In addition to frequent quotations from its prices-current list, there were many other borrowings, more than twice as many as from the *Gazette*.[63] All three of these papers, then, knew and made some use of the *Mercury,* the Maryland and Virginia journals especially. Once again we have evidence that Bradford's sheet was familiar to, and presumably respected by, his fellow-editors.

* * * * *

The *Mercury,* we have already seen, attempted to satisfy the desire of its local readers for information about events and people in distant places — chiefly across the ocean, but in other colonies as well. For the pleasure or advantage of the same group it also included "domestic" news, feature articles, and advertising. The twenty-six years in which its weekly publication almost never faltered are a proof of its success in giving its local customers what they wanted. In addition, the examination of various colonial papers contemporary with it reveals unmistakably that from north to south, from 1720 to at least 1740 the *Mercury* was an important source of news for "authors" of other colonial weeklies. No doubt when they borrowed news items from Philadelphia, they borrowed other things too — foreign intelligence or features. These we can only speculate upon, but even without them we can be sure of the essential point: that in other colonies as at home, for more than two decades, the *Mercury* was read. Long after a more able man than Andrew Bradford had established a rival paper, the *Mercury* continued to win the

61. For example, *S.C.G.* 544 (August 27, 1744) and *Merc.* 1270 & 1271, and *Gaz.* 809-812, *S.C.G.* 548 and *Merc.* 1281, *S.C.G.* 549 and *Gaz.* 817. Since Lewis Timothy, for a time the editor of the *South Carolina Gazette,* was sent to Charleston by Franklin, one would expect him to have used the *Gazette* more than the *Mercury* as a source of news.

62. *V.G.* 9 (October 1, 1736) and *Merc.* 871, *V.G.* 10 and *Merc.* 868, 870, & 872, *V.G.* 14 and *Merc.* 874, *V.G.* 45 and *Merc.* 907 & 908, *V.G.* 47 and *Merc.* 909, *V.G.* 49 and *Merc.* 912, *V.G.* 65 and *Merc.* 923, *V.G.* 77 and *Merc.* 931 & 936 and *Gaz.* 470, *V.G.* 81 and *Merc.* 935, *V.G.* 90 and *Merc.* 949 and *Gaz.* 482, *V.G.* 92 and *Merc.* 954, *V.G.* 106 and *Merc.* 968, *V.G.* 119 and *Gaz.* 515, *V.G.* 136 and *Gaz.* 528, *V.G.* 140 and *Merc.* 1000, *V.G.* 147 and *Merc.* 1009, *V.G.* 149 and *Merc.* 1012, *V.G.* 151 and *Merc.* 1014, *V.G.* 155 and *Merc.* 1017, *V.G.* 157 and *Merc.* 1020, *V.G.* 163 and *Gaz.* 559, *V.G.* 165 and *Merc.* 1026 & 1027, *V.G.* 167 (October 12, 1739) and *Gaz.* 563.

63. Parks occasionally cited or referred specifically to the *Mercury* or the *Gazette,* for example, in Numbers 49, 81, 90, 180.

approval of both the man in the street and the newspaper printer. However the *Mercury* may appear to our sophisticated eyes, it was beyond doubt a success. Moreover, here as elsewhere, first impressions are deceiving; despite its superficially unprepossessing appearance Bradford's paper — perhaps like his shop — casually included a fascinating variety of materials suited to many needs and many tastes. Indeed, Cowper might well have been thinking of the *Mercury* when he wrote:[64]

> This folio of four pages, happy work! ...
> What is it, but a map of busy life,
> Its fluctuations, and its vast concerns?

64. *The Task*, IV, 50 ff.

PART III

The American Magazine

On Thursday, November 6, 1740, Number 1088 of the *American Weekly Mercury* ran the longest advertisement of its history, two and three-quarter pages, in order to announce "The Plan of an Intended Magazine." Nine years earlier, in London, Edward Cave had founded the *Gentleman's Magazine*, the first important English miscellany. According to its preface of 1738, twenty imitations had promptly followed the instant success of the *Gentleman's*, the most notable being the *London Magazine* of 1732. Quite frankly the English magazine was an extension of the newspaper, being made up very largely of extracts from the weeklies and dailies, not only of news and summaries of current events but also of entertaining features such as essays and poetry. Both the influence of the British magazine and certain modifications of its plan are apparent in the first paragraphs of the *Mercury's* advertisement:

> The Success and Approbation which the Magazines, published in Great Britain, have met with for many Years past, among all Ranks and Degrees of People, Encouraged us to Attempt a Work of the like Nature in America. But the Plan, on which we intend to proceed, being in many respects different from the British Models; it therefore becomes necessary, in the first Place, to lay before the Reader a general Prospect of the present Design.
>
> It is propos'd to publish Monthly, An Accunt of the publick Affairs transacted in His Majesty's Colonies, as well on the Continent of America as in the West India Islands: Under this Head will be comprehended, the Speeches of the several Governors, the Addresses and Answers of the Assemblies, their Votes, Resolutions and Debates. So that this Part of the Work will contain Journals of the most important Proceedings of each particular Assembly. Moreover, at the End of every Sessions, we shall give an Extract of the Laws therein passed, with the Reasons on which they were founded, the Grievances intended to be remedied by them, and the Benefits expected from them.
>
> That the Reader may be the Better enabled to form a Judgment of the various Transactions intended to be set in View; Succinct Accounts will be given, in the Course of the Work, of the Situation, Climate, Soil, Productions, Trade and Manu-

factures of all the British Plantations; the Constitutions of those several Colonies, with their respective Views and Interests, will be opened and explained; and the Nature and Extent of the various Jurisdictions exercised in each Government particularly described.

In handling so great a Variety of Matter, Mistakes, thro' misinformation or otherwise, will probably be committed; but as the Magazine will be Monthly distributed among the Persons residing on the Spot, which the Affairs therein intreated of regard, the Errors, that may intervene, will be quickly discovered, and, on the least Intimation, corrected in the succeeding Numbers. By this Means the Reader will be furnish'd with such Descriptions of the British Plantations as may be relied on. A Work the more to be desired, as the general Relations, hitherto Published, of these Parts of the World, have been found to be grossly erroneous and partial in several Respects.

The advertisement goes on to say that the magazine will contain accounts of remarkable trials, both civil and criminal; the rate of exchange between each colony and London; the prices of goods in the principal trading centers of the colonies; accounts of party controversies within the various colonies, provided they throw light on the governments of the places involved; abstracts from other papers; and communications "worthy of publick Notice" sent to the editor. On this last point the advertisement speaks further:

> As several Colonies have no Printing-Press; and in others where there is but one, and even in those Places where there are more, it is Complained (whether with Justice or no we do not undertake to determine) that the Printers are often under the Influence of Parties, & cannot, without much Difficulty, be prevailed upon to publish any Thing against the Side of the Question they are of themselves: This Magazine, therefore, is Offered as a Remedy against those several Inconveniencies. Here any Person, in whatever Colony residing, will find a ready Admittance to a fair and publick Hearing at all Times. In the Disputes, that may be thus transmitted to us for Publication, we shall inviolably observe an exact Neutrality, and carefully avoid mingling with the Arguments on either Side, any Reflections or Remarks of our own.

The greater part of the remainder of the advertisement is a well-expressed but extremely diffuse and repetitive essay upon freedom of speech and of the press and upon liberty in general. It begins with the statement that though the magazine will "promote the Liberty" it will "carefully avoid contributing to the Licentiousness of the Press," that it will have no part in libel or defamation or in personal invective directed against "those Infirmities, which, as incident to human Nature, we are all subject to more or less." On the other hand, the editor does not condemn the use of satire, only its abuse, and will therefore welcome censure of "Affectation, Foppery, Vanity, Impertinence or any reigning Folly . . . ." The advertisement then asserts that in refusing countenance to personal censure the magazine is voluntarily limiting its audience to those who have "the true Interest and the true Peace of Society at Heart," and in order to make clear its distinction between proper and improper criticism it quotes — shades of the great controversy! — two paragraphs from Hamilton's defense of Zenger and supports Hamilton's arguments by references to and quotations from the Bible. This in turn leads to the assertion that the promotion of the liberty of mankind is "the most effectual Method we can pursue, for recommending us to the Favour of our Creator" and that the press "under right Application has been found to have had an admirable Influence on Magistrates, in restraining them within the Prescribed Bounds of their Duty." The writer hopes that the magazine about to be launched will have "like good Effects" by affording to all those who are genuinely oppressed an opportunity of making known their grievances. Casually at this point he lets fall the information that "considerable Numbers" of the magazine are to be printed for exportation to England. Then, following a quotation from Horace, the advertisement explains that the magazine will also enable the subjects under each government to be well informed on the conduct of their representatives and that knowledge of the political experiences of one colony will assist in the advance and improvement of another. Further, the writer points out that the magazine "may prove of great Use to any future Historian, that shall undertake to write the History of the present Times," since it will include not only public occurrences but such other material as "may enable Posterity to form an Idea of the Learning, Wisdom, and abilities; the Temper, Taste, Politeness, Customs, Manners, Morals, Religion and Politics of their Fore-fathers. With a View to this End we shall endeavour to obtain from the Curious such Observations as may serve to illustrate any of these Particulars." Finally, the writer says, the magazine will include a digest of "the General Affairs of Europe, Asia and Africa," which, it is hoped, "will yield greater Pleasure and Profit, than the scattered, unconnected Articles of News in the common Prints."

The final paragraphs, perhaps the most interesting part of this extraordinary prospectus, read thus:

As the City of Philadelphia lies in the Center of the British Plantations, and is the Middle Stage of the Post, from Boston in New-England Northwards, down to Charlestown in Carolina Southwards, and as that City, besides its frequent Intercourse with Europe, drives a continual Trade with the West-India Islands, & has also a considerable Commerce with the rest of the Colonies on the Continent; We Therefore, fixed upon it as the properest Place, and more commodiously situated than any other, for carrying on the various Correspondences, which the Nature of the Work renders necessary.

To conclude, The Reader is desired to consider the Undertaking, as an Attempt to Erect, on Neutral Principles, A Publick Theatre in the Center of the British Empire in America, on which the most remarkable Transactions of each Government may be impartially represented, and fairly exhibited to the View of all His Majesty's Subjects, whether at Home or abroad, who are disposed to be Spectators.

> This is True Liberty, when free-born Men,
> Having to advise the Publick, may speak free,
> Which he who can, and will, deserves high Praise;
> Who neither can, nor will, may hold his Peace;
> What can be juster in a State than this?

From Euripides, by Milton, for a Motto to his Vindication of the Subject's Right to the Liberty of the Press.[1]

In a postcript the advertisement comes at last to practical matters:

> It is proposed to publish a Magazine Monthly; each to contain four Sheets, or what will be equivalent to four of such as the *American Mercury* is printed on. Price to Subscribers Twelve Shillings a Year Pensylvania Currency. The first Number will be published in March next, if by that Time there are a sufficient Number of Subscriptions. Such as may be inclined to encourage the Undertaking, are desired to signify their Intention, by sending their Names, to be entred, to Andrew Bradford Printer in Philadelphia.

The next week, and for several weeks thereafter,[2] the *Pennsylvania Gazette* bore an admirably succinct advertisement of the *General Magazine And Historical Chronicle,* scheduled to appear in "January next." A concise note followed:

1. That is, *Areopagitica.*
2. *Gazette* 622-625, 628.

"THE AMERICAN MAGAZINE"

This Magazine, in Imitation of those in England, was long since projected; a Correspondence, is settled with Intelligent Men in most of the Colonies, and small Types are procured, for carrying it on in the best Manner. It would not, indeed, have been published quite so soon, were it not that a Person, to whom the Scheme was communicated in Confidence, has thought fit to advertise it in the last *Mercury,* without our Participation; and, probably, with a View, by Starting before us, to discourage us from prosecuting our first Design, and reap the Advantage of it wholly to himself. We shall endeavour, however, by executing our Plan with Care, Diligence and Impartiality, and by Printing the Work neatly and correctly, to deserve a Share of the Publick Favour: — But we desire no Subscriptions. We shall publish the Books at our own Expence, and risque the Sale of them; which Method, we suppose, will be most agreeable to our Readers, as they will then be at Liberty to buy only what they like; and we shall be under a constant Necessity of endeavouring to make every particular Pamphlet worth their Money. Each Magazine shall contain four Sheets, of common sized Paper, in a small Character: Price Six Pence Sterling, or Nine Pence Pennsylvania Money; with considerable Allowance to Chapmen who take Quantities. To be printed and Sold by B. Franklin in Philadelphia.

The accusation contained in Franklin's announcement caused the writer of the advertisement in Bradford's paper to give up his anonymity and reply directly to the charge leveled against him. In three consecutive numbers of the *Mercury* between November 20 and December 4 appeared "The Detection," signed by John Webbe, quondam "Z." of the Hamilton episode. The first part of the essay presented Webbe's version of the arrangement previously made between him and Franklin. According to Webbe's story Franklin had expressed his interest in printing a magazine or pamphlet if Webbe would undertake to "compose" it. Webbe had therefore planned it; in fact, he had in his possession at the moment, he said, the various drafts of his scheme. He had also Franklin's memoranda, which he now presented, primarily to show that Franklin had intended to be only the printer of the publication, but also to indicate the nature of the financial bargain which Franklin had proposed.[3] Before he had signed the contract Webbe had decided that Franklin's claim to three-quarters of the profits of the magazine — to

---

3. They show also that the original plan had called for a magazine of three sheets to cost fifteen shillings a year. Bradford proposed to print four sheets at a cost of twelve shillings a year. Franklin's response was to increase the size of his magazine to four sheets and to cut the price to nine pence for a single issue.

which he, not Franklin, would devote his entire time — was not just. He had, therefore, refused to complete the agreement and, though he does not say so, no doubt had made a more equitable arrangement with Bradford. This self-defense — which sounds plausible and, if true, was certainly valid — was followed the next week by the statement that Webbe had published the "Plan" both to indicate the subject matter of the proposed magazine and to present to the critical judgment of the possible subscriber his own capacities as a writer, without implying "a vain Confidence in his own abilities." He further admitted that he had met no encouragement — unlike the Gazetteer, he mockingly added, not having laid himself under obligation to supply petty chapmen with large quantities of wit. Then came what appears to be a most disingenuous remark:

> In Opposition to so inimitable a Writer [as the Gazetteer], it would be a vain Attempt for the other to persist in his Undertaking. Besides that, he is informed that another Magazine, or rather a monthly News-Paper, like that advertised in the *Gazette,* will be carried on by the Printer of the *Mercury.* Therefore, That which was proposed by the Plan is dropped for the present; and the Publisher of it humbly craves Pardon of the Public for troubling them with his Proposals.

It is possible, although it seems unlikely, that Webbe was speaking truth: that he had given up his plan; that Bradford, unwilling to drop the whole idea, had decided on a modification of it more likely to compete with Franklin; and that Webbe was not yet a party to the new arrangement.

The remainder of "The Detection" was to be devoted to Webbe's attempt to vindicate himself, as he put it, "from the Charge of being a bad Man"; but when the third part appeared Webbe stated that, since the facts of his self-defense had been "confessed" by Franklin's silence, he would drop "The Detection." Then came the counterchallenge against Franklin and the conclusion:

> ... he has since my first Letter, in Quality of Post-Master, taken upon him to deprive the *Mercury* of the Benefit of the Post, and will not permit it to travel with his *Gazette,* that charges me with the most infamous Practices. His Resentment against his Brother Printer is altogether unreasonable; for a Printer should be always acquitted from being a Party to any Writing when he discovers the Author, or when the Author subscribes his Name; except the other knows he publishes a Falsehood at the Time, which cannot be supposed to be the Case in Respect to what Mr. Bradford printed for me.

"THE AMERICAN MAGAZINE"

I take this Occasion to return him my sincere Thanks for the Opportunity he has so generously, so humanely, tho' it was to his own Prejudice, furnished me with, of vindicating myself from the most scandalous Insinuations. But I presume he will not from thence assume to himself a Right of having me at his Mercy hereafter, and to spare or cut my Throat at his Pleasure. On that Presumption, I subscribe my self, with the greatest Gratitude and Respect,

his most obliged,
humble Servant,
John Webbe.

If Webbe's intention was to arouse Franklin to reply, he succeeded. The following week, December 11, the *Gazette* dropped the advertisement of the *General Magazine* and included instead a letter answering the accusation, which began — with an ironical echo of Webbe at the close of the first paragraph — thus:

The Publick has been entertain'd for these three Weeks past, with angry Papers, written expressly against me, and publish'd in the *Mercury*. The two first I utterly neglected, as believing that both the Facts therein stated, and the extraordinary Reasonings upon them, might be safely enough left to themselves, without any Animadversion; and I have the Satisfaction to find, that the Event has answered my Expectation: But the last, my Friends think 'tis necessary I should take some Notice of, as it contains an Accusation that has at least a Shew of Probability, being printed by a Person to whom it particularly relates, who could not but know whether it was true or false; and who, having still some Reputation to guard, it may be presum'd, could by no Means be prevail'd on to publish a Thing as Truth, which was contrary to his own Knowledge.

Franklin then quoted Webbe's accusing remarks, italicizing the word *knows*, and continued:

It unluckily happens, that this not only may be supposed to be the Case, but really is the Case, in respect to this very Paragraph.

For the Truth is, that 'tis now upwards of a Twelvemonth since I refus'd to forward Mr. Bradford's Paper free by the Post, in Obedience to a positive Order from the Hon. Col. Spotswood, then Post-Master General.

To prevent any Suspicion of the Reality of such an Order, or that I obtain'd it by some Misrepresentations of Mr. Bradford, or that it was given hastily, thro' Caprice, or without just Reason, I am sorry I am oblig'd to mention, That his Detaining the Ballance of his Accounts, and his Neglecting to render any Account for a long time, while he held the Post-Office himself, as they were the Occasion of his Removal, so they drew upon him, after long Patience and Forbearance, the Resentment of the Post-Master General.

There followed a letter to Franklin from Spotswood, dated October 12, 1739, in which Spotswood asserted that he had not been able to collect the post-office accounts from Bradford after 1734 and therefore ordered Franklin to bring suit against Bradford and also to forbid him henceforward free use of the post for his papers and his private correspondence.[4] Franklin ended with a blast which embraced both Webbe and Bradford:

Upon the Receipt of this Letter it was, that I absolutely refus'd to forward any more of Mr. Bradford's Papers free by Post; and from that time to this, he has never offered me any to forward. This he cannot but KNOW to be True.

---

4. Franklin himself added a note of explanation here: "The Privilege of Free-Postage was allow'd Mr. Bradford, on Condition of his acquitting himself fairly of the Office, and doing Justice to the Revenue." If Franklin is to be believed, this privilege was continued even after Bradford had ceased to be postmaster.

In defense of Bradford and other colonial postmasters, nearly all of whom were slow in bringing in their accounts, it should be said that the position, though an honor, was a constant vexation. As late as 1735, for example, Henry Flower, who had been postmaster in Philadelphia before Bradford, advertised (*Mercury* 804) that those who owed him money for postage should pay him. Andrew Hay, postmaster at Amboy, inserted a notice in the *Mercury* (Number 826) asking for the payment of postage, some of it due for four years. In 1736 (*New York Gazette* 557, July 5) the New York postmaster announced that he would cease to give credit for mail, because there was at that time sufficient small change in the colony. In the same year (*Mercury* 877) Bradford advertised thus in his paper:

All Persons who are Indebted to Andrew Bradford, Post-Master, for Postage of Letters, are desired forthwith to come and Pay the same; some having been of above four Years standing. And all Persons are desired to take notice, That whereas the giving Credit, and keeping Accounts of Postage of Letters is found to be very troublesome (and has been a great Loss to the Post-Master, who has lost some Pounds by it) so, for the Future, he desires all Persons whatsoever to send Pay for their Letters, there being small running Cash enough in this Province: And for the Future there will be no Accounts kept for Postage, nor any Letters delivered without Postage paid.

Franklin, who had probably learned by the experience of others and was too shrewd to be victimized, almost as soon as he had acquired the postmastership announced (*Pennsylvania Gazette* 473, January 3, 1738):

To prevent the unnecessary Trouble of keeping Accounts, and the Loss that attends delivering Letters on Trust; No Letters will be delivered hereafter to any Person whatever, without the Money immediately paid. Which it's hoped will not be taken amiss.

Title Page of the *American Magazine*
Courtesy of The New-York Historical Society, New York City

I must however do Mr. Bradford the Justice, to vindicate him from an injurious Suspicion which I apprehend may arise on this Occasion, to wit, That he has impos'd that Story on his unhappy Writer, and misled him by a wrong Account of Facts he might be ignorant of. —— For this, in my Opinion, cannot possibly be: Inasmuch as that Person is thoroughly acquainted with the Affair, was employ'd as Attorney in the Action against Bradford, and had, at the very Time he was writing the Paragraph in Question, the Original Letter from Col. Spotswood, in his own Possession.

Webbe could not remain silent. On December 18 a six-page issue of the *Mercury* included a long postscript in which "J.W." answered Franklin's charges. After the inevitable preamble (with a quotation from Steele) defending his right to self-defense, Webbe ironically noted that the original advertisement, the cause of the conflict, had been dropped from the *Gazette*. He then came to the real point of his remarks:

> ... it is true that after the Orders mentioned by the *Gazetteer*, Mr. Bradford never sent him any of his Papers to be forwarded in the Mail. But it is as true, that, as they were made up in unsealed Packets, he sent them to the Riders who used to distribute them on their several Routs. This Method, which Mr. Bradford was obliged to have Recourse to a considerable Time past for the Conveyance of his News-Papers, was NO SECRET; and consequently could not be unknown to Mr. Franklin; and therefore it must be presumed to have had his Approbation. Moreover, I was well assured that He had declared, some Time before he laid me under the Necessity of writing against him in my own Defence, that as he favoured Mr. Bradford by permitting the Postman to distribute his Papers, he had him therefore under his Thumb; and was confident, in Regard he could at any Time deprive him of that Privilege, that he would not, if he understood his own Interest, be prevaild upon to publish any Thing against him the *Gazetteer*....

Again, Mr. Bradford, on whom I ought to relie, informed me before I wrote my last, that the Postman who generally carried his News-Papers lately mentioned he was apprehensive it wou'd be displeasing to Mr. Franklin, were he to know he destributed them. Now such Apprehensions which could only be judged to arise from some Declaration of Mr. Franklin; (whether directly or indirectly is left to his Choice to say;

for either is equal for our Purpose) being considered with the Information I had of his previous Resolution to stop the Passage of the *Mercury,* whenever he should think himself disobliged by it: I therefore, and justly therefore, inferred, That he had already begun to put his Threats against the *Mercury* in Execution. . . .

This Edict in Regard to the Postman was what I meant by depriving the *Mercury* of the Benefit of the Post. And I expressly charge it on Mr. Franklin that he was sensible I so meant before he wrote his abusive Letter, which I call upon him to deny if he can. . . .

Webbe went on to insist that in quoting Spotswood's letter Franklin had been drawing a red herring across the trail, proving — what nobody would deny — that the order against Bradford's use of the post existed and implicitly denying Webbe's previous charge in order to conceal his own chicanery. Webbe asserted that Franklin's true purpose had been to defame Bradford; accordingly, step by step, he analyzed Franklin's letter, pointing out particularly that it was Franklin, not Spotswood, who alleged that Bradford's failure to render his accounts was the cause of his removal from the postmastership, and that Franklin raised rather than allayed a suspicion when he said that he was printing Spotswood's letter to show that he had not received the order because of any misrepresentation of Bradford. Webbe further maintained that Bradford considered the loss of his position due to "the false Representations, and private Sollicitations of the Gazeteer," that Spotswood might have been misinformed about Bradford's health by Franklin himself, and that Franklin had failed to communicate Spotswood's order to Bradford.

After this not unconvincing statement of the Webbe-Bradford side of the controversy, there was silence for several weeks while each printing office evidently concentrated its energies on preparing as rapidly as possible for the publication of its magazine. On December 25 the advertisement of the *General Magazine* appeared once again in the *Gazette.* On February 5 each newspaper advertised that the magazine sponsored by its printer would appear during the following week, though the *American Magazine* had been originally announced to begin in March. Neither magazine, however, appeared as scheduled, for on February 12 each paper contained another announcement — Bradford's to the effect that his magazine would appear the next day, Friday, Franklin's stating that his would come out on Monday. The next week each printer advertised his magazine, the January issue, as "just published"; for lack of contrary evidence it is assumed, therefore, that the magazines appeared at the times specified and that Bradford's antedated Franklin's by three days. Whereas in his advertisement of February 19 Franklin confined himself to printing his magazine's table of contents and the price, Bradford omitted the table of contents and included a note on the size and the price of his miscellany and the originality of much of the material in it. In the *Gazette* of February 26 was published what was represented as a letter to Franklin mocking the advertisement in the previous *Mercury* and particularly assailing Webbe, who was held responsible for it, as writing nonsense. This was doubtless Franklin's retaliation for Webbe's statement in the *Mercury* of December 18 that Franklin's explanation of his closing the mails to Bradford was a tissue of illogicalities and inconsistencies. The *Gazette's* attack was a gross exaggeration and crudely written, but in raising a laugh against Webbe and Bradford it may have served its purpose. Once again Franklin had struck home, for instead of ignoring the Gazetteer's derision the *Mercury* of March 5 contained a dignified, though somewhat pedantic, reply signed by Andrew Bradford.[5] This answer in the *Mercury* at last brought the newspaper war to a close. The following week, March 12, Bradford announced that on the seventeenth the February issue of the *American Magazine* would appear. On March 19, while the *Mercury* advertised that Bradford's monthly had come out, the *Gazette* announced that the February number of the *General Magazine* would be ready on March 24. On the twenty-sixth Franklin advertised the magazine as published and once again gave the table of contents. Strangely, the third and final number of the *American Magazine* was not mentioned in the *Mercury*, but Franklin continued to announce regularly the publication of his magazine until it came to an end late in July with the sixth issue.[6]

The *American Magazine or A Monthly View of the Political State of the British Colonies* was printed on pages measuring about 4½ by 7¾ inches. Across the top of the title-page ran the picture of the Philadelphia waterfront which had already been used by the *Mercury;* below it was the title, the date, and the phrase "To be Continued Monthly." Then came the table of contents in a double column, and at the bottom appeared the imprint: "Printed and Sold by Andrew Bradford: (Price One Shilling Pennsylvania Currency, or Eight Pence Sterling.)"[7] Except for the reprinting of the "Plan" in the first number most of the maga-

---

5. In spite of the signature this defense sounds like Webbe's writing, though it is more concise than he usually manages to be. Since we have very little of Bradford's composition with which to compare it, however, we are not in a position to deny his authorship.
6. See *Gazette* 645, 646, 649, 650, 654, 658, 659.
7. The imprint of the first number had the additional information that single copies of the "Plan" could be had at three pence Pennsylvania money.

zine was printed in double columns. The types were the same size as those ordinarily used in the *Mercury*, but much broken, so that many of the pages were blurred and slovenly in appearance. The pagination throughout the magazine was continuous: the first number contained eight pages in Roman numerals and thirty-four in Arabic; the February issue began with page 35 and ran through page 76; the March number ended with page 120.[8] Since several topics discussed in the third issue were described as to be continued, it is obvious that at the time that number came from the press Webbe expected to carry the magazine further.

The "Plan," which immediately followed the title-page of the January issue, was substantially the same as that which had appeared in the *Mercury*, but two changes of some importance had been made. Whereas the original "Plan" had announced that a considerable number of copies of the magazine would be printed for exportation to England, the revision said that the magazine was "proposed to be Printed Monthly in London," though whether or not an actual arrangement was ever effected we cannot tell. In the second place, though the first scheme had ambitiously offered to discuss "the General Affairs of Europe, Asia and Africa," the revision dropped "Asia" and "Africa" as well as the comment on the disjointedness of the news accounts in the regular journals. The "Plan" was supplemented by a "Postscript," which promised impartiality in presenting disputes between colonial governors and assemblies and once again insisted on the liberty of the individual to remark upon political matters. Surely Webbe was thinking of the current argument between the Pennsylvania Assembly and Governor Thomas over the defense of the province, but the final paragraph supported the previous implication that he was also looking beyond the colonies and intended to interpret them, especially Pennsylvania, to England.

The greater part of the first number was nominally devoted to the activities of the Assemblies of New Jersey, Pennsylvania, and Maryland "in Relation to the King's Instructions recommending to them the victualling and transporting the Troops, that were afterwards sent from thence against the Spanish West-Indies." First appeared an abstract of the proceedings of the Assembly of New Jersey from June 26 to July 31, 1740. Then came a five-page account of Pennsylvania and the address of the speaker of the Assembly at the close of the session of August 1739, both of which were evidently intended to form an introduction to the proceedings of the Assembly of the province. Each, however, has interest in its own right. The first, entitled "A Description of Pennsylvania, in Answer to a Misrepresentation of it, in the Drapier's Letters,"

---

8. In the January and February issues the title-pages and versos were not included in the numbering; in the March issue they were.

was a well-written essay which first pointed out the contribution made by the colonies to the prosperity of England and then denied Swift's contention that people emigrated to America only because of their "insupportable Condition at home" and that the lot of these immigrants in the new country was a miserable one. Speaking of Pennsylvania, against which he believed Swift's remarks were especially directed, Webbe insisted on the friendliness of the Indians and on the cheapness of land and the large profits from raising crops; he mentioned the several ironworks already supplying tools to the people of the colony, the navigability of the Delaware and the Schuylkill, and religious freedom and the extent of the franchise. Though his remarks were generally sound, Webbe's picture of the province was somewhat idealized — for example, when he turned the tables on Swift in speaking of the Indians:

> Such a Simplicity of Manners prevails amongst them (we mean amongst those of them whose Settlements are remote from the English, and who are not yet corrupted with Rum) that one would be almost tempted to swear, they are the same individual People, that Captain Gulliver met with in his Travels, and allegorically describes under the Name of the Houynhnms.

The address of the speaker of the Assembly was probably introduced to lend support to the account of Pennsylvania, as well as to pay tribute to a man whom Webbe admired. For, though his name was not mentioned, the speech was the political farewell of Andrew Hamilton,[9] a dignified and eloquent expression of his faith in the liberal principles which the government of the province embodied. There followed Webbe's abstract of the proceedings of the Assembly from October 15, 1739, to January 11, 1740, which entirely concerned the conflict of Thomas and the legislature over the question of defense. With a note that from January to July "the Dispute stopt," Webbe then went on to abstract the proceedings of the Maryland Assembly, beginning with April 20, 1740. After a few pages, however, he interrupted himself to insert "Remarks on the Maryland Government," intended to "enable the Reader to form an Idea of the Nature of the Maryland Constitution." The "Remarks" was a typical Webbe essay, written in good prose, but very discursive: he quoted from Locke's *Treatises on Government* and from James Logan's charge to the grand jury of Pennsylvania in 1723; he discussed the senates of ancient Athens and Sparta, the nature of Athenian aristocracy, and the origin of the British House of Lords; he pointed out the differences between the Councils of Pennsylvania and

---

9. Hamilton's speech was reprinted in the magazine exactly as it had appeared a year and a half earlier in the *Gazette* (Number 563, September 27, 1739).

of Maryland; and he argued against the introduction into the American colonial system of a power comparable to the House of Peers. Having considered these points and having touched only obliquely upon the real subject of the essay — the struggle of the elected lower branch of the Maryland legislature against the power of the upper house, nominated by and responsible to the proprietor — Webbe found that his space was running out. Accordingly, just as he was ready to "take another View" of the Maryland constitution, he announced that the subject would be further discussed in the next issue, and filled out the remaining three columns of the January number with an item from the *London Magazine* of July 1740, "The Characters of the Worthies at Stowe."

The February issue opened with a sixteen-page continuation of Webbe's remarks on Maryland, which developed further, by quotation and argument, the implications of the previous article. As a whole the essay, though too diffuse to be entirely effective, resembled Cato in its emphasis on democratic procedures in government and in the author's assumption of the right to discuss basic political concepts. There followed further abstracts of the proceedings of the Assemblies of Maryland and of Pennsylvania, and for the first time the proceedings of the New York Assembly, beginning with June 30, 1740. Thereafter came comment upon the conflict in New Jersey between the governor and the legislature and appropriate quotations to illustrate that struggle. This topic was broken off to make room for an article entitled "The State of the War," a section of a little over three pages containing items similar to the regular news reports in the *Mercury*. The most interesting of these was the story of the celebration in Dublin of Admiral Vernon's birthday: " . . . the Anniversary Birth Day of this Admiral, was observed . . . with great Demonstrations of Joy: In the Morning the Bells of St. Patrick's Church rang (by Order of Dr. Swift Dean of that Cathedral) *Britons strike Home &c.* with great Variety of Changes."[10] On the final page of this issue was printed Vernon's line of battle, which was presented also to readers of the *Mercury* on March 19.

After calling attention on the verso of the title-page to two errors in the printing of the February issue, the third number of the magazine briefly summarized the proceedings of the Assembly of New York. Then came Webbe's best-known work, "An Essay towards explaining the Nature of Money in general, and of Paper Money in particular." The article, a clear and orderly exposition of "the Nature, Power and Effects"[11] of a currency based on precious metals, was the introduction to a discussion of paper currency which, because of the abrupt ending

10. *American Magazine*, 74.
11. *Ibid.*, 90.

of the *American Magazine,* was not printed. The subject was even more lively in 1741 than the question of the relation between the two houses of the colonial legislatures, and Webbe's unusual concision and the lucidity with which he expounded his theory of money made this essay the most able and vigorous piece of writing in the magazine. "The Religion of the Indian Natives of America," which followed it, is probably the closest approach in the magazine to the periodical essay of the English prose writers. It propounded the familiar, though not undisputed, eighteenth-century view that "Christianity . . . is only the Religion of Nature in its original Purity and Perfection,"[12] and it concluded with the unanswerable reply of an Indian to a Swedish missionary at "Conestogoe" in 1690, the end of which ran:[13]

> Are the Christians more virtuous, or rather are they not much more vicious than we are? If so, how comes it to pass they are the Objects of God's Beneficence while we are neglected? Does the Deity confer his Favours without Reason, and with so much Partiality? In a Word, we find the Christians much more depraved in their Morals than our selves; And as we judge of their Doctrine by the Badness of their Lives, we therefore cannot believe that the just God has left us with a Revelation inferior to theirs.

"The Wiles of Popery: Or, the Popish Emissary instructed," from the *South Carolina Gazette* of October 16, 1740, was a diatribe against Roman Catholicism;[14] a letter from "A.B." attempted "A Vindication of the Conduct of the Upper House of Maryland"; and the proceedings of the Assembly of Pennsylvania were continued. More interesting was a second letter to the publisher, this one upholding the right of private persons "to inquire into the Nature of Government, and into the Conduct of Governors."[15] Except for an introductory paragraph and a brief conclusion, the entire letter consisted of a quotation from "a great Author" of "not many Years ago,"[16] who ably supported the writer's convictions. Though Webbe's correspondent never acknowledged the identity of the "great Author," once again it was Cato who was called upon to bolster the colonial argument — specifically Letter 38, of July 22, 1721, entitled "The Right and Capacity of the People to judge of

---

12. *American Magazine,* 91.
13. *Ibid.,* 94. It is interesting to note the conception of the noble savage both here and in Webbe's previous remarks on the resemblance of the Indians to the Houyhnhnms.
14. The attack is in the form of a dialogue.
15. *American Magazine,* 109.
16. *Ibid.,* 110.

Government," of which all but the first three pages was used.[17] A third letter, part of which the editor deferred to the next issue, was a complaint against the exorbitant grants to particular people of the free lands of America, whereby "the rest of the Subjects have been obliged to buy it for their Use at an extravagant Price."[18] Finally came an interesting piece of local information, an "Account of the Snows that have fallen this last hard Winter in and near Philadelphia," from October 27, 1740, to April 19, 1741.[19] There were forty-four snowfalls; by December 17 the snow was a foot deep "where level"; on December 19 "the Ice stuck between Town and Gloucester"; and by February 1 the snow was "2 Foot deep on a Level in the Woods about 18 Miles from Town, in Merion . . .; 20 Miles further 'twas many Inches deeper." On March 14, at last, two vessels "came from Sea up to Town," and several more arrived two days later. On March 26 the aurora borealis was seen, but the weather remained dry. The account concludes with a homely remark on the fruit crop: "Probably we shall have a great Apple Year, and Cherries of some Kinds pretty plenty, but few Peaches." Thus the *American Magazine* came to an end.

Since both Bradford's and Franklin's magazines failed after a few months, it seems obvious that the time was not yet ripe in Philadelphia in 1741 for a more ambitious and expensive journalistic venture than a newspaper. But it is also clear that Webbe was not versatile enough to be a good magazine editor. He should certainly be commended for his own contributions to the *American Magazine,* especially since even the British miscellanies contemporary with it contained almost no original work. Indeed, his conception of the magazine as primarily a forum for first-hand discussion of political issues was in advance of his day. Moreover, the March issue with its several letters, its satirical attack upon the proselyting of the Roman Catholic Church, its essay on the Indian religion, and its touch of local color suggests that Webbe was beginning to realize the need for greater variety and liveliness than the earlier issues had possessed. Nevertheless, Webbe was essentially too one-sided and pedantic to edit a magazine successfully, and the *Mercury* offers presumptive evidence that Bradford unaided would have been more likely to put out a salable miscellany than Webbe. For Bradford would probably have been content to follow the pattern of the English magazines; with the help of his scissors he would have brought together,

---

17. Almost twenty years before, this essay had been the first of *Cato's Letters* to be reprinted in the *Mercury* (February 20, 1722). The letter in the *American Magazine* was signed with Webbe's familiar initial "Z."; it is quite possible that Webbe himself inserted the letter in defense of his frankness in discussing the Maryland Assembly.

18. *American Magazine,* 115.

19. Note that this was the magazine for March.

as they did, news and political essays, familiar essays and verse — the same sort of thing he had found eminently profitable in his newspaper. Not that this would necessarily have proved successful. When Franklin made his first proposal to Webbe, so Webbe stated,[20] he had mentioned that the editing of the magazine "would only require about 3 or 4 Days in a month"; if he meant what he said, Franklin must have been thinking of a clip-and-paste job. Franklin's own magazine, indeed, bears out this assumption; though it was much more various and entertaining and much less weighty than the *American Magazine,* it contained little but borrowings, such as I imagine that Bradford might have used if left to his own methods. Yet Franklin's magazine also failed.[21] On the other hand, the first successful American miscellany, the *American Magazine and Monthly Chronicle* of Boston, which began in September 1743 and ran for more than three years, was modelled even more closely on the British magazines than Franklin's had been and used relatively more material from English sources.

Bradford's magazine, then, was probably foredoomed to failure. The undertaking was hastily contrived; it lacked the financial security of a subscription list, which the Boston *American Magazine* wisely established in advance; and there was no time to prepare for its proper distribution in other colonies, which Bradford in initiating the *Mercury* had arranged with great care. Possibly the feud between the *Gazette* and the *Mercury* damaged both magazines, though it is equally likely that the conflict was good publicity. Finally, Webbe's editorial shortcomings severely limited the appeal of the *American Magazine.* But, although it was a failure, it is interesting as an early experiment in journalism. Webbe's initiative in supplying a great part of his own copy and his courage in polemics were matched by Bradford's initiative and courage in interrupting the comfortable monotony of middle age and financial ease to launch another pioneer work and to assume responsibility once again for the publication of opinions suspect and explosive.

20. *Mercury* 1090.
21. The *General Magazine* was printed on smaller sheets than the *American Magazine,* just as the *Gazette* was smaller than the *Mercury.* The type-faces were generally in better condition than those used by Bradford, but the reader cannot share Franklin's enthusiasm for the "small Letter that no other Printer in America had besides himself" (Webbe, of Franklin, in "The Detection," *Mercury* 1090). This uncommonly fine print appeared in the *Gazette* also at this period, regularly in the advertising column and often in other parts of the paper. Its only possible recommendation is that it saved space.

Conclusion

It is unfortunate that we have no record of Andrew Bradford's personal characteristics. We know nothing of his ordinary way of life, of his appearance or manner of speech; we have no picture of him and only a handful of business letters. The single episode of his family life that gossip has brought down to us — Thomas's account of the dissolution of his partnership with his nephew — suggests that he was henpecked, at least by his second wife, but we can neither confirm nor deny the story. We cannot be sure what or how much he wrote for his newspaper. Even the great battle over Hamilton throws no light on Bradford's character because we do not know why he fought and whether or not the cause which he seems to have espoused was just. We can infer his stubborn courage in resisting control of his press, but we know little of the details of the struggle.

Though we cannot, therefore, draw a portrait of the man, some aspects of his business activities indirectly reveal his reputation or his character. For example, though his father had been a backslider and had suffered harsh treatment from the Philadelphia Meeting, and though he himself was a staunch Anglican, Bradford amicably conducted business with the Society of Friends for a quarter of a century — a fact which indicates good sense and tolerance on both sides. In the establishment of the Durham Iron Company he was associated with several of the most respected and financially substantial men of the province. His purchases of real estate, especially in the area west of what is now Broad Street — towards which the city, if it grew at all, must necessarily have expanded — show his business acumen. And his success as printer and publisher, even against the competition of the most able of all of his contemporaries, indicates enterprise and sound judgment of no mean order. In addition to considering the implications of such facts as these, we can readily correct several persistent misconceptions of Bradford and his work. Particularly misleading is Franklin's accusation that he was "very illiterate."[1] We can hardly doubt that Bradford had less interest in intellectual matters than Franklin; and the *Mercury*, though its evidence is only negative, does not suggest that Bradford had discriminating literary taste. On the other hand, we have samples of Bradford's practiced and legible handwriting, and such pieces of his composition as we are able to identify — a few business letters, and probably advertisements and notices in his newspaper —

---

1. *Autobiography*, 257. Franklin's comment that Bradford had not been bred to his trade was either a careless misstatement or a deliberate misrepresentation. Three years after Franklin was born, Bradford was listed as a printer among the freemen of New York City.

Conclusion

indicate, if no grace of style, at least order and clarity of expression. More important, it is hard to imagine a "very illiterate" person successfully managing a store, editing and printing a newspaper, publishing a magazine, and holding offices of trust and responsibility from church, city, and province — not to mention the postmastership.

The *Mercury*, like its "author," has suffered from unjust disparagement. In the heat of founding the *Universal Instructor* and no doubt smarting from his skirmishes with Bradford, Keimer made the absurd statement that "the late *Mercury* has been so wretchedly perform'd, that it has been not only a Reproach to the Province, but such a Scandal to the very Name of Printing, that it may, for its unparallel'd Blunders and Incorrectness, be truly stiled Nonsense in Folio, instead of a Serviceable News-Paper."[2] Franklin, originally in a position not very different from Keimer's and even in retrospect, probably, piqued at a competitor's success, asserted in the *Autobiography* that the *Mercury* was "a paltry thing, wretchedly manag'd, no way entertaining, and yet was profitable."[3] Neither the *Universal Instructor* nor the *Pennsylvania Gazette* in its first decade, however, showed any genuine superiority to the *Mercury* either in format or in content. Until after the death of Andrew Bradford and the founding of the *Pennsylvania Journal*, no appreciable decline in the *Mercury* in comparison with its rivals occurred. Indeed, in both appearance and subject matter the *Mercury* is well able to stand comparison with its contemporaries among colonial journals; among the newspapers of the middle colonies it deserves special mention because it led the way; and its long career betokens that, whatever ridicule Keimer and Franklin may have directed against it, their opinions were not those of the people for whom it was printed.

While there is much reason to believe that Andrew Bradford had a good reputation and unusual success in business, we have no cause to imagine that he was in any way a great man. We are likely, however, because we know so little of him as a person, to underestimate rather than to overestimate his importance. He has, without question, several claims to respect and interest. First, the *American Weekly Mercury* and the *American Magazine* assure him a significant place in the history of American journalism. Second, he fought and won his small part in the great battle for freedom of the press. Third, in the books he imported from England and in the columns of his newspaper he helped to form the tastes and opinions of his contemporaries. Finally, in the daily course of fulfilling his more-than-average responsibilities as business man and citizen he contributed to the economic and cultural prosperity which even in his lifetime was rapidly transforming Philadelphia from a colonial town to one of the first cities of the British Empire.

2. Advertisement of the *Universal Instructor*, October 1, 1728.
3. *Autobiography*, 302.

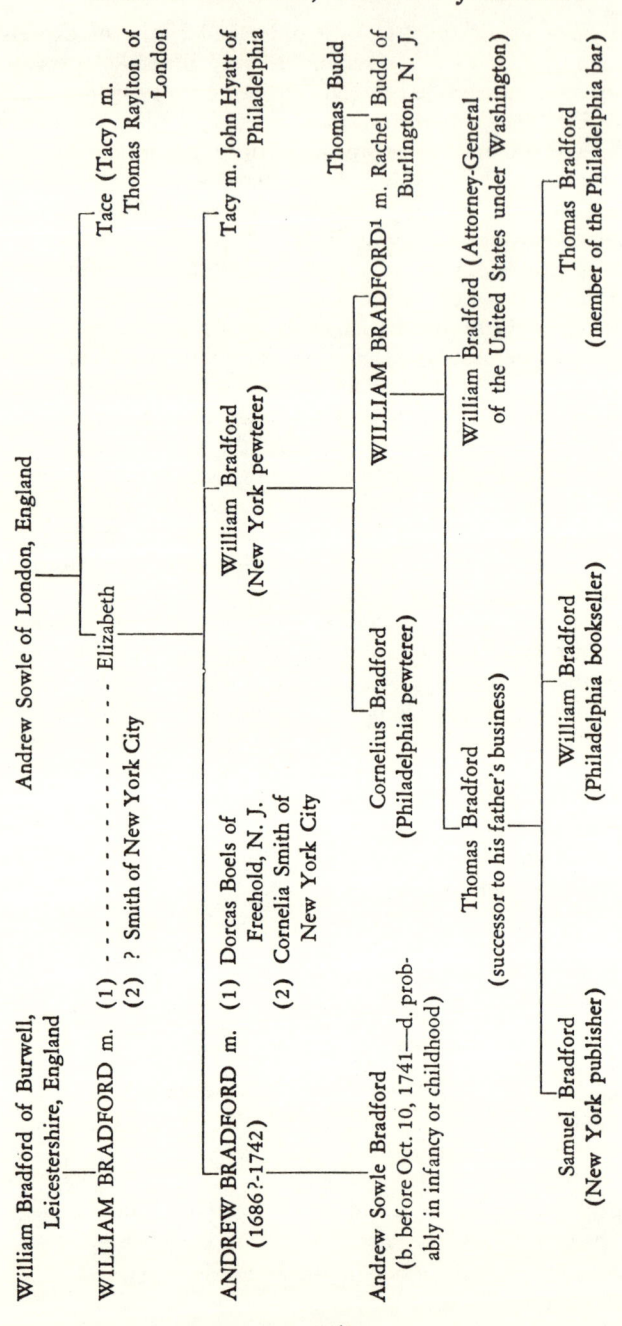

Andrew Bradford's Will

In the Name of God Amen this tenth Day of October in the year of our Lord one thousand seven hundred & forty one I Andrew Bradford of the City of Philada. Stationer & Printer being of health of Body and of perfect Mind & Memory Thanks be given unto God but calling to mind the mortality of my Body knowing that it is appointed for all men once to Dye Do make and ordain this my Last Will and Testament in manner & form following That is to say First and principally I give my Soul into the Hands of God who gave it me And for my Body I recommend the same to the Earth to be buried in a Christian manner at the Discretion of my Executrix hereinafter named nothing doubting but at the General Resurrection I shall receive the same by the mighty Power of God and as touching such Worldly Estate wherewith it hath pleased God to bless me with in this Life I Give Devise Bequeath & Dispose the same in manner & form following that is to say All that my Tract of Land situate in Lower Dublin in the County of Philadelphia Containing five hundred Acres of Land And also All that my sixteenth part of Durham Iron Works I Give and devise to Cornelia my Wife To hold the same to her the said Cornelia her Heirs & Assigns to the End she may be enabled to make Sale of the same for the Uses herein after mentioned Also I give to my said Wife All my Household Goods Shop Goods Plate Bille Bonds and Books Debts and all other my personal Estate of what nature or kind soever My printing Press Letters and the Appurtenances thereunto belonging only Excepted She my said Wife out of the Money arising by the Sale of the said ffive hundred Acres of Land Durham Iron Works and my said personal Estate paying all such Debts as shall be due from me at the Time of my decease Also I give unto my said Wife all other my Houses Lands Tenements and Real Estate And the Use of my Printing Press Letters and the Appurtenances aforesaid To hold to her during her Life only And on her decease I give and devise unto Andrew Sole Bradford All those my Houses and Lotts of Land in the City of Philadelphia Bounded Northward by the Messuages & Lot of Land now in the Tenure of John Kearsley Eastward by the Front Street Southward by Tenements in the Occupation of Samuel Hasel and Westward by Laetitia Court Also I give to the said Andrew Sole Bradford on the decease of my said Wife All that my Messuage & Lot of Land with the Appurtenances situate in the high Street of Philada. aforesaid which I purchased of Joseph Jones To have & to hold the said Houses Lots of Land with their Appurtenances unto the said Andrew Sole Bradford and to the Heirs of his Body to be begotten and on default of such Issue I give and Devise the same to my nephew Cornelius Bradford and his Heirs & Assigns for ever Also I Give & Devise unto my Niece Elizabeth Bradford All those my Lots of Land on Society Hill which I purchased of the Trustees appointed by Act of Assembly for the Society To hold to her the said Elizabeth her Heirs & Assigns for Ever Also I give unto the aforesd. William Bradford younger Son of my Brother William Bradford of New York on the decease of my said Wife if he shall behave himself handsomely towards her my said Printing Press Letters and the Appurtenances thereunto belonging To hold to him and his Assigns for Ever. Also I give to my Sister Tacy Hyat one English silver Shilling Lastly I nominate and appoint my said Wife Cornelia Sole Executrix of this my last Will and Testament And I do devise and bequeath unto her the Residue of my Estate Real and Personal And I do hereby Revoke and declare Null and Void all former Wills by me made And declare this only to be my Last Will and Testament In Witness whereof I have hereunto Affixed my Hand & Seal Dated the Day & Year above written — Andrew Bradford — [Seal]

Cornelia Bradford's Will

In the Name of God Amen I Cornelia Bradford of the City of Philadelphia in the Province of Pensylvania Widow, being at present in a poor state of Health, but of sound and well Disposing Mind & Memory thanks be to God for the same, and all other his Mercys, & Considering the Certainty of Death, and the uncertainty of the time thereof, Do make my last Will and Testament, in Manner following, (to say) First it is my Mind and Will, that all my Just Debts and Funeral Expences be Duly paid, And I Do give and Devise unto my nephew James Hamm, all that my Messuage or Tenement wherein he now Dwells, and Lott of Ground thereunto belonging Situate in a Street called Smiths Street, in the City of New York; in the Province of New York together with the Appurtenances unto the same Tenemt. & Lott of Ground belonging, To hold the sd. Tenement & Lott of Ground unto him the sd. James Ham his Heirs & Assigns forever, And I Do Give unto the said James Ham the sum of One Hundred Pounds Pensylvania Currancy to be paid to him the sd. James Ham his Executors Adminrs. or Assigns in two Years after my Decease, And I do hereby give and Devise unto my Niece Elizabeth Flew her Heirs and Assigns for Ever, The one half of my Land or Lott of Ground in the Township of Germantown in the County of Philada. in the sd. Province of Pensylvania, which I Purchased from Dominicus Gassner together with the Houses and Tenement wherein she now dwells, And the other half of the sd. Land or Lott of Ground I do give and Devise unto my Nephew George Smith of the City of Philada. Merchant, & Cornelia his Wife, their Heirs & Assigns for ever, together with all the Appurtenances thereunto belonging, And it is my mind & Will that the Front of the said Land or Lott of Ground in Germantown high road be Divided by A propper Surveyor into two Equal parts and a Line of Division run through ye Middle of the sd. Land or Lott as far as the Lane where the sd. Land or Lott Terminates, And that half nexto the Lutheran Church I Give and Devise unto Elizabeth Flew, and the other half thereof I Do give and Devise unto George Smith & Cornelia his Wife their Heirs & Assigns for Ever And I Do give and Devise unto my Niece Catherine Degrowgh (the Daughter of my Sister Mary) her Heirs & Assigns forever,

All my House and Lott of Ground thereto belonging wherein she now Dwells Situate in Beaver Street in the sd. City of New York together with the Appurtenances, & it is my Mind & Will that my two negroes Henry, & Sylvia, be freed & Discharged by my Executors from all Duty & Service, And I Do desire my Sd. Executors to give such Security for my sd. Negroes as the Law requires And I do give my sd. Negroe Woman Sylvia all her Wearing Apparrell together with her Bed, Bed Cloaths, Bed Stead, two Iron Potts, two Pewter Dishes, Six pewter Plates, three Cane Chairs with Matted Bottoms, one Black Elbow Cane Chair, and one Cedar Chest, and it is my Will that if my sd. Negroes by Lameness Sickness or other casualtys be rendred incapable of Geting their Living, that my Sd. Executor pay them three Pounds ℔ Year to Each of them, or to the one which Shall be so rendred incapable of getting their Livelyhood And I do give Devise & Bequeath unto my Nephew George Smith of the sd. City of Philada. Mercht. & Cornelia his Wife, (my Niece) All and Singular the rest and residue of my Messuages, Lotts, Lands, Tenements, Rents and Hereditaments whatsoever or Wheresoever, together with their and every of their Appurtenances To hold to them the sd. George Smith & Cornelia his Wife, their Heirs and Assigns forever Moreover I do give & Bequeath unto the sd. George Smith & Cornelia his Wife all the rest and residue of my Goods, Chattels, Plate, Moneys, Mortgages, Bonds, Book Debts, Rights, Credits, Effects and Personal Estate whatsoever or wheresoever, either in the Province of New York or in the sd. Province of Pensylvania or Elsewhere And I do Nominate and appoint the sd. George Smith & Cornelia his Wife to be the sole Executors of this my last Will and Testament And I do hereby Revoke all former Wills by me made, And do Declare this only, to be my last Will & Testamt. In Witness whereof I the sd. Cornelia Bradford have hereunto sett my Hand and Seal this Eleventh day of January in the Year of our Lord One Thousand Seven Hundred & fifty five,

Cornelia   her   Bradford   [seal]
         x
      mark

Bibliography[1]

Files of the following British newspapers and magazines: the *Bee*, the *British Journal*, *Common Sense*, the *Craftsman* (the *Country Journal*), the *Daily Advertiser*, the *Daily Courant*, the Dublin *Evening Post*, the *Gentleman's Magazine*, the *Grub Street Journal*, the London *Evening Post*, the London *Gazette*, the London *Journal*, the *London Magazine*, Mist's *Weekly Journal*, the *Old Whig*, the *Plain Dealer*, the *Political State of Great Britain*, the *St. James Evening Post*, the *Spectator*, the *Tatler*, the *Universal Spectator*, the *Weekly Miscellany*, the *Whitehall Evening Post*.

Files of the following American newspapers and magazines, in addition to the *American Weekly Mercury* and the *American Magazine*:

I. New England: the *American Magazine* (Boston), the Boston *Evening Post*, the Boston *Gazette*, the Boston *News Letter*, the Boston *Weekly Post Boy*, the (Boston) *Weekly Rehearsal*, the *New England Courant*, the *New England Weekly Journal*, the *Rhode Island Gazette*.

II. New York: the New York *Evening Post*, the New York *Gazette*, the New York *Weekly Journal*, the New York *Weekly Post Boy*.

III. Philadelphia: the *General Magazine*, the *Pennsylvania Gazette*, the *Pennsylvania Journal*, the *Universal Instructor*.

IV. The South: the *Barbadoes Gazette*, the *Maryland Gazette*, the *South Carolina Gazette*, the *Virginia Gazette*.

The American Magazine. Reproduced from the Original Edition, Philadelphia, 1741, with a Bibliographical Note by Lyon N. Richardson. New York, 1937. (There is no complete file of the magazine in existence. The John Carter Brown Library, the Library of Congress, and the New-York Historical Society have incomplete files.)

The American Weekly Mercury. (I have used the files of the Library Company of Philadelphia, the American Antiquarian Society, and the Historical Society of Pennsylvania.)

The American Weekly Mercury, 1719-1723. Facsimile reprint by the Colonial Society of Pennsylvania. Philadelphia, 1898-1907. 4 volumes.

Articles of the Fellowship Fire Company. HSP.[2]

Bezanson, Anne; Gray, Robert D.; and Hussey, Miriam. *Prices in Colonial Pennsylvania*. Philadelphia, 1935.

[Blenman, Jonathan.] *Remarks on Zenger's Tryal*. [Philadelphia, 1736.] HSP.

Bourne, H. R. Fox. *English Newspapers*. London, 1887. 2 volumes.

Bradford Manuscripts (uncatalogued). HSP.

Bradford Papers. HSP.

Brigham, Clarence S. "Bibliography of American Newspapers, 1690-1820," *Proceedings of the American Antiquarian Society*, New Series, volume 23, part II, October 1913, to volume 37, part I, April 1927.

—————. *History and Bibliography of American Newspapers, 1690-1820*. American Antiquarian Society, Worcester, Massachusetts, 1947. 2 volumes.

Brown, David Paul. *The Forum; or Forty Years Full Practice at the Philadelphia Bar*. Philadelphia, 1856. 2 volumes.

Bucks County Deed Book 16 (F-1)

---

[1]Since this is not a bibliographical study, I have not listed the Bradford imprints which I have examined or referred to. The bibliography as a whole is selective rather than exhaustive; it contains items actually mentioned in the text with the addition of those others which seem most important.

[2]Historical Society of Pennsylvania.

Bullen, Henry Lewis. "The Bradford Family of Printers," *The Americana Collector*, volume I, January and February 1926, 148-156, 164-170. (The title of this periodical was changed to *The American Collector* with volume II, number 4.)
The Burghers of New Amsterdam and the Freemen of New York, 1675-1866. Collections of the New-York Historical Society (1885), Publication Fund Series, volume XVIII. New York, 1886.
Burial Records of Christ Church, Philadelphia.
Burney, Charles. *A General History of Music*. London, 1789. 4 volumes.
Calendar of [New York] Council Minutes, 1668-1783. Albany, 1902.
Caribbeana. London, 1741. 2 volumes.
Clark, Edward L. *A Record of the Inscriptions on the Tablets and Grave-Stones in the Burial-Grounds of Christ Church, Philadelphia*. Philadelphia, 1864.
Cohn, Albert. *Shakespeare in Germany in the Sixteenth and Seventeenth Centuries*. London, 1865.
Cook, Elizabeth Christine. *Literary Influences in Colonial Newspapers, 1704-1750*. New York, 1912.
Crane, R. S., and Kaye, F. B. *A Census of British Newspapers and Periodicals, 1620-1800*. Chapel Hill, 1927.
Cross, Wilbur L. *The Life and Times of Henry Fielding*. New Haven, 1918. 3 volumes.
Darrach, Henry, *Bradford Family, 1660-1906*. Philadelphia, 1906.
DeArmond, Anna Janney. "Andrew Bradford," *The Pennsylvania Magazine of History and Biography*, volume LXII (1938), 463-487.
Deed-Books in the Office for the Recording of Deeds in Philadelphia, A-1, D-14, F-5, F-10, G-6.
The Documentary History of the State of New York. Arranged by E. B. O'Callaghan. Albany, 1849-1851. 4 volumes.
Documents Relative to the Colonial History of the State of New-York. Albany, 1854.
Dorr, Benjamin. *A Historical Account of Christ Church, Philadelphia*. New York and Philadelphia, 1841.
Dunton, John. *The Life and Errors of John Dunton*. London, 1818. 2 volumes.
Durham Iron Company: Original Deed. Bucks County Historical Society.
Etting Papers. HSP.
Evans, Charles. *American Bibliography*. Chicago, 1903-1934. 12 volumes.
Fackenthal, B. F., Jr. *Durham Iron Company*. 1936. Bucks County Historical Society. (This is the most important of several collections of unpublished material on the Durham ironworks compiled by Mr. Fackenthal and in the possession of the Bucks County Historical Society.)
——————. "Genealogical Notes and Land Titles," *Publications of the Genealogical Society of Pennsylvania*, volume XII (1934), 111-126.
Faÿ, Bernard. *Franklin, The Apostle of Modern Times*. Boston, 1929.
"The First Philadelphia Newspaper and Its Republication by the Colonial Society," *The Pennsylvania Magazine of History and Biography*, volume XXII (1898), 217-220.
Franklin, Benjamin. *Autobiography* (volume I of *The Writings of Benjamin Franklin*, next title).
——————. *The Writings of Benjamin Franklin*. Collected and edited... by Albert Henry Smyth. New York and London, 1905-1907. 10 volumes.
Friends' Miscellany. Edited by John and Isaac Comly. Philadelphia, 1834-1839. 12 volumes.
Genzmer, George Harvey. "Zinzendorf," *D.A.B.*
[Gordon, Thomas, and Trenchard, John.] *Cato's Letters*. London, 1755 (6th edition). 4 volumes.
[——————————————————.] *The Independent Whig*. Philadelphia, 1724.
Gordon, Thomas, editor. *The Works of Tacitus*. London, 1728 and 1731. 2 volumes.

BIBLIOGRAPHY

Graham, Walter. *English Literary Periodicals.* New York, 1930.
Hildeburn, Charles R. *A Century of Printing. The Issues of the Press in Pennsylvania, 1685-1784.* Philadelphia, 1885-1886. 2 volumes.
Hunter, Dard. *Papermaking.* New York, 1943.
Jackson, Joseph. *Encyclopedia of Philadelphia.* Harrisburg, 1931-1933. 4 volumes.
Jackson, M. Katherine. *Outlines of the Literary History of Colonial Pennsylvania.* Lancaster, Pennsylvania, 1906.
Jones, Horatio Gates. *Andrew Bradford, Founder of the Newspaper Press in the Middle States of America.* Philadelphia, 1869.
Kalm, Peter. *Travels in North America.* Revised and edited by Adolph B. Benson. New York, 1937. 2 volumes.
Keith, Charles P. *Chronicles of Pennsylvania from the English Revolution to the Peace of Aix-la-Chapelle, 1688-1748.* Philadelphia, 1917. 2 volumes.
Kite, Nathan. "Antiquarian Researches Among the Early Printers and Publishers of Friends' Books," *The Friend: A Religious and Literary Journal,* volume XVII (1843), 12-13, 21-22, 28-29, 44-45, 54.
Kobre, Sidney. *The Development of the Colonial Newspaper.* Pittsburgh, Pennsylvania, 1944.
Konkle, Burton Alva. *The Life of Andrew Hamilton, 1676-1741.* Philadelphia, 1941.
Landon, Fred. "Benjamin Lay," *D.A.B.*
Lee, James Melvin. "Andrew Bradford," *D.A.B.*
———. *History of American Journalism.* Boston and New York, 1917.
Logan Papers. HSP.
Magee, James F. *Watermarks of Early American Paper.* MS. The Free Library of Philadelphia.
Marriage Records of Trinity Church, New York. (Typed copy in the possession of the New York Genealogical and Biographical Society.)
Martin, John Hill. *Bench and Bar of Philadelphia.* Philadelphia, 1883.
"Mayors of Philadelphia," *Autograph Collection of Simon Gratz.* HSP.
McCulloch, William. "William McCulloch's Additions to Thomas's History of Printing," *Proceedings of the American Antiquarian Society,* New Series, volume XXXI (1921).
McMurtrie, Douglas C. *A History of Printing in the United States* (volume II, Middle and South Atlantic States). New York, 1936.
Metzger, Ethel. *Supplement to Hildeburn's Century of Printing, 1685-1775.* Unpublished master's essay, Columbia University, June 1930.
Minutes of the Board of Property and Other References to Lands in Pennsylvania. Edited by William H. Egle. Harrisburg, 1894. (*Pennsylvania Archives,* Third Series, volumes I and II.)
Minutes of the Board of Property of the Province of Pennsylvania. Edited by William H. Egle. Harrisburg, 1893. (*Pennsylvania Archives,* Second Series, volume XIX.)
Minutes of the "Commissioners or Overseers" of the William Penn Charter School (beginning December 4, 1712). MS.
Minutes of the Common Council of the City of Philadelphia (1704 to 1776). Philadelphia, 1847.
Minutes of the Monthly Meeting of Philadelphia, 1682-1714 and 1715-1744. MS.
Minutes of the Provincial Council of Pennsylvania. Philadelphia, 1852. 2 volumes.
Minutes of the Union Fire Company. MS. The Library Company of Philadelphia.
Minutes of the Vestry of Christ Church. MS.
Minutes of the Yearly Meeting of Philadelphia, 1681-1746. MS.
Morison, Stanley. *The English Newspaper.* Cambridge, 1932.
Mott, Frank Luther. *A History of American Magazines, 1741-1850.* New York and London, 1930.
———. *American Journalism.* New York, 1941.
Munsell, Joel. *A Chronology of Paper and Papermaking.* Albany, 1864.

New Jersey Deed Books, A-2, E-2, F-2, K.
New Jersey Will Book C. (The will of Thomas Boels appears on pages 45-47. An abstract of this will is contained in *Archives of the State of New Jersey,* First Series, volume XXX, Somerville, N. J., 1918.)
Oberholtzer, Ellis Paxton. *The Literary History of Philadelphia.* Philadelphia, 1906.
Ordinances . . . of Philadelphia for 1858, 1895, 1897.
Paltsits, Victor H. "William Bradford," *D.A.B.*
Papers Relating to Provincial Affairs in Pennsylvania, 1682-1750. Harrisburg, 1891. (*Pennsylvania Archives,* Second Series, volume VII.)
Penn Accounts. HSP.
Penn Manuscripts. HSP.
Penn, William. *William Penn's First Charter To the People of Pennsylvania, April 25, 1682.* Edited by Albert Cook Myers. Philadelphia, 1925.
Philadelphia Will Book G, pp. 28-29 (Andrew Bradford's will).
Philadelphia Will Book K, pp. 344-346 (Cornelia Bradford's will. An abstract of this will, which was probated in New York as well as in Philadelphia, may be found in *Collections of the New-York Historical Society* [1893], Publication Fund Series, volume XXVI, New York, 1894. The abstract is inaccurate in several details.)
Plomer, Henry R. *A Dictionary of the Booksellers and Printers Who Were at Work in England, Scotland and Ireland from 1641 to 1667.* London, Bibliographical Society, 1907.
"Prospectus for the reprinting of the *Mercury,*" The Colonial Society of Pennsylvania. Two-page leaflet, dated March 20, 1897.
Proud, Robert. *The History of Pennsylvania.* Philadelphia, 1797. 2 volumes.
Purple, Samuel S. *Bradford Family.* New York, 1873.
Realey, Charles B. "*The London Journal* and Its Authors, 1720-1723," *University of Kansas Humanistic Studies,* volume V, number 3 (December 1935).
Records of the Colony of Rhode Island and Providence Plantations, in New England. Edited by John Russell Bartlett. Providence, 1856-1865. 10 volumes.
Richardson, Lyon N. *A History of Early American Magazines, 1741-1789.* New York, 1931.
Rutherford, Livingston. *John Peter Zenger, his Press, his Trial and a Bibliography of Zenger Imprints.* New York, 1904.
Scharf, J. Thomas, and Westcott, Thompson. *History of Philadelphia, 1609-1884.* Philadelphia, 1884. 3 volumes.
Schuyler, Livingston Rowe. *The Liberty of the Press in the American Colonies Before the Revolutionary War.* New York, 1905.
Shaaber, Matthias A. "Forerunners of the Newspaper in the United States," *Journalism Quarterly,* volume XI (1934), 339-347.
Shepherd, William Robert. *History of Proprietary Government in Pennsylvania.* New York, 1896.
"Ship Registers for the Port of Philadelphia, 1726-1775," *The Pennsylvania Magazine of History and Biography,* XXIII (1899), 254-264, 370-385, 498-515 (and continued in later volumes).
Smith, Joseph. *A Descriptive Catalogue of Friends' Books.* London, 1867. 2 volumes.
Smyth, Albert Henry. *The Philadelphia Magazines and Their Contributors (1741-1850).* Philadelphia, 1892.
Society Collection. HSP.
Spangenberg, August Gottlieb. *The Life of Nicholas Lewis Count Zinzendorf.* Translated by Samuel Jackson. London, 1838.
Thomas, Isaiah. *The History of Printing in America.* Albany, 1874. 2 volumes. (*Transactions and Collections of the American Antiquarian Society,* volumes V and VI.)
Votes and Proceedings of the House of Representatives of the Province of Pennsylvania. Philadelphia, 1752-1754. 3 volumes.

Bibliography

Wallace, John William. *An Address Delivered at the Celebration by the New York Historical Society, May 20, 1863, of the Two Hundredth Birth Day of Mr. William Bradford, Who Introduced the Art of Printing into the Middle Colonies of British America.* Albany, 1863.

——————. *An Old Philadelphian, Colonel William Bradford, The Patriot Printer of 1776.* Philadelphia, 1884.

——————. "Early Printing in Philadelphia: The Friends' Press—Interregnum of the Bradfords," *The Pennsylvania Magazine of History and Biography,* volume IV (1880), 432-444.

Wallace Papers. HSP.

Watson, John F. *Annals of Philadelphia.* Enlarged . . . by Willis P. Hazard. Philadelphia, 1881. 3 volumes.

Wilson, James Grant, editor. *The Memorial History of the City of New-York.* New York, 1892-1893. 4 volumes.

Wroth, Lawrence C. *The Colonial Printer.* Portland, Maine, 1938 (second edition).

[Zenger, John Peter, et al.] *A brief Narrative of the Case and Tryal of John Peter Zenger, Printer of the New-York Weekly Journal.* Boston, 1738.

Index to the Issues of the *Mercury*

1	Tuesday	December	22,	1719	74		May	18, 1721
2			29		75			25
3		January	5,	1719/20	76		June	1
4			12		77			8
5			19		78			15
6			26		79			22
7		February	2		80			29
8			9		81		July	6
9			16		82			13
10			23		83			20
11		March	1		84			27
12			8		85		August	3
13	Thursday		17		86			10
14			24		87			17
15			31,	1720	88			24
16		April	7		89			31
17			14		90		September	7
18			21		91			14
19			28		92			21
20		May	5		93			28
21			12		94		October	5
22			19		95			12
23			26		96			19
24		June	2		97			26
25			9		98		November	2
26			16		99			9
27			23		100			16
28			30		101			23
29		July	7		102			30
30			14		103		December	7
31			21		104	Tuesday		12
32			28		105			19
33		August	4		106			26
34			11		107		January	2, 1721/22
35			18		108			9
36			25		109			16
37		September	1		110			23
38			8		111			30
39			15		112		February	6
40			22		113			13
41			29		114			20
42		October	6		115			27
43			13		116	Thursday	March	1
44			20		117	Saturday		10
45			27		118	Thursday		15
46		November	3		119			22
47			10		120			29, 1722
48			17		121		April	5
49			24		122			12
50		December	1		123			19
51			8		124			26
52	Tuesday		13		125		May	3
53			20		126			10
54			27		127			17
55		January	3,	1720/21	128			24
56			10		129			31
57			17		130		June	7
58			24		131			14
59			31		132			21
60		February	7		133			28
61			14		134		July	5
62			21		135			12
63	Thursday	March	2		136			19
64			9		137			26
65			16		138		August	2
66			23		139			9
67			30,	1721	140			16
68		April	6		141			23
69			13		142			30
70			20		143		September	6
71			27		144			13
72		May	4		145			20
73			11		146			27

Index to the Issues of the "Mercury"

No.	Day	Month	Date	Year
147		October	4,	1722
148			11	
149			18	
150			25	
151		November	1	
152			8	
153			15	
154	Friday		23	
155	Thursday		29	
156	Tuesday	December	11	
157			18	
158	Wednesday		26	
159	Tuesday	January	1,	1722/23
160			8	
161			15	
162			22	
163			29	
164		February	5	
165			12	
166			19	
167			26	
168	Thursday	March	7	
169			14	
170			21	
171			28,	1723
172		April	4	
173			11	
174			18	
175			25	
176		May	2	
177			9	
178			16	
179			23	
180			30	
181		June	6	
182			13	
183			20	
184			27	
185		July	4	
186			11	
187			18	
188			25	
189		August	1	
190			8	
191			15	
192			22	
193			29	
194		September	5	
195			12	
196			19	
197			26	
198		October	4 [sic]	
199			10	
200			17	
201			24	
202			31	
203		November	7	
204			14	
205			21	
206			28	
207		December	5	
208	Tuesday		10	
209			17	
210			24	
211			31	
212		January	7,	1723/24
213			14	
214			21	
215			28	
216		February	4	
217			11	
218			18	
219			25	
220		March	3	
221	Thursday		12	
222			19	
223			26,	1724
224		April	2	
225			9	
226		April	16,	1724
227			23	
228			30	
229		May	7	
230			14	
231			21	
232			28	
233		June	4	
234			11	
235			18	
236			25	
237		July	2	
238			9	
239			16	
240			23	
241			30	
242		August	5 [sic]	
243			13	
244			20	
245			27	
246		September	3	
247			10	
248			17	
249			24	
250		October	1	
251			8	
252			15	
253			22	
254			29	
255		November	5	
256			12	
257			19	
258			26	
259		December	3	
260			10	
261	Tuesday		15	
262			22	
263			29	
264		January	5,	1724/25
265			12	
266			19	
267			26	
268		February	2	
269			9	
270			16	
271			23	
272	Thursday	March	4	
273			11	
274			18	
275			25,	1725
276		April	1	
277			8	
278			15	
279			22	
280			29	
281		May	6	
282			13	
283			20	
284			27	
285		June	3	
286			10	
287			17	
288			24	
289		July	1	
290			8	
291			15	
292			22	
293			29	
294		August	5	
295			12	
296			19	
297			26	
298		September	2	
299			9	
300			16	
301			23	
302			30	
303		October	7	
304			14	

305		October	21, 1725		384		May	11, 1727
306			28		385			18
307		November	4		386			25
308			11		387		June	1
309			18		388			8
310			25		389			15
311		December	2		390			22
312			9		391			29
313	Tuesday		21		392		July	6
314			28		393			13
315		January	4, 1725/26		394			20
316			11		395			27
317			18		396		August	3
318			25		397			10
319		February	1		398			17
320			8		399			24
321			15		400			31
322			22		401		September	7
323		March	1		402			14
324			8		403			21
325	Thursday		17		404			28
326			24		405		October	5
327			31, 1726		406			12
328		April	7		407			19
329			14		408			26
330			21		409		November	2
331			28		410			9
332		May	5		411			16
333			12		412			23
334			19		413			30
335			26		414		December	7
336		June	2		415	Tuesday		12
337			9		416			19
338			16		417			26
339			23		418		January	2, 1727/28
340			30		419			9
341		July	7		420			16
342			14		421			23
343			21		422			30
344			28		423		February	6
345		August	4		424			13
346			11		425			19 [sic]
347			18		426			27
348			25		427		March	5
349		September	1		428	Thursday		14
350			8		429			21
351			15		430			28, 1728
352			22		431		April	4
353			29		432			11
354		October	6		433			18
355			13		434			25
356			20		435		May	2
357			27		436			9
358		November	3		437			16
359			10		438			23
360			17		439			30
361			24		440		June	6
362		December	1		441			13
363	Tuesday		13		442			20
364			20		443			27
365			27		444		July	4
366		January	3, 1726/27		445			11
367			10		446			18
368			17		447			25
369			24		448		August	1
370			31		449			8
371		February	7		450			15
372			14		451			22
373			21		452			29
374			28		453		September	5
375		March	7		454			12
376	Thursday		16		455			19
377			23		456			26
378			30, 1727		457		October	3
379		April	6		458			10
380			13		459			17
381			20		460			24
382			27		461			31
383		May	4		462		November	7

254

Index to the Issues of the "Mercury"

No.	Day	Month	Date	Year
463		November	14,	1728
464			21	
465			28	
466		December	5	
467	Tuesday		18 [sic]	
468			24	
469			31	
470		January	7,	1728/29
471			14	
472			21	
473			28	
474		February	4	
475			11	
476			18	
477			25	
478		March	4	
479	Thursday		13	
480			20	
481			27,	1729
*482		April	3	
483			10	
484			17	
485			24	
486		May	1	
487			8	
488			15	
489			22	
490			29	
491		June	5	
492			12	
493			19	
494			26	
495		July	3	
496			10	
497			17	
498			24	
499			31	
500		August	7	
501			14	
502			21	
503			28	
504		September	4	
505			11	
506			18	
507			25	
508		October	2	
509			9	
510			16	
511			23	
512			30	
513		November	6	
514			13	
515			20	
516			27	
517		December	4	
518	Tuesday		9	
519			16	
520			23	
521			30	
522		January	6,	1729/30
523	Wednesday		14	
524	Tuesday		20	
525			27	
526		February	4 [sic]	
527			10	
528	Thursday		19	
529	Tuesday		24	
530		March	3	
531	Thursday		5	
532			12	
533			19	
534			26,	1730
535		April	2	
536			9	
537			16	
538			23	
539			30	
540		May	7	
541			14,	1730
542			21	
543			28	
544		June	4	
545			11	
546			18	
547			25	
548		July	2	
549			9	
550			16	
551			23	
552			30	
553		August	6	
554			13	
555			20	
556			27	
557		September	3	
558			10	
559			17	
560			24	
561		October	1	
562			8	
563			15	
564			22	
565			29	
566		November	5	
567			12	
568			19	
569			26	
570		December	3	
571	Tuesday		8	
572			15	
573			22	
574			29	
575		January	5,	1730/31
576			12	
577			19	
578			26	
579		February	2	
580			9	
581			16	
582	Wednesday		24	
583	Tuesday	March	2	
584			9	
585	Thursday		18	
586	Friday		26,	1731
587	Thursday	April	1	
588			8	
589			15	
590			22	
591			29	
592		May	6	
593			13	
594			20	
595			27	
596		June	3	
597			10	
598			17	
599			24	
600		July	1	
601			8	
602			15	
603			22	
604			29	
605		August	5	
606			12	
607			19	
608			26	
609		September	2	
610			9	
611			16	
612			23	
613			30	
614		October	7	
615			14	
616			21	
617			28	
618		November	4	
619			11	

*Damaged

255

620		November	18, 1731	699		May	24, 1733
621			25	700			31
622		December	2	701		June	7
623			9	702			14
624	Tuesday		14	703			21
625			21	704			28
626			28	705		July	5
627		January	4, 1731/32	706			12
628			11	707			19
629			18	708			26
630			25	709		August	2
631		February	1	710			9
632			8	711			16
633			15	712			23
634			22	713			30
635			29	714		September	6
636		March	7	715			13
637	Thursday		16	716			20
638			23	717			27
639			30, 1732	718		October	4
640		April	6	719			11
641			13	720			18
642			20	721			25
643			27	722		November	1
644		May	4	723			8
645			11	724			15
646			18	725			22
647			25	726			29
648		June	1	727		December	6
649			8	728	Friday		14
650			15	{729			21}
651			22	{729	Saturday		22}
652			29	730			29
653		July	6	731	Tuesday	January	1, 1733/34
654			13	732			8
655			20	733			15
656			27	734			22
657		August	3	735			29
658			10	736		February	5
659			17	737			12
660			24	738			19
661			31	739			26
662		September	7	740		March	5
663			14	741			12
664			21	742	Thursday		21
665			28	743			28, 1734
666		October	5	744		April	4
667			12	745			11
668			19	746			18
669			26	747			25
670		November	2	748		May	2
671			9	749			9
672			16	750			16
673			23	751			23
674			30	752			30
675		December	7	753		June	6
676	Tuesday		12	754			13
677			19	755			20
678			26	756			27
679	Thursday	January	4, 1732/33	757		July	4
680			11	758			11
681			18	759			18
682			25	760			25
683	Tuesday		30	761		August	1
684		February	6	762			8
685			12 [sic]	763			15
686	Wednesday		21	764			22
687	Tuesday		28 [sic]	765			29
688		March	6	766		September	5
689			13	767			12
690			20	768			19
691			27, 1733	769			26
692	Thursday	April	5	770		October	3
693			12	771			10
694			19	772			17
695			26	773			24
696		May	3	774			31
697			10	775		November	7
698			17	776			14

Index to the Issues of the "Mercury"

No.	Day	Month	Date	Year
777		November	21,	1734
778			28	
779		December	5	
780			12	
781	Tuesday		17	
782			24	
783			31	
784		January	7,	1734/35
785			14	
786			21	
787			28	
788		February	4	
789			11	
790			18	
791			25	
792		March	4	
793			11	
794	Thursday		20	
795			27,	1735
796		April	3	
797			10	
798			17	
799			24	
800		May	1	
801			8	
802			15	
803			22	
804			29	
805		June	5	
806			12	
807			19	
808			26	
809		July	3	
810			10	
811			17	
812			24	
813			31	
814		August	7	
815			14	
816			21	
817			28	
818		September	4	
819			11	
820			18	
821			25	
822		October	2	
823			9	
824			16	
825			23	
826			30	
827		November	6	
828			13	
829			20	
830			27	
831		December	4	
832			11	
833			18	
834	Tuesday		23	
835			30	
836		January	6,	1735/36
837			13	
838			20	
839			27	
840		February	3	
841			10	
842			17	
843			24	
844		March	2	
845			9	
846			16	
847			23	
848	Thursday	April	1,	1736
849			8	
850			15	
851			22	
852			29	
853		May	6	
854			13	
855			20	
856		May	27,	1736
857		June	3	
858			10	
859			17	
860			24	
861		July	1	
862			8	
863			15	
864			22	
865			29	
866		August	5	
867			12	
868			19	
869			26	
870		September	2	
871			9	
872			16	
873			23	
874			30	
875		October	7	
876			14	
877			21	
878			28	
879		November	4	
880			11	
881			18	
882			25	
883		December	2	
884			9	
885			16*	
886			23	
887	Tuesday		28	
888	Thursday	January	6,	1736/37
889			13	
890	Tuesday		18	
891			25	
892	Thursday	February	3	
893	Tuesday		8	
894			15	
895			22	
896		March	1	
897			8	
898	Thursday		17	
899			24	
900			31,	1737
901		April	7	
902			14	
903			21	
904			28	
905		May	5	
906			12	
907			19	
908			26	
909		June	2	
910			9	
911			16	
912			23	
913			30	
914		July	7	
915			14	
916			21	
917			28	
918		August	4	
919			11	
920			18	
921			25	
922		September	1	
923			8	
924			15	
925			22	
926			29	
927		October	6	
928			13	
929			20	
930			27	
931		November	3	
932			10	

*A note indicates that this paper was not issued until December 17.

Andrew Bradford, Colonial Journalist

No.	Day	Month	Date	Year
933		November	17,	1737
934			24	
935		December	1	
936			8	
937			15	
938			22	
939			29	
940	Tuesday	January	3,	1737/38
941			10	
942			17	
943			24	
944			31	
945		February	7	
946			14	
947			21	
948			28	
949		March	7	
950	—Missing			
951	Thursday		23	
952			30,	1738
953		April	6	
954			13	
955			20	
956	—Missing			
957		May	4	
958	—Missing			
959			18	
960			25	
961		June	1	
962			8	
963			15	
964	Thursday	June	22,	1738
965			29	
966		July	6	
967			13	
968			20	
969			27	
970		August	3	
971			10	
972			17	
973			24	
974			31	
975		September	7	
976			14	
977			21	
978			28	
979		October	5	
980			12	
981			19	
982			26	
983		November	2	
984			9	
985			16	
986			23	
987			30	
988		December	7	
989			14	
990			21	
991			28	
992		January	4,	1738/39
993			11	
994	—Missing			
995	Tuesday		23	
996			30	
997	Thursday	February	8	
998	Wednesday		14	
999	Thursday		22	
1000	Wednesday		28	
1001	Thursday	March	8	
1002	Wednesday		14	
1003	Thursday		22	
1004			29,	1739
1005		April	5	
1006			12	
1007			19	
1008			26	
1009		May	3	
1010			10	
1011			17	
1012		May	24,	1739
1013			31	
1014		June	7	
1015			14	
1016			21	
1017			28	
1018		July	5	
1019			12	
1020			19	
1021			26	
1022		August	2	
1023			9	
1024			16	
1025			23	
1026			30	
1027		September	6	
1028			13	
1029			20	
1030			27	
1031		October	4	
1032			11	
1033			18	
1034			25	
1035		November	1	
1036			8	
1037			15	
1038			22	
1039			29	
1040		December	6	
1041			13	
1042			20	
1043			27	
1044		January	3,	1739/40
1045	Tuesday		8	
1046			15	
1047			22	
1048			29	
1049		February	5	
1050			12	
1051			19	
1052			26	
1053		March	4	
1054			11	
1055	Thursday		20	
1056			27,	1740
1057		April	3	
1058			10	
1059			17	
1060			24	
1061		May	1	
1062			8	
1063			15	
1064			22	
1065			29	
1066		June	5	
1067			12	
1068			19	
1069			26	
1070		July	3	
1071			10	
1072			17	
1073			24	
1074			31	
1075		August	7	
1076			14	
1077			21	
1078			28	
1079		September	4	
1080			11	
1081			18	
1082			25	
1083		October	2	
1084			9	
1085			16	
1086			23	
1087			30	
1088		November	6	
1089			13	
1090			20	

Index to the Issues of the "Mercury"

No.	Date		No.	Date	
1091	November	27, 1740	1170	June	3, 1742
1092	December	4	1171		10
1093		11	1172		17
1094		18	1173		24
1095		25	1174	July	1
1096	January	1, 1740/41	1175		8
1097		8	1176		15
1098		15	1177		22
1099		22	1178		29
1100		29	1179	August	5
1101	February	5	1180		12
1102		12	1181		19
1103		19	1182		26
1104		26	1183	September	2
1105	March	5	1184		9
1106		12	1185		16
1107		19	1186		23
1108		26, 1741	1187		30
1109	April	2	1188	October	7
1110		9	1189		14
1111		16	1190		21
1112		23	1191		28
1113		30	1192	November	4
1114	May	7	1193		11
1115		14	1194		18
1116		21	1195	December	2
1117		28	1196		9
1118	June	4	1197		16
1119		11	1198 Tuesday		21
1120		18	1199		28
1121		25	1200	January	4, 1742/43
1122	July	2	*1201		13
1123		9	1202		18
1124		16	1203		27
1125		23	1204	February	1
1126		30	1205		10
1127	August	6	1206		14
1128		13	1207		24
1129		20	1208	March	1
1130		27	1209		10
1131	September	3	1210		16
1132		10	1211		24
1133		17	1212		30, 1743
1134		24	1213	April	7
1135	October	1	1214		14
1136		8	1215		21
1137		15	1216		28
1138		22	1217	May	5
1139		29	1218		12
1140	November	5	1219		19
1141		12	1220		26
1142		19	1221	June	2
1143		26	1222		9
1144	December	3	1223		16
1145		10	1224		23
1146		17	1225		30
1147		24	1226	July	7
1148		31	1227		14
1149	January	7, 1741/42	1228		21
1150		14	1229		28
1151		21	1230	August	4
1152		28	1231		11
1153	February	4	1232		18
1154		11	1233		25
1155		18	1234	September	1
1156		25	1235		8
1157	March	4	1236		15
1158		11	1237		22
1159		18	1238		29
1160		25, 1742	1239	October	6
1161	April	1	1240		13
1162		8	1241		20
1163		15	1242		27
1164		22	1243	November	3
1165		29	1244		10
1166	May	6	1245		17
1167		13	1246		24
1168		20			
1169		27			

*After Number 1200 there are no further indications of the day of the week.

259

1247	December	2,	1743	1312		February	26, 1744/45
1248		8		1313		March	5
1249		15		1314			12
1250		21		1315			19
1251		29		1316			26, 1745
1252	January	4,	1743/44	1317		April	4
1253		12		1318			12
1254		18		1319			18
1255		25		1320			25
1256	February	3		1321		May	2
1257		8		1322			9
1258		16		1323			16
1259		23		1324			23
1260	March	1		1325			30
1261		7		1326		June	6
1262		15		1327			13
1263		22		1328			20
1264		30,	1744	1329			27
1265	April	5		1330		July	4
1266		12		1331			11
1267		19		1332			18
1268		26		1333			25
1269	May	3		1334		August	1
1270		10		1335			8
1271		17		1336			15
1272		24		1337			22
1273		31		1338			29
1274	June	7		1339		September	5
1275		14		1340			12
1276		21		1341			19
1277		28		1342			26
1278	July	5		1343		October	3
1279		12		1344			10
1280		19		1345			17
1281		26		1346			24
1282	August	2		1347			31
1283		9		1348		November	7
1284		16		1349			14
1285		23		1350			21
1286		30		1351			28
1287	September	6		1352		December	5
1288		13		1353			10
1289		20		1354			17
1290		27		1355			24
1291	October	4		1356		January	1, 1745/46
1292		11		1357			8
1293		18		1358			15
1294		25		1359			21
1295	November	1		1360			29
1296		8		1361		February	4
1297		15		1362			11
1298		22		1363			18
1299		29		1364			25
1300	December	6		1365		March	4
1301		14		1366			11
1302		20		1367			18
1303		28		1368			27, 1746
1304	January	1,	1744/45	1369		April	3
1305		9		1370			10
1306		15		1371			17
1307		23		1372			24
1308		29		1373 — Missing			
1309	February	5		1374		May	8
1310		12		1375			15
1311		20		1376			22

General Index

The general index includes the names of all persons mentioned in the text or in the footnotes. Footnote references are indexed individually except when inclusive page numbers are given. Titles of books, pamphlets, poems, etc. are listed if their authors are unknown or likely to be unfamiliar; otherwise, except for periodicals, the works are indexed by the authors' names only. Those topics which are likely to be of general interest or which are treated extensively in the text are also included.

A

Account of the Torments, the Protestants Endure, 26
Acts and Laws of the Province of Pennsylvania, 1713, 10
Adam of Orlton, Bishop of Hereford, 191
Addison, Joseph, 29, 30, 45, 94, 133, 183, 185-186, 187, 187 n., 188, 188 n., 201 n. See also *Spectator* and *Tatler.*
Advice and Caution from Our Monthly Meeting, 31
Advice and Information To the Freeholders, 15, 15 n.
Æsop, 29
Alexander the Great, 140, 141
Allen, William, 20 n., 88 n.
American Almanack for 1711 (Daniel Leeds), 8 n.
American Antiquarian Society, 39 n.
American Magazine, 2, 37, 37 n., 112, Pt. III, 241; advertisement in the *Mercury* 223-226; quarrel with Franklin 37, 227-233; first issue 232-233, 234-236; format, etc. 233-234; second issue 236; third issue 236-238; importance 239. See also illus. facing p. 240.
American Magazine (Boston), 56, 173 n., 190 n., 239
American Weekly Mercury: see chapter titles of Pt. II and illustrations; title 39; first issue 39-41 and illus. facing p. 48; files 39 n.; purpose 41, 45; size and format 42, 42 n., 48, and illus. facing pp. 48, 112, 144, 192; prices current 41, 42, 85, 216, and illus. facing p. 192; cuts 42, 47-48, and illus. facing pp. 48, 112, 144, 192; shipping news 40, 42, 70, 85, 216, and illus. facing p. 192; advertisements 42, 43, 43 n., 151-159, and illus. facing pp. 144, 192; obituaries 42 and illus. facing p. 192; births and burials 42, 42 n.; distribution 41, 44; subscriptions 41, 180-181, and illus. facing pp. 144, 192; circulation 43-45; type and printing errors 46-47, 66; news coverage 45, 51-52; inaccuracies in news items 53, 63-65; epidemics and disease 115-116, 150-151; crimes and criminals 136-142; monstrosities and the supernatural 142-143; natural phenomena 143-145, 149-150; inventions and scientific investigations 145-146; exploration 146; archeology 147; personal advertisements 158-159; editorial policy 160-161; religion and politics 170-175, 195; education 174; letters to the editor 176-180; poetry 183-186, 197-209; and *passim.*
"Americo-Britannus," 166
Amerman, John, 8 n.
Amsterdam *Courant,* 55, 55 n.
Amsterdam *Gazette,* 55, 55 n.
Ancient Testimony of the People called Quakers, 27
Ancre, Concino Concini, Marshal and Marquis d', 98-100, 103
Anne, Empress of Russia, 71
Anne, Princess Royal (daughter of George II), 131, 132, 197
Annerch Ir Cymru, 32 n.
Annis, Capt. Thomas, 26 n.
Appeal from the twenty-eight Judges to the Spirit of Truth, 5
Arbuthnot, Dr. John, 182
Argyll, John Campbell, Duke of, 138, 138 n.
Aristophanes, 208
Arnold, Jonathan, 126
Artemidorus, 29, 29 n.
Atkins, John, 157
Atkins, Samuel, 4 n.
Atterbury, Francis. See Rochester, Bishop of.
Augusta, Princess of Wales, 132, 135, 197

Augustus II of Poland, 136
Austrian Succession, War of the, 71, 83, 117. See also Jacobite invasion of Scotland, 1745.

B

Bacon, Sir Francis, 187, 190, 190 n.
Baird, Patrick, 151
Baker, Henry ("Henry Stonecastle"), 188 n., 210
Bancroft, Archbishop Richard, 28 n.
Bank of England, 70
Barbadoes Gazette, 56, 105 n., 107, 176
Barbier, Mrs., 67
Barclay, John, 41
Barsi, Laura Maria Kathrina, 147
Bathurst, Allen, Earl Bathurst, 190
Bayard, Peter, 8 n.
Bedford, Wriothesley Russell, Duke of, 63
Bee, 54, 54 n., 171, 175 n.
Behring, Capt. Vitus, 146
Belcher, Gov. Jonathan, 59 n., 60, 63, 74-75, 76, 82
Bell, Robert, 2
Bell, Tom, 135, 135 n.
Benedict XIII, Pope, 68, 120, 197
Benedict XIV, Pope, 64
Berkeley, Bishop George, 135
Berwick, James Fitzjames, Duke of, 63 n., 66, 171
Bezanson, Anne, 42 n.
Bible, 2, 2 n., 187 n., 225
"Bickerstaff, Isaac." See Steele, Sir Richard.
Birkett's almanacs, 50 n.
Bishop, George, 25 n.
Blackwell, Gov. John, 5 n.
Blair, Samuel, 129, 129 n.
Blenman, Jonathan, 105 n.
Bockett, Elias, 199
Boehler, Peter, 129, 129 n., 130
Boels, Thomas, 36, 36 n.
Bolingbroke, Henry St. John, Viscount, 133
Boston *Evening Post*, 122, 217-218
Boston *Gazette*, 12, 14 n., 42 n., 44 n., 53, 56, 60, 74, 216, 216 n.
Boston *News Letter*, 12, 12 n., 14 n., 39, 44 n., 51, 51 n., 56, 133, 215-216
(Boston) *Publick Occurrences*, 12
Boston *Weekly Post Boy*, 46 n., 47, 56, 192 n., 217, 217 n.
(Boston) *Weekly Rehearsal*, 56, 155 n., 217, 217 n.
Boulter, Archbishop Hugh, 134
Bourne, H. R. Fox, 55 n.
Boyle, Roger, 29
Bradford, Andrew: birth 2, 7-8; proposal to print Pennsylvania laws 7; early life 8-9; earliest autograph 8 n.; early printing in Philadelphia 10; printing for government and Friends 11; beginning of *American Weekly Mercury* 11; conflict with government 12-20; freeman of Philadelphia 20; city councilman 20; vestryman of Christ Church 20; postmastership 20, 22, 30, 33, 33 n., 44, 45, 60, 105 n., 212 n., 213, 228-233; Durham Iron Co. 20-21; store 21-31; stationer and bookseller 23-31; printing in foreign languages 32; investments in real estate 34-35; civic activities 35; partnership with William B. III 35-36; *American Magazine* 37 and Pt. III; death 37-38, 49, and illus. facing p. 192; Hamilton controversy 87-113; importance 240-241; genealogy 242; will 243-244; and *passim*. See also frontispiece.
Bradford, Andrew Sowle, 37 n., 242, 243-244.
Bradford, Cornelia Smith, 24 n., 34 n., 36, 36 n., 38, 38 n., 49, 49 n., 50 n., 64, 65, 122, 176, 190 n., 214, 240, 242, 243-244, 245-246, and *passim*
Bradford, Cornelius, 242, 242 n., 244
Bradford, Dorcas Boels, 36, 36 n., 38 n., 214, 242
Bradford, Elizabeth (Andrew's niece), 244
Bradford, Elizabeth Sowle, 2, 3, 3 n., 242
Bradford, Rachel Budd (wife of William B. III), 242
Bradford, Samuel, 242
Bradford, Thomas, 242
Bradford, Thomas, Jr., 242
Bradford, William I, 2-6, 7 n., 8, 8 n., 9, 10 n., 11, 12, 13, 27 n., 30 n., 32, 34, 34 n., 35 n., 36 n., 40, 41, 43, 49, 79 n., 98, 211, 211 n., 218, 219, 242
Bradford, William II, 34, 34 n., 35 n., 37, 242, 242 n., 244
Bradford, William III, 6 n., 31 n., 33, 35, 35 n., 36, 36 n., 37, 37 n., 49, 50 n., 214, 242, 242 n., 244

General Index

Bradford, William IV, 242
Bradford, William V, 242
Bradford, William, of Burwell, 2, 242
Bradford Street, Philadelphia, 34 n.
Bradley, Richard, 29, 29 n.
Brady, Nicholas, 27, 214
Breintnall, Joseph, 16, 16 n., 39 n., 168, 168 n., 194, 196, 203, 205, 205 n.
Brief Narrative of the Case and Tryal of John Peter Zenger, 96 n., 105 n.
Bristol *Journal* 54, 54 n., 62, 175
"Britannicus," 167, 167 n.
British Journal, 16 n., 54, 54 n., 61
British Mercury, 39
Broglie, François Marie, Duke of (Marshal "Broglio"), 175
Brooke, Henry, 197, 197 n., 203
Brooker, William, 44 n.
Brown, Daniel, 30 n.
Brown, David Paul, 19 n.
Brown, Michael, 157, 157 n.
Browne, Sir Thomas, 29, 30
Brownell, George, 155, 155 n.
Bucks County Historical Society, 20 n., 21 n.
Budd, Thomas, 3, 242
Budgell, Eustace, 132, 186
Bullen, Henry Lewis, 3 n., 35 n.
Bunyan, John, 29, 194, 196
Burgundy, Peter, 28, 28n.
Burnet, Bishop Gilbert, 29, 29 n., 171
Burnet, Gov. William, 11, 72, 73-74; wife 197, 197 n.
Burney, Dr. Charles, 132 n.
Burns, Robert, 191 n.
Busy-Body, 16-19, 44, 44 n., 45, 87, 106 n., 108 n., 166 n., 168, 168 n., 170, 194-197, 205 n., 213
Butler, Samuel, 183, 184
Byrd, William, 81

C

Caesar, Julius, 208
Caligula, 111
Calvert, Gov. Charles, 73
Calvin, John, 28
Cambrai, Congress of, 68
Cambridge Platform. See *Plat-form of Church-Discipline.*
Campbell, John, 44 n., 51, 51 n.
Campbell, Thomas, 159

Campbell, Mr. (parson in New Castle County), 18
Campbell, Mr. (postmaster at Rhode Island), 41
Cannibalism, 136, 136 n.
Cario, Michael, 157
"Carissimi," 174
Carolina, Princess, 131
Caroline, Queen (consort of George II), 46, 138, 147, 155, 155 n.
Carpenter, Samuel, 4
Caribbeana, 105 n., 109 n.
Catherine I of Russia, 68
Catlin, Robert, 148
Cato, 29, 106, 169
"Cato, Jr.," 87, 88, 89, 107, 108, 108 n., 110, 166 n., 169-170, 214
Cato's Letters (Gordon and Trenchard), 16 n.-17 n., 17, 19 n., 29, 30, 45, 87, 89, 92, 92 n., 106 n., 166-170, 173, 182, 195, 236, 237-238
Catte, Monsieur de, 171
Cave, Edward, 223
Centlivre, Mrs. Susannah (*The Busy-Body*), 154 n.
Cervantes, Miguel de, 208
Chalkley, Thomas, 10
Chambers, Dr. Ephraim, 132, 194 n., 196
Champion, 54, 54 n., 190, 191, 191 n.
Charles I, 133, 142
Charles VI (Holy Roman Emperor), 71, 143, 209
Charles XII of Sweden, 33
Charles, Robert, 100, 100 n.
Charter of Privileges (of Pennsylvania), 1, 33, 98
Chew, Samuel, 81, 100, 158
Christ Church, Philadelphia, 8 n., 20, 20 n., 30 n., 35, 35 n., 36 n., 38, 38 n., 43 n., 50 n., 115 n., 124, 201, 213
Christian VI of Denmark, 46
Christianity as Old as the Creation, 132
Christianity of the Quakers Asserted, 11
Cibber, Colley, 132 n.
Cicero, 169, 208
Claridge, Richard, 27
Clark, Edward L., 8 n., 38 n.,
Clarke, Gov. George, 79
Clarke, Dr. Samuel, 174, 174 n.
Clauberg, Johann, 28, 28 n.
Claudian, 208
Clement XI, Pope, 120

263

Clement XII, Pope, 70, 120
Cohn, Albert, 155 n.
Coke, Sir Edward, 14
Colden, Cadwallader, 27, 27 n.
Colonial Society of Pennsylvania, 39 n., 50 n.
Comes Commercii, 27
Common Sense, 54, 54 n., 105 n., 109 n., 175 n., 190, 190 n.
Conductor Generalis, 11, 11 n., 27
Conti, Armand de Bourbon, Prince of, 26
Cook, Elizabeth Christine, 194
Cope, Gen. Sir John, 65, 122, 122n.
Copson, John, 12, 26, 39, 49, 211
Corn Cutter's Journal, 54, 54 n.
Cork *News Letter,* 54, 54n., 62
Cosby, Gov. William, 76-79, 82, 84, 90 n., 96, 97, 160, 219
Costard, John, 41
Cottonian library, 147
Country Journal. See *Craftsman.*
Cowell, Mr., 144
Cowley, Mary, 158
Cowper, William, 222, 222 n.
Cox, Abraham, 152
Craftsman, 29, 54, 54n., 105, 106, 107, 107 n., 109 n., 139 n., 171 n., 172 n., 190, 190 n.
Craggs, James, 67, 183
Cranmer, Archbishop Thomas, 28 n.
Crellius, Joseph, 156
Crisis (Sir Richard Steele), 25, 33
Cromwell, Oliver, 133, 165
Cromwell, Richard, 133
Cross, Wilbur L., 191 n.
Crousaz, Jean Pierre de, 177, 177 n.
Culpeper, Nicholas, 27
Cumberland, William Augustus, Duke of, 135
Cumming, Sir Alexander, 211, 211 n.
Cummins, Archibald, 30 n.
Curtius, Marcus, 140

D

Darnell, Henry, 81
Darrach, Henry, 8 n.
Davenport, James, 127, 127 n., 128
Davis, William, 7
Defoe, Daniel, 30 n., 186-187, 188 n.
de Foreest, Henry, 220
Denmark, King of. See Christian VI.
Degrowgh, Catherine, 245

DeLancey, James, 78
Dereham, Sir Richard, 22
Dereham, Richard, 22
Dialogues betwixt a Christian and a Quaker, 28
Diodorus Siculus, 33
Domitian, 111
Dommett, John, 200
Dorr, Benjamin, 35 n.
Drelincourt, Charles, 30, 30 n.
Drummond, Mrs., 131, 171, 201, 201 n.
Dryden, John, 189-190, 197, 197 n.
Dublin *Daily Post Boy,* 54, 54 n.
Dublin *Evening Post,* 54, 54 n., 210
Dublin *Journal,* 54, 54 n.
Duborn, Daniel, 156
Duchée, Anthony, 151, 156
Duck, Stephen, 132
Dudley, Gov. Joseph ("Gov. D———y"), 15
Dummer, Gov. William, 73, 74, 74 n.
Dunlap, Elizabeth, 159, 159 n.
Dunton, John, 25, 25 n.
Durham Iron Co., 20-21, 33, 36 n., 240, 243

E

Edinburgh *Evening Post,* 54, 55 n.
Edward II, 191
Edwards, Jonathan, 123
Edwards, Thomas, 156 n.
Elizabeth, Queen of England, 101
Elizabeth Farnese of Parma (consort of Philip V of Spain), 132
Ellicott, Roger, 153
Ellis, Robert, 20 n., 36 n.
Ellwood, Thomas, 27
English Physician, 27
Épernon, Jean Louis de Nogaret, Duke of, 98-100
Epictetus His Morals, 25, 33
Epicurus, 171
Erasmus, Desiderius, 29, 29 n., 30
"Essay on Scripture-Prophecy," 27
Essay upon Literature, 29
Essays on the Preservation and Recovery of Health, 27
Estella, Diego de, 28 n.
Euclid, 28
Eugene, Prince of Savoy, 123
European Secretary of State, 54, 55 n., 61
Eusden, Laurence, 132

General Index

Eusebius, 29
Evans, Charles, 10 n., 15 n.
Examples of Virtues & Vice, 28

F

Fackenthal, B. F., Jr., 20 n.
Falconar, Magnus, 126, 126 n., 156, 212
Farinelli, 132, 132 n.
Farley's Bristol *News Paper,* 54, 54 n., 171
Farmer, Samuel, 158
Farquhar, George (*The Recruiting Officer*), 154 n.
Faÿ, Bernard, 214 n.
Fellowship Fire Co., 35, 35 n.
Fénelon, François de Salignac de la Mothe, Archbishop of Cambrai, 26, 26 n., 30, 30 n., 171 n.
Ferdinand, crown prince of Spain (later Ferdinand VI), 132
Ferdinand III (Holy Roman Emperor), 143
A Few Words in Favour of Free-Thinking, 15, 15 n.
Fielding, Henry ("Hercules Vinegar"), 190-191
Fleury, Cardinal André Hercule de, 71
Flew, Elizabeth, 245
Flower, Henry, 230 n.
Fog's Weekly Journal. See *Mist's Weekly Journal.*
Forcing A Maintenance Not Warrantable, 10
Fox, George, 3
Francis of Lorraine (consort of Maria Theresa), 208-209
Franklin, Benjamin, 2, 16 n., 25, 25 n., 32, 32 n., 33, 33 n., 35, 37, 38, 42 n., 44, 44 n., 45, 47 n., 50 n., 58, 59 n., 60 n., 63, 63 n., 84 n., 85 n., 89 n., 90, 91, 92 n., 98, 98 n., 104, 105 n., 125 n., 126, 126 n., 139, 139 n., 155 n., 158 n., 175 n., 181, 182, 194, 194 n., 195, 211 n., 212-215, 218, 220 n., 221, 221 n., 227-233, 238, 239, 239 n., 240, 240 n., 241, 241 n.
Franklin, James, 14, 14 n., 15, 160, 214, 216
Franklin, Josiah, 214, 214 n.
Franklin & Hall, 25 n.
Frederick, Prince of Wales, 123, 132, 135, 197
Free Briton, 175

Free Gift to the Clergy, 32
Freedom of the press, 4-5, 12-20, 35, 52, 68, 78, 84-87, 90-96, 98, 105-111, 118, 129, 160, 169, 185, 224-226, 234, 239, 240, 241
"Freeman, R.," 97, 97 n., 98, 98 n.
Friends, Society of, 1, 2, 2 n., 3, 4, 5, 5 n., 6, 9, 9 n., 10, 10 n., 11, 11 n., 25, 25 n-26 n., 31, 31 n., 32, 32 n., 82, 85 n., 86, 114, 117, 131, 169, 205, 205 n., 206, 206 n., 214 n., 240
Fruits of a Father's Love, 27, 28, 31

G

Galigai, Leonora, 99-100
Garth, Sir Samuel, 184, 184 n.
Gassner, Dominicus, 245
Gay, John, 94, 183, 184 n.
General History of the Pyrates, 29
General Magazine And Historical Chronicle, 37, 226-233, 238, 239
Genzmer, George Harvey, 129 n.
Gentleman's Magazine, 54, 54 n., 55 n., 57, 61, 61 n., 63, 103 n., 107 n., 109 n., 122 n., 126, 172, 172 n., 175 n., 206 n., 223
George I, 52, 66, 69, 73, 122, 163, 185, 185 n., 197
George II, 46, 69, 69 n., 71, 121, 122, 132, 135, 148, 198, 200
Georgia: founding of 80-81, 125 n.; Whitefield's orphanage in, 125-128
Gilmore, Mr. (apothecary at Williamsburg), 154 n.
Gin Act of 1736, 70, 70 n.
Goddard, William (pilot), 157
Goddard, William (printer) 2
"Goforth, Aaron, Senior," 212
Goldney, Henry, 13 n.
Gooch, Gov. William, 73, 154 n.
Good Order Established in Pennsylvania and New Jersey (Thomas Budd), 3
Goodere, Sir John, 137
Gordon, Gov. Patrick, 18, 46, 85, 85 n., 86, 86 n., 87, 88, 88 n., 89, 89 n., 90, 93, 97, 99, 100, 100 n., 103, 209
Gordon, Philadelphia, 100 n.
Gordon, Thomas, 16 n.-17 n., 92 n., 166, 170 n. See also *Cato's Letters, Independent Whig,* and *Tacitus, Discourses upon.*

265

Gospel Ordinances, 10 n.
Graham, Walter, 188 n.
Gray, Robert D., 42 n.
Great Law of 1682, 1, 1 n.
Green, Bartholomew, 133
Green, Jonas, 47 n.
Green, Timothy, 212
Grew, Theophilus, 156, 156 n.
Grinaway, Prudence, 159, 213
Growdon, Joseph, 4 n.
Grub Street Journal, 54, 54 n., 55, 57, 171 n., 175 n., 191, 191 n., 201 n., 210
Guardian, 29, 195
Gustavus Adolphus, 175
Guyon, Mme. Jeanne Marie Bouvier de la Mothe, 171, 171 n.

H

Haarlem *Courant,* 55, 55 n.
Hackett, Theobald, 156
Hague *Courant,* 55 n.
Hall, David. See Franklin & Hall.
Hall, Bishop Joseph, 172
Halley, Edmund, 131
Hamilton, Andrew, 14 n., 19, 35, 35 n., 79 n., 84 n., 88-113, 118, 152, 160, 161, 165, 167 n., 173, 174 n., 176, 184, 184 n., 185, 186, 187, 206, 206 n., 209, 213, 225, 227, 234, 235, 235 n., 240
Hamilton, Margaret, 88, 100
Hamm (Ham), James, 245
Handel, George Frederick, 131-132
Hannibal, 108 n.
Hardy, Thomas, 148 n.
Harvard College, 147
Hasel, Samuel, 243
Hay, Andrew, 230 n.
Henderson, Jacob, 84, 84 n.
Henry, Mathew, 26
Henry E. Huntington Library, 8 n.
Hetherington, W., 156 n.
Higinbotham, Charles, 104 n.
Hildeburn, Charles R., 5 n., 6 n., 10 n., 11 n., 15 n., 25, 25 n., 31 n., 32, 32 n., 50 n., 206 n., 214 n.
Hill, Hannah, 10 n.
Hill, Richard, 10, 10 n., 26 n.
Hill, Thomas, 41
Historical Society of Pennsylvania, 15 n., 31 n., 34 n., 39 n.
"History of Ethiopia," 29

History of Magick, 28
History of the Five Indian Nations, 27
History of the Kingdom of Basaruah, 27
History of the Quakers (Sewel), 25, 25 n., 26 n.
Holland Spectator, 191 n.
Homer, 200 n.
Hopkinson, Francis, 39 n.
Hopkinson, Thomas, 39 n.
Hopson, Vice-Admiral Edward, 63
Horace, 29, 30, 113 n., 174, 206, 208, 209, 225
Horner, Elizabeth, 157
Howel, Philip, 34 n.
Huber, Mr., 81
Hughes, John, 24 n., 27
Hulsius, Henricus, 29, 29 n.
Hunter, Dard, 40 n.
Huntington Library, 8 n.
Husband, Charles, 138
Husband-Man's Guide, 11, 27
Husband's Relief, 146
Hussey, Miriam, 42 n.
Hyatt, John, 37 n., 242
Hyatt, Tacey Bradford, 37 n., 242, 244

I

Iliad, 91 n.
Independent Whig, 16 n., 25, 32, 166
Indians, 27, 27 n., 28, 36 n., 62, 72-73, 81, 82, 83, 86, 86 n., 103, 117, 117 n., 119, 148, 235, 237, 237 n., 238
Interest at one View, 29

J

Jackson, Joseph, 1 n.
Jacobite invasion of Scotland, 1745, 64-65, 71, 83, 83 n., 121-122, 173, 197. See also Stuart, Charles Edward.
Jamaica Courant, 56
Jansen, Reiner, 6, 6 n., 9
Jenkins' Ear, War of, 69, 71, 80, 114
Jerman, John, 11
Johnson, Tiberius, 6, 6 n.
Jones, Evan, 106 n., 138-139, 151, 213
Jones, Evan (of Annapolis), 41
Jones, Horatio Gates, 8 n., 24 n., 31, 31 n.
Jones, Jenkin, 213, 214
Jones, Joseph, 244
Jonson, Ben, 99, 99 n.
Juvenal, 29, 206, 208

General Index

K

Kalendarium Pennsilvaniense, 3
Kalm, Peter, 49 n.
Kearsley, John, 201, 243
Keimer, Samuel, 10, 15 n., 16 n., 25, 26 n., 32, 32 n., 33, 44 n., 47 n., 59 n., 105 n., 119, 166 n., 176 n., 194, 194 n., 196, 205, 205 n., 212-213, 241
Keith, Charles P., 100 n.
Keith, George, 4-5
Keith, Gov. William, 11, 11 n., 13 n., 14, 14 n., 43, 72 n., 85, 85 n., 88, 97, 154, 154 n., 215.
Kentish Post, 54, 54 n.
Key . . . to discern the Difference betwixt the . . . Quakers, 11, 11 n.
Kinnersley, Ebenezer, 213, 214
Kinsey, John, 214 n.
Kite, Nathan, 3 n., 6 n., 9, 9 n., 31, 31 n.
Kneeland, Samuel, 212
Kneeland & Green, 212
Kneller, Sir Godfrey, 183, 185, 185 n.
Knight, Samuel, 148
Kolbe, Peter, 175, 175 n.
Konkle, Burton Alva, 91 n., 111 n.
Kyneall, Richard, 156 n.

L

Lamb, Andrew, 156
Landon, Fred, 107 n.
Langhorne, Jeremiah, 20 n.
Lauder, Andrew, 156 n.
Law, Tom, 207
Lawrence, Thomas, 44 n.
Laws of the Province of Maryland, 11
Laws Of the Province of Pennsilvania, 11
Lay, Benjamin, 106, 107, 139 n., 214
Layer, Christopher, 142 n.
Lee, James Melvin, 19, 19 n., 21, 21 n., 40 n., 66, 66 n.
Leeds, Daniel, 8 n.
Leeds, Felix, 24 n., 27, 212
Leeds, Titan, 10, 24 n., 27, 212
Legacy for Children, 10 n.
Lentulus, Cicero's letter to, 169
Letter to His Majesty's Justices of the Peace, 11 n.
Lewis, Barbara, 158
LeVassor, Michel, 98, 98 n., 100, 103, 160
Leyden *Courant*, 55 n.

Library Company of Philadelphia, 39 n., 40 n., 155, 214 n.
Lisbon *Gazette*, 53, 55 n.
Livy, 108 n.
Lloyd, Thomas, 157
Loan, Mr., of Bristol, 131
Locke, John, 174, 235
Logan, James, 11, 13 n., 20 n., 44 n., 85 n., 86, 88, 99, 100, 100 n., 103, 128 n., 154 n., 235
(London) *Daily Advertiser*, 54, 54 n., 210
(London) *Daily Courant*, 53, 54, 54 n., 55
(London) *Daily Gazetteer*, 54, 54 n., 61, 97 n., 172, 193 n., 198 n.
(London) *Daily Journal*, 54, 54 n., 62
London *Daily Post*, 54, 54 n., 62
London *Evening Post*, 54, 54 n.
(London) *Flying Post*, 54, 54 n.
London *Gazette*, 54, 54 n.
(London) *General Evening Post*, 54, 54 n., 122 n.
London *Journal*, 16 n., 41 n., 97 n., 165, 166, 166 n., 167 n., 173, 174 n., 175
London Magazine, 54, 54 n., 55n., 57, 62, 63, 103 n., 105 n., 107 n., 109 n., 138, 171, 171 n., 172 n., 173 n., 175, 188 n., 190 n., 191 n., 198 n., 207 n., 208, 209 n., 223, 236
(London) *Post Boy*, 54, 54 n., 55
(London) *Post Man*, 54, 54 n.
(London) *Weekly Journal*, 54, 54 n.
(London) *Weekly Medley*, 54, 54 n.
(London) *Weekly Miscellany*, 54, 54 n., 90, 173 n., 175 n.
(London) *Weekly Register*, 54, 54 n., 190, 190 n.
"Lord Penn" affair, 4 n., 13
Louis XIII, 98-100
Louis XIV, 101
Louis XV, 53, 64, 68, 132, 135-136
Louisburg, Siege of (Cape Breton), 83, 197
Lucan, 29
Lucian, 208
Lucretius, 171, 208
Luther, Martin, 28
Lyly, William, 29
Lyneall, Richard. See Kyneall, Richard.

267

M

Mackenzie, Alexander, 156 n.
Macpherson, John, 2
Magee, James F., 40 n.
Mahmud, 68, 68 n.
Manly, George, 140-141
Mapp, Mrs. Sally (the bonesetter), 146, 146 n.
Marchmont, Hugh Hume, Earl of, 133
Maria Theresa, 71, 174, 208-209
Marie de' Medici, Regent of France, 99-100
Marlborough, John Churchill, Duke of, 122-123, 140, 182, 183, 208
Marlborough, Sarah Churchill, Duchess of, 123
Marlowe, Christopher, 191 n.
Martin, John Hill, 19 n.
Martin's *Physical Dictionary*, 28
Martyr, Peter, 28, 28 n.
Maryland: first press in Middle Colonies 1 n.; printing of Charter 32; Maryland-Pennsylvania boundary dispute 75 n., 100, 104 n.; tobacco trade 81, 213; and *passim*
Maryland Gazette, 44 n., 47 n., 56, 56 n., 81, 81 n., 175, 212, 220, 220 n., 221
Masonic Order, 106, 106 n., 107 n., 138-139
Massachusetts: salary of governor 73-75; money shortage 82; and *passim*
Massachusetts Historical Society, 217 n.
Mather, Cotton, 123-124, 150 n., 160, 187
Maydman, Henry, 28, 28 n.
McCulloch, William, 40 n.
McMurtrie, Douglas C., 6 n., 220 n.
Menshikov, Prince Alexander Danilovich, 70
Mercantilism, 75-76
Meredith, Reese, 35, 157
Metzger, Ethel, 32 n.
Miller, Mrs., 131
Milton, John, 2, 185, 185 n., 226, 226 n.
Mir Wa'iz, 68 n.
Mist, Nathaniel, 133
Mist's *(Fog's) Weekly Journal*, 54, 54 n., 61, 103 n., 171, 191, 191 n.
Montgomerie, Gov. John, 73, 75, 76, 77
Moore, Sir Jonas, 28, 28 n.
Moravians. See Zinzendorf.
Morgan, Joseph, 10 n.
Morison, Sir Stanley, 42 n.

Morning Exercises, 28
Morris, Anthony, 20 n.
Morris, Lewis, 43, 77, 78, 78 n., 79, 79 n., 82
Mulhallond, Lewis, 156 n.
Munsell, Joel, 40 n.
Myers, Albert Cook, 3 n.
Mystery of Husbandry, 29

N

Nash, Richard ("Beau"), 127, 132
Nero, 92 n., 101 n., 111
Newcastle *Courant*, 54, 55 n.
New England Courant, 14, 14 n., 15, 56, 160, 214, 216-217
New England Weekly Journal, 41 n., 56, 198 n.
New Help to Discourse, 27
Newton, Sir Isaac, 131
Newton, Samuel, 28, 28 n.
New York: Cosby case (see Cosby); and *passim*
New York *Evening Post*, 220
New York *Gazette*, 12, 12 n., 21 n., 34 n., 36 n., 43, 56, 60, 78, 79 n., 98, 101 n., 104 n., 107 n., 126, 138 n., 155 n., 165 n., 192 n., 211, 218-219, 230 n.
New York *Weekly Journal*, 19 n., 56, 60, 78, 78 n., 79, 79 n., 84, 93 n., 94 n., 98 n., 105 n., 125, 160, 166 n., 205, 205 n., 219, 219 n.
New York *Weekly Post Boy*, 56, 219-220
Nicholas, Abraham, 154 n.
Nixon, Richard, 36 n.
Nixon, Sarah Boels, 36 n.
Noailles, Marshal Adrien-Maurice, Duke of, 175
Norris, Isaac, 96, 100; I.[saac?], 26 n.
Norton, Richard, 175, 175 n.

O

Oglethorpe, Gen. James, 80
Old English Journal, 109 n.
Oldfield, Mrs. Anne, 132
Orange, William, Prince of, 197
Orleans, Augusta, Duchess of, 64, 135
Osborne, Francis, 174
Osborne, George Lucas, 158
Ottoboni, Cardinal Pietro (1667-1740), 197

General Index

Ovid, 208, 209
Owen, Owen, 19 n.

P

Paltsits, Victor H., 2 n., 3 n.
Pamphlets, 26-30, 31, 32, 33. See also individual titles.
Paris *A la Main,* 55, 55 n.
Paris *Gazette,* 55
Parker, James, 211, 211 n., 219, 220, 220 n.
Parks, William, 44 n., 212, 212 n., 220, 221, 221 n.
Parliamentary Press Act of 1662, 5
Penn, Hannah, 89 n.
Penn, John, 44, 89 n., 95, 99
Penn, Richard, 89 n.
Penn, Thomas, 44, 44 n., 87, 89 n., 100, 100 n., 115, 115 n., 181 n., 197
Penn, William, 1, 3, 4 n., 11, 13, 27, 28, 31, 33, 34, 86, 87, 89 n., 97, 103, 130, 131, 133
Penn, William (son of the first proprietor), 85
Penn Charter School. See William Penn Charter School.
Pennsylvania: Charter of Privileges 1, 33, 98; Charter 3, 3 n., 4 n.; "dying credit" 12-14, 45, 85; chancery dispute (court of equity) 43, 85, 96-98; Pennsylvania-Maryland boundary dispute 75 n., 100, 104 n.; Walking Purchase of 1737 117, 117 n.; Provincial Council *passim;* Assembly *passim*
Pennsylvania Evening Post and Daily Advertiser, 2
Pennsylvania Gazette, 8 n., 33 n., 35 n., 36 n., 37, 38 n., 40 n., 42 n., 44 n., 46 n., 47, 47 n., 49, 52 n., 59 n., 60 n., 63, 63 n., 79, 81, 81 n., 83 n., 84 n., 88 n., 89, 89 n., 90, 91, 96 n., 97, 98, 98 n., 100, 100 n., 101, 101 n., 102, 102 n., 104, 104 n., 105, 105 n., 106, 106 n., 107, 107 n., 108, 108 n., 112, 114, 114 n., 117 n., 122 n., 126, 126 n., 128 n., 129, 129 n., 130, 130 n., 139, 144 n., 151, 152, 152 n., 159, 159 n., 160, 165 n., 167 n., 175 n., 180, 180 n., 182, 187, 187 n., 211, 213, 213 n., 214, 214 n., 215 n., 216 n., 217, 217 n., 218, 218 n., 219, 219 n., 220, 220 n., 221, 221 n., 226, 226 n., 228, 229, 230 n., 231, 232, 233, 233 n., 235 n., 239, 239 n., 241. See also *Universal Instructor.*
Pennsylvania Journal, 50 n., 122 n., 220, 241
Perpoint, Samuel, 156
Persius, 29, 91 n., 206, 208
Peter the Great, 64, 165
Peter II of Russia, 70
Petty, Sir William, 29
Philadelphia: population 1, 116 n., 117; printing and the book trade 1-2; education 1, 126 n., 155-156; printing (interregnum of the Bradfords) 6, 6 n.; picture of waterfront 47, 233, and illus. facing pp. 112, 240; weather 149-150, 238; smallpox 151; chemists and physicians 151-152; fires, crimes, etc. 152-153; entertainment 153-155; inns and taverns 153, 158, 158 n.; trade and business 157-158, 226; poems on 203-207; position among the colonies 226; and *passim*
"Philalethes," 171
"Philanthropos," 174
Philip V of Spain, 51, 64, 67, 132, 141, 142, 198
Philipse, Frederick, 78 n.
Philop, C., 89
Philosophical Transactions of the Royal Society, 55, 55 n.
Phipps, Thomas, 156 n.
Phrases of the Poets, 29
"Pickle Herring," 154 n., 155, 155 n.
Pitt, Andrew, 131
Plague of 1720-22, 67-68
Plat-form of Church-Discipline, 8 n.
"Plato," 166, 166 n.
Pliny, 208
Plomer, Henry R., 2 n.
Plumley, George, 157
Plumstead, Clement, 20 n.
Plutarch, 195, 208
Poland, King of. See Augustus II and Stanislaus.
Polish Succession, War of the, 69, 69 n., 70
Political Mercury, 54, 54 n.
Political State of Great Britain, 54, 54 n., 59 n., 61, 74, 166, 166 n., 170, 174, 192 n.
Pope, Alexander, 45, 133, 183, 183 n., 184, 185 n., 190, 190 n., 197, 197 n., 201, 201 n.

269

Pope. See Benedict XIII, XIV; Clement XI, XII.
Popish Labyrinth, 28
Porteus, John, 137-138
Portsmouth and Gosport *Gazette,* 54, 55 n.
Postal service in the colonies, 44 n., 56, 59-61
Postmastership of Pennsylvania, 20, 33, 44, 44 n., 45. See also Bradford, Andrew.
Potter, Dr., 154 n.
Powell, Samuel, 20 n.
Presgrave, Mr., 207
Preston, Samuel, 7; S.[amuel?], 26 n.
Price Current, 2
Prideaux, Humphrey, 29
Princeton University, 128 n.
Printing press: importance in early Pennsylvania 1-2; Maryland's priority in Middle Colonies 1 n. See also Freedom of the press, and *passim.*
Prior, Matthew, 182-183
Prompter, 190, 190 n.
Proud, Robert, 5 n.
Psalms of David (Brady and Tate), 27, 214
Pugh, Ellis, 32 n.
Pulteney, William, Earl of, 70
"Pythagoras," 171

Q

Quakers. See Friends, Society of.

R

Ralph, James, 191 n.
Rawle, Francis, 13 n., 14 n.
Raylton, Tacey Sowle (Mrs. Thomas), 25, 25 n., 30, 34, 34 n., 36, 242
Read, Alexander, 28, 28 n.
Read, Charles, 19 n., 20 n.
Read's *British Gazetteer,* 54, 54 n.
Realey, Charles B., 17 n.
Religious freedom in Pennsylvania, 1, 1 n., 235
Remarks on Zenger's Tryal, 105, 105 n., 107, 107 n., 108, 109, 109 n., 110
Remarks upon Mr. Hamilton's Arguments in the Tryal of J. P. Zenger, 107 n., 110
Remarks upon the Advice, 15 n.
Reynard the Fox, History of, 29

Reyners, Joseph, 6, 6 n.
Rhode Island Gazette, 218 n.
Richardson, Samuel, 2
Rittenhouse, Klaas (Nicholas), 40 n.
Rittenhouse, William, 4
Rittenhouse, William (son of Klaas), 40 n.
Rittenhouse paper mill, 1, 4, 40, 40 n., 46, 66
Robinson, John, 159, 213
Robinson, Mr. (postmaster at Williamsburg), 41
Rochester, Bishop of (Francis Atterbury), 68, 68 n., 120, 167, 167 n.
Rogers, James, 157
Rogers, John, 53
Rogers, Thomas, 28 n.
Rose, Aquila, 199-200, 206, 214
Ross, John, 104 n.
Royal Dublin Society, 55, 55 n.
Royal Society, 55, 55 n., 131, 211
Ryan, John, 159, 159 n.
Ryley, Dr., of New Castle, 41

S

St. James Evening Post, 54, 54 n., 171 n., 175 n.
Salkeld, John, 205
Salomon, John, 156, 208, 209
Saunders, John, 143
Savoy, Charles Emmanuel III, Duke of, 63
Scharf, J. Thomas, 106 n., 107 n.
Schenck, Martin, 8 n.
Schuyler, Livingston Rowe, 19 n.
Scott, Sir Walter, 137
Scull, Nicholas, 151
Seaton, Alexander, 156 n.
Secrets of the Jesuits, 28
Sejanus, 91, 91 n., 93, 99
Selden, John, 29, 29 n., 30
Seneca, 208
Seville, Treaty of, 69
Seward, William, 126, 126 n.
Sewel, William, 25, 25 n., 26 n., 27
Shaftsbury, Anthony Ashley Cooper, third Earl of, 187
Shakespeare, William, 2, 186, 186 n.
Shepherd, William R., 13 n., 98 n.
Shields, John, 156 n.
Shipping, 58-59, 117. See also *American Weekly Mercury:* shipping news.
Shirley, Gov. William, 82 n., 116 n.

General Index

Sloane, Sir Hans, 146
Smith, Cornelia, 21 n., 245-246
Smith, George, 245-246
Smith, Mary, 245
Smith, William, 126
Smollett, Tobias, 2
Smyth, Albert H., 16 n., 44 n.
Sober mindedness Pressed upon Young People, 26
Socrates, 208
"Socrates," 173, 173 n., 180 n.
Soissons, Congress of, 63, 63 n., 69
Some Necessary Precautions, 15, 15 n.
Some Remedies Proposed, for the Restoring the sunk Credit of the Province of Pennsylvania (Francis Rawle), 12-14
Sonmans, Peter, 151
South Carolina Gazette, 40 n., 56, 155 n., 217 n., 220-221, 237
South Sea Bubble, 16 n.-17 n., 67, 67 n., 130
Sower, Christopher, 2 n., 32 n., 33, 129
Sowle, Andrew, 2, 2 n., 3, 25, 34, 34 n., 242
Sowle, Jane, 34 n.
Spangenberg, Bishop August Gottlieb, 130 n.
Spectator, 29, 92, 96, 176, 177, 187, 187 n., 188, 188 n., 190
Spencer, Charles (Lord Spencer), Duke of Marlborough and Earl of Sunderland, 123, 133
Spinoza, Baruch, 91, 91 n.
Spotswood, Gov. Alexander, 22, 33, 60 n., 72, 72 n., 215, 229, 230, 231, 232
Stanislaus of Poland, 93
Stanhope, Charles, 67
Steel, James, 86 n.
Steele, Sir Richard ("Isaac Bickerstaff"), 25, 29, 30, 33, 133, 187, 187 n., 188, 210, 231. See also *Crisis, Spectator,* and *Tatler.*
Sterling, Henry Alexander, Earl of, 46
Stevens, John, 156 n.
Stevenson, Thomas, 7
Stobaeus, Joannes, 29, 29 n.
"Stonecastle, Henry." See Baker, Henry.
Stuard, Dr. Alexander, 147
Stuart, Charles Edward (Young Pretender), 64-65, 83 n., 120-122
Stuart, James (Old Pretender), 64, 68, 103, 120-121, 130, 167 n., 168, 197

Sugar and Molasses Act of 1733, 76, 76 n.
Swift, Jonathan, 68, 133-135, 182, 187, 234-235, 236, 237 n.
Sydenham, Dr. Thomas, 28, 28 n.

T

Tacitus, Discourses upon, 92 n., 166, 170 n., 208. See also Gordon, Thomas.
Tackerbury, Mr., 139
Tate, Nahum, 27, 214
Tatler, 29, 176, 187, 187 n.
Taylor, Dr. Chevalier, 146, 146 n.
Taylor, Jacob, 6, 6 n., 7, 10, 203, 205, 205 n., 212
"Telemachus," 176
Télémaque, 26, 26 n., 27 n., 91 n.
Temple, Sir William, 29, 173, 173 n., 187
Tencin, Cardinal Pierre Guérin de, 172, 174
Tennent, Gilbert, 128, 128 n., 129, 130, 173
Tennent, William, 128 n.
Terence, 208
Testament of the Twelve Patriarchs, 27
Thales, 199
Theatre at Williamsburg, Va., 154 n.
"Theodore, King," of Corsica, 69
Thomas, Gov. George, 111, 112, 114, 115, 116, 116 n., 117, 117 n., 213 n., 234, 235
Thomas, Isaiah, 5 n., 6 n., 7 n., 8 n., 15, 15 n., 36, 36 n., 37 n., 40 n., 47, 47 n., 49 n., 50 n., 240
Thomas, Philip, 81
Thomson, James, 200 n.
Tiberius, 111
Tigellinus, 101, 101 n.
Tillotson, Archbishop John, 172, 187
Timoleon, 195
Timothy, Lewis, 221 n.
Tindal, Dr. Matthew, 132
Titus, 111
Torre, Count de la, 136-137
Torres, Francis, 151-152
Trajan, 111
Trenchard, John, 16 n.-17 n. See also *Cato's Letters* and *Independent Whig.*
Trevisa, John, 208
Trinity Church, New York, 36 n., 73
"Truman, A," 98
"Trueman, Tom," 126

271

"Truths Triumph over Trent," 28
Tryal of Capt. Samuel Goodere, 30
Turpin, Dick, 131, 131 n.
Tyrrell, William, 158

U

Udall, John, 29, 29 n.
Union Fire Co., 35, 35 n.
Universal Dictionary, 132, 194 n., 196
Universal Instructor, 16 n., 44 n., 47, 47 n., 119, 194, 194 n., 196, 212, 213, 213 n., 216 n., 218, 218 n., 220, 220 n., 241, 241 n. See also *Pennsylvania Gazette*.
Universal Spectator, 54, 54 n., 55, 57, 172, 188-190, 210

V

van Bebber, Hendrick, 151
Van Dam, Rip, 77-79, 97
Varro, Marcus Terentius, 164
Vatinius, 92 n.
Venables, Admiral Robert, 165
Vermigli, Pietro. See Martyr, Peter.
Vernon, Admiral Edward, 236
Vespasian, 111
Villars, Marshal Claude Louis Hector de, 171
Virgil, 29, 30, 197, 197 n., 208
Virginia Gazette, 56, 176, 210, 212, 212 n., 221, 221 n.
Virginia Miscellany, 212
Voltaire, 132

W

Wade, Field Marshal George, 122, 122 n.
Walby, John, 156
Wales, Prince and Princess of. See Frederick, Prince of Wales, and Augusta, Princess of Wales.
Walker, Jacob, 41
Wallace, John William, 3 n., 5 n., 6 n., 9, 9 n., 31 n., 34 n., 35 n., 36 n.
Walpole, Horatio (Sir Robert's brother), 130
Walpole, Horatio (the novelist), 130
Walpole, Sir Robert, 69, 70, 71, 119, 130, 130 n., 172, 172 n., 175, 197-199
Walpole, Lady Robert (Maria Skerrett), 130
Walton, Nathaniel, 156 n.
War with the Devil, 27
Ward, Bishop Seth, 28, 28 n.
Warner, Isaiah, 49, 214

Warner & Bradford, 214
Warren, Vice-Admiral Sir Peter ("Commodore Warren"), 209
Webb, George, 203
Webbe, John ("Z."), 37, 101, 102, 103, 104, 108, 108 n., 109 n., 110, 111, 112, 157 n., 167 n., 227-239
Weis, G. Michael, 156
Welsted, Leonard, 185
Wesley, Charles, 184
Wesley, John, 127, 184
Westcott, Thompson, 106 n., 107 n.
Whiston, William, 28, 28 n.
Whitebread, William, 151
Whitefield, George, 30, 30 n., 50 n., 124-128, 129, 129 n., 130, 130 n., 153, 175, 184, 197, 201, 214
Whitehall Evening Post, 54, 54 n., 61, 63, 198 n.
Whole Art of Fishing, 29
Whole Duty of Man, 27
Wickes, Ebenezer, 156 n.
William Penn Charter School, 1, 1 n., 5, 6 n., 9, 10, 10 n., 31
Wilson, Andrew, 138
Winthrop, John, 150 n.
Wood, Robert, 29 n.
Wood, William, 68
Wooley, Hannah, 29, 29 n.
Woolston, Thomas, 32
Wormley, Eleanor, 158
Wrigglesden, William, 162 n.
Wright, Capt. Edward, 44, 44 n., 181 n.
Wroth, Lawrence C., 1 n., 2, 2n., 4 n., 5 n., 6 n., 11 n., 12, 12 n., 20 n., 23 n., 24 n., 25 n., 32 n., 40 n., 66 n., 84, 84 n.

Y

Yale College, 135, 147, 150
Young Man's Companion, 8 n., 11, 27

Z

"Z." See Webbe, John.
Zenger, John Peter, 19 n., 20, 78, 78 n., 79, 79 n., 91 n., 95, 96 n., 97, 105, 105 n., 107, 107 n., 110, 160, 211 n., 219, 225
Zenger's Tryal. See *Remarks on Zenger's Tryal*.
Zinzendorf, Benigna von, 130 n.
Zinzendorf, Nicholas Ludwig, Count von, 30, 124, 129-130, 208
Zionitischer Weyrauchs-Hügel, 32 n.

WITHDRAWN
UST
'Libraries'

DATE DUE			
MAR 1 1975			
MAY 15 1978			
GAYLORD			PRINTED IN U.S.A.